THE AWAKENING GIANT:
China's Ascension in World Politics

THE AWAKENING GIANT
China's Ascension in World Politics

HARISH KAPUR

Professor, The Graduate Institute
of International Studies, Geneva

WITHDRAWN

SIJTHOFF & NOORDHOFF   1981
Alphen aan den Rijn, The Netherlands
Rockville, Maryland, USA

Copyright © 1981 Sijthoff & Noordhoff International Publishers B.V., Alphen aan
den Rijn, The Netherlands

All rights reserved. No part of this publication may be reproduced, stored in a retrieval
system, or transmitted, in any form, or by any means, electronic, mechanical, photo-
copying, recording or otherwise, without the prior permission of the copyright ow-
ner.

ISBN 90 286 0230 5

Library of Congress Catalog Card Number: 81-50363

Printed in The Netherlands

256236

DS
740.4
K348

CONTENTS

V

TRANSLITERATION TABLE

Wade and Pinying Systems*

Wade		Pinying	
a		a	
ai		ai	
an		an	
ang		ang	
ch	Chiang Ch'ing	j	Jiangqing
ch	Chou En-lai	zh	Zhou Enlai
ch'	Ch'en I	ch	Chen Yi
ch'	Ch'iao Kuan-hua	q	Qiao Guanhua
e		e	
ei		ei	
en		en	
eng		eng	
erh		er	
f		f	
h		h	
hs	Hsü Hsiang-ch'ien	x	Xu Xiangqian
i	I-ching	yi	Yijing (a classical book)
ieh		ie	
ien		ian	
j	Je-he	r	Rihe (Province)
k	Kuang-tung	g	Guangdong
k'	K'ang Yu-wei	k	Kang Youwei
l	Lin Piao	l	Lin Biao
m	Mao Tse-tung	m	Mao Zedong
n	Nieh Jung-chen	n	Nie Rongzhen
o		o	
ou		ou	
p	Pa-ch'üan	b	Baquan (Hegemonism)
p'	P'eng Te-huai	p	Peng Dehuai
s		s	
sh	Shanghai	sh	Shanghai
szu	Szu-ch'uan	si	Sichuan (Province)

* The Pinying system has been used in this book.

Wade			Pinying	
t	Teng Hsiao-p'ing		d	Deng Xiaoping
t'	T'ang		T	Tang (Dynasty)
ts	Tsai-chien		z	Zaijian (Goodbye)
ts'	Ts'ai		c	Cai (Family name)
tz'u	Tz'u-hsi		ci	Cixi (Empress)
tzu	Tzu-pen-chu-i		zi	Ziben Zhuyi (Capitalism)
ü			u	
ung			ong	
w			w	
y			y	
yeh	Yeh Chien-ying		ye	Ye Jianying
yin			yin	
ying			ying	
yu	Yu-p'ai		you	Youpai (The rightist)
yü	Yüan Shi-k'ai		yu	Yuan Shikai

PREFACE

China's ascension in world politics has been rapid and unprecedented—rapid in the sense that within a span of thirty years she is generally recognised to have acquired a significant role in the central strategic balance of the international system, unprecedented in the sense that she is the only developing country to have acquired this status. While this has been principally caused by the Chinese Communist Party's (CCP) own internal and external efforts to develop and project China, it can be legitimately asked whether it corresponds to her real capacity to influence global trends and whether this status has not in part been thrust on her by those nations whose declining power has led them to build her up in order to establish a credible counterbalance in the international configuration of forces—however marginal it may be. The answer to this conundrum is by no means easy. Those who are partisans of China tend to exaggerate her strength, while those who are her adversaries have a tendency to play it down. In this study an attempt is made to explore this question, not so much by focusing on the issue itself but rather by presenting a detailed analysis of China's foreign policy behaviour towards the principal actors and towards the principal regions of the globe.

The foreign policy behaviour of any nation cannot be adequately explored through a heavy reliance on a particular discipline or a specific framework of analysis. The inputs that go into the shaping of the foreign policy of a nation are so diverse, so complex, and so interrelated that to highlight any one of them would give an inadequate picture. This is all the more valid in the case of China, whose foreign policy declarations are clearly ideological but whose operational policies are power-oriented, whose emotional sense of belonging is with the Third World but who functions within the central strategic balance, and who formally rejects great power status but is in the process of acquiring one. Without opting for any particular approach, an attempt has therefore been made in the following pages to confine this study to a straightforward analysis, while incorporating wherever appropriate and wherever necessary the determinants that may shape her policy. At any one point of time in the history of China's development a single determinant may be important, only to cede its place to another one with the evolution of the situation.

By commencing the study with a brief chapter on China's perception of the world, an inadvertent impression may be gained that, in the view of this writer, ideology is central to Chinese thinking. This is, however, not the case. By starting off with perceptions, an attempt is made to highlight what the Chinese themselves think about the international system and how they are attempting to reconcile it to their ideological pattern before analysing the operational aspects of Chinese diplomacy.

In the preparation of this study I have particularly benefited from the collective discussions I have had with students participating in my seminar on "China in World Politics" at the Graduate Institute of International Studies in Geneva. Though the responsibility for analysis and interpretations presented here is of course mine alone, it would have been difficult to complete the study without the intellectual inspiration of the classroom.

In conclusion, my thanks go to Dr. Jau Jan-Seng, the Executive Secretary of the Asian Centre in Geneva, for his continuous advise and invaluable assistance, to Mrs. Wiley Woodruff for her editorial help with parts of the manuscript, to Miss Catherine Marti for having typed the first draft of the text and the final draft of the notes and bibliography, and to Mrs. Zina Grunder for having typed the final text in record time.

Harish Kapur

Geneva

Chapter 1

CHINA'S PERCEPTION OF THE WORLD: AN OVERVIEW

Legacy of the Past

Until the arrival of the Western nations on her shores in the nineteenth century, China was an autonomous and self-contained civilization. Geographically protected by barren steppe and desert in the north, high mountains and arid plateaus in the west, the endless sea in the east, and inaccessible jungles in the south, she was able to establish a self-sufficient and highly developed pre-industrial civilization. Largely devoid of any major external imprints, the political and social order designed, the philosophy incarnated, the culture diffused, and the language written were all indigenous.

Even the two most significant exceptions to this general rule have had little impact. The introduction of Buddhism in the second half of the first century A.D., for example, remained essentially marginal in the totality of Chinese culture. China never became a Buddhist country. Buddhism never played the role of a dominating creed or of central religious and philosophical tradition comparable to that of Christianity or Islam.[1] Even at the time of its great vitality in the early Tang period, Buddhism, propagating the ideal of personal salvation, had to bear up against the overwhelming power and prestige of the Confucian tradition, which was essentially a pragmatic and secular doctrine and which sought, in this world and in this life, a harmonious and hierarchical social order.

The second exception was the multiple pressures that emanated from Inner Asia. Nomadic tribes often united to invade China establishing Sino-barbarian dynasties: the first along the Great Wall (The Toba dynasty in 550 and the Liao dynasty of the Khitan Mongols in 907-1125), then in North China (The Jin dynasty between 1125-1279), and finally over the whole country with the Yuan dynasty of the Mongols between 1279-1368, and the Qing dynasty of the Manchus between 1644-1911. But all of them were absorbed by the superior Chinese culture and civilization.[2] When the nomadic Toba Tartars overran North China, their emperors prohibited the use of their own language and ordered all their people to adopt the Chinese language and Chinese customs. The Khitans were absorbed into the Chinese civilization. A century later they were conquered by the Kins who, in turn, were seduced by the Confucian society. The Mongols and then the

1

Manchus, who ruled over the whole of China, suffered the same fate. While the Mongols were assimilated, the Manchus became even "more Chinese than the Chinese, adopting and suffocating the civilization they had conquered placing it with murderous reverence under an airless glass case."[3]

The Chinese perception of the outside world was thus hardly influenced by external factors and remained, like its civilization, essentially indigenous during the entire pre-industrial period of Chinese history. Based on a belief in their own superiority, they viewed the world in four concentric circles. The innermost zone was metropolitan China, Tibet, and Mongolia. The second consisted of nearby culturally similar states, Korea and North Vietnam, parts of which had in ancient times been ruled by the Chinese empire. The third circle was principally formed by the Japanese, a sovereign people who had adopted much of the Chinese civilization. And the last consisted of the "outer barbarians" living beyond the pale of civilization. To be non-Chinese was to be despicable. An eleventh-century writer held that the foreigner, that is, barbarian, "must be regarded as resembling birds and beasts."[4] In the nineteenth century, the Chinese believed or were taught that other people lived in holes and dressed in leaves for the lack of wisdom of the sage kings.[5]

Though the Chinese hardly exercised any control over the borderlands, the neighbouring countries were expected to pay tribute. The tribute bearers were treated with great contempt, often being kept waiting for months before having to kowtow in a manner designed to inflict maximum punishment. Foreign princes were also expected to accept investiture from the emperor. And all foreign powers were held to be subordinate. For example, in 607 A.D. the Sui emperor refused to accept a letter from a Japanese ruler addressed to him in terms of equality. In 1596, the Ming emperor sent a patronising letter graciously investing the Japanese emperor with the kingship of his islands.[6]

Acculturation process

In the first half of the nineteenth century, the whole edifice of the Chinese civilization collapsed. Like other dynasties in the past, the Manchus entered the stage of decline. The causes were multiple and complex. At the base were essentially socio-economic factors. There was, for example, an unprecedented growth of population which could not be absorbed by industry and which increased pressures on land. There was also a tendency towards concentration of land ownership, the avoidance of taxation by powerful landowners, and a general impoverishment of the rural population.

Though the internal elements were important, they were not the key factors in the final collapse of the Chinese civilization; in the past, whenever dynasties declined, they were replaced by new ones without inflicting any damage to the Chinese way of life. This time it was different. In the nineteenth century, the Chinese were not going through their usual pattern of "dynastic cycles" but were actually facing the collapse of their whole civilization.

The decisive elements were twin external pressures. The one was caused by a geopolitical revolution on China's frontiers, and the other was occasioned by the forcible intervention inside the country by industrial powers of the Western world.

China had acquired two powerful neighbours. With the final and firm installation of Russia on her northern frontiers and the meteoric rise of Japan just across the narrow sea—and with both of them pushing in the direction of China—the Middle Kingdom was no longer an isolated civilization. She had now to reckon with the new phenomenon of having to behave like a country in the midst of other countries, of having to respond to the actions and reactions of others, and of having to take into account potential security threats. The geographical isolation in which China had lived and prospered and which had permitted her to establish a self-sufficient civilization had disappeared.

With the coercive entry into China of Western industrial powers, China had to face another and even greater danger—the danger not to her frontiers but to her civilization. The forcible opening up of China to industrial goods, the setting up of some industries within the country, compounded with the inevitable problems involved in the acculturation process, destroyed the delicate balance the Chinese system had created after centuries of intellectual and economic efforts. The authority of the emperor, upon which the Chinese order reposed, was ended; the hand-labour-based industry, on which the Chinese economy depended, was destroyed, the population, which benefited from pre-industrial civilization, was pauperised, and the favourable balance of trade, which existed up to 1830 and which had brought about an uninterrupted flow of silver from the outside, became lopsided.

The combined effect of these twin pressures put an end to the universalist Chinese vision of their own society and that of the world. Apparently, it was no longer relevant to the new reality both inside and outside the country.

The imperative need to replace their irrelevant and discredited worldview by a new one generated among Chinese elites an intense process of reflection and discussion as to how they should respond and what they should do in the face of this massive acculturation. Should they reject it outright as alien to their way of thinking or should they adapt themselves to the new phenomena?

The Chinese Response

Like most countries of the Third World which had been subjected to acculturation processes, the Chinese elite was divided—perhaps even more

3

so since what was at stake was a civilization which had established a social order far superior to other developing countries. As much as one can conceptualise and categorise a complex phenomenon, it could be argued that four currents of thought emerged in response to the new situation.

There were first of all those who believed that China must focus her attention on strengthening the traditional structures, recovering the ancient power and expelling the foreigner. They appeared to be convinced that China's difficulties were not due to inadequacies in the traditional structures but were caused by defects that had seeped into society over centuries due to bad rulers or defective human behaviour. The only way out, in their view, was to correct the situation by reinterpreting the Confucian texts in the light of modern conditions.

But all this was fallacious and was not even remotely connected to the existing state of affairs. For while they were advancing their panaceas, China was already pushed onto the road of industrialisation from which there was no going back. Once a nation is locked into this process, it is no longer possible to return to the original point of departure.

It is important to note that this process of Westernisation and industrialisation was in many ways unique—for it was neither completely colonial nor completely indigenous. The Japanese were able to forestall Western domination by modernising themselves. In this manner they were able to pick whatever they needed—be it technology or ideology—and adapt it to their own conditions, thereby minimising the level of alienation and destabilisation that is often unavoidable under such conditions. Most of the other countries in Asia and Africa suffered a different fate. Colonial powers administered these countries. They were certainly exploited, dominated, and even alienated. But since the control was exercised by one colonial power, they also benefited from Western ideas, education, and statecraft.

The Chinese did not benefit from either of these processes. They were not dominated by one colonial power but by many of them who were busy dividing up the country into spheres of influences. The Chinese thus found themselves in the paradoxical position of being formally independent but in fact dependent, and of being formally engaged in an initiatory process of modernisation without any guidance from those who had pushed them onto this road. They had the worst of the two worlds. As Sun Yat-sen affirmed:

> China is a colony of all the countries with whom she has concluded the treaties. All the countries which had concluded treaties with China are the masters of China. China is therefore not the colony of one country but all of them. We are not slaves of one of them but all of them. Let us compare: is it better to be slave of one country or slave of all of them? If one is a slave of one single country at the time of natural disasters, the metropole gives assistance. By giving assistance the people of the metropole will be fullfilling their duties of a master. This is their duty to do so.

4

And the people who are slaves would also consider that it is their master who must come to their assistance. A few years ago northern China was afflicted by natural disasters. No country considered it her duty to assist . . . [translated].[7]

The second school argued in favour of change, but only for a limited change. Those who represented this current were neither interested in what the foreigner could do in the realm of industry and pure science, nor were they attracted by the Western political and economic system. Their principal interest was the acquisition of valuable techniques in the field of weaponry and of military training in Western methods.

But this school too proved inadequate. For one thing, the inexorable but slow process of modernisation, in which they were not interested, fell entirely into foreign hands, further increasing the dependence of China on foreign powers; for another, it was unrealistic to think that China could build a modern arsenal and train officers at Western-style military academies and still expect them to behave and act as good Confucianists. It was "tantamount to letting the fox into the henhouse and then naively assuming that he could not eat the chicken."[8]

The third school supported total Westernisation. Its partisans considered as pure fantasy the idea that Chinese traditional behaviour could co-exist and even interact with Western military technology. Techniques do effect values, means do determine ends. Liang Qichao considered, for example, that it simply was not possible to borrow Western technology while maintaining Chinese thought and institutions, since China "definitely cannot make use of new institutions with an old psychology."[9] The Western world had to be emulated in its totality. Everything that the West represented, whether in the domain of learning or technology or political institutions or ideas, was therefore encouraged. Hu Shih, inspired by the pragmatism of John Dewey, considered scientism as a weapon with which to destroy all elements of the past which were dear to the conservatives. And there was Sun Yat-sen, a liberal and intellectual, who believed during the initial years of his political career that China's political salvation lay in the attainment of democracy on the Western model and who was even prepared to leave the unequal treaties intact.

This attempt at total Westernisation plunged the country into one of the most chaotic, confusing, and disunited periods in her history. Nothing worked. The 1911 revolution effectively pushed China from her old system of central control into war-lordism. The sinews of military and industrial strength, for which the revolution was staged, were not developed. The political institutions were a travesty of democracy. Neither were the people ready for it, nor were the Western powers prepared to give a hand. The Chinese leaders were unable to make China a better place to live, nor were they able to make the country into an united and independent nation.

The fourth current to which the Chinese elite group finally turned to was heavily influenced by Marxism-Leninism. Though the partisans of this school also believed in Westernisation, they offered different solutions and different models from that of the Western world. They proposed a united and independent China and declared their determination to make her into a better place to live through a more ethical system of production based on cooperation rather than competition.

Marxism-Leninism had also other attractions for China: (*a*) it corresponded more closely to Chinese thinking concerning unrestricted universalism than the multistate system of the West; (*b*) it was an effective tool to criticise the West from the Western point of view; (*c*) it gave the Chinese a new methodological framework to understand their own past; and (*d*) it permitted China to give first priority to domestic problems, and thereby to move the country away from an exaggerated focus on her foreign policy, as had been the case since 1860.

The Chinese Marxists in sum appeared to incorporate "in their modernised structures all those traditional elements and subconscious yearnings to which the Westernised 'modernists' refused to render full justice."[10]

It is perhaps important to underline the fact that China was attracted to Marxism-Leninism through the Russian Revolution which embodied these ideas. The Chinese elite began to take an interest only after the revolution had transformed the foreign policy of Russia. Until then Tsarist Russia had been perceived as an enemy. Everything she represented, whether it was economic or political, was of no interest to them. Besides this, she had the reputation of being the most reactionary of all European nations. With the Russian Revolution everything changed. Here was a new Russia that had unilaterally renounced all her unequal treaties, abolished all concessions, opposed intervention by other powers, and showed readiness to treat China and other Asian nations as equals. This change in Russian foreign policy behaviour could not be explained in terms other than the fact that a new ideology was the basis of the revolution and that new non-exploitive economic system had come into effect.

All this had a tremendous impact on Chinese intellectuals. Left-wing movements fermented in universities. A significant element of Chinese literary elite manifested an interest in socialism. Regarding the October Socialist Revolution, Hu Sheng affirmed:

> The great victory could not but capture the attention of the Chinese people who were writhing under the iron heel of imperialist powers. Its repercussions were first felt in China in the ideological field. Almost all the intellectuals who were seriously concerned with the destiny of the nation began to watch the development of revolution in Russia and eagerly sought acquaintance with the socialist ideology—Marxism-Leninism—by which the revolution was guided.[11]

But what about China's perception of the world order? Did it change too? Did the different currents underlying internal modernisation generate a corresponding view about the universe and the way it functioned?

Here again the inadequacies of the traditionalist and the Western liberal approach rapidly became apparent. For the traditionalist it was vital for China to become strong within the Confucian framework. The major thrust, for example, of Kang Youwei's thinking on the world, was focussed on conceiving of a utopian universal state which would be free from all national constraints and which would also be free from all distinctions of class, race, sex, family, property, profession, etc. This modernised and adapted version of the original Chinese notion of universal kingship was hardly relevant to the nationalistic requirements of the day.

The supporters of the Western school broke with the traditional world view without really replacing it with a new one. Their principal concern was not so much with maintaining the Chinese tradition of looking at the world globally, but rather of focussing attention on making China strong, of restoring her old status, of reacquiring sovereignty or suzerainty over tributary areas detached from the mainland. For Sun Yat-sen, it was vital for China to become powerful and to assume greater responsibility towards the world. The opinions about the world were limited to such general and vague considerations as that of the acceptance of its multistate character, of its assymetrical nature, and of its division between the weak and the strong. Like most of the nationalist perceptions in the Third World, the Chinese view was too pragmatic, too ad hoc, and too nationally oriented to establish or conceive of a global perception.[12]

Once again it was Marxism-Leninism that offered the opportunity for a synthetic perception both of the international system and China's place in it. It gave the Chinese elite the necessary tool to understand and meet the national aspirations within a well-defined transnational world order.

Since all Marxist-Leninist analysis is made within a conceptual framework of "contradictions", which is based on the theory of dialectical materialism, the Chinese Marxists applied this methodological tool to investigate the international system and China's role in it. For the practical implementation of the contradictions analysis, Mao considered it essential to localise the principal contradiction in a given situation. "In studying any complex process in which there are two or more contradictions," he wrote, "we must devote every effort to find its principal contradiction. Once this principal contradiction is grasped all problems can be readily solved."[13]

As far as the international system was concerned, Mao considered the establishment of Socialist Russia in 1917 a crucial turning point, as it changed the nature and dimension of international conflicts. They were no longer only between national states, as was the case before, but also between systems which cut across national frameworks and which were defined in ideological and socio-economic terms. The international system, essentially bipolar in character, was composed of different levels of contradictions: (*a*) between Soviet Russia and imperialism; (*b*) between the imperialists; (*c*) between proletariat and bourgeoisie within capitalist states and (*d*) between the colonies and the imperialists. Though each of these contradictions functioned within their autonomous frameworks they were also linked with each other insofar as socialist Russia was supported by colonial people and the proletariat in developed countries and insofar as internationally well-

7

established economic groups, cutting across national frontiers, sustained the imperialists.

Within this broad bipolar conflictory international framework, revolutionary China's place within the global system was on the Soviet side, which was viewed as the leader of the transnational movement. However, while making this clear, Mao did not consider China's role as necessarily subservient to Soviet Russia. On at least three major issues he weaned himself away from the generally accepted Marxist view of the international system.

First of all, he did not consider it necessary that an identity of interest must prevail between the different revolutionary forces when they are faced with different sets of contradictions in their separate struggles for survival. He thought it perfectly normal, for example, that revolutionary China and revolutionary Russia might have to pursue different policies in the light of different conditions in which they might find themselves in their respective areas. If the Nazi-Soviet agreement of 1939 and the Soviet-Japanese neutrality pact of 1941 were understandable in the light of the Soviet needs of the period, so too were the Chinese attempts to seek an alliance with Western capitalist and imperialist countries against their principal enemy, Japan. Mao Zedong declared:

> In the field of foreign relations, we regard those who assist us as our friends and whose who aid the enemy as our foes. Germany and Italy for instance have helped the enemy in the past, and for that reason Wang Ching-Wei's demand for rapprochement with those two nations are wrong and treasonable. Should Germany and Italy cease aiding the enemy, we would not be opposed to improving our relations with them in order to weaken Japan. Should Britain assist our enemy, then we should abandon all hope of aid from her and vigilantly guard against being caught by any traps she might set to endanger our war of resistance.
>
> As for the Soviet Union, we must strengthen the friendship between our country and her and form a true united front of the two great nations; and thus even get more aid and strengthen our position. The same should be our attitude in general towards America.[14]

Secondly, Mao also visualised a diversity of revolutionary developmental models. He did not see any reason why the Soviet developmental model —formulated in the light of her own national experience—would automatically be relevant to all the revolutionaries and to all the nations. While the broad general framework would understandably be the same, the national specificities would give them a different orientation.

Thirdly, revolutions in the colonies and semi-colonies were also conceived of in essentially national terms. Though a part of the international revolutionary movement, they were expected to have their own national momentum and were expected to be different from capitalist and Soviet models supported by a cross-section of groups cutting across class lines. Before they reach the socialist stage, wrote Mao in 1940, "a third form of state must be adopted in the revolutions of all colonial and semi-colonial countries, namely the new Democratic Republic . . ."[15]

The international system, once some revolutions had succeeded, would thus consist of multitude of states representing the socialist, the capitalist, and the developing world. Though the developing world would be a part of the world proletariat socialist revolution, it would not be controlled by one power centre, and it would be inspired by nationally oriented revolutionary and developmental models.

Chinese Revolution

In the immediate aftermath of the Chinese Revolution, the Chinese party leaders abstained from expressing too openly some of the discordant views they had voiced earlier, though the abstention was not that total, since some emphasis was laid on China's role[16] and that of the Third World in international politics.[17]

The initial euphoria of Sino-Soviet solidarity was apparently too strong to permit the expression of any major disagreements. The main thrust of the Chinese declarations was therefore on Sino-Soviet amity and on the faithful enunciation of the bipolar picture that the Soviet leadership had painted of the international system.

But all this did not last long; for the appearance of the first major difficulties within the bipolar system in the mid-1950s resulted in the reappearance of some of the discordant notes and the commencement of the new Chinese search for their own perception of the international system and their role in it.

It all began with the introduction of some theoretical innovations by the Communist Party of the Soviet Union (CPSU) at its 20th Party Congress in 1956, and the explosion of turmoils in Hungary and Poland during the same year. These two major developments were viewed to have generated a series of "non-antagonistic contradictions" within and among the socialist countries. In addition, China's participation in the Bandung conference of independent Afro-Asian countries in 1955, her autonomous role in Eastern Europe in 1956, and her decision to work out her own developmental model in 1957 opened new perspectives for her to function autonomously within the bloc.

Thus by 1956, all the three themes (national foreign policies, independent model of development, the Third World) on which Mao had struck independent notes before the Revolution had reappeared in Chinese actions.

Parallel to these events, the 1956 Suez crisis accelerated some of the basic contradictions between the imperialist countries and between them and the Third World. In effect, in the Chinese view, the capitalist world had become less coherent. Though the developing world was still tied to the

9

capitalist camp, it had nonetheless begun increasingly to manifest signs of seeking out its own autonomous goals.

The development of the different levels of contradictions, compounded by the successful launching of the Soviet Sputnik in 1957 had, in the Chinese view, modified the configuration of forces. Within a still bipolar world, the Chinese began to consider that the balance of forces had tilted in favour of the Socialist bloc. Any confrontational policy directed against the capitalist world, they were convinced, would serve the dual purpose of placing the capitalist countries in a defensive position and would, at the same time, diminish, if not eliminate, the "non-antagonistic contradictions" within the socialist bloc, provided the Soviet Union was prepared to take up the role of the leader.

The Soviet position was different. Fully aware of the destructive capacity of their own nuclear weapons and those of the United States, Moscow was concerned with the holocaust that any confrontational situation might create both for the Soviet Union and for the United States.

Without going into the details of the Sino-Soviet dispute (dealt with elsewhere) suffice it to say that this first major fissure within the Socialist bloc set off a slow process of change in the Chinese view of the bipolar framework and finally resulted by 1974 in the projection of a new Chinese perception of the international system.

Ad Hoc Modifications

The most significant response to the new situation created by the Sino-Soviet dispute was the designing of a new framework which broke away from some of the basic tenets of Marxist-Leninist theory. Instead of continuing to reiterate the cosmic aspects of Marxism or according equal importance to the revolutionary movements in the developed capitalist, as well as the Third World countries, the CCP projected a modified picture of the international system in which the national liberation movements in the Third World figured as the main force of the whole revolutionary process.

The emphasis on the revolutionary potential of the Third World began in March 1963 with CCP's letter addressed to the CPSU. In it, it was argued that while all the four "fundamental contradictions" with which the world was afflicted were still operational, the national liberation movements were accorded a special place. The letter noted:

> The various types of contradictions in the contemporary world, are concentrated in the vast areas of Asia, Africa and Latin America; these are the most vulnerable areas under imperialist rule and the storm centres of world revolution dealing direct blows at imperialism ... In a sense, therefore, the whole cause of the international proletarian revolution hinges on the outcome of revolutionary struggles of the people of these areas who consitute the overwhelming majority of world's population. Therefore the anti-imperialist struggle of the people of Asia, Africa and Latin America is definitely not merely a matter of regional significance

10

but one of overall importance for the whole cause of proletarian world revolution.[18]

In May 1965, the national liberation movement was promoted to the rank of being "the most prominent and most acute of all the fundamental contradictions,"[19] and in October of the same year, it was clearly argued that the future of world revolution would be decisively settled by revolutions in the Third World. Stressing this point, Lin Biao wrote:

> Taking the entire globe, if North America and Western Europe can be called the 'cities of the world', then Asia, Africa and Latin America constitute 'the rural areas of the world'. Since World War II, the proletarian revolutionary movement has for various reasons been temporarily held back in North American and West European capitalist countries while the people's revolutionary movement in Asia, Africa and Latin America has been growing vigorously.[20]

Reduced to its bare essentials, the series of Chinese statements attributing an independent and primordial revolutionary role to the Third World in effect means that they were no longer operating within the tight bipolar framework.

Parallel to this revolutionary process, the Chinese introduced a diplomatic dimension—the dimension of the process of disengagement of the medium capitalist countries which were supposedly striving to free themselves from American domination.

Thus the two main components of the capitalist system which had constituted an integral part of the bipolar framework had varyingly sparked off a process of disintegration. By the mid-1960s, the United States was all that was left of an integrated capitalist world. It is interesting to note that the Chinese did not look at the United States through Marxist lenses. They did not appear to attach any importance to the class character of the American society nor did they appear to make any serious evaluation of the so-called "monopoly stage" of American capitalism—apart of course from the systematic utilisation of ideologically oriented polemical language to condemn the country. Long years of Western domination had apparently led them to reduce the United States policies solely to terms of a system of colonial enslavement.

American imperialism was not considered a reflection of a social system but a policy of a state solely directed at setting up, expanding, and retaining empires. They tended to associate the destiny of the United States mainly with the process of the collapse of the colonial system. They tended to reduce the struggle against the American system principally to a fight against colonialism. Simultaneously the Chinese also perceived the fragmentation of the Socialist bloc and the disengagement of some of the members from the dominant Soviet influence. This began with the characterisation of the Soviet Union as "revisionist" in the early 1960s, as "social imperialists" in the late 1960s, and as "anti-socialist" in the early 1970s.

By 1970, the major basic contradictions in the world were no longer between two opposing social systems but were between imperialism headed by the two superpowers and those whom they dominated (i.e., their allies) or those whom they attempted to oppress (i.e., the Third World). There had thus developed, in the Chinese view, a continuum between opposing super-powers at one end and practically the rest of the world at the other.

Having arrived at this basic view, China logically had to move herself out of the Socialist bloc. This was done in 1971 when she declared that she was a part of the Third World. "Like the overwhelming majority of the Asian, African, and Latin American countries", declared Qiao Guanhua, head of the Chinese delegation to the 26th Session of the U.N. General Assembly on 15 November 1971, "China belongs to the Third World."[21]

The Third World was now assigned an even more important position as representative of change than had been the case in the early 1960s. "The awakening and the growth of the Third World" was not only considered "a major event" in day-to-day contemporary international relations where its role was becoming "ever more significant,"[22] but was also viewed as the main motivating force "impelling forward the wheel of history."[23] In this part of the world, according to an often-used Chinese formula, "countries want independence, nations want liberation, and people want revolution."[24]

Three-Worlds Theory

All these *ad hoc* modifications, introduced slowly through the 1960s and early 1970s, led the CCP to finally make a new global and synthetic evaluation of the entire international system. Though this began with remarks made by some Chinese leaders in early 1974, the first public evaluation was made by Deng Xiaoping in April 1974 at the 6th Extraordinary Session of the General Assembly. Expounding the three-worlds theory, he completely revamped the Chinese view by giving a new dimension to the configuration of the international forces. No longer was the world viewed as bipolar. No longer was it divided ideologically but rather in terms of level of power, stage of economic development, and common interests. In the new analysis, the United States and the Soviet Union were put together as belonging to the "First World"; Japan, Europe and Canada were classified into the "Second World," and the whole of Asia, Africa, and Latin America were characterised as the "Third World".[25]

What was perhaps new in this new perception was that though the two superpowers were placed in the same group, they were no longer considered equally as the main adversaries. The Soviet Union was viewed as "the more ferocious, the more reckless, the more treacherous, and the most dangerous source of world war."[26] Moscow, in the Chinese view, had become a "state under Fascist dictatorship,"[27] even worse than the United States. The United States at least is on the decline. Everything in her daily policies and in her global posture seemed to reflect it. The Soviet Union, on the other hand, is on the ascendant. Her "state monopoly capitalist economy which is centralised to a degree unattainable by the United States"[28] and her state apparatus which puts "the entire economy on a military footing" makes it possible for her to be more aggressive than the United States.[29]

China's perception of the world had come full circle. From a view that had considered the United States her principal enemy, against which all forces were expected to unite, she had swung to the other extreme—the extreme of considering the Soviet Union the principal enemy against which everyone must join hands, including, if necessary, the United States. In this increasingly confrontational situation, China, by implication, sees herself playing a crucial role. For one thing, as a country with considerable experience of the Soviet Union, she considers that she is able to judge and evaluate Soviet actions more markedly than others; for another, being the most powerful of the Third World countries with a unique pattern of economic and social development, she probably sees herself as one of the few nations possessing the appropriate capacity of being able to mobilise most of the peoples and most of the countries.

Conclusion

China has a long-established tradition of regarding all phenomena conceptually and globally.

For over two thousand years, the Chinese perceived a hierarchical world order at the base of which were people of inferior culture living beyond the frontiers of Chinese civilization. This perceptual outlook was linked with another Chinese trait—the trait of according China a significant place within that system. During the long period of her history, she had always attempted to assign an important place to herself within the world order. Under the Confucian system, she was the centre of the world, representing the civilised world and claiming some kind of a universal authority to which all non-Han people were expected to pay tribute.

However, when the traditional view of the world order had been thoroughly discredited and was no longer considered to offer a valid explanation of the changing international reality of the 19th and 20th centuries, the Chinese elite turned to Marxism-Leninism. The principal explanation for this orientation can be found in the fact that Marxism-Leninism offered a conceptualised view of the international and national reality. On the one hand, the Chinese elite was able to construct a global image of the world which cut across national frontiers and which perceived the international reality in socio-economic terms. On the other hand, while operating within their national frontiers, they were able to comprehend the agonising developments that were taking place within their own country. The domination of China by the European powers, the disintegration of the country, the development of pre-Marxist revolutionary processes—all of these and other events could be analysed in socio-economic terms.

However, as soon as the Marxist theory began to take roots in China, it went through two processes: the process of sinification and the process of projecting on to the international scene what had been sinicised. The sinification process, set off in the 1930s and accelerated after the Chinese revolution, finally resulted in (a) the adoption of an independent developmental model for China's modernisation and (b) the formulation of an independent perception of the outside world. The process of projection really began after the revolution, with the Maoist assertion that the centre of world revolution has shifted again to China,[30] that the Chinese revolutionary and developmental models were relevant to other Third World countries, and that China, with the dissolution of the Socialist bloc, was one of the very few countries, if not the only one, that represented genuine socialism.

Notes

1. See E. Zurkher, *The Buddhist Conquest of China* (London: Hutchins, 1959).
2. Amaury de Riencourt, *The Soul of China,* Revised Edition (New York: Harper and Row, 1965).
3. Dennis Bloodworth, *Chinese Looking Glass* (London: Penguin, 1967), p. 328.
4. M. Frederick Nelson, *Korea and the Old Order in Eastern Asia* (Baton Rouge: Louisiana University Press, 1946), p. 12.
5. Justus Doolittle, *Social Life of the Chinese* (New York: Harper, 1865), Vol. II, p. 421.
6. Robert G. Weston, *The Imperial Order* (Berkeley and Los Angeles: University of California Press, 1967).
7. S. J. Pascal M. D'Elia, *Le triple Démisme de Suen Wen* (Shanghai: Bureau Sinologique de Zi-ka-we, n.d.).
8. Franz Schurmann and Orville Schell, *Imperial China* (New York: Vintage, 1964), p. 241.
9. Ibid., p. 302.
10. Amaury de Riencourt, op cit., p. 206.
11. Hu Sheng, *Imperialism and Chinese Politics* (Peking: Foreign Languages Press, 1955), p. 241.
12. Sun Yat-sen, *San Min Chu I* (Shanghai: China Committee, Institute of Pacific Relations, 1927).
13. Mao Zedong, *Selected Works* (Peking: Foreign Languages Press, 1965), Vol. I, p. 332.
14. Cited from John Gittings, "The Statesman" in Dick Wilson (ed.), *Mao Tse-Tung in the Scales of History* (Cambridge: Cambridge University Press,1977), pp. 250-251.
15. *Selected Works of Mao Tse-Tung,* op cit., Vol. II, p. 350.
16. See Liu Shaoqi's Speech to the Asian and Australasian Trade Union Conference held in November 1949, *New China News Agency,* 23 November 1949.
17. See Mao's *Selected Works,* op cit., Vol. IV.
18. From a letter of the Central Committee of the CCP to the Communist Party of

the Soviet Union of 30 March 1963; full text in *The Polemic on the General Line of the International Communist Movement* (Peking: Foreign Languages Press, 1965), p. 13.

19. Peng Chen's speech to the Indonesian Communist Aliarcham Academy on 25 May 1965; for text see *Peking Review*, 24 (1965), p. 12.

20. Lin Biao, *Long Live Victory of People's War* (Peking: Foreign Languages Press, 1965), pp. 48-49.

21. *Peking Review*, 47 (1971), p. 8.

22. Zhou Enlai, Report to the Tenth National Congress, *Peking Review*, 35 and 36 (1973), p. 22.

23. Speech of Deng Xiaoping to the Special Session of the U.N. General Assembly, ibid., 16 (1974), p. 7.

24. Chinese Representatives speech at the ECAEE Session, ibid., 5 April 1974, p. 22.

25. Ibid.

26. See editorial of *People's Daily:* "Chairman Mao's Theory of the Differentiation of the Three Worlds is a Major Contribution to Marxism-Leninism," *Peking Review*, 45 (1977), p. 22.

27. Ibid., p. 23.

28. Ibid., p. 20.

29. Ibid.

30. John Gittings, "The Statesman" in Dick Wilson (ed.), op cit.

15

Chapter 2

CHINA AND THE SOVIET UNION

Russian Expansion: The Early Years

Relations between China and Russia have indeed a long history. Much before the arrival of the West European maritime powers on the shores of China, geopolitical imperatives had caused the centres of two civilisations to come into contact with each other in the vast expanse of the "permanently frozen" and nearly uninhabited Siberia. For almost seven centuries—from 1223 when Mongolian warriors defeated the Russian forces on the bank of Kalka (present-day Kalchik) until the October 1917 Russian Revolution when the Bolsheviks seized power—the pattern of relationship was essentially conflictual.[1]

Without going into the chronological details of this abiding relationship—for this would take us beyond the scope of this short study—it is intended to highlight some of the salient aspects of Sino-Russian links.

The early years were essentially characterised by a continuous Russian drive eastward. With the exception of the Mongolian offensive westward during the 13th and 14th centuries, practically all the major movements were Russian. The initial thrust was made by waves of private adventurers who conquered all of eastern Siberia and the whole of Lena valley in the 17th century. This was followed by the subjugation of the extreme northeast, beyond the Kamchatka peninsula and the Sea of Okhotsk. By the end of the 17th century, Muscovy was already bordering on the Pacific. Further Russian advance, especially beyond the Amur River, was stopped by the Manchus by successful military initiatives and finally through the conclusion of the Treaties of Nerchinsk and Kiakhta in 1689 and 1727 which fixed boundaries between the domains of the Tsar and Manchu emperors.

But this was only a temporary interlude. In the middle of the 19th century the expansionary process was once again set off. This time it was carried out officially by the Russian authorities themselves with a new forcefulness that had appeared in Russian foreign policy, personified by Nicholas Muraviev, Governor General of Eastern Siberia. Taking swift advantage of the chaos in China as a result of the wars with Britain and France, a new process of expansion was inaugurated; and through a subtle combination of bold diplomatic initiatives and rapid military action, the Chinese were forced to sign a series of "unequal treaties" that finally enabled them to seize more territory and obtain more privileges than any maritime power. The Treaty of Aigun of 1858, for instance, secured for the Tsar a territory as large as France. The Treaty of Tianjin, signed in 1858, gave Russia all the privileges secured by England, France, and the United States; and the Treaty of Beijing, signed in 1860, not only recognised Russian sovereignty over territories ceded previously, but extended Russian jurisdiction over the vast region between the Ussuri and the Gulf of Tartary and granted trading privileges in Mongolia and Chinese Turkestan.[2] Russia's predominance over China probably reached its climax in 1895-1905 when she firmly implanted herself in Manchuria. The diplomatic treaties concluded with China to extend the Trans-Siberian Railway in 1896, where it was known as the Chinese Eastern Railway, and to obtain a lease of Port Arthur and Darien in 1898, bore the character of Russian dictates.[3] This seemingly irresistible expansion in the area can be attributed to a number of factors. There was, first of all, the human urge to discover unknown areas, to enhance the grandeur of the empire, to add to its glamour, and to increase the glory of its monarch. The Tsar was heir to a long line of leaders who had pushed the borders of their small principality farther and farther to establish the greatest land mass of the world. The dominant view in the nineteenth century was that this process could not be considered as having been fully achieved as long as the huge emptiness that seperated Russia from China had not been completed. Secondly, Russian expansion can also be attributed to the constant Russian urge to seek first control over partages and rivers that would give access to the open sea and thereafter the open sea itself.[4] Thirdly, the rapid Russian transformation from an agricultural state to a modern capitalist and industrial system in the 19th century pushed successive governments to intensify their efforts to seek markets beyond the defined Russian frontiers; and fourthly, the Russian policy was also designed to offset other imperial powers expanding in the area, and to strengthen the Russian position in the Pacific region where expanding empires had begun to converge.

Each of these elements have had their role to play in Russian expansion eastward. The grandeur of Russia was uppermost in the minds of the Russian leaders during the occupation of Siberia. To it was added the economic dimension when the Russian army sailed down the Amur river, only to be compounded with strategico-political considerations and the "urge to the sea" when they moved into China proper.

The Manchu dynasty was unable to halt this secular onslaught. With the first popular uprising that began in the province of Shandong in 1774, a process of internal decline set in from which the country as a whole never recovered until the 1949 revolution. Corruption spread rapidly among officials of the government. The army was allowed to become effete. The treasury was depleted in the aftermath of Qianlong emperor's extravagant campaigns. The enormous increase in the population in the 18th century was not followed by a corresponding technical revolution, as in Europe,

18

which would help to feed new mouths; and as a result, popular discontent began to explode with metronomic regularity.[5]

The Russian Withdrawal

Finally, Russian pressures from the north were checked by two extraneous developments—the rise of Japan and the 1917 October Russian Revolution.

Having rapidly developed into a powerful industrial nation with a series of relatively well-defined colonial interests on the Asiatic mainland, the Japanese attempted to contain the further expansion of Russian influence. They seized Korea from the Chinese after the Sino-Japanese War of 1894 and provoked the Russo-Japanese War of 1904-1905 with an attack on Inchon and Lüshun (Port Arthur). Severely defeated, Russia abandoned most of the recent gains acquired in Manchuria. Her power in the area had indeed suffered a serious retrogression.

The Russian response to this declining situation was two-pronged. On the one hand, abandoning all plans of any further expansion, Russia staged a general retreat from the area by returning to Europe. It was a development that was encouraged by Great Britain and France, the former linked to Japan, the latter to Russia, and both of them linked to each other by an *entente cordiale*. It is noteworthy that the same thing had happened in 1878—but in reverse direction: badly mauled in Europe after the Crimean War, she had turned to the East. By the very nature of her geo-strategic location, the choice—either Europe or the East—was always open and depended on the nature and the level of counter-pressures. Balked in the East, she abandoned all attempts at further expansion and turned her sights on Europe. On the other hand, the apparent Japanese predominance in the Far East led her to seek a *modus vivendi* with Tokyo in order to save whatever could be saved in the region. As many as four treaties were concluded between Japan and Russia within a span of a decade (1907-1916) defining their mutual interests.

If Japan had sucessfully contained Russian expansion, the 1917 Bolshevik Revolution further shrivelled Russian interests in China. Whatever had remained of Tsarist imperial interests had either been renounced by the new revolutionary government or had been unilaterally seized by China or Japan. This withdrawal from China continued for more than two years after the revolution. Apart from rhetorical and highly inflammatory declarations in which appeals were made to the Chinese people to revolt against the West, the Bolshevik leaders had hardly designed any policy to speak of as far as China was concerned. Even basic information on what really went on in China was unavailable in the Soviet capital.

There were a number of new reasons for this neglect, in addition of course to the Japanese barrage which had become ever more significant after the Russian Revolution. In the first place, the eyes of almost all the Bolshevik leaders were focussed on Europe where Communist revolutions were considered to be around the corner. The revolution in Russia was perceived as a prelude to the explosion of a series of revolutions in the developed countries which would finally culminate in the communisation of Europe and eventually of the whole world. All this was in line with the Marxist expectation that Socialist revolutions would inevitably take place in the industrially developed countries of the West. Secondly the area under direct Soviet control at the time was separated from China by a number of independent governments in Siberia. Therefore, most of the time when the Soviet leaders talked about the East during this period, they were thinking about Baku, Batum, Tashkent, rather than Beijing or Shanghai. However important China might have been, the Bolshevik leaders had more urgent work at home. Thirdly, the civil war, foreign intervention, and foreign blockade had created a situation marked by so much confusion, suffering, violence, and privation that it was out of the question for the Bolshevik leaders to assume the additional task of concentrating on China or any other country of Asia.

Resurgence of Russian Interest: Interwar Years

By 1920, however, the general situation in Russia and in Europe had undergone an important change which encouraged the Soviet leadership to turn to Asia. With the defeat of Kolchak and Denikin in the civil war it became possible for Soviet Russia to bring under her control the eastern borderlands which had declared their independence from Moscow after the October Revolution. Once again she found herself contiguous with China and a few other Asian countries. No longer was it then possible for the Bolsheviks to take only a theoretical interest in Asia or simply issue appeals to the peoples of the area to revolt against their internal and external oppressors. Obviously, something more palpable was needed to draw the revolutionary Asian masses into an alliance with revolutionary workers and peasants of Russia.

In addition to the breaking down of the geographical barrier there was another factor of even greater importance: the Communist revolutions in Europe, on which so much hope had been laid, had failed. The revolutionary uprising staged by the German Communist Party in Berlin (January 1919) not only failed to touch off a revolution but ended in disastrous defeat and physical elimination of Rosa Luxembourg and Karl Liebknecht, the two outstanding leaders of German Communism. The Munich Soviet collapsed after a few weeks and the Hungarian Soviet Government (1919) quickly disintegrated under heavy internal and external pressures. Hope again flickered in the summer of 1920 when the Red Army was pounding at the gates of Warsaw; but this again did not last long as the Poles counterattacked, leading to a general retreat of the Red Army and along with it the virtual disappearance of all hope of successful revolutions in Europe.

20

The Asian continent, on the other hand, was seething with discontent in the early 1920s; almost all the neighbouring countries were in the process of undergoing profound revolutionary changes. Afghanistan under Amanullah had become independent. Turkey under Kemal Pasha was in the throes of revolutionary changes; and India under Gandhi was rapidly mobilising the masses against the British.

In China, the situation was even more volatile. The political vacuum created by the final collapse of the Qing dynasty in 1911 was becoming wider and deeper. Waves of mass protest against the Japanese had been launched, and the working class movement in Shanghai and other cities had gained momentum.

All these momentous upheavals could not but impress the Bolshevik leaders. If Europe had failed them, at least there was Asia to revive their drooping spirits. Lenin, who had immediately grasped the importance of these events, did not hesitate to express his satisfaction over the manner in which Asia was changing. In almost all his communications and reports during the first few months of 1920 the Bolshevik leader made a point of referring to Asia. In his report to the All-Russian Central Executive Committee on 2 February, he confidently expressed the importance of "our relations with the East."[6] In his interview with *New York Evening Journal* on 21 February 1920, he pointedly referred to the awakening of the Eastern people "to a new life, a life without exploitation, without landlords, without capitalists, without merchants."[7] In still another report made at the All-Russian Congress of Toiling Cossacks on 1 March 1920, Lenin stressed that in every country in Asia there was "an awakening of political consciousness and the revolutionary movements grow from day to day."[8]

Moscow's United Front Strategy 1921-27

As far as China was concerned, the Revolutionary Soviet Government adopted a three-pronged policy of attempting to establish official relations with the Beijing government; of developing ties with the rapidly developing nationalist movement of Sun Yat-sen in the South; and of encouraging the Chinese Marxist revolutionary leaders to establish a Communist party. In the initial stages, relations with one were not allowed to influence or interfere with the other. They were clearly compartmentalized. However, as it became increasingly evident that Chinese nationalism was becoming the principal political force in the country, the three-pronged policy was slowly abandoned. On the one hand the increasingly discredited Beijing government, which was rapidly losing power and which had indicated its anti-Soviet proclivities, was relegated to second place; on the other, the members of the CCP, were pushed to join the nationalist party, the Kuomingtang, in order to transform it into a driving force of the revolution.

The new strategy was based on the theory that in the colonial and

21

semi-colonial countries, nationalism was the principal force and national independence the primordial objective. The aim of Communist parties was therefore to gain influence within the decision-making process of the nationalist parties so that they could be oriented in a given revolutionary direction. Though alternative strategies were proposed at the 2nd Comintern Congress, where the issue was extensively discussed, Communist alliance with nationalism carried the day.[9]

China was the first major experimental laboratory where an attempt was made to operationalise this strategy. When Sun Yat-sen, having failed to obtain any promise of aid from Britain or America, turned to Moscow, a concerted effort was made by Soviet Russia to take over the Kuomingtang. That Moscow's attempts were almost successful can be gauged from the remarkably high level of influence exercised by the Soviet advisers and the CCP members within the nationalist party. By 1924 most of the aid to the Kuomingtang emanated from Moscow, and pivotal positions within the party were held by Soviet advisers. Such Kuomingtang auxiliary societies as the "Federation of Farmers, Workers, Soldiers, and Students," and the "Youth Movement" were controlled by CCP members aided by Russian experts who had been specially brought into China for this purpose. The revolutionary movement that spread like a wildfire over south and central China in the spring of 1927 was guided by CCP members. Most of the successes achieved by the Kuomingtang against the Beijing government in the north and the independent war lords was substantially due to the CCP.

But this near success did not come through. The establishment of the hold over the Kuomingtang generated a strong nationalist sentiment against Moscow. In July 1923, one of the leaders, Dai Jitao, warned against the dangers of Soviet domination;[10] and Chiang Kai-shek, who had succeeded Sun Yat-sen and who had begun to have doubts about Soviet intentions, took an open stand against the CCP in 1926. By the end of the year he had completely disassociated himself from the leftist Kuomingtang government in Hankou. His headquarters in Nanjing assumed the status of a rival government challenging the authority of the Hankou regime. While the Kuomingtang leftists and the Communists rallied around Borodin, the conservatives turned to Chiang Kai-shek. When Chiang's forces occupied greater Shanghai in March 1927, he received financial support from the Chinese banking group which relieved him of any further reliance on Soviet Russia.

The final break took place in July 1927 after an Indian Representative of the Comintern, M. N. Roy, confided to Wang Jingwei, the Kuomingtang leader in Hankou, that he and key Soviet adviser Borodin had received orders to plan a takeover. Following this, the Kuomingtang Central Executive at Hankou formally adopted a resolution in July 1927 for the expulsion of all Communists. At this meeting Borodin's resignation was accepted. A Kuomingtang coup was finally staged during that year under which Soviet advisers were forced to leave the country, Soviet consulates were closed, diplomatic relations with Moscow were broken, and the CCP members were driven underground.[11]

Moscow's Second United Front Strategy 1935-1945

After a confused period of shifting policies and changing leadership for almost a decade, the CCP was compelled to rely largely on its own resources and to develop an indigenous strategy of armed revolution organised from the rural areas. However, within this new and autonomous framework, the party was nonetheless once again faced with the necessity of having to take a decision on the united front strategy proclaimed at the 7th Congress of the Comintern held from 20 July through 30 August 1935. On this occasion, the new line, as elaborated by Wang Ming, instructed the Chinese leaders (a) to cease the decade-old struggle against the Nationalist government; (b) to rename and broaden the Chinese Soviet government established in Kiangsi to include non-Communist groups; (c) to subordinate the Red Army to the Nationalist government; and (d) to relax their stringent economic and political policies.[12]

While the CCP leadership did not see any difficulty in accepting the Soviet line and even proclaiming it in its Politburo meeting of December 1935, it was reluctant to accept the specific form in which the propositon was made. The central issue was the role of Chiang Kai-shek and the Kuomingtang in the movement. Moscow appeared to consider that Chiang and his party were still pivotal elements in any united front strategy without whom it would be indeed difficult to rally the country against the Japanese;[13] the CCP and Mao Zedong, on the other hand, viewed Chiang as a "traitor to the nation"[14] and were not prepared to cede the leadership role either to him or to his party in any united front strategy. The final resolution of the Wayaopao conference where the issue was discussed reflected Mao's position. It called for a united front but without Chiang and under the CCP's leadership. The resolution declared that:

> The party's strategic line is to rally and organise all revolutionary forces of the whole Chinese nation to oppose the presently superior enemies—Japanese imperialists and traitor Chiang Kai-shek. All persons, all factions and all armed units, as long as they are opposed to Japanese imperialists and traitor Chiang Kai-shek should unite . . . The Communists should seek to obtain their right to leadership of the anti-Japanese front.[15]

This reluctance to join Chiang was not due only to ideological considerations—though they were important—but was also based on internal political reasons. Completely echoing Comintern's policy by Mao would have been tantamount to swinging over to the position of his rival Chang Guotao, who had advocated it all along and would have at the same time meant deserting some of his hard-line opponents.[16] Mao waited until Chang's fate was sealed. Once this had happened, which was the case by August 1936, Mao accepted completely the Comintern line.[17]

However, even if the final acceptance of the New United front strategy in the 1930s was comparable in many ways to that of the 1920s, the relations between the CCP and Moscow were no longer the same. For one thing, the areas from which the party operated in the 1930s were situated in the remote regions of Jiangxi and in even more inaccessible areas of Shanxi after the long march. Communications with the outside world were at best tenuous. The fourth plenum of the Central Committee of the CCP held in January 1931 was probably the last identifiable occasion of a direct Comintern presence in the person of Pavel Mif, formerly the director of Sun Yat-sen University and, since the spring of 1930, Comintern's principal agent in China. For a party which had been constantly under Moscow's control during the first ten years of its existence, the new situation was indeed a respite for the new leadership which permitted them to reflect independently.

By no means is it suggested that all contact was lost or all relations were broken or that the CCP was no more constrained to follow policies shaped in the Soviet capital; it only meant that within the broad policy framework designed in Moscow, the geographical remoteness permitted the party to have a much greater leverage in its day-to-day operations than before. Moreover, the general level of resistance against Moscow was higher among the new Chinese leaders with their rural backgrounds than those who were at the helm of party affairs in the 1920s. While accepting the challenge to forge the second united front, the CCP carefully avoided subordinating itself to the Kuomingtang. In fact, it was an alliance between two mutually suspicious governments, each of which had its own autonomous territorial base and its separate constituencies. Even this facade of a joint strategy evaporated with the "New Fourth Army Incident" of January 1941 as a result of which an entire unit of 10,000 men belonging to the New Fourth Army of the CCP was annihilated by nationalist troops, generating thereby considerable tension and open polemical exchanges between the two political parties. The Kuomingtang Military Council ordered the disbandment of the Fourth Army, and the CCP Revolutionary Military Commission condemned the nationalist action as an "anti-Communist onslaught" making it clear that the CCP "can no longer be easily deceived and crushed as it was in 1927."[18] Finally, even more important for the widening of the gap between Moscow and the CCP was the attempt by the new leadership, personified by Mao, to independently think out its own problems through the Marxist prism. All of Mao's predecessors—despite their training in philosophy and philology—had been too bogged down with day-to-day problems to seriously investigate the relevance of Marxism to China. Residing in the relative security of Yenan, Mao was the first leader to devote his mind to larger theoretical issues. During this period he was most productive, and his writings ranged from reflections on Marxist theory to a

24

detailed analysis of the different stages through which the Chinese Revolution was expected to pass through before reaching the goal of socialism.[19] All this had given the CCP a firm and independent ideological base which made it possible for the party leadership to eventually confront Moscow more effectively than many of the other Communist parties.

This trend towards autonomous decision-making became increasingly pronounced with the consolidation of Mao's hold over the organisational framework of the movement, particularly the party, army, and the state apparatus. Wang Ming, the last of the great pro-Moscow partisans within the party hierarchy, lost control over all the bases of his strength, including the Fourth Army, by early 1941.[20]

While drifting away from Moscow, Maoist leadership was careful in maintaining a pro-Soviet stance in foreign policy. While attempting to design its own strategy on national issues, it carefully continued to recognise Moscow as the headquarters of world revolution and continued to accept the Soviet lead in international issues. All the major turns in Soviet foreign policy during these years, including treaties with Germany and Japan in 1939 and 1941 respectively, were applauded without equivocation, regardless of the adverse effects they may have had on some of the plans of the CCP.

The climactic level in this process was reached during the party's so-called rectification campaign of the early 1940s during which Soviet influence was weakened even further. Mao had succeeded in applying "the theory of Marxism-Leninism to the specific circumstances of China"[21] inculcating in his comrades the habit of viewing political problems in their specific Chinese context and in affirming the independence of his leadership from Moscow.

If the CCP was moving towards greater autonomy, the Soviet Union was losing interest in her Chinese comrades and was turning more and more towards Kuomingtang China. The imperatives of the rapidly changing international situation, including the growing establishment of a linkage between Nazi Germany and expansionist Japan, conjured up terrible visions among Soviet leaders regarding a potential two-front confrontation. She perceived herself as pinned between two aggressive anti-Communist powers with no counterbalance to deter either of them. The European governments were either not interested in forging an alliance with Moscow against Nazi Germany or—at least in the Soviet view—were not making the appropriate concessions. In the Far East, practically the whole area was a vast colonial territory with which hardly any viable arrangements could be made. In the Soviet perception, the only exception apparently was the Chinese nationalist government which appeared to possess at least some political and military sinews to face Japan.

Soviet diplomacy in the Far East was thus focussed on the objectives of generating Chinese nationalist resistance and of foreclosing the fearful prospects of any rapprochement between the Chinese nationalists and the

Japanese. A close relationship was therefore established with the official Chinese government. A Sino-Soviet non-aggression pact was concluded in August 1937, important credits were given, arms were despatched and even a number of Soviet pilots were flown into China.[22] "Soviet Russia," declared the Chinese Foreign Minister W. W. Yen, "has rendered, perhaps more than any other power, material aid to China, in the form of arms, ammunition and planes."[23]

The heavy Soviet involvement in the European sector of the World War in 1941 once again relegated China to the lowest rung on the Soviet diplomatic ladder. Whatever interest Moscow then showed in the area was principally focussed on the task of avoiding any action that might irritate Japan and might impel her to declare war on the Soviet Union, thus forcing Moscow to face the terrible prospects of a two-front confrontation. All aid to China was therefore suspended; even all discussions of Far Eastern events was muted in the Soviet press.

But this was only temporary. As soon as the tide of the war turned in favour of the Allied powers in Europe, the Far East once again reappeared in Soviet strategy. Though some signs of this renewed interest were discernible in Stalin's conversations with US emissaries in 1942,[24] substantial indications of Soviet interest appeared at the Teheran Conference in November 1943, where Stalin outlined the concessions he would expect to gain in the Far East in exchange for Soviet entry in the war against Japan.[25] During the fourteen months following the Conference, the Russians formulated their requirements more and more concretely and finally received assurance that they would be granted in the secret agreement in Yalta which set forth the terms for Soviet entry into the war against Japan.[26]

In addition to guaranteeing the internationalisation of Dalian and the Soviet acquisition of the southern part of Sakhalin and Kurile Islands, the Yalta agreement provided for (a) the maintenance of the status quo in Outer Mongolia; (b) the joint Sino-Soviet operation of the Chinese Eastern and South Manchurian railways; and (c) the restoration of Russia's lease on Port Arthur as a naval base.

In return for these extensive concessions, Russia undertook to enter the Pacific war within "two or three months" after the surrender of Germany. Although the agreement stipulated that the provisions regarding Outer Mongolia, ports and railways would require the concurrence of Chiang, the three powers unilaterally agreed that the Soviet claim "shall be unquestionably fulfilled after Japan has been defeated."[27]

Moscow's Third United Front Strategy 1945 - 1948

Having obtained the formal and irrevocable commitment of the US and Great Britain for the fulfillment of Soviet claims, the Soviet effort was principally directed at assuring for itself that nothing untowards would happen that would endanger Soviet objectives.

The Soviet leaders therefore made a point of lulling American fears by repeatedly disclaiming any interest in Chinese Communism,[28] and by giving assurances to Chiang that his government was the only government recognised by Moscow.[29]

So far as the CCP was concerned, while giving them material aid in Manchuria, Moscow attempted to persuade them that Chiang Kai-shek was too strong, they were still too weak to stage a revolution, and "that they should join Chiang Kai-shek's government and dissolve their army."[30]

If Moscow succeeded in partially lulling American fears and in forcing Chiang's hand to conclude the Sino-Soviet treaty which formalised Soviet claims, they did not succeed in persuading the CCP to once again resort to a united front strategy in which they would have to subordinate themselves to the nationalist government. After having respectfully listened to their "Soviet comrades" in their meetings with them in Moscow, they returned to China to carry out the military offensive against the Kuomingtang which finally installed them in power in 1949.[31]

History was repeating itself. For the third time within a span of almost three decades the Soviet leaders were in effect pressing the CCP to once again follow the united front strategy. Presumably the Soviet Union was pushed to make this recommendation either by a fear that the CCP was not strong enough to win the civil war or by cold calculation that an indefinite continuation of instability—which would inevitably follow the united front strategy—could deeply embroil the United States, thereby opening the possibility for an unhindered Soviet push further into Europe.

The situation of the CCP was certainly very different in 1945 from the preceding periods (1921 and 1937) when it was pressed by Moscow to follow the united front strategy. By the end of the war the party had already established a firm base in the country and was led for almost a decade by a nationalist leadership whose dependence on Moscow was minimal. No longer was it prepared to follow Moscow if the policies proposed did not correspond to its own perception of the national interest.

What is most significant and perhaps an indication of its determination to remain independent of Moscow was that before and even during the final offensive that brought the CCP to power in 1949, it attempted to establish a working relation with the United States, presumably in the hope of establishing a measure of independence vis-à-vis the superpowers.

But this did not come through. Having failed in her efforts to mediate between the Kuomingtang and the Communists to establish a coalition government, the United States lost all interest in the CCP and refused to respond to Communist initiatives.[32]

The failure of this diplomatic initiative apparently left no choice to the CCP but to turn to the Soviet Union. Jettisoning its ambiguous and prudent position, the party then decided to move towards the policy of "leaning on one side"[33]— the Soviet side—in the international power game dominated by the two contending superpowers.

"Lean on one Side" 1949 - 1954

The implementation of this stance took place after the Chinese Revolution, the most dramatic manifestation of which was Mao's two-month-long official visit to Moscow and the conclusion of wide-ranging agreements in February 1950. The importance of these accords can be gauged by the fact that they offered to China appropriate external security, and, at the same time, provided the much-needed economic and technological assistance for the modernisation of the country, including a credit of $300 million spread over a period of five years.[34]

However, the forging of institutionalised ties with Moscow and the publication of myriad Chinese declarations accepting Soviet leadership did not imply any intention on the part of the Chinese leaders to accept an unquestionable subordination to the USSR.[35] Despite the critical level of Chinese dependence on Moscow for her twin goals of external security and internal modernisation, they enjoyed a wide degree of autonomy which, under the existing circumstances of monolithic Soviet hegemony, would have been unthinkable for any other Socialist country short of being expelled, as was the case with Yugoslavia.

While publicly and spontaneously accepting Soviet leadership, they made a point, for example, of upgrading their own revolutionary model and underlining its relevance to Asian conditions. Implicit in this argumentation was the Chinese contention that China had a far greater right to influence and to orient policies of Asian Communist parties than her senior partner.[36]

The initial Soviet reaction to Chinese claims was clearly negative. While acknowledging that the coming Chinese revolution was expected to become a major event in Asia, Soviet theoretical journals attempted to put across the thesis that what was taking place in China was less than socialist and therefore could not claim equality with the October Revolution of 1917. Concomitantly they also attempted to challenge the relevance of Chinese revolution to other Asian countries by underlining its specificity to China and by insisting that the classical revolutionary model, with all the improvements and modifications made by Lenin and Stalin, remained the only valid path for all countries, including Asia.[37]

That these conflicting viewpoints advanced in the Chinese and the Soviet press were not simple academic exchanges but were real tussles for influence was reflected through the strategic options taken by the Asian Communist parties on the contending revolutionary models. To risk a generalisation, it could be suggested that though all the Asian parties varyingly experienced intra-party crises following Sino-Soviet disagreements, the Asian response was essentially sub-regional. In areas such as South Asia, which had been spared the convulsions of World War II and which possessed more developed socio-economic structures, including a burgeoning proletariat, the Communist parties opted for the Soviet Union. In areas such as East Asia, which had been victims of Japanese occupation and had, as a result, experienced violent upheavals, the attraction to the Chinese model was more rampant.

The Indian Communist Party, for example, after some acrimonious debate between pro-Maoist and pro-Stalinist factions, publicly accused Mao Zedong of having presented strategies which were "horrible and reactionary" and which were "against every tenet of Marxism-Leninism."[38] On the other hand, most of the East Asian parties increasingly turned to Beijing. By the end of 1949 when the Chinese Red Army had overrun all of South China, direct liaison was established with the Burmese and Vietnamese parties which were reported to have been given assistance and which were inspired by the Chinese model in their peasant-based guerilla strategies. The Malayan Communist Party clearly influenced by Mao's "Strategic Problems of China's Revolutionary War," written in 1936, declared that a coalition of classes on Chinese lines was necessary for Malaya, and that the Malayan liberation struggle possessed the character of a "new democratic revolution".[39] After the abortive revolt of Madiun in 1948, the Indonesian Communist Party, under the leadership of Aidit and Lukman—both of whom had been to China—had absorbed much of Maoist thinking on revolutionary strategy:[40] and the Japanese Communist Party (JCP), pressed by Moscow and Beijing to jettison its moderate policy, opted for the Chinese line, and even attempted—despite different conditions—to follow Chinese strategy in the early 1950s.[41]

The final outcome of this first Sino-Soviet ideological competition was the Soviet acceptance of the Chinese revolutionary model for other Asian countries. In an editorial in the Soviet-controlled Cominform journal, it was formally declared in February 1950 that the Chinese model was relevant to many colonial and dependent countries and the Indian Communist Party, where the dispute had become serious, was called upon to formulate a strategy that would "draw on the experience of the national liberation model of China and other countries."[42]

That this was indeed a major development in the international Communist movement can be gauged from the fact that it was the first occasion on which the CPSU had accepted the validity of a revolutionary model other than its own for other countries. In many ways it was this major concession that set off the process of erosion of the hitherto unchallenged Soviet leadership within the Socialist bloc. Moscow was of course still perceived by all Communist parties, including China, to be the leader of the international Communist movement, but in the new situation, China had acquired the position of being considered more equal to the CPSU than the others.

Why this concession by the Russians? Did the overall international situation dictate it? Can it be argued that under the circumstances the Soviet leadership had no other reasonable choice than to cede to China?

Given the paucity of archival documentation on the subject, only a tentative hypothesis can be advanced regarding the possible reasons that might have contributed to this major Soviet shift.

During the period of continuous escalation of the cold war, any attempt to have a showdown with Beijing might have been viewed by Moscow as a risky operation insofar as it might weaken its confrontational capacity vis-à-vis the United States. Furthermore, given the apparent existence of a favourable consensus among Asian Communists regarding the relevance of the Chinese model to the area, any open challenge to the CCP might have contributed to the emasculation of Soviet influence among the Asian parties. Presumably neither the time nor the theme were considered as propitious for assailing the Chinese party. The general euphoria in the aftermath of the Chinese Revolution was probably too great to contain Chinese influence, and the Yugoslav Communist Party's successful defiance of Moscow in 1948 was too recent to stage another exclusion, particularly that of the CCP whose influence among Asian and even other Communist parties was weighty. Under the circumstances, papering over the differences with China appeared to be the least risky solution.

If the ideological differences between the two parties on the validity of contending revolutionary models had finally resulted in the assignation of a privileged status to China in the bloc itself, her role in the Korean war had given her an autonomous position within the international system. Whatever may have been the level of Sino-Soviet cooperation—views on which seem to differ—the successful and independent Chinese defense of her frontiers and the stalemating of US troops on the battlefield exploded on the one hand the US myth that China was a satellite of the Soviet Union, and on the other, foreclosed all Soviet attempts to confine China to a state of subordination.

However, despite this privileged status within the bloc, China's dependence on Moscow for her twin goals of modernisation and security remained inordinate. Her trade in the mid-1950s with Moscow had, for example, reached a peak—the highest among Socialist countries (see Table 2.1). Her annual average rate of industrial growth of 25 per cent between 1952-59 was made possible by a significant Soviet and East European financial support (see Table 2.2), and the flow of Soviet equipment and technical assistance "had a vital effect on the quality of China's industrialisation,"[43] enabling the country to produce such prestige items as jet aircraft, large electricity-generating equipment, metal-cutting machine tools, tractors, trucks and electronic equipment (see Table 2.3).

China's dependence on the Soviet Union for her security and for the acquisition of sophisticated weaponry was also great. While any threat from the United States was neutralised by a formal Soviet commitment to come to China's assistance, Moscow's help was equally crucial to acquire the much-needed weaponry for the ill-equipped Chinese army. Most of the weapons that China received emanated from the Soviet Union. "We'd given them," wrote Kruschev in his memoirs, "tanks, artillery, rockets, aircraft, naval and infantry weapons. Virtually our entire defence industry had been at their disposal."[44]

In the nuclear field, too, the Chinese needed Moscow. The extensive training given by the Russians to a large number of Chinese scientists and technicians in the nuclear sciences, the supplying of experimental nuclear reactors, the establishment of joint Nuclear Research Institute in Dubna near Moscow in 1956 contributed to the great leap China made in the field of nuclear weaponry.

The importance of the Soviet Union to China was thus undeniable. The successful attainment of the twin goals of modernisation and security were contingent on the maintenance of ties with the Soviet Union. At the same time a situation of such dependency on her senior partner was contrary to China's third basic goal of being sovereign and independent, one of the major elements that had catalysed the 1949 Revolution.

Clearly China was in a state of dilemma. What could she do to become more independent? What course could she take to enlarge the area of her autonomy in decision-making without compromising her goals of modernisation and security for which Russian help seemed necessary?

In order to extricate themselves from what was indeed a difficult situation, the Chinese leaders attempted to introduce some modifications in foreign policy objectives in the mid-1950s. While maintaining relations with Moscow, they attempted to neutralise the situation of over-dependence by mapping out a new and outgoing diplomacy of peaceful coexistence with the Third World, and by endeavouring to seek out the United States to relax tension in the Far East. The successful operationalisation of this new line, it was hoped, would permit the Chinese (*a*) to enlarge their area of autonomous decision making; (*b*) to neutralise the US threat to their security; and (*c*) to open alternative channels of assistance for modernisation.

But all this proved fruitless. Though ties with the Third World were beneficial insofar as they permitted China to widen her contacts with the outside world, they could hardly be considered as a credible substitute for their relations with the Soviet Union, for the poor and vulnerable Third World countries were hardly in a position to provide China with what the Soviet Union had provided so far. Similarly, the attempts to seek out the United States proved abortive. Though a process of negotiations was inaugurated in 1955, Washington was not interested in seeking any understanding on substantive issues that divided the two countries.

Table 2.1 *Derivation of Chinese Communist Trade with the USSR,[1] 1950-58 (US dollars in millions)*

Year	Trade reported by China	Trade reported by the USSR	Trade reported by China as a per cent of trade reported by the USSR[2]	Soviet imports from China	Derived trade Imports[3]	Exports[4]
	(1)	(2)	(3)	(4)	(5)	(6)
1950[5]	$ 320	$ 575	(5)	$ 190	$ 135	$ 190
1951	750	810	92,6	330	445	305
1952	965	960	99,5	415	550	415
1953	1,165	1,170	99,6	475	690	475
1954	1,270	1,340	94,8	580	720	550
1955	1,700	1,390	(5)	645	1,055	645
1956	1,460	1,495	97,7	765	715	745
1957	1,295	1,280	101,2	740	545	750
1958[6]	—	1,515	—	880	635	880

1. Assuming that the ratio of exports to imports in the trade data reported by the trading partners is the same as in the trade data reported by China. Value data are rounded to the nearest $ 5,000,000.
2. Unless otherwise indicated, col. 1 divided by col. 2.
3. Unless otherwise indicated, col. 6 subtracted from col. 1.
4. Unless otherwise indicated, col. 3 multiplied by col. 4.
5. The wide discrepancies between Chinese and Soviet reports of Sino-Soviet trade in 1950 and 1955 suggest major differences in procedures for recording trade. Because these procedures are more likely to have varied in the reporting of Chinese imports from the USSR (especially aid goods for the Korean war and goods for the joint-stock companies) than in the reporting of Chinese exports, the data on China's exports are assumed to be identical in value to Soviet-recorded imports from China and China's imports are calculated as the residual of total reported by China and exports.
6. Imports and exports as reported by the USSR.

Source: Congress of the United States Joint Economic Committee, *An Economic Profile of China*, vol II, (Washington: Government Printing Press, 1967) p. 645.

Table 2.2 *Soviet Aid to Bloc Countries, 1945-1962*
(In millions of U.S. dollars)

Recipients	1945-62	1959	1960	1961	1962
Albania	245.9	92.6			
Bulgaria	569.2				
Czechoslovakia	61.5				
East Germany	1,352.9		162.5	475.0	310.0[a]
Hungary	381.1				
Poland	913.9				
Rumania	188.7				
Communist China	790.0			360.0	
North Korea	690.0				
North Vietnam	368.9	25.0	200.0	3.9	—[b]
Outer Mongolia	658.0		186.3	135.4	
Total	6,221.1	117.6	548.8	974.3	

[a] Presumably part of 1961 credit of $ 475 million.

[b] Amount of credit unknown.

Note: The $ 360 million credit to China shown above for 1961 contains a large element of double-counting. In 1961, short-term credits of $ 320 million were extended to cover China's inability to meet her long-term debts to Russia, apparently due in 1960 and 1961. The $ 360 million figure also includes a $ 40 million credit extended for the purchase of Cuban sugar in 1961.

Source: US Department of State, *Soviet Aid to Less-Developed Countries Through Mid-1962*, Research Memorandum RSB-173, dated 14 November 1962, p. 19.

Table 2.3 *Planned "above-norm" Projects in Communist China 1953-1957*[a]

Industry	No. planned	No. to be designed by USSR	Import requirements
A. Heavy industry			
1. Iron and steel	15	3	Soviet machinery and equipment for 3.
2. Non-ferrous metals	18	18	Soviet machinery and equipment for 18.
3. Electric power	107	24	Soviet machinery and equipment for 24. 70% of the equipment for 80 projects also to be imported.
4. Machine-building	63	63	Soviet machinery and equipment for 63.
5. Coal	194	27	Soviet machinery and equipment for 27.
6. Oil	13	2	Soviet machinery and equipment for 2.
7. Chemicals	15	5	Soviet machinery and equipment for 5. in addition 1 cinematographic film plant was to be imported from Czechoslovakia.
B. Light industry			
8. Food	34	0	Equipment for 6 sugar refineries to be imported from East Germany, Poland, and Czechoslovakia.
9. Drugs and medical supplies	4	2	Soviet machinery and equipment for 2.
10. Paper	10	1	Soviet machinery and equipment for 1.
C. Others	221	11	
Total projects	694	156	

[a] These projects include re-equipment of existing industries. Not all the planned projects were started or completed during the First Five-Year Plan. The "norm" for heavy industry ranges between 5 and 10 million *yuan* and that for light industry between 3 and 5 million *yuan*.

Source: *First Five-Year Plan for Development of the National Economy of the People's Republic of China in 1953-1957,* Foreign Languages Press, Beijing, 1956, pp. 55-96, as summarized in Mah Fenghwa, "The First Five-Year Plan and Its International Aspects" in C. F. Remer (ed), *Three Essays on the International Economics of Communist China,* Univ. of Michigan Press, 1959, p. 90.

Search for Greater Independence

It was this impasse that led the Chinese leadership to radically reconsider its policies. Modification of some of its diplomatic goals was apparently not sufficient. What was needed was a real revamping of its internal and external options so as to obtain a greater leverage in her relations with Moscow.

Internally, the Chinese party, under the personal impulsion of Mao Zedong, abandoned the Soviet developmental model and oriented itself towards a more autonomous and self-reliant approach under which the need for Soviet assistance would become minimal. But it involved a radical revision of some of the key ideas of socialism. So far, it had been argued from Marx to Stalin that industrialisation was a major prerequiste for any socialist transformation. This had been generally understood to mean that communism could only follow from a higher economic base.

The new Maoist framework placed a great faith in development through the revolutionary fervor of man rather than on technical information or material incentives, supported the extensive development of a low level of industry in the countryside, and gave priority to the transformation of agriculture.

The new developmental model seemed to offer a new kind of goal—the goal of attaining a low level of communism. "It seems," declared a Central Committee resolution, "that the attainment of communism in China is no longer a remote future event. We should effectively use the form of People's Communes to explore the practical road of transition to communism."[45]

If the new model was an attempt to attain modernity autonomously, it was noteworthily also a consequence of decline in Soviet aid. The post-Stalinist leadership, concerned with problems of internal development and preoccupied with designing a new policy towards the Third World which involved financial assistance, had already indicated to the Chinese leaders that the flow of funds from Russia to China was not likely to be maintained at the existing level.

Within the framework of her new politics of self-reliance, China also decided to embark on a programme of strengthening her own defenses, the objective of which was to diminish dependence on Moscow for her external security. Here, too, the real catalyst was an increasing realisation that they could not rely on the Russians. For during the Taiwan crisis of August 1958, the Chinese, having bombarded Jinmen (Quemoy) and having threatened to blockade the offshore islands, received no Soviet assistance in the face of hard U.S. response. In fact the Soviet Union rescinded the Sino-Soviet agreement on atomic cooperation in June 1959 and decided at the last minute against sending an atomic bomb prototype which they had agreed to do in 1957.

If the basic Chinese goals of internal modernisation and external security had been seriously compromised by Soviet reluctance to give appropriate economic or military assistance, the Chinese saw no reason to continue a privileged and close relationship with Moscow. 1957-58 was the watershed period in China's internal and external policies. Not only was the Chinese leadership spurred into framing new policies and mapping out new goals, but it was also induced to set in motion the process of parting company with the Russians. This began slowly but finally escalated into a major dispute over a wide spectrum of issues pertaining to the important principles of Marxist theory and practice, to the assessment of the international situation, to the type of strategy and tactics required to confront the West, and to the issue of the alignment of the Sino-Soviet frontier.

Sino-Soviet Schism

Whereas a host of different factors provided the appropriate fuel for the evolution of the dispute, the crucial turning points that escalated it to new heights can be invariably traced to specific problems relating to security issues.

The 1958 Taiwan crisis was the first major issue on which the national interests of the two giants had clearly become discordant. It was probably during this juncture that Beijing began to question the usefulness of maintaining Sino-Soviet amity. The second major issue related to the Sino-Indian border dispute during which Moscow adopted a posture of neutrality, and the third was in 1968-69 concerning Sino-Soviet border alignment when differences were transformed into a limited military confrontation.

To risk a generalisation, it could be suggested that the moving apart of the two countries followed an escalatory pattern. From a level of differences on concrete issues in 1958, it developed into a polemical dispute on theoretical issues in 1960, and thereafter dilated into a serious conflict in 1969, first centring around the border issue but soon spreading in all directions on all major issues.

Evolution of the Dispute: de-Stalinization

Differences between China and the Soviet Union, as examined earlier, date back to the Stalinist period. But they did not then follow an escalatory pattern and did not move beyond a simple but discreet assertion of their respective viewpoints. Moreover, there was presumably an implicit understanding between the two countries not to openly air their differences since the advantages accruing to both of them from such an alliance outweighed the disadvantages.

The real origination of the schism can be traced to the CPSU's 20th Party Congress where, without any consultations with any of the parties, Khruschev dramatically inaugurated a process of de-Stalinisation with a harsh denunciation of Stalin personally. Whereas the Soviet leader was convinced that the CPSU alone had the right to decide on the timing and the nature of the anti-Stalinist offensive, the Chinese considered that the implications of such an action, particularly on the international Communist movement, could be so serious that any unilateral decision on the part of the CPSU on such a major issue was unacceptable. Besides, they argued, Khruschev's assessment of and charges against Stalin were not completely correct since he had "made a great contribution to the progress of the Soviet Union and the development of the international Communist movement"[46] and since he had "creatively applied and developed Marxism . . . and proved himself to be an outstanding Marxist-Leninist fighter."[47]

While defending Stalin, the Chinese also made it a point to underline some of his "serious mistakes in regard to the domestic and foreign policies of the Soviet Union"[48] and to congratulate the CPSU on having "taken measures to correct the mistakes and eliminate the consequences."[49]

This attempt to present a balanced picture of Stalin, after having deliberated at the highest level (politbureau) was not so much because the CCP was really Stalinist, but rather because of the serious consequences that it could have on the unity of the international Communist movement. For almost three decades, the Communist parties all over the world had eulogised and unquestionably accepted the authority of Stalin. To summarily condemn him and question his contribution to the Soviet system in such violent terms, without any preparations and without even any forewarning to other parties was tantamount to the opening of Pandora's box, which could only prove disastrous to international Communism.

That the Chinese fears turned out to be correct became evident from the subsequent developments in the international movement. Though Khruschev's unilateral initiative to condemn Stalin did not as such have any major repercussions on the Communist parties, it certainly was instrumental in setting off a process of disintegrating the cohesive character of the entire movement. The Chinese apprehensions of de-Stalinisation can also be attributed to the fear of dire consequences it could have within China. People in China could well ask the question: if the "cult of the personality" had finally led to serious errors in the Soviet Union, could such a situation not reproduce itself in their own country where Mao Zedong had acquired a position equivalent to that of Stalin?

Well aware of the situation, the Chinese attempted to suggest that all errors committed within the party occurred before Mao assumed control over the party; at the same time the party made a point of underlining the distinction between "the cult of the personality" of which the CPSU had become victim during the Stalinist period, and the non-authoritarian character of the Chinese leadership.

The discordant voices emanating from Beijing in defense of Stalin could also be viewed as an expression of defiance towards and a challenge to Khruschev's leadership. If the CCP since 1949 had accepted, though sometimes reluctantly, the decisions taken under the supreme authority of Stalin, it was not prepared to blindly submit to the uncertain and doubtful judgements of his weak successors—particularly on such an important issue as the role of Stalin in Soviet politics.

The Chinese attempt to present a different and more balanced view in widely diffused and lengthy articles containing all the theoretical jargon could also be viewed as an implicit challenge to and competition with the Soviet leadership on major issues with the objective of gaining influence and authority over the international Communist movement.

The ground for turning away from each other had thus been laid. The process of what later degenerated into a real and open schism had commenced, and with the passage of time the kaleidoscopic events that successively appeared on the international horizon widened the gap between the two countries.

With effect from 1956, the Chinese were apparently no more prepared to toe the Soviet line. While maintaining the facade of formal unity, they were determined, at least within the confines of Communist conclaves, to assert their own viewpoint. When the rumblings of discontent began in Hungary and Poland in 1956, the Chinese protected the Polish revolt from being suppressed, but pushed the bemused Russians to nip in the bud the Hungarian revolution, which, in their view, had gone beyond the limits established by the international Communist movement. When the 1957 conference of office-holding Communist parties met in Moscow to discuss global strategy for the future, the Chinese accepted the inclusion of the Soviet thesis on peaceful transition to socialism in the common declaration, but only on the condition that the other thesis—the thesis of violent revolutions—was given equal importance.[50] And when on the same occasion, the CPSU, mindful of the considerable and dangerous growth in nuclear weaponry, argued in favour of reducing conflicts through a policy of peaceful coexistence, the Chinese urged a more militant line.

Conflicting Foreign Policy Perceptions and Actions

Though all these issues were undoubtedly considered important, the one that had the maximum effect on and led to the most palpable ramifications in the foreign policies of the two countries in 1957 was the issue of peaceful coexistence. Disagreement on this point in effect meant that every time a confrontational situation presented itself in any part of the globe, the Chinese, on the one hand, proposed such risky actions as pushing the United States into a defensive position, while the Russians, on the other hand, followed a policy of prudence and sought solutions through a process of negotiations and accommodation. Consider the Middle East crisis of 1958. The Iraqi coup of 13 July 1958 and the subsequent British and American landings in Lebanon and Jordan presented the first test case of divergent strategic views. For the Russians this had created an explosive situation

38

which needed careful political and diplomatic action to prevent any further escalation. Their principal concern was therefore directed at getting the US and UK to the conference table to resolve the crisis politically. When their own proposal of convening an emergency summit meeting was rejected, they accepted the Western counterproposal for a summit meeting within the framework of the UN Security Council.[51] For the Chinese, energetic military response by the Socialist countries was the only answer should the Western countries refuse to withdraw from Lebanon and Jordan and should they make any attempt to attack the Iraqi Republic. An editorial of the *People's Daily* therefore clearly declared on 20 July that "if the US-British aggressors refuse to withdraw from Lebanon and Jordan and insist on expanding their aggression then the only course left to the people of the world is to hit the aggressor on the head."[52]

Consider the Taiwan crisis of August-September 1958. Since it involved direct national interests, the Sino-Soviet disagreement and tension was even more clearly established. Since 1949 the Chinese had regarded the recovery of Taiwan as one of their prime goals. In 1954-55, they vainly attempted to recover Taiwan through military pressure. In 1956, they initiated moderate diplomacy, which also failed. In August 1958, they once again switched to pressure by expanding their military build-up opposite the islands, by directing a heavy artillery barrage on Jinmen, and by extending their territorial waters up to 12 miles, which in effect constituted a challenge to American ships convoying Nationalist supply vessels to Jinmen and Matsu.

Though the new militant posture was partly the result of an internal swing to the left, the prime element was the Chinese conviction that the international balance had decisively shifted as a result of the successful launching of the Soviet sputnik in 1957. The moment had therefore arrived for the Socialist countries to take advantage of the situation in order to place the capitalist world on the defensive. For the Chinese the "new turning point"[53] meant that, with firm Soviet backing to defend China in the event of a US nuclear threat, they could probably achieve at least their objective of integrating Taiwan and the offshore islands to the mainland.

The Soviet Union, however, did not perceive the international situation in the same manner. If it had improved for the socialist bloc, the military balance had by no means tilted since the nuclear arsenal possessed by the United States was more than sufficient to deter any Soviet action.

Therefore when the question came up for discussion—for the question was evoked—[54] the Soviet Union was reluctant to make any commitment which might embroil her in a situation that could prove disastrous.[55] The Chinese nonetheless decided to go ahead with their offensive, regardless of Soviet reluctance, with the probable expectation that whatever formal decision the Soviet leaders might take would in any event place them in a difficult position. If they decided to come to the aid of the Chinese, this would clearly undermine the Soviet objective of seeking entente with the Americans. If, on the other hand, they decided to remain neutral, it would

39

become formally evident that the defense provisions of the Sino-Soviet alliance were valueless. Furthermore, such an attitude could well weaken the position of those in the Chinese leadership who were still firm partisans of maintaining the alliance.

Moscow found its own solution, as it had in the Suez crisis of 1956. Kruschev's strongest pledge of support to the Chinese came only after the crisis had passed its critical stage.

While much of this is speculation, it does seem safe to assume that the Chinese were greatly disappointed by the Soviet failure to provide prompt nuclear backing during the crisis. It clearly demonstrated that the linchpin of Sino-Soviet alliance—external security—which had originally impelled the Chinese to conclude the agreement, had lost much of its force.

In all probability it was this particular crisis that led the Chinese to question the usefulness of the alliance; at the same time, these events also convinced them of the vital necessity of acquiring their own nuclear deterrence. Since Soviet assistance still was of critical importance, the Chinese opted to remain silent about their disappointment over Taiwan and attemped to play down the significance of the offshore bombardment. They claimed that their initiatives were nothing more than a simple exercise to demonstrate the continuation of the civil war with the Kuomingtang and thus frustrate the would-be "two-China plotters". Publicly, therefore, the Chinese maintained the myth of the alliance. At the 21st Congress of the CPSU in January 1959, Zhou Enlai declared that: "Since the Great October Socialist Revolution, the Soviet Union has always been ahead of the times, and by its brillant example of socialist and communist construction inspires the proleteriat and the working people of the world. They see their future in the Soviet Union's present day."[56] At the April 1959 session of the National People's Congress, the Chinese leaders noted the great importance of Sino-Soviet economic cooperation. "The countries of the socialist camp, led by the Soviet Union," declared Zhou Enlai once again, "have given us all-round assistance in socialist construction in our country."[57] And on the occasion of the 10th anniversary of the Chinese Revolution, the Chinese Prime Minister once again went on record to publicly express the "utmost gratitude" of the Chinese people "to the Soviet Union which gave our country assistance since the revolution."[58]

But the Chinese intention to maintain the myth of solidarity with the Russians did not work; for the events of 1958, which could have culminated in a general conflagration, made Khruschev realise not only the diversity of Soviet and Chinese national interests but also the terrible risks the Chinese leaders were prepared to take on issues which were not of general interest to the Socialist countries as a whole. What would China do if she possessed nuclear weaponry? Would she not run similar risks and involve the Soviet Union in conflicts which were not of her making and from which she would have nothing to gain? Was it really safe to give the appropriate military knowhow to the Chinese?

These doubts must have began to develop in the minds of the Soviet leaders in the aftermath of the 1958 crisis and must have been instrumental in the unilateral Soviet cancellation of the nuclear agreement of June 1957 under which China was to be given appropriate technology to develop nuclear weaponry. But this was not the only reason. The discreet anti-Soviet campaign among the other Communist parties and the equally still-discreet territorial demands on the Russians also had something to do with the Soviet decision to renege on the Sino-Soviet atomic agreement. Explaining these events, Khruschev declared:

> We convened a meeting and tried to decide what to do. We knew that if we failed to send the bomb, the Chinese would accuse us of reneging on an agreement, breaking a treaty, and so forth. On the other hand, they had already begun their smear campaign against us and were beginning to make all sorts of incredible territorial claims as well. We did'nt want them to get the idea that we were their obedient slaves who would give them whatever they wanted, no matter how much they insulted us. In the end we decided to postpone sending them the prototype.[59]

The Sino-Indian border skirmishes in July-October 1959 further aggravated the Sino-Soviet dispute. For the Chinese, the Soviet decision to publicly adopt a neutral attitude[60] on the border question and to privately dissuade them from escalating the conflict [61] was perceived as even worse than their attitude on the Taiwan crisis. At least during the Sino-American offshore island confrontation the Russians had given their moral support. During the Sino-Indian skirmishes, Moscow had simply declined to give any help whatsoever and had refused to accept the Chinese suggestion not to issue the Tass statement through which Moscow had declared its neutrality.[62] Furthermore during the same period, the Soviet government had almost doubled its aid to India.[63]

The compounding of all these developments (offshore islands, nuclear assistance, and Sino-Indian skirmishes) had undoubtedly created a critical situation. For the first time national interests had clearly clashed; and for the first time it was no longer simply a question of expressing opposite views on such issues as de-Stalinisation, the Great Leap Forward, or on the relative military power of the two blocs, but clearly involved concrete national issues of major importance to China.

It is noteworthy that it was at this critical point in bilateral relations when some basic decisions had to be taken on both domestic and external issues that divisions within the Chinese leadership began to appear on what to do next. Should China opt for further intensification of her programme for independent modernisation focussed on agriculture or should she revert to the earlier Soviet model based on heavy industry? Should she decide for a bootstrap nuclear development or should she, despite Sino-Soviet tension, accept the Soviet nuclear umbrella? Should she continue to incorporate "Soviet advanced experience" in the development of modern military techniques and military science or should she turn her attention principally to the task of mobilising the masses, relying on them for the defense of the country?

The crucial factor behind all these options was the Soviet Union. Whether the options pertained to modernisation or nuclear strategy or the organisational framework of the armed forces, the pivotal element of the domestic debate was China's relations with the Soviet Union.

The debate was finally resolved with the decision of the Central Committee plenum to opt for the Maoist strategy of self-reliance and autarchic development with a minimum of dependence on the outside, including the Soviet Union.

The pursuit of such a line was accompanied by the removal of Peng Dehuai as Minister of Defense who had challenged Mao's strategy of the Great Leap Forward and had probably favoured the formula under which China, while accelerating the modernisation of her economy and the armed forces, would continue to rely on the Soviet nuclear umbrella even if it involved making, in exchange, some military concessions to the Russians.

The removal of Peng was not due only to his disagreement with Maoist strategy. It was also because of some indiscretions he had committed during his meetings with the Soviet leaders at a time when anti-Soviet options were increasingly gaining support in Chinese politics.[64] Furthermore, during his 1959 Moscow trip he had been publicly too admiring of the professional skills of Soviet officers and of the technological sophistication of Soviet weaponry.

With the political elimination of Peng and his friends, domestic obstacles to the emergence of the dispute were removed. The forum and the themes to initiate the dispute were well-chosen. Since China's first objective at the time was to obtain the support of the international Communist movement, differences were aired within the framework of the Communist organisations, and the themes evoked were given a heavy ideological colouration. The process of airing divergent views began in February 1960 at the meeting of the Warsaw Pact countries, where Kang Sheng represented China as an observer, and was successively continued in Beijing in June at the meeting of the General Council of the World Federation of Trade Unions; in Bucharest at the Romanian Party Congress; in November at the important meeting of the 81 Communist parties; in October 1961 at the 21st Congress of the CPSU where Zhou Enlai was personally present; and at the Communist party congresses in Hungary, Italy, Bulgaria and Czechoslovakia. With the publication of *People's Daily* editorial, "Proletariat of all countries unite against the common enemy, " in March 1963 the dispute came out in the open.

The Ideological Dimension

The form given to the Sino-Soviet dispute in the early 1960's was essentially ideological. For one thing, any attempt on the part of the two giants to highlight their conflicting opinions in terms of a simple clash of national interests would not have had the desired effect of swinging the international Communist movement to their side, which appeared to be their major objective; for another, ideologically-orientated argumentation within the Communist movement had always been the traditional means of communicating with each contestant projecting himself as the defender of the doctrine.

If the massive documentation through which the two parties repeatedly presented their respective views were to be conceptualised and capsulised, the area of dispute on the theoretical front could be narrowed down to three basic interacting and interconnected themes: the issue of war and peace; the peaceful transition to socialism; and the importance of the Third World in international revolutionary strategy.

Since the 20th Congress of the CPSU, the Soviet leadership has argued that the acquisition of nuclear weapons by the United States and the Soviet Union makes a global conflict unacceptable as an instrument of social change. Any superpower conflagration would not any more lead to the advancement of social revolutions as it had done in the past, but to the massive annhilation of all social systems. Such a situation must therefore be avoided through a concerted policy of seeking detente with the United States and through a vigilant policy of avoiding eventualities susceptible of becoming confrontational and conflictual. The only acceptable way left to reach the communist goal of world revolution therefore is through a process of peaceful transition to socialism of the capitalist societies and through a collateral process of coexistence with the United States. This can be achieved by demonstrating that the socialist model of development and distribution can satisfy the material and spiritual needs of humanity far more effectively than the existing capitalist system in the Western world; the only way this can be convincingly done is through the continuous development of socialist economies until the entire bloc becomes the most powerful and the most attractive force in the world, at which point the final revolutionary offensive could be effectively launched. That the Socialist bloc could economically surpass the capitalist countries; that it could eventually cause the continual "multiplication of benefits" for its citizens leaving the capitalist world far behind: of all this the Soviet leaders were convinced, since in their view, the stimuli for secular economic growth was built into the Socialist system.

However, parallel to this process of peaceful evolution, the numerous contradictions within the capitalist system would, in the Soviet line of thinking, continue to generate non-global conflicts. While some of them, like local wars, would need "maximum vigilance"[65] because of the risk of

43

their escalation into a nuclear holocaust, the others, like national liberation movements, civil wars, and popular uprisings are unavoidable and as such should be encouraged in order to place the capitalist world more and more on the defensive. Through this two-pronged strategy of accelerated socialist economic development and localised conflicts in the Third World, it should be possible to finally bring about the collapse of the capitalist world.

If the rapid development of socialist economies has a demonstrative effect on the capitalist world insofar as ever larger groups of people may be attracted in this way to socialism, it is still by no means sufficient to actually push the developed capitalist countries to swing towards socialism. Revolutionary efforts within each of the capitalist countries obviously would be the main catalyst in bringing about the evolution of the capitalist society from one social system to the other. Though there are different ways of achieving this goal, the gradualist revolutionary strategy, ran the Soviet argument, is both advantageous as well as possible in developed capitalist countries. It is advantageous because it involves "minimal destruction" of the economy making it thereby possible for the working class to take over "the production from the capitalist monopolies intact and, after the necessary reorganisation, immediately put it into operation in order that all sections of the population may rapidly convince themselves of the advantage of the new mode of production and distribution."[66] Peaceful transition was furthermore seen as possible because objective conditions within the capitalist countries had indeed evolved since World War II.

In the first place, it had become increasingly possible for the working class to gain access to centres and levers of political and economic power in capitalist countries even before the revolution. In some cases it was possible "to win a solid majority in Parliament and turn it from an organ of bourgeois democracy into a genuine instrument of peoples' will."[67] In other cases the working class might be able to gain access to State power through the "extension of working class influence in the economy through greater control over the various forms of activity by the entrepreneurs and their agencies."[68] By this penetrative process the Communist parties are able to constantly champion the socialist alternative in every practical issue and are thereby able "to establish links between day-to-day tasks and the end objectives."[69]

Secondly, the establishment of "state monopoly capitalism" has accentuated contradictions of such dimensions within the capitalist society that it has now become possible for the working class to rally to itself increasingly deprived and alienated social groups in order to obtain the arithmetical majority necessary to come to power.

Thirdly, a new and favourable international situation has cleared the way for revolutions to develop without any external hinderance. Since the East-West balance had clearly tilted in favour of the Socialist bloc, it was no longer possible for "international reaction to forestall or undermine the revolutionary process" within countries as had been done in the past when

44

the Soviet Union was weak and when socialism had not as yet spread beyond the frontiers of Russia.

If the Soviet framework regarding a peaceful transition from capitalism to socialism remained essentially faithful to some of the original Marxist tenets, it broke new ground on the question of the transformation of national liberation revolutions into socialism. The new Soviet thinking advanced the thesis that the pre-industrial societies could also "grow over into socialist revolutions"[70] and eventually even adopt a "socialist course"[71] without having to pass through the successive stages of development outlined in Marxist theory and without necessarily having to resort to an armed struggle. Such an evolution was feasible if they would first of all adopt the transitional road of "non-capitalist development", the basic content of which is internally moderately socialistic and is externally nationalistic. Though such a model of development, in the Soviet view, had already become operational in a number of countries (Algeria, Guinea, Tanzania, People's Republic of Congo, Syria, Iraq, Somalia, the People's Democratic Republic of Yemen, Burma and UAR during the Nasser period), the prospects of its future expansion into other countries was viewed as almost inevitable. For one thing, long periods of colonial rule had created innate contradictions between them and the advanced capitalist countries, thereby generating a strong trend towards nationalism; for another, many of these countries "are feeling today the great drawing power of socialism" as an alternative developmental model.[72] Though the very existence of the Socialist bloc is a guarantee for the maintenance of the independence of the Third World, the acceleration of the developmental process can be assured by the Soviet deployment of its military and political power against any external threats and by the utilisation of its economic power to help in their disengagement from the tentacles of the Western economic system.

From the foregoing analysis of Soviet innovations in Marxist theory, three basic conclusions could be tentatively advanced: First, one of the interconnecting themes in all these modifications is the Soviet attempt to highlight the importance of gradually moving from one transitory phase to another in the process that leads to communism. Whether it is the issue of war versus peace or a peaceful versus a violent shift to socialism, the new Soviet tendency, at least on the theoretical level, is to underline the relevance and feasibility of non-conflictual methods and processes to reach the eventual goal of world revolution. Secondly, the Soviet theoretical framework has established a clear linkage between "the three main revolutionary currents" within the international system.[73] They are perceived as indivisible, constantly interacting and influencing the orientations of each other. However, while carefully distributing significant roles to all three of them, in the Soviet revolutionary framework, the decisive element nonetheless remains the developed countries, since in the Soviet view the national liberation movements, not being socialist, "cannot play the deci-

45

sive role in mankind's transition from capitalism and socialism"[74] and since the international working class—principally centred in the developed countries—"has been and remains the decisive force in the development of world revolution."[75] Thirdly, as the success of global socialism was contingent upon the economic success of the socialist model, the developed countries acquired even greater importance in the international revolutionary balance. The more the socialist countries were able to satisfy the material and spiritual needs of their citizens, the more chance they had of convincing other nations and other peoples to move in the socialist direction.

Implicitly, the Soviet conception of demonstrative effect placed the Third World countries in an even more secondary position—for premature socialist revolutions in economically backward countries would only slow down the original socialist objective of becoming more powerful than the Western world, since the Socialist bloc would have to provide these countries with massive assistance instead of focussing, attention on the task of developing its established socialist economies. The objective of the Socialist bloc in the Third World, in the Soviet view, therefore should be to encourage them to opt increasingly for the non-capitalist road of development under the leadership of revolutionary democrats, and to help them, politically and economically, to become more and more disengaged from the Western world. In short, the Soviet Union was implicity suggesting a holding operation in the Third World while the decisive battle of world revolution was conducted in the West.

The Chinese rejected all these arguments. That the Socialist countries should focus their attention on the rapid expansion of their economies, that they should strive to significantly improve the standard of living of their citizens was a goal which obviously merited considerable effort by and sympathetic attention of all communist governments. But to identify all this with the fundamental objective of world revolution was tantamount to national chauvinism, which had no place in the international Communist movement. Furthermore, to argue that the economic advancement of the socialist world system would automatically and inevitably rally the rest of the world around the communist flag was patently absurd, since there was neither any past evidence nor any present indications to suggest that such an evolution was possible. If anything, both the past as well as the present pointed to the opposite direction—the direction of violent conflict and change. "War," declared China," is an inevitable outcome of the systems of exploitation, and the imperialist system is the source of modern war. Until the imperialist system and the exploiting classes come to an end, wars of one kind or another will still occur."[76] No socialist country wants global nuclear conflicts, but should they be unleashed "the result will only be the very speedy destruction of those monsters themselves encircled by the peoples of the world and certainly not the so-called annihilation of mankind."[77] On "the debris of civilisation," continued the Chinese argument, "the victorious people would create very swiftly a civilisation thousands of times

46

higher than the capitalist system and a truly beautiful future for themselves."[78]

The Soviet thesis of a peaceful transition of advanced capitalist countries, in the Chinese view, was equally unrealistic, since "there is still not a single country where this possibility is of any practical significance."[79] Any attempt therefore to "overemphasize the possibility of peaceful transition"[80] would be tactically dangerous since it would lull the parties into a false sense of security from which it might be indeed difficult to extricate themselves should the circumstances make it imperative for them to seek alternative and less peaceful solutions. Besides, sweeping generalisations regarding peaceful transitions without emphasizing clearly the areas in and the conditions under which this might be possible, would only generate considerable "confusion among the majority of the parties where it is distinctly impossible."[81] Furthermore, it was not possible to square the new Soviet thesis with the original Marxist scheme of things under which "the smashing of the bourgeois state by the proletarian state" was necessary.[82] The Chinese clearly argued that "Marxism has always proclaimed the inevitability of violent revolutions. It points out that violent revolution is the midwife to society, the only road to the replacement of the dictatorship of the proletariat and a universal law of proletarian revolution."[83]

Differences with the Russians regarding the Third World were even greater. The crucial task faced by these countries was not so much one of economic development in cooperation and coordination with the socialist world system but of successfully resisting continuous imperialist aggressions of which they were the principal victims. Moreover, their transition from national liberation to the socialist phase could by no means be conceived of as a peaceful evolution stretching over a long period under the leadership of non-communist parties. On the contrary, the two revolutions "were closely linked together"[84] and "the struggle of the socialist revolution could be waged without interruption immediately after the nationwide victory of the democratic revolution."[85] The key to ensuring a rapid transition to socialist revolution "is the firm grasping of hegemony in democratic revolution through the Communist party."[86] Any other strategy under which nationalist parties would be permitted to maintain a command over the democratic revolution would inevitably endanger the revolutionary process and could cause these countries to gravitate back to the Western camp. The Chinese, furthermore, contested the Soviet thesis that the decisive tilting of the global balance in favour of the socialist countries was contingent on the successful operationalisation of the revolutionary process in the developed countries. On the contrary, they are centred in the Third World. "In a sense", they argued, "the whole cause of the international proletarian revolution hinges on the outcome of the revolutionary struggle of the peoples of these areas who constitute the overwhelming majority of the world's population."[87]

If the new Soviet theoretical framework was essentially a search for non-conflictual solutions to Marxist conundrums, the Chinese conceptualisation was an attempt to uphold the original tenets of Marxist thought which linked change to violence and revolution. These conflicting views were largely an expression of their assymetrical power situations within the international system. If the Soviet Union, having acquired the status of an established nuclear power and having attained the essentials of foreign policy goals, was prepared to abstain from taking any major risks vis-à-vis her principal adversary, the United States, China, still a regional non-nuclear power, was remote from attaining some of her foreign policy objectives: the goal of integrating Taiwan remained unfulfilled, and the United States was threateningly installed on her periphery. It was thus inevitable that the different situations in which the two giants found themselves would have an effect on their ideological views—for theory, however abstract, is viewed by Marxist methodology as changing through a constant process of interaction with practice. Furthermore, the silent and public acceptance of the Soviet thesis of a non-conflictual transition to socialism would virtually imply that the Chinese revolutionary model was internationally irrelevant, which in effect would have meant that Beijing had hardly anything to offer to other Communist parties in terms of ideological inspiration.

By the early 1960s, the Sino-Soviet dispute had become irreversibly fixed, dialogue had ceased, and different communist platforms were used by both parties to assert their own views, although this was conducted discreetly. The public airing of opinion by both parties was limited to either an assertion of their respective views or alternatively to an indirect criticism of each other. By the end of 1962 China, however, did not see any point in continuing the facade of unity. On 15 December 1962, the Chinese party leadership therefore took the initiative of publicly criticising the Soviet Union and some of the European Communist parties.[88] This was just the starting point: there then followed a ceaselessly escalating public campaign of sharp polemical exchanges repeating, *ad nauseaum,* points that had already been made and arguments that had already been put forward. By the mid-1960s the ferocity with which each of the two countries attempted to undermine the position of the other was as striking as the ardor with which they had earlier indulged in indigestible encomiums underlining their friendship for each other.

Territorial Dispute

The events of 1958 had transformed Sino-Soviet differences into a dispute the most climactic manifestation of which was, as noted above, the Chinese decision in December 1962 to directly criticise the Russians on a number of ideological issues. Similarly, the events of 1962 in the Xinjiang sector escalated the dispute into a real confrontation, the most dramatic manifestation of which was the March 1963 decision to openly raise the issue of

48

their territorial claims against Russia, thereby giving a new dimension to the rapidly escalating dispute.

Though there had been a number of frontier incidents in the 1950s, the first critical outbreak took place in Xinjiang in the spring of 1962 when accelerated Chinese attempts—already begun in 1949—to sinicise the Kazakhs, Uighurs and Kirghiz, and other semi-nomadic minorities resulted in their massive departure. As many as 67,000 fled into Soviet territory between April and June 1962 and threw themselves under Soviet protection.[89]

Though it is impossible to determine what train of events led the dissidents to flee across the border, the existence of a general atmosphere of persecution, of which the local population had become the victims, compounded with the sudden Chinese decision in early 1962 to end their normal practice of issuing exit visas to those wishing to leave, may have contributed to this exodus. In any event, what was important about the Xinjiang incidents was not whether the exodus was provoked by the subversive activities of Soviet diplomatic and consular personnel, as alleged by the Chinese, or by brutal Han repression in the town of Kuldja in May 1962, as alleged by the Russians, but that the Sino-Soviet relations had reached such a point of hostility that armed clashes occurred, leading to the closing down of the Soviet Consulate General in Urumchi and the recalling of Soviet officials from the border stations of Horgis and Turuquard.[90]

The Xinjiang clashes were to be the prototype of similar outbreaks all along the vast frontier, including the Mongolian borders and on the disputed islands on the Amur and Ussuri rivers where Chinese fisherman were alleged to have trespassed into Soviet territory. Undoubtedly all this contributed to the aggravation of the dispute, for within a span of few months after these incidents, the Chinese leadership decided to bring their differences into the limelight. In an editorial in the *People's Daily* on 8 March 1963, they announced that all the territorial agreements concluded between Imperial China and Tsarist Russia were "unequal" and would have to be settled peacefully through negotiations "when the time is ripe".[91] On 10 July 1964, Mao Zedong jumped into the fray. In an interview with a Japanese Socialist Party delegation he attacked Soviet expansion in Europe and supported the Japanese claims on the Kurile Islands. On the same occasion, he claimed the whole area east of Lake Baikal. He declared:

> There are too many places occupied by the Soviet Union . . . About a hundred years ago, the area to the east of Lake Baikal became Russian territory and since then Vladisvostok, Khabarovsk, Kamchatka and other areas have become Soviet territory. We have not presented our account for this list.[92]

On 1 August of the same year, Zhou Enlai declared that the USSR "is holding a large amount of territory which was taken from others since the Tsarist period and it is logical and justifiable for new independent countries to claim their former territories."[93] In May 1965, Foreign Minister Chen Yi went even further by suggesting that the Soviet Union had occupied even more territory than claimed by China.[94]

The purpose of all these and many other declarations was not so much to reach an agreement but rather to maintain a certain level of tension and to conduct psychological warfare against the Russians. The incidence of border clashes consequently increased. Tension mounted. According to Soviet sources in 1962 there were as many as 5,000 incidents. In 1963, they were reportedly to have exceeded 4,000. The decrease in 1963 was more than made up for by the number of people involved—rising to 100,000.

Though it is impossible to delineate responsibilities regarding all these incidents, from all evidence that is available the Chinese appeared to have been more active than their northern neighbour. In the first place, a general consensus appears to exist that, more often than not, it was the Chinese who encouraged frontier population to move into areas claimed by them, often provoking conflictual situations which culminated in massive demonstrations by the Chinese, most of whom were transported from the interior. Secondly, Chinese authorities established a series of regulations covering the inspection of incoming and outgoing ships. That these were hardly necessary is evident from the fact that all these questions were already covered by a wide range of Sino-Soviet agreements including those on navigation and construction along boundary waterways in January 1951, on the joint investigation and comprehensive utilizations of natural resources in the Amur Valley of August 1956, and on the opening of the boundary rivers and lakes to commercial navigation in December 1957. Though most of these issues served only to irritate, some regulations were nonetheless potentially explosive and were capable of generating serious friction if properly enforced, as for example the regulation that gave the port supervisor authority to arbitrarily forbid foreign vessels from leaving port or the rule that prohibited crews and passengers of foreign vessels not only from taking photographs or making maps but also from swimming, fishing, or hunting. The interdiction of vessels to load or unload people or goods on the way was equally provocative.[95] Thirdly the Chinese attitude at the February 1964 Sino-Soviet border talks was also indicative of their intention to maintain tensions. Though at this conference very little of substance kept them from wrapping up an agreement, nothing was agreed upon. Procedural questions apparently raised by the Chinese delegation were the main stumbling block.[96] If one were to set aside the unacceptable Chinese demands that the disputed area was about one and one-half million square kilometres, that the Russians must formally declare the original treaties unequal and illegal, and that the new treaty must specify that even the new borders agreed upon between Moscow and Beijing perpetuated an injustice foisted on China over a hundred years ago, the real focal points of dispute are limited.[97] The most important points are a large number of small islands that separate the two countries in the northeast and an area of several thousand square kilometres in the Pamir mountain region

50

overlapping China's Xinjiang province and the Soviet Union.[98]

With one exception the disputed islands are not important to either country, and yet both of them are extremely sensitive to any violations of their assumed rights concerning them. From the very beginning, the Chinese have consistently maintained that the river borders should follow the middle of the main channel of the river, according to the "Thalweg"principle, and that the Russians are illegally occupying many islands that are on the Chinese side of the channel.

Initially, the Russians insisted that the border line, delineated on the original treaty maps, followed the Chinese bank of the river in many places, and that they had not violated that line. But in the course of the negotiations, they finally accepted the main channel idea, which meant relinquishing control over most of the islands. They made one exception, however. They made it clear that they would not, under any circumstances, abandon HeiXiachu (in Russian, Chimnaya and Tarabarovsky) which is adjacent to the city of Khabarovsk and is perceived by them to be strategically important.

The Pamir area is also of no great strategic or economic significance. The most important point on which the two countries disagreed was the status of the Pamir mountains, which was not included in any treaty. While the Chinese maintained that these mountains belonged to China, the Russians insisted that since the Pamir region was populated by Tadzhiks, they were therefore a part of the Soviet Tadzhik Republic.[99] The border dispute thus reached a total impasse. The Sino-Soviet border negotiations broke down in August 1964. Though an agreement was reached to reopen talks on 15 October 1964, they were not resumed. With the inauguration of the Cultural Revolution in 1966, relations became worse. Polemical exchanges proliferated. Large and unacceptable territorial demands reappeared in the Chinese press. Anti-Soviet demonstrations abounded. Border incidents were provoked, and finally, as is often the case with such escalatory situations, the whole dispute climaxed into a series of armed clashes on the Ussuri river in March 1969, on the Xinjiang border in June 1969, and a serious confrontation on the Amur river in July 1969.[100]

Mutual Exclusion from the Socialist Club

The clashes pushed the Sino-Soviet confrontation to a new pitch—the pitch of no longer considering each other socialist. Internally the Chinese accused the CPSU of having become a "revisionist fascist party,[101] of having "totally undermined the socialist economic base,"[102] of having restored "all-round capitalism" in the country,[103] and of having "turned the homeland of the Soviet working people into a land of terror."[104] Externally they charged the Russians with having become "social imperialists," "the new Tsars"[105] and of collusion with the United States, Japan, and Taiwan.

The Russians countered by accusing the Chinese of having eroded the

51

very "foundations of socialism"[106] and of having embraced "nationalistic and voluntaristic theories"[107] and of having excluded themselves "from the Socialist community."[108]

The new polemical game of placing each other outside the pale of socialism was undoubtedly a watershed in Sino-Soviet relations; thereafter it was no longer a question of simple disputes on national or international issues, but was rather embodied in depicting each other as belonging to conflicting socio-economic frameworks. In a sense this new and unprecedented situation had brought the relations to a point of no return. The dispute was no longer political or national but had become systemic insofar as it was no longer a question of removing their adversaries but instead implied for each the transformation of the socio-economic structures of the other before a Socialist community could once again be established. Admittedly, this exclusion of each other from the Socialist club was, like the territorial issue, a consequence of the dispute, but by having inserted this new element in the dispute both China and Russia decided to move still further away from the possibility of reverting to their original form of relationship.

Concluding Remarks: Problems and Prospects

The long history of Sino-Russian relations has been largely conflictory. From the thirteenth century until the present, there were only brief interludes—mainly after the Bolshevik and Chinese revolutions—of warmth and friendliness, only to regress to the normal escalatory patterns of disagreements, suspicion, and even conflict.

Until 1949, this process could be principally attributed to the increasingly assymetrical character of bilateral relations from which Russia gained the most. After the revolution, the Chinese determination to remedy this factual and objective situation, compounded with their attempts to project themselves as the alternative power centre of socialism sparked off an even more acute process of tension and disagreement—to a point that the two giants, whose aspirations are based upon the same ideology, have become major adversaries within the international system.

What about the future prospects of their relations? Have they reached a point of no return and has the likelihood of even a minimal understanding been obliterated?

Insofar as no pattern of inter-state relations can be viewed as permanent, it would be imprudent and short-sighted to attach the label of irreversibility to the normalisation of Sino-Soviet relations. If within a span of two generations Sino-Soviet relations have become conflictual, new developments may well de-escalate the relationship to a state of normality and even friendliness. Such an evolutionary process occurred in the case of Sino-American relations, and one can hardly exclude it where Sino-Soviet relations are concerned. In any event it is evident that the current level of

52

Sino-Soviet tension has greatly influenced the behaviour of the two socialist states on a wide array of foreign policy issues. There has been, first of all, considerable expansion of the defenses of the two countries. The Chinese, who now consider the Soviet Union as their "most dangerous and most important enemy . . . waiting an opportunity to wage large-scale war,"[109] have intensified their nuclear programme; created an atmosphere of war hysteria by massive mobilisation of the population to build fortifications, bomb shelters, etc; and stationed, according to the Russians, more than two million men in the border regions.[110] For the Russians, heavily involved as they were in safeguarding their security in the West, the sudden awakening and activation of their Far Eastern border created a new and difficult situation. They attempted to respond to this new threat, according to US government studies, by quadrupling the number of their divisions in the area from twelve to forty-five between 1967 and 1974, by increasing five-fold their frontal aviation in the last ten years, and by tripling their level of spending in 1977 in constant roubles in comparison to 1967. Admittedly, this Soviet military build-up is much larger than what would be really needed to cope with limited border clashes. But it is obviously not sufficient to pursue a long and large-scale conventional war. China's capacity—inferior weapons notwithstanding—for facing such a confrontation is probably greater than that of the Soviet Union.

Compounded to this is the new US dimension. Washington's growing interest, since Nixon's visit to China in 1972, in maintaining and even safeguarding Chinese independence within the new international system, has further weakened the Russian capacity to face a confrontation in the Far East. The real Russian nightmare of having to face a potential two-front threat is no longer farfetched but something with which they have to live and operate.

The aggravation of the Sino-Soviet dispute after 1969 has also had an important impact on the attitude and influence of the Soviet and Chinese parties over the international Communist movement. Though the quantum of polemical exchange has considerably increased in Chinese and Soviet mass media, their real interest in the international movement has become strikingly disproportionate. While the Chinese appeared to manifest a growing indifference, the Russians have shown an increasing interest. While the Chinese appeared to be focussing their limited attention principally on the task of maintaining their narrow circle of ideological friends, the Russians continued a relentless but discreet campaign to persuade many of their erstwhile comrades, who had drifted to a form of neutralism, to return to the Soviet fold.

This disproportionate level of activity had resulted in the isolation of the CCP. With the exception of a few parties and a few dissident groups, the party had been unable to make any real progress with the Communist parties of most of the countries. The Soviet Union, on the other hand, had clearly come out as the winner. As many as 75 out of about 90 official communist parties[111] attended the June 1969 meeting in Moscow. The declaration that was issued at the end of the conference clearly took a pro-Soviet line. At the 24th Congress of the CPSU in March-April 1971 the Soviet record was even better. Though 73 parties were officially present—two less than in the June 1969 international meeting—six of the participating delegations, who where also presumably communist; were left unidentified.[112] The total number of Communist party delegations was therefore even higher at the 24th congress.

How can one explain this Soviet success and Chinese failure? What were the elements that advantaged the Russians and disadvantaged the Chinese? Why was it that even among the Third World parties the Chinese record was uneven—in fact, poor. Without going into the details of the regional factors (dealt with elsewhere[113]) some of the global explanations can be examined here.

First of all, practically all the Communist parties of the world had a long and traditional record of pro-Sovietism. For years, during the Leninist and Stalinist periods, they had sought inspiration from the CPSU. Most of their operational policies were influenced, if not totally designed, by general directives emanating from Moscow. It was, therefore, hardly possible to disown and discredit what the parties had believed so profoundly and for so long.

Secondly, the form and level of polemical exchanges was indeed very different. Whereas the Chinese moved from indulging in excessive encomiums of friendship for Moscow to severe and at times even abusive personal attacks on the Russian leaders, the Soviet Union, on the whole, had maintained a critical but nonetheless sober attitude even during the height of these exchanges. Though this may not, on the face of it, appear to be an important element, it cannot be overlooked as a contributory factor, howsoever marginal, in swinging the Communist parties around to the Soviet direction or at least in restraining them from getting too close to the Chinese.

Thirdly, carried away by the euphoria of the Cultural Revolution, the CCP gave the impression of becoming increasingly intransigent in their dealings with the CPSU. Even on occasions when *ad hoc* unity was proposed either by the Soviet Union or other parties on specific issues where such an understanding was possible, the Chinese invariably rejected the suggestion Consider, for example, the Chinese attitude towards the Vietnam crisis. During the mid-1960s, at the height of U.S. intervention, a number of Communist parties attempted to persuade the CCP to accept the Soviet proposition of adopting a united front to help Vietnam. This was rejected by the Chinese. Though evidence is not available on the exact nature of its impact on the international Communist movement it must have been a source of considerable disappointment for a number of parties. At least in the case of the Japanese Communist Party it is known that the negative Chinese response greatly contributed in swinging the party from a pro-

Chinese to a neutral and subsequently to a pro-Soviet stance.

Fourthly, in the aftermath of the radical evolution of international and even national systems, the Soviet leadership attempted to adapt Marxist theory to the new conditions. Considerable in-depth work in this direction was carried out by Soviet scholars on a wide spectrum of major theoretical issues, ranging from pre-industrial Africa to the developed countries of the West.[114] Furthermore, the CPSU, in order to maintain its leadership over an increasingly diversified international Communist movement, tolerate—within limits, of course—some dissident thinking. Consider, for example, the Soviet attitude towards Eurocommunism. While the Soviet Union has on numerous occasions expressed reservations on some, but not all, aspects of Eurocommunist thinking, it has nonetheless maintained contact with West European Communist parties. The CCP, on the other hand, has made no attempts to tread new Marxist paths nor has it shown any degree of ideological toleration towards new attitudes developed by other Communist parties.

Finally, while continuing to advance its own national foreign policy goals, the Soviet leadership has, in general, carefully projected an image of a progressive state by supporting what are usually considered by Communist parties to be revolutionary movements. On the other hand, the imperatives of their national foreign policy has led the Chinese, at least since 1969, to support causes and establish relations with states or parties which are generally attacked by the international Communist movement. Supporting the Shah in Iran, Strauss in the Federal Republic of Germany, Pinochet in Chile, and Franco in Spain could hardly endear the CCP to the Communist parties.

Another major result of the dispute has been considerable activation of global diplomacies of the two communist giants. Abandoning their politics of self-imposed isolation during the Cultural Revolution—which had indeed proved disastrous—the Chinese, within a span of a few years, have designed a completely new pattern of operational diplomacy. In their search for a countervailing power against the Russians, they dramatically turned to the developed capitalist world with the object of not only normalising relations but of seeking a global understanding. Within a span of a decade (1969-1979) the relations with the trilateral world have indeed gone beyond a simple level of normalisation: so much so that the maintenance of an independent and viable China has become a pivotal objective of United States diplomacy.

On the other hand, the imperatives of security and modernisation have considerably downgraded the importance of the Third World in Chinese calculations, with the exception, of course, of the outer periphery. In fact, the Third World has become marginal in current Chinese diplomacy. Admittedly, Chinese press and official declarations are full of rhetoric regarding the importance of the developing world. Admittedly, the understandable Chinese goal of gaining acceptance as a global power has led the

55

Chinese leadership to interest itself in all international issues, including, of course, the Third World issues. But the two crucial Chinese objectives, modernisation and security, have decisively shifted the focal point of its activity to the West.

Soviet diplomacy, however, appeared to be more balanced and more diversified. While seeking out the developed countries, it did not ignore the developing world. While multiplying its initiatives towards the United States and Western Europe, it made significant inroads in the Third World. On the one hand, Moscow accelerated the process of normalisation and detente in the West through a series of bilateral and multilateral accords; on the other, it attempted to use its newly developed military power in the area to dissuade Western countries from overplaying the Chinese card. That this objective has been attained is evident from the prudent attitude the Western countries have adopted towards China. While developing significant economic relations with Beijing—to which Moscow does not seem to object—most of them who have an equal stake in detente appeared to have abstained, at least for the moment, from seeking any understanding against Moscow or giving any major arms assistance to Beijing.

Moscow has also made considerable headway in the Third World. Through a subtle mix of military aid, economic assistance and hard political pressure, it has succeeded in keeping the Chinese at bay in a number of strategic points of the globe. In Africa, the Chinese have been unable to make any real headway. In Latin America their influence is only minimal. Even on China's southern periphery, where she has considerable geostrategic advantage, Vietnam's decision to opt decisively in favour of the Soviet Union has created major hurdles for the Chinese in the area, which even the Chinese military initiatives of February 1979 have been unable to remove. Furthermore, the activation of numerous Soviet initiatives in Southeast Asia, particularly towards the ASEAN countries, has made it possible for Moscow to establish some meaningful footholds in the area.

Having thus reached what may seem to be, at least on the face of it, the point of no return in Sino-Soviet relations, it may perhaps be appropriate to briefly reflect upon the future prospects.

Has the Sino-Soviet conflict really reached a point from which they can only move in the direction of open and escalated conflict? Are there no other options, no other directions, and no other solutions?

While the prospects of an open conflict cannot be ruled out—least of all between the two communist giants who have already given the world a spectacle of open animosity and barbed exchanges—the scenario of slow de-escalation and some mutual accommodation appears to be more real, particularly since the death of Mao Zedong, who, from the evidence that is available, was the main, if not the sole, architect of Sino-Soviet animosity. Despite the strident anti-Soviet policy of the new Chinese leaders, there is nonetheless an intriguing possibility that the assymetrical nature of the military equation may well move them to consider some bargaining with

Moscow as essential, in particular if China concludes—which appears to be the case—that the United States is a weak side in the triangular competition. Indeed some of the recent developments in Sino-Soviet relations appear to indicate that limited detente with the Russians has become an important element of new Chinese thinking. Trade increased by roughly 300 million dollars in 1977-78. The intensity of polemical exchanges diminished, and a high level of diplomatic parleys was re-established. Interestingly enough, this is a radical departure from China's previous line when pre-conditions were invariably tagged to all proposals of talks.

If the prospects for an actual confrontation are remote, the possibility of a Chinese return to a unified Communist bloc is even more improbable; for much, as we have seen, has happened to make the dispute irreversible. The scope of any talks can, therefore, only be limited, which may lead to the establishment of normal or nearly normal diplomatic relations between the two countries. In the event of this happening, the configuration of power in the international system would surely be modified, but it will hardly transform the basically triangular character of relations in which two global powers (US and USSR) and a superpower (China) will continuously interact with each other, trying to benefit as much as they can from the situation.

Notes

1. For details of the period see, O. Edmund Clubb, *China and Russia: The Great Game* (New York: Columbia University Press, 1971); Aitchen K. Wu, *China and the Soviet Union: A Study of Sino-Soviet Relations* (London: Metuen and Co, 1950).
2. See R. K. I. Ouested, *The Expansion of Russia in East Asia 1857-1860* (Kuala Lumpur: University of Malaya Press, 1968).
3. See William L. Tung, *China and the Foreign Powers: The impact and Reaction to Unequal Treaties* (New York: Oceana Publications, 1970).
4. R. J. Kerner, *The Urge to the Sea* (California: University of California Press, 1942).
5. See Wolfram Eberhard, *A History of China* (Berkeley and Los Angeles: University of California Press, 1977).
6. V. I. Lenin, *The National Liberation Movement in the East* (Moscow: Foreign Languages Publishing House, 1957), p. 238.
7. Ibid., p. 240.
8. Ibid., p. 244.
9. For details, see *The Second Congress of the Communist International*, Proceedings of the Petrograd Session of 17 July and Moscow Session of 19 July to 7 August 1920 (America: 1921).
10. See C. Martin Wilbur and Julie Lien-Ying How, *Documents on Communism Nationalism and Soviet Advisers 1918-1927* (New York: Columbia University Press, 1956).
11. See Chiang Kai-shek, *Soviet Russia in China: A Summing-up at Seventy*, Revised abridged edition (New York: Farrar Straus and Giroux, 1965); also see M. N. Roy, *Revolution and Counter-Revolution in China* (Calcutta: Renaissance Publishers, 1946).

57

12. Kuo "United Front Strategy", *Issues and Studies*, Part II, 9 (1978).

13. Van Min (Wang Ming), "15 let borby za nezavisimost i svobodu Kitaiskogo naroda", *Kommunisticheskii internatsional*, 14 (1936).

14. *Inprecor*, 14 (1936).

15. Cited in *Issues and Studies*, loc cit., p. 29.

16. For details about intraparty controversies, see Charles B. McLane, *Soviet Policies and the Chinese Communists 1931-1946* (New York: Columbia University Press, 1958).

17. Ibid.

18. *Mao's Selected Works*, Volume II, p. 455.

19. For the writings of the period, see ibid.

20. For a criticism of Mao, see Wang Ming, *China's Cultural Revolution or Counter-Revolutionary Coup* (Moscow: Novosti Press Agency Publishing House, n.d.).

21. Mao's *Selected Works*, Volume II, p. 209.

22. For details, see Aitchen K. Wu, op cit.

23. *Pacific Affairs*, XIII, 3 (1940), p. 265.

24. United States Government, Committee on Armed Forces and Foreign Relations, Eighty Second Session, *Military Situation in the Far East* (Washington D.C.: US Government Printing Press, 1954).

25. See Herbert Feis, *The China Tangle* (Princeton: Princeton University Press, 1953).

26. Full text in Aitchen K. Wu, op cit.

27. Ibid., p. 397.

28. *Military Situation in the Far East*, op cit.

29. Chiang Kai-shek, op cit.

30. Remarks Stalin made to a Yugoslav delegation prior to Yugoslavia's expulsion from the Cominform; Vladimar Dedijer, *Tito* (New York: Simon and Schuster, 1953), p. 322.

31. Ibid.

32. See Chapter 3.

33. Expression used by Mao Zedong. See Mao's *Selected Works*, Vol. IV, 1969, p. 417.

34. For texts of the agreements, see *Milestones of Soviet Foreign Policy 1917-1967* (Moscow: Progress Publishers, 1967).

35. According to recently published Soviet accounts, relations between Stalin and Mao were by no means easy and smooth; see N. S. Khruschev, *Khruschev Remembers: The Last Testament*, Vol. 2 (London: Penguin Books, 1977); also see Victor Louis, *The Coming Decline of the Chinese Empire. With a Dissenting Introduction by Harrison E. Salisbury* (New York: Times Books, 1979).

36. Liu Shaoqi declared in 1949 at the Asian and Australasian Trade Union Conference in November-December 1949 that "the path taken by the Chinese people in defeating imperialism and its lackeys and in founding the People's Republic is the path that should be taken by the peoples of various colonial and semi-colonial countries in their fight for national independence and people's democracy." *New China News Agency*, 23 November 1949.

37. E. Zhukov, "Obostrenie Krizisa Kolonialnoi systemy," *Bolshevik*, 23 (1947).

38. *Communist*, 4 (1949).

39. For full text of the report, see "Strategic Problems of the Malayan Revolutionary War" in Gene Z. Hanrahan, *Communist Strategy in Malaya* (New York: Institute of Pacific Relations, 1954).

40. Ruth McVey, *The Development of the Indonesian Communist Party and its Relations*

with the Soviet Union and the Chinese People's Republic (Ithaca: Cornell Southeast Asia Programme, 1959).

41.　Paul F. Langer, *Communism in Japan: A Case of Political Naturalisation* (Stanford: Hoover Institution Press, 1972).

42.　*For a Lasting Peace, For a People's Democracy,* 27 January 1950.

43.　*An Economic Profile of China,* Studies Prepared for the Joint Economic Committee Congress of the United States, 2 (Washington: US Government Printing Office, 1967), p. 591.

44.　*Khruschev Remembers: The Last Testament,* Vol. 2 (London: Penguin Books, 1977), p. 319.

45.　*People's Communes in China* (Peking: Foreign Languages Press, 1958), p. 8.

46.　*More on the Historical Experience of the Dictatorship of the Proletariat* (Peking: Foreign Languages Press, 1957), p. 13.

47.　Ibid., p. 9.

48.　Ibid., p. 14.

49.　Ibid., p. 19.

50.　Full text in *The Current Digest of the Soviet Press,* 1 January 1958.

51.　For details about Soviet declarations regarding the crisis, see *The Policy of the Soviet Union in the Arab World, A Short Collection of Foreign Policy Documents* (Moscow: Progress Publishers, 1975).

52.　*Peking Review,* 22 (1958), p. 5.

53.　Term used by Mao to describe the new situation in his 18 November 1957 speech in Moscow. *New China News Agencey,* 31 October 1958.

54.　See O. B. Borisov and B. T. Koloskov, *Sino-Soviet Relations* (Moscow: Progress Publishers, 1975).

55.　There are, however, conflicting views regarding the Soviet reaction to the Chinese decision to create the crisis. Khruschev claims in his memoirs that Moscow was exasperated with the Chinese for not going through with their assaults on the islands; see N. S. Khruschev, *Khruschev Remembers,* Vol. 2, pp. 310-312. The more recent Soviet line criticises Mao for picking a fight in the first place. Two Soviet authors have characterised the Chinese decision as an "adventurist policy"; Borisov and Koloskskov, op cit., p. 150.

56.　*Pravda,* 29 January 1959.

57.　Ibid., 10 April 1959.

58.　Zhou Enlai, *The Great Decade* (Peking: Foreign Languages Press, 1959), p. 10.

59.　N. S. Khruschev, op cit., p. 318.

60.　See Tass statement regarding Sino-Indian relations of 9 September 1969; text in *Soviet News,* 10 September 1959.

61.　See Soviet government statement of 21 September 1963, *Pravda,* 21 and 22 September 1963.

62.　See *People's Daily* editorial of 2 November 1963, *Peking Review,* 48 (1963).

63.　The agreement to give India US$ 375 million was concluded on 13 September 1959.

64.　According to Edward Crankshaw, Peng had shown an elaborate memorandum setting forth his views to Khruschev before presenting to his colleagues at home; see Edward Crankshaw, *The New Cold War: Moscow and Peking* (London: Penguin Books, 1963); for the Marshall Peng story, see David A. Charles, "The Dismissal of Marshall Tuh-huai", *China Quarterly,* 8 (1961).

65.　Expression used by the Soviet party in its letter of 21 September 1963.

66.　O. V. Kuusinen, et al, *Fundamentals of Marxism-Leninism Manual,* Second revised edition (Moscow: Foreign Languages Publishing House, 1963), p. 500.

67. Resolution of the 20th Congress of the CPSU, p. 13.

68. Konstantin Zarodov, *Leninism and Contemporary Problems of the Transition from Capitalism to Socialism* (Moscow: Progress Publishers, 1972), p. 180.

69. Ibid.

70. V. Solodovnikov, V. Bogoslovisky, *Non-Capitalist Development. A Historical Outline* (Moscow: Progress Publishers, 1975), p. 88.

71. R. Ulyanovsky, *Socialism and the New Independent Nations* (Moscow: Progress Publishers, 1974), p. 544.

72. Zhokov, et al, *The Third World. Problems and Prospects* (Moscow: Progress Publishers, 1970), p. 207.

73. *The National Liberation Movement—A Component of the Alliance of the World Revolutionary Forces* (Prague: International Publishers, 1976).

74. *Development of Revolutionary Theory by the CPSU* (Moscow: Progress Publishers, 1971), p. 343.

75. Ibid., p. 344.

76. *Long Live Leninism* (Peking: Foreign Languages Press, 1960), p. 30.

77. Ibid., pp. 22-23.

78. Ibid., p. 22.

79. "Outline of views on the Question of Transition" in *The Polemic*, op cit., p. 106.

80. Ibid., p. 106.

81. Ibid., p. 106.

82. "The Proletarian Revolution and Khruschev's Revisionism", editorial in *People's Daily* and *Red Flag*, 31 March 1964; for text see ibid., p. 367.

83. Ibid., p. 106.

84. Liu Shaoqi, *The Victory of Marxism-Leninism in China* (Peking: Foreign Languages Press, 1959), p. 4.

85. Ibid., p. 4.

86. Ibid., p. 4.

87. Letter of the Chinese Party to the CPSU of 30 March 1963; text in *The Polemic*, op cit., p. 13; also see Lin Biao, *Long Live the Victory of the People's War* (Peking: Foreign Languages Press, 1965).

88. For full text, see *Prolétaires de tous les pays unissons-nous contre l'ennemi commun* (Peking: Foreign Languages Press, 1963).

89. See Borisov and Koloskov, op cit.

90. Ibid.

91. Text in Denis J. Doolin, *Territorial Claims in the Sino-Soviet Conflict: Documents and Analysis* (Stanford: Stanford University Press, 1965), pp. 44-45.

92. Ibid., p. 45.

93. Ibid.

94. Partial text in "JCK, The Border Issue Reappears" *Radio Free Europe Research*, 3 June 1966.

95. Texts in I. F. Kuidiukov, et al, *Sovetsko-Kitaiskie otnosheniia 1917-1957* (Moscow: Izdatestvo vostochnoi literatury, 1959).

96. For details, see G. Ginsburgs and C. Pinkels, *The Sino-Soviet Territorial Dispute 1949-1964* (New York: Prager, 1978).

97. A Soviet article on Sino-Soviet relations in 1976 cited 13,000 square miles as the disputed area, *China Quarterly*, 67 (1976); also see Tai Sung An's, *The Sino-Soviet Territorial Dispute* (Philadelphia: Westminster Press, 1973), which cites the figure of 12,000 square miles.

98. See ibid.

99. *Khruschev Remembers,* op cit.

100. For an exhaustive compilation of documents of the Sino-Soviet armed clashes, see *Studies in Comparative Communism: An Interdisciplinary Journal,* 3 and 4 (1969).

101. *People's Daily,* 6 January 1969.

102. Ibid., 19 March 1969.

103. Ibid.

104. *Peking Review,* 14 (1969), p. 17.

105. Ibid., 49 (1973), p. 15.

106. *Pravda,* 11 January 1969.

107. *Maoism Through the Eyes of Communists* (Moscow: Progress Publishers, 1970); also see *Present-Day China: Collected Articles* (Moscow: Progress Publishers, 1975); B. Zanegin, *Nationalist Background of China's Foreign Policy* (Moscow: Novosti Press Publishing House, n.d.).

108. *Literaturnaya Gazeta,* 23 May 1979.

109. See "Confidential Documents", edited and printed by the Propaganda Division, Political Department of Kunming Military Region on 2 April 1973; text published in *Chinese Communist Internal Politics and Foreign Policy. Reviews on Reference Materials concerning Education on Situation. Issued by the Kunming Region* (Taiwan: Institute of International Relations, 1974), pp. 130-134.

110. *Foreign Broadcast Information Service: Daily Report Soviet Union,* 9 January 1974.

111. This does not include the seccessionist groups.

112. Keith Devlin identified five of them: Nepal, Morocco, Algeria, Nigeria, and Lesotho. See *Soviet Survey,* 54 (1965).

113. See Chapters 3, 4 and 5.

114. See Evgueni Varga, *Essais sur l'économie politique du capitalisme* (Moscow: Progress Publishers, 1967); *Fundamentals of Marxism-Leninism Manual* (Moscow: Foreign Languages Publishing House, 1963); I. G. Blyumin (ed.), *Theories of "Regulated" Capitalism* (Moscow: Foreign Languages Publishing House, n.d.); A. Rumyantsey, *Categories and Laws of the Political Economy of Communism* (Moscow: Progress Publishers, 1969); A. Frumkin, *Modern Theories of International Economic Relations* (Moscow: Progress Publishers, 1969); Konstantin Zarodov, op cit.: R. Ulyanovsky, op cit.

Chapter 3

CHINA AND THE UNITED STATES

The Background

The American role in China until the nineteenth century was essentially indirect and marginal:[1] indirect in the sense that the role of individuals was more important than that of the state. Commercial relations were established by New England merchants who arrived on the shores of China with an eye for profit. American missionary work was carried out by missionaries who, surrendering the comforts of their families, went off on overseas crusades. Political relations were established by American representatives on the spot who had acquired a comparatively free hand in designing a China policy with minimal intervention from Washington. Even the treaty revision movement in the middle of the nineteenth century was carried out by American commissioners rather than by authorities in Washington. Their policies were based upon their private judgements. None of them seemed to care what their predecessors did, and none of them even waited for the arrival of their successors to transfer their official duties in person.[2]

US policy was also marginal in the sense that its role in the opening up of China was negligible. She sought and enjoyed privileges which other nations had wrested from the Chinese. The opening of five Chinese ports to American traders in 1840s, for example, would not have been possible without the British victory in the Opium War. American boats could not have sailed on the Yangtze in the 1860s had the British initiatives not opened it to foreign trade. Even the effective security of American citizens pursuing trade or missionary work would not have been possible without some assurance of protection from Great Britain.

Only towards the close of the 19th century did the United States policy towards China become less indirect and more assertive. Many of her leaders then began to conjure up visions of a nation acting as a world power, participating in the white man's burden beyond the frontiers of their continent. A number of factors had generated this new mood. First of all, there was the rapidly expanding economy. By the 1890s, the United States had emerged as the foremost industrial state of the world. Since this major development coincided with the closing of the American frontier, the opportunities for developing the internal market no longer appeared to be unlimited. The 1893 Depression, the worst ever faced by the young nation, aggravated the economic difficulties, spreading a sense of impending disaster throughout the country. The business community became increasingly convinced that external markets were essential and, given the necessary protection and equal opportunity, the country would be able to find appropriate solutions.

Second, since expansion beyond their own frontiers had become standard behaviour for most industrial nations, the United States too became afflicted by this malady. During the last decade of the 19th century, a number of American public figures began to advocate the reversal of American foreign policy, until then the basic theme of which had been to remain uninvolved in global politics. They advocated active participation in international affairs and urged the transformation of the United States into a world power. There was, for example, Alfred Thayer Mahan, a naval officer who strove to persuade those who were at the helm of the affairs to expand the naval power, to look outwards, to push commerce everywhere in the world, and to actively intervene in international controversies facing Europe and Asia. There was Josiah Strong, a militant protestant missionary, who lectured and wrote on the subject. In his book, *Our Country,* he declared that the Anglo-Saxon race was chosen by God to civilise the world and that the major responsibility for running this crusade had fallen on the United States. There was Theodore Roosevelt, who, having cast himself in a big role, which led him to the presidency, was convinced that expansion beyond the continental frontiers had become vital. The country, he feared, had become too "soft"; another war was needed to redress the moral virtues and activate the people. And there was Senator Henry Cabot Lodge, son of a Boston merchant, who, having become wealthy in China trade, preached the gospel of expansionism.

Third, and most important, was the actual American expansion beyond its continental boundaries towards Hawaii, Guam, and the Philippines in 1898. With these annexations, particularly the Philippines, the United States, in the view of one historian, "emerged from its habitual self-sufficient abode in the Western hemisphere and entered the limitless realm of world politics, naval rivalry and imperial domain."[3]

The cumulation of all these factors resulted in the formulation and operationalisation of an outgoing policy—a policy which was neither as indirect—or as marginal as before. The US government was more actively and more independently involved with a perspective of its own.

This by no means implies that the "open door policy," designed in September 1899, was a completely new framework or that the United States was able to extricate herself from a position of dependence on other powers, particularly Great Britain; it only means that by the end of the century she had become more conscious of her interests, and that the Secretary of State, John Hay, architect of the policy, had injected a certain element of systematisation and coherence into American perception and policies.

"Open Door Policy"

The new policy, as perceived by the Americans, was based on the principle that their interests, economic as well as strategic, were best served by making the other powers already installed in China (*a*) to agree to an equality of commercial opportunity for all nations, and (*b*) to respect China's territorial and administrative integrity. These two principles became the linchpin of Washington's policy. With only minor variations and emphasis they were thereafter consistently followed by presidents and secretaries of state for almost four decades. Though the United States, throughout these years, did not possess the political and military strength to obtain an effective implementation of these principles by other powers, she nonetheless had the consolation of having established a framework to which she formally adhered until World War II. Whenever any of these principles were violated, the US government did not fail to launch a protest. For example, Washington opposed Russian expansionism in Manchuria in 1902-1903; appealed for the respect of China's neutrality and integrity during the Russo-Japanese war in 1904-1905; proposed the neutralisation of Manchurian railways in 1908 to prevent foreign domination; and condemned Japan's attempts to control China through the notorious Twenty-one Demands in May 1919. In 1922, the US attempted to codify the "open door" principles at the Washington conference. After Japan invaded Manchuria in 1931, Secretary of State Stimpson, through his famous non-recognition doctrine, clearly informed Japan that his country "does not intend to recognize any situation, treaty or agreement" which would impair her treaty rights in China.[4]

Repeatedly thereafter Washington protested Japanese expansionist designs. Consider Roosevelt's "quarantine speech" of 5 October 1937 warning against the "epidemic of world lawlessness,"[5] the economic measures taken against Tokyo in 1939, the formal proposal sent out to Japan to withdraw her forces from China in 1941, and the decision taken to freeze Japanese assets in the United States.

If the Americans perceived their role in China to be essentially benevolent and altruistic, it was not viewed as such by the Chinese. For many of them, the US record was equally expansionist. It was considered to be part and parcel of a general Western imperialist offensive which had decimated the Qing dynasty, undermined Chinese sovereignty, and obstructed the development of Chinese nationalism. Any difference in degree between European and American actions was due more to American weakness than to the absence of any expansionist intentions. Even a cursory glance at the US historical record, in the Chinese view, spoke for itself. The Sino-American Treaty of Wangxia, concluded in 1844, guaranteed that the United States would be entitled to all treaty rights and privileges that the Chinese accorded to other imperialist powers with respect to trade, tariffs, residence rights, etc. Thus, whenever Great Britain and other powers pushed China to accord them more and more extraterritorial privileges, the US was also a beneficiary. In common with all the other treaty powers, the United States viewed it as in her basic interest to maintain the unequal treaty system. And the "open door policy" was aimed less at protecting Chinese interests than at deterring Japan and Russia from any actions that could erode American interests.[6]

The US attitude towards Japanese expansion in China was also considered as rather benign. While the American declaration regarding the Twenty-one Demands was critical of Japan, she recognised that "territorial contiguity" created special rights between countries.[7] While the Lansing-Ishii agreement of 1917 respected the independence and territorial integrity of China, it contained a stipulation which recognised "territorial propinquity" justifying Japan's claims that "she had special interests in China particularly in the part to which her possessions are contiguous."[8] While concluding world peace talks at Versailles in 1919, the US finally acquiesced to the Japanese takeover of the Shandong Province in the face of the Chinese opposition.[9] Two years later at the Washington Conference for the Limitations of Armaments, the American performance was no better. While formally upholding the principle of Chinese territorial integrity in the Nine Power Treaty, she was no more willing than other imperialist powers to revise the unequal treaties and surrender extraterritorial rights.

The Chinese were also disappointed at the lack of action taken by the United States to restrain Japanese aggression in the 1930s; the United States was no more prepared than in the past to offer direct aid to China—and finally the strong measures that were taken in 1941 were provoked less by any obligation towards China than by Japanese threats to Western interests in Southeast Asia.

US activity within China was also a source of general disappointment to the Chinese. She did not extend open support to Chinese nationalism, but instead remained essentially neutral between the imperial government in Beijing and Sun Yat-sen's provisional republican regime in Nanjing. Only after Chiang Kai-shek's successful northern expedition in 1926 did the US begin to consider recognising the new regime, and finally did so in 1928. Similarly, Washington refused to unilaterally surrender any of the privileges enjoyed by Americans, expressing instead a willingness to participate in any international conference to discuss these matters.

Thus during a century in which an unequal treaty system existed, American policy in China suffered from an ever-widening gap between theory and practice. While vigorously supporting an "open door" doctrine, she persistently backed away from doing anything about it; and while cultivating an image of being different from other expansionist nations, she participated in all the privileges of the treaty system.

World War II

During World War II, the configuration of international forces changed radically. The United States, along with Japan, became the dominant elements in China, to the exclusion of other powers. The original American "open door policy" lost much of its relevance since most of the traditional imperialist nations to which it was designed to apply, had withdrawn from China either due to the erosion of power or due to heavy involvement (as was the case for the Soviet Union) in the European sector of the war. With regard to Japan, this policy had lost much of its credibility, since hardly anything was done to implement it until Japan attacked Pearl Harbour. Only then, having been directly brought into the Pacific War, did she focus her attention on giving military support to China. But then there was nothing open-door-like in such a policy, for military assistance and political support were being given to most nations fighting Japan.

Inevitably, as is often the case in such asymmetrical situations, the United States found herself increasingly embroiled in the Chinese domestic situation—even more than Japan, for the latter had lost her credibility and much of the political leverage necessary to influence the situation by the brutal military intervention in China.

Since the fundamental American goal was to win the war, the whole weight of American policy in China was directed at (*a*) encouraging the Kuomingtang and the CCP, the two major forces in the country, to jointly mobilise their efforts against Japanese imperialism and (*b*) persuading the Soviet Union to enter the conflict in the Far East.

However, so strong was the level of suspicion and enmity between the two contending forces that all American efforts to unite them proved abortive. Both the political parties were prepared and even eager to solicit Washington's support, but neither of them were willing to collaborate with each other except on their own terms. The previous two decades of Chinese history had more than clearly proved that a *modus vivendi* between them was not feasible, and all endeavours directed at such an end had failed. Yet a new attempt was made. The prime objective of winning the war had apparently pushed the United States to make the effort even if it seemed unrealistic. But this was not the only reason. The American failure can also be attributed to her own indecisiveness. The internal disagreements among diplomatic personnel in China had deprived her of the firmness that was necessary to reach the goal of establishing a united front against Japan. Though both Patrick Hurley, Roosevelt's emissary in China, and diplomatic career men, particularly John S. Service, accepted the national government as that of all China, they diverged over its ability to maintain public support. While the former had great confidence in Chiang Kai-shek's leadership, the latter was convinced that he was rapidly losing all popular support and was in effect becoming politically bankrupt.[10] Even more important, and in part a source of American indecisiveness, were the conflicting evaluations received by Washington regarding the CCP. While Hurley felt that it was not strong enough to exercise decisive influence, Service was convinced that a communist victory was inevitable.[11] Faced with such conflicting evaluations, the decision makers in Washington were unable to establish a clearcut and prompt policy.

US policy, however, was not only ambivalent; it was also contradictory. While, on the one hand, the American decision makers were ideologically favouring the Chiang regime, they were, on the other, implicitly undermining it by continuing to work on the unrealistic task of forging a coalition government between two irreconcilable and mutually contentious forces. While they viewed the establishment of democracy as a legitimate goal, they favoured the inclusion of a political party (CCP) into a government which was not even remotely committed to the setting up of a democratic society as conceived by the United States. And while working for a strong China, they favoured a coalition government; yet it was evident that the establishment of such an authority would only further paralyse the already weak and unstable government. Instead of establishing a strong China it would only have weakened the country further.

The net result of all this was the further destabilisation of the country and the generation of considerable ill-will. None of the parties involved in this triangular relationship were satisfied with or confident of the policies or the intentions of the others. The US administration was becoming even more dismayed by the corruption and inefficiency of the Chiang regime, but it was reluctant to back the CCP in Yenan. Chiang Kai-shek was becoming deeply resentful of what he regarded as a distorted evalutation of the Chinese situation and an unjustified intervention in Chinese affairs; and the Chinese communists were frustrated by American ambivalence and irritated by American hesitation in giving them arms aid. Despite the establishment of harmonious relations with the American Military Observer Group established in Yenan in July 1944,[12] they began to wonder whether the US government had the capacity necessary to force Chiang to establish a coalition government.[13]

Post-War Mediatory Efforts

If Washington had utterly failed in influencing the domestic scene it was, however, successful in obtaining a Soviet commitment to enter the Far Eastern conflict "two or three months after Germany has surrendered and the war in Europe has terminated."[14] But the Soviet entry into the Far Eastern conflict and the subsequent occupation of Manchuria and North China rendered the Chinese situation more complicated. The American task in China became even more difficult. Already during the war, Washington had failed to create a strong China and had failed to unite the Communists and the Nationalists; now with the Soviet presence in China the task became even more herculean. For one thing, the political balance within the country had tilted. The already weak, corrupt, and isolated Kuomingtang had to confront a far more more hazardous and uncertain situation than ever before. Not only did it have to face the prospects of confronting the continuously expanding CCP but it also had to take into account the Soviet factor, which had already squeezed out from Chiang major diplomatic and territorial concessions in agreement with the Yalta accords.[15]

The US attempted another major diplomatic initiative in December 1945 by sending General George Marshall to China.[16] His task was to try to avert a Chinese civil war by encouraging the formation of a broader-based goverment. At first, his mission appeared to meet with some success. It brought about a cease-fire and negotiations between the Nationalists and the Communists. But soon it became clear that differences were too great and suspicion too high to permit a political accord. Neither side was ready to make the concessions necessary for a coalition government. Chiang was too confident of his forces to unite the country and Mao, disappointed with the earlier Hurley mission which had finally sided with Chiang, had become too skeptical of the effectiveness of any mediatory efforts.

By the close of 1946, Marshall had no alternative but to accept that his mission was a complete failure, and on 6 January 1947 President Truman announced his recall from China.

Why another attempt at mediation when the first American initiative, carried out under more favourable circumstances, had proved abortive? Were there any new elements that catalysed Washington to take this step?

Myriad explanations have been given for the mission, but there were in any case two factors that proved decisive in moving the United States to take the initiative: first, she appeared to have become convinced that Chiang no longer had the capacity to reunify the country by military means; and second, Washington, having clearly opted against any massive intervention to redress the situation and to contain the extension of Soviet influence, was left with no other option but to attempt another diplomatic initiative.

It is interesting to note that in the formulation of a mediatory strategy, the United States made a distinction between Moscow and the CCP. Whereas she was fearful of any extension of Soviet influence, she appeared to accept the prospects of a CCP presence in a coalition government at the time; the exclusion of one in American thinking did not automatically involve the exclusion of the other.

In making this distinction between Soviet and Chinese Communists, the United States was in all probability influenced by her diplomatic career personnel in China, who had persistently advanced the thesis that the Chinese Communists were essentially inspired by nationalist aspirations, and that they were ideologically more open and more flexible than the Soviet Communists.

These general evaluations were of course reinforced by the considerable flexibility and open-ness shown by the CCP towards the United States. During the war years, the CCP's operational diplomacy seemed to be geared to the objective of developing relations with Washington. It had, for example, agreed to the stationing of a US military observer group in Yenan during the war in 1944 and close working relations were established with this group. It had accepted US mediatory missions led by Patrick Hurley and George Marshall, with whom long and extensive negotiations were conducted in order to seek Nationalist-Communist compromise. It had furthermore given its accord to the placing of Chinese Communist troops under American command, had acknowledged the importance of the American role in China's modernisation after the war, and had even proposed sending a high-powered delegation to Washington for an "exploratory conference" with Roosevelt, presumably to discuss, among other things, military cooperation.[17]

Even after the war, the CCP attitude continued to remain flexible. As late as the spring of 1949, when the balance of the war had clearly tilted in favour of the Chinese Communist troops, the party was careful to informally maintain contact with the US representatives and to communicate to the US Ambassador its interest in seeking US recognition of Communist China.[18] Approximately at the same time Zhou Enlai personally established contact with the US representative in Beijing to assure him that China after the revolution would not be a communist country and could therefore play a mediatory role.[19]

This attempt to maintain a prudent attitude can be attributed to two reasons. Firstly still uncertain of winning the civil war, the CCP wished to neutralise any future possibility of US intervention on the Kuomingtang side. By attempting to establish relations with Washington, the Chinese Communist leaders presumably hoped that they would be able to obtain the appropriate guarantees on the question. Secondly, though ideologically sympathetic to the Soviet Union, the CCP nonetheless wished to play a role independent from Moscow as well as from Washington. Some understanding with Washington was therefore considered necessary as an assurance against over-dependence on the Soviet Union and as a probable guarantee for greater independence in international affairs.

Whatever the possible reasons may have been for such an attitude—about which observers even today tend to disagree—one thing is certain: it never got off the ground. By 1948, the US administration had changed its attitude towards the CCP. Though highly critical of the Nationalists[20] and though even prepared to maintain local contact with CCP leaders through its diplomatic personnel, it was either unable or unwilling to recognise the Chinese Communists or to establish any form of formalistic relations with them. This was in part due to the resurgence of strong domestic pressure groups against any recognition, but it was principally due to the onset of the cold war and the new American perception regarding the place the CCP occupied in the bipolar system. The increasing globalisation of the cold war had led the US administration to move away from its earlier evaluation in which it distinguished between Chinese and Soviet Communists, and as a result it considered the CCP a part of a monolithic international Communist movement and therefore subservient to the Soviet Union. American security interests were viewed globally and the American policy towards China was perceived as a part of an overall strategy towards the Communist bloc.

Sino-American Hostility

The failure of all these attempts to obtain American recognition, compounded with the increasing certainty that the US administration had decided not to embroil itself in the civil war on the losing Nationalist side, constituted the real catalyst in swinging the CCP towards a more anti-American stance.

Jettisoning its position of ambiguity and prudence in 1949 and particularly after the revolution, the CCP fell in line with the Soviet bipolar perception of the international system. On the one hand, it rapidly inaugurated a harsh campaign of anti-Americanism coupled with the seizure of American property, the harassment of American nationals—including denial of exit permits except upon extortionary payment of large sums of money—and the open condemnation of the US "as a rotten imperialist nation" which constituted the "headquarters of reactionary degeneracy in the whole world."[21] On the other hand, it made a clear decision to lean to one side—the Soviet side—the first most dramatic manifestation of which was the conclusion of a series of Sino-Soviet agreements in February 1950.

The US influence in China had thus completely eroded. Nothing substantial was left of a century of bilateral relations—only harsh mutual recriminations and the hope of seeing each other weakened. Now that most of the country was in the hands of the CCP, the US administration appeared determined to remain disengaged even if it meant the CCP would take over the entire Chinese territory that still remained in the hands of non-communist forces. Presumably the risks of getting sucked into the conflict were so inordinate and so incalculable that it was not considered worth the candle. It is only in this context that one can understand the series of American decisions announcing the intention to remain uninvolved in what was left of the Chinese conflict. On 5 January 1950, three months after the proclamation of the People's Republic of China, President Truman announced that the United States would not defend the island of Taiwan to which the remnant Nationalist forces had retreated.[22] On 12 January, Secretary of State Dean Acheson declared the administration's decision to exclude Taiwan (and South Korea) from the American defense parameters.[23]

But this decision to disengage concerned only the Chinese sector and not the whole area, for the US administration had become firmly installed in Japan and had publicly defined a defense perimetre on the Pacific which it would defend to contain any further expansion of communism in the area.

The situation, however, changed fundamentally as a result of the sudden outbreak of the Korean conflict in June 1950. In the ensuing weeks and months, both Washington and Beijing took a series of steps that brought them on a collision course. Washington decided to intervene in Korea against the North, a decision that alarmed Beijing since it involved major US action in areas not too far away from the Chinese borders. More important and even more threatening to China's security was the unexpected American decision to re-intervene in the Chinese civil war. Reneging upon its previous policy of non-intervention, the US government decided to interpose the Seventh Fleet between the Chinese mainland and Taiwan, with the limited objective of neutralising Taiwan. At the same time, it challenged Beijing's claim to Taiwan by declaring that her future would have to "await the restoration of security in the Pacific or settlement with Japan or consideration by the United Nations."[24]

If the US decision to intervene in the Korean war had alarmed the Chinese,[25] her decision to re-intervene in the civil war enraged them. Zhou Enlai gave vent to this rage in his statement of 28 June 1950. He declared that it constituted.

> . . . aggression against the territory of China and a total violation of the United Nations Charter. This violent predatory action by the US government comes as no surprise to the Chinese people, but only increases their wrath because the Chinese people have, over a long period, constantly exposed all the conspiratorial schemes of the American imperialists for aggression against China and grabbing Asia by force.[26]

Without going into the details of the Korean War, as this would take us beyond the scope of this chapter, suffice it to say that as the Korean conflict progressed, the Chinese fear about a direct attack on their territory increased. While the 1949 attacks on American imperialism were essentially a rhetorical device, in 1951 the United States came to be perceived as an actual threat to Chinese security. A crucial turning point occured in September and October 1950 when it appeared that the American-dominated UN force might cross the 38th parallel and move north. Beijing no longer considered the Korean War the exclusive concern of the North Koreans. It warned that should American troops advance to the north, China would have no choice but to respond. When the Americans chose to ignore such warnings—probably believing that Beijing was bluffing—Chinese volunteers entered Korea, transforming the war into a direct Sino-American conflict. Though for a long time observers debated the level and the nature of Soviet influence on Chinese initiatives in Korea,[27] it has now been established that there were extensive Sino-Soviet consultations at the highest level during the war, and that the Chinese intervention was initiated after Stalin had personally given his accord.[28]

From 1950 until 1953, China and the US fought a limited but a bitter war. Whatever chance there might have existed for the two countries to normalise relations disappeared; it was replaced by an escalating pattern of mutual hostility, the most dramatic and virulent manifestation of which was the rapid growth of McCarthyism in the United States and the intensification of the "hate-American campaign" in China.

The broad outlines of American policy were shaped and crystallized during and immediately after the Korean war. Based on the new perception that the People's Republic of China was aggressively expansionist and ideologically an integral part of the Communist bloc, the US undertook practically everything short of war to contain and even weaken her. It blocked, for example, her admission to the UN, pressed American allies not to recognise Beijing, cut off all commercial and cultural relations, and expanded, under the Eisenhower administration, alliance structures uniting South Korea, Pakistan, and Thailand. What was perhaps most dangerous and considered most provocative by China was the American decision to establish close relations with Taiwan, including a mutual defense treaty concluded in 1954. These avowedly anti-PRC policies persisted without any change during the 1950s and 1960s. In fact, twice in 1954-55 and 1958 tense relations brought the two countries close to a military conflict.

Hostility against the United States also persisted in China, and the quantum of virulent attacks from China were easily matched by those emanating from Washington. Mao Zedong personally set the tone of this new campaign. On 20 June 1950, he declared that the United States had now "exposed its own aggressive nature" and that "the entire country . . . is solidly united and making preparations to defeat American imperialists in any quarrel they may provoke."[29] On the same day Zhou Enlai, elaborating on the theme, stated that the American move was no surprise "because the Chinese people have long been ceaselessly exposing the secret plot of American imperialism to invade China and occupy all of Asia."[30] But in operational terms, the Chinese could hardly do more than what they had done. Their capacity for taking initiatives—unlike that of the United States—was severely limited at the time.

Negotiations and Confrontation

However, within the general framework of this escalating pattern of Sino-American hostility, there was a short peaceful interlude in the mid-1950s when an attempt was made by the Chinese to re-establish contact with the Americans. At first it was carried out discreetly during the 1954 Geneva Conference. The Chinese expressed through the UK delegation an interest in establishing direct contact with the Americans. On 26 May, the spokesman of the Chinese delegation, Huang Hua, even publicly hinted of the willingness of his government to talk directly with the American delegation regarding the release of prisoners of war in China and the return of some 5.000 alien Chinese from the United States to mainland China.[31] Thereafter the circle of diplomatic brokers was enlarged to a number of Asian countries in order to send out signals to Washington.

In February 1955, for example, U. Nu of Burma informed Dulles of Zhou Enlai's willingness to negotiate the problem of American airmen held in China and other issues directly with the United States. At the same time similar signals were sent out to Washington through certain delegations at the United Nations.[32]

Then suddenly, at Bandung, where independent Afro-Asian countries were holding their first historic conference, Zhou publicly declared on 23 April 1955 that his government was "willing to sit down and enter into negotiations with the United States government to discuss the question of relaxing tension in the Far East and especially the question of relaxing tension in the Taiwan area".[33] Thereafter, the Taiwan issue, principal source of Sino-American hostility, was evoked in very moderate terms. On 17 May, in a report to the Standing Committee of the national People's Congress, Zhou renewed his offer to "sit down and enter into negotiations with the United States to relax tension in the Taiwan area."[34] On 30 January 1956, he declared that Taiwan's liberation by peaceful means was possible,[35] and on 16 April, on the occasion of a banquet given in honour of the Soviet President, Voroshilov, he was even more explicit. He stated that "the internal questions of China can always be settled through consultations. Taiwan is no exception."[36]

All these initiatives elicited a response from the American side. Though the United States formally and publicly declined to hold any direct talks, Zhou's repeated initiatives served the very useful purpose of activating the process of reaching an accord to hold ambassadorial level talks. On 25 July, it was agreed, after hard bargaining, to raise the consular-level talks initiated during the 1954 Geneva Conference to ambassadorial level.

That this was indeed a major development can be gauged from the facts that this negotiatory process (a) continued right up to Henry Kissinger's first visit to Beijing in 1971; and (b) it provided the two countries "with more continuous diplomatic contact and diversified dialogue . . . than any of the non-communist Western governments with embassies there."[37]

On the Chinese side, the agreement to hold talks can be viewed first as part of a general Chinese policy in the mid-1950s of seeking out the non-communist world and of de-escalating the tense situation in the Far East. Since there was a significant American presence in the area, no major breakthrough was possible without reaching some understanding with the United States. Secondly, the September 1954 Chinese campaign to liberate Taiwan and the offshore islands was a failure. Military pressures against the islands neither demoralised the Nationalists nor did they lead to any disengagement of the United States. In fact, the results were just the opposite. Although China was able to take over one of the islands, Dachen, the United States appeared as determined as ever to continue and even reinforce her presence in the area. She therefore went ahead to conclude a mutual defense treaty with the Nationalist regime, which stipulated that the two countries would "maintain and develop their individual and collective capacity to resist armed attack and communist subversive activities directed from without against their territorial integrity and political stability".[38] In addition, the US Congress passed a resolution authorising the president "to employ the Armed Forces of the United States as he deems necessary for the specific purpose of securing and protecting Formosa and the Pescadores against armed attack."[39] If China wished to obtain the liberation of Taiwan—which she did—it had become apparent that this was impossible without working out some *modus vivendi* with Washington.

Thirdly, in retrospect, one could also wonder whether initiatives in the direction of Washington were not dictated by the state of Sino-Soviet relations. Though formal relations with Moscow were still fairly smooth, some undercurrents of disagreement and even tension were not completely absent.[40]

The American acceptance of the suggestion to talk to the Chinese was due to concrete reasons. For one thing, obtainment of the release of American airmen held in China had become a pressing problem in domestic politics. Since the Chinese had made it clear, albeit informally through the British and a number of Asian nations, that they were prepared to discuss the matter only with an American representative,[41] it would have been difficult for Dulles to reject the Chinese public offer outright; for another, serious tension over Taiwan had set off a process, characterised by intense diplomatic pressures, to talk to the Chinese, which Washington found it difficult to resist. "The Asian neutrals", confirmed Kenneth T. Young, US Ambassador involved in preliminary Sino-American exchanges, "had much to do with activating the ambassadorial talks when it became evident that nothing could be worked out to relieve the tension over Taiwan or to solve the issue of prisoners either under United Nations auspices or at the consular level in Geneva."[42]

After the removal of these preliminary difficulties, the two countries then had to overcome another hurdle—the hurdle of reaching an agreement on the agenda of the proposed meeting. This, too, was by no means easy. For one thing, the two countries held divergent views on the issues to be discussed; for another they had to be resolved through a series of indirect exchanges conveyed by British diplomatic channels. Whereas Beijing wanted to discuss a number of wide-ranging issues, including a foreign ministers' conference, withdrawal of US forces from Taiwan, etc., Washington insisted on limiting the agenda to a discussion of repatriation of American civilians and the renunciation of force. Such distant positions jeopardized the prospects of even holding any talks. Finally an ingenious formula proposed by the Americans and accepted by the Chinese ended the impasse. The US suggested a simple two-point agenda: first the return of citizens, and second "other practical matters now at issue."[43]

The process of holding ambassadorial talks formally began on 1 August 1955, first in Geneva and thereafter in Warsaw. So far as substantive issues were concerned, these talks were an exercise in sheer futility. Throughout all these meetings—and there were 134 by 1969—only an agreement on the repatriation of civilians was reached in six weeks. Thereafter they slid into a stalemate. No agreement was concluded, not even on non-controversial issues. Yet it cannot be denied that these meetings provided a useful forum through which the two countries could clarify positions and thereby reduce any prospects of miscalculations and misunderstanding. Outside of this highly irregular and severly deadlocked bilateral framework, Sino-American relations did not exist. There were no formal trade ties, no cultural relations—not even an exchange of newsmen.

In the early 1960s, during the Kennedy administration, attempts were made to break the deadlock. Discarding the rigidities of the cold war, the US administration appeared eager to break new ground. John Kennedy hinted at the possibility of providing food to China, broadening non-official contacts, and expressed the need to include China in disarmament efforts.[44]

Chinese interest in the US, on the other hand, had considerably declined during the Kennedy and Johnson administrations. Beijing refused all proposals for developing contacts and even backed out of its original position, held during the first two years of the ambassadorial talks, that negotiation and agreement on subsidiary issues might make it easier to come to an understanding on matters of principle. Furthermore, it openly condemned Kennedy's strategy of flexible response and censured American assistance to India during and after the Sino-Indian border conflict of 1962. To cap it all, Mao Zedong personally denounced the Kennedy administration for its handling of the domestic racial issue.[45] The refusal on the part of Beijing to respond favourably to Washington's overtures can be attributed principally to developments within the CCP. A major shift in its position was underway. Carried away by revolutionary euphoria, the hardliners within the party refused to have anything to do with either the Russians or the Americans. While the one was characterised as "revisionist" the other was considered as "the greatest threat to world peace"[46] and as "the most ferocious common enemy of the people of the world."[47]

By any standard, the adoption of such a belligerent line against the two superpowers would be viewed as dangerous and even counterproductive. Yet China, weak and disunited as she was, did not make any attempt to extricate herself from this precarious position by either discontinuing any further escalation of the Sino-Soviet dispute or by responding favourably to cautious American signals to defreeze Sino-American relations. On the contrary, it seemed that the Chinese leadership intentionally allowed its

76

relations with the Russians to degenerate even more and refused to have anything to do with the normalisation of relations with the United States.

This policy was eloquently voiced during 1964-65, when the issue came up for discussion within the party hierarchy of whether, in the light of the deepening Vietnam conflict, it was not in the interest of China to re-establish a common front with the Soviet Union. Despite pressures from such leaders as Liu Shaoqi, Deng Xiaoping, Peng Chen and other party bureaucrats, Mao and his followers refused to deviate from opposition to imperialism and revisionism.

Such a policy was continued even more assiduously during the Cultural Revolution, with open attacks being launched at both the United States and the Soviet Union.

Detente and Normalisation

Then by the late 1960s things began to change. Both Beijing and Washington began to undertake basic foreign policy appraisals which led them to establish a less hostile relationship.

The process was initiated by the Chinese in November 1968 when a Foreign Ministry spokesman proposed the reopening of the Warsaw talks to conclude an agreement based "on the five principles of peaceful co-existence."[48] The importance of this initiative can be gauged from the fact that this was the first time since 1964 that such a proposal was made.

The timing too was significant. In the first place, the Soviet invasion of Czechoslovakia in August 1968 and the proclamation of the Brezhnev doctrine had clearly alarmed the Chinese regarding possible Soviet intentions on the Sino-Soviet border. Secondly, the new Republican administration was about to be installed. Though President-elect Nixon had the reputation of belonging to the vanguard of cold warriors, he had a year earlier broached the question of US-China relations and had expressed the view that American policy "must come urgently to grip with the reality of China."[49]

Two days before the scheduled meeting, however, the Chinese cancelled it. Though the ostensible and formal reason for this last-minute decision was the defection of a Chinese communist diplomat to the United States, the more likely explanation was that the internal debate in the party hierarchy on the question was not completely over. Those who had taken the initiative to propose the resumption of the Warsaw talks had probably miscalculated in the belief that the three-month interval before the meeting would be sufficient to resolve what remained of the internal political struggle. To judge from the anti-US campaign in the Chinese press, resistance within the party to the normalisation of relations was still too strong.

Two elements finally proved decisive in tilting the internal balance in favour of those who were eager to open up to the United States. Both of them were external. The first was the series of violent skirmishes on the Sino-Soviet border. The Chinese apparently became very concerned with the risks of a conflict with the Soviet Union. With the United States still involved in Vietnam, a two-front battle was perceived as highly dangerous. Secondly, the new Nixon administration, having taken the major decision to explore the "possibilities of rapprochement with the Chinese"[50] a few week after its installation, had begun to send out signals to this effect. To risk a generalisation, it could be suggested that these signals were simultaneously declarative, operative and discreet, the objective of which was to put across unambiguously to the Chinese that Washington was interested in a rapprochement.

The declarative aspect of American diplomacy appeared to be well concerted. Nixon personally declared in his inaugural address in 1969—with China in mind—that "we seek an open world . . . a world in which no people, great or small, will live in angry isolation."[51] Secretary of State Rogers announced in Canberra in August 1969 that his government recognised the reality of mainland China and was "therefore seeking to open channels."[52] The Under-Secretary of State, Elliot Richardson, went even further. In a declaration to the New York Convention of the American Political Science Association on 5 September, he stated that (a) improving relations with China was in American interest, and (b) the escalation of Sino-Soviet dispute concerned the United States.[53]

The most serious and perhaps the most unambiguous public signal was the reference made by Nixon to China in his first foreign policy report in February 1970. He declared:

> The Chinese are a great and vital people who should not remain isolated from the international community . . . The principles underlying our relations with Communist China are similar to those governing our policy toward the USSR. United States policy is not likely soon to have much impact on China's behaviour, let alone its ideological outlook. But it is certainly in our interest, and in the interest of peace and stability in Asia and the world, that we take what steps we can toward improved practical relations with Beijing.[54]

Simultaneously, the Nixon administration made a number of administrative and political decisions to de-escalate the Sino-American tension. In July and December 1969, trade and travel restrictions concerning China were relaxed. They were taken unilaterally and without request for a *quid pro quo*. Even more important was that on 7 November the United States stopped active patrolling in the Taiwan straits.

Parallel to these formal declarations and decisions, the United States attempted to assure the Chinese through Rumanian and Pakistani diplomatic channels that (a) the US had no intentions of joining hands with the Russians against the Chinese; (b) the administration was opposed to Soviet attempts to create an Asian security system, and (c) they did not wish China to remain isolated any longer.[55]

This three-pronged initiative had the appropriate effect. The Chinese response was favourable. Though there were still disagreements within the CCP leadership regarding foreign policy options, it would seem that in the aftermath of the 9th Party Congress held in April 1969, the balance had tilted in favour of those who recommended a more outgoing policy and who had arrived at the conclusion that two-front strategy directed simultaneously against Moscow and Washington was counterproductive. China, in their view, must accord greater priority to the continuation of a confrontational policy against the Soviet Union while discreetly seeking out the United States.

China therefore began to send out return signals to the United States. The formal declarations against the US, though still critical, had lost some of their belligerence. They seemed to give the distinct impression that they were less hostile than the declarations of the earlier years. Furthermore, on 24 July 1969, they released the two American citizens who, having capsized off Hongkong, had drifted into Chinese waters. Chinese officials no longer avoided American diplomats at official functions. And in December 1969, Beijing informed Washington through Pakistani channels that it was prepared to resume Warsaw talks without any conditions. An agreement was reached to meet on 20 January 1970.

At the 135th meeting, the atmosphere was completely different from all the previous Sino-American encounters. The United States proposed sending or receiving a representative to hold "direct discussions."[56] Though the Chinese delegate did not respond to the American proposal, the statement he made was conciliatory. He declared that his government was willing to discuss any matter that US might put forward and was prepared to conduct talks at any level acceptable to both the countries.[57] The 136th meeting, held on 20 February was even more conciliatory. The Chinese agreed to receive an American emissary.[58]

The 137th meeting, scheduled to be held on 20 May, was, however, suddenly cancelled by the Chinese. The reason advanced for this cancellation was the American intervention in Cambodia as a result of which Sihanouk, who had been overthrown, surfaced in Beijing to establish his government in exile. That this was probably the real reason can be discerned from the fact that while publicly expressing their discontent at American action in Cambodia,[59] the Chinese were careful to avoid breaking off relations with the United States. On 10 July, for example, Beijing announced the release of Bishop James Walsh, who had been arrested in 1958 and sentenced in 1960 to twenty years imprisonment as a spy.[60] On 1 October 1970, Mao Zedong invited Edgar Snow and his wife to stand beside him on the public rostrum on China's national day. On the face of it this may seem a banal event. But since "nothing China's leaders do publicly is without purpose"[61] this was China's way of signalling that the development of Sino-American relations now had Mao's "personal attention".[62] In December, he informed Snow in an interview that he would welcome a visit by Nixon to Beijing.[63]

In April 1971, the Chinese response became even clearer. In addition to informing Washington through Pakistani channels of their final accord to meet an American emissary in China, they suddenly and unexpectedly invited, in the same month, the American table tennis team that was participating in the world championship competition in Tokyo, and Zhou Enlai personally met the team and hailed the visit as a "new page" in Sino-American relations.[64]

Thereafter things moved rapidly. Kissinger set out on his secret visit to China in July 1971. Though the purpose of this visit was to seek the normalisation of relations between the two countries and to prepare the way for Nixon's visit,[65] Kissinger's more than seventeen hours of talks with Zhou were principally devoted to the presentation of "their respective views of the world with a frankness rarely achieved among allies."[66]

Nixon's Journey to China

Nixon's visit in February 1972 was indeed a watershed in Sino-American relations. From a phase of non-relations and utter hostility for almost two decades, with this visit they went beyond the simple level of normalisation.

The approaches of the two countries at the talks were in many ways similar. As in Kissinger's first visit, the purpose was not so much to argue the bilateral issues that separated the two countries, but to ascertain whether there existed a commonality of perception on global issues and whether they had common security concerns. "The fundamental objective of both sides," wrote Kissinger "was not territorial but geopolitical;" it was not bilateral but was "to deal across the gulf of ideology with common security concerns."[67]

Once this was achieved, the goal then of the two delegations was to avoid jeopardizing this general agreement and general understanding by discord on bilateral issues. The common attitude appeared to be that since it was neither practically feasible nor humanly possible to reach agreement on bilateral issues, they should agree to disagree while underlining their agreement on more basic issues.

The Shanghai Communiqué, signed on 28 February 1972 by President Nixon and Premier Zhou Enlai, was a reflection of this frame of mind. Skillfully drafted after days of negotiation, it frankly stated the differences that separated them. No attempt was made to hide them by using fuzzy diplomatic language.

While the United States proclaimed her support for the eight-point peace proposal made by the United States and South Vietnam, China gave her firm support to the seven-point proposal made by the Vietcong. While the US supported South Korean efforts to seek relaxation of tensions, China came out in favour of the eight-point North Korean plan for unification of the peninsula. While Washington placed "the highest value on its friendly relations with Japan," Beijing went on record to stress its opposition to "the revival and outward expansion of Japanese imperialism."[68] And while the United States supported "the rights of peoples of South Asia to shape their own future . . .," the Chinese highlighted their support to the "Pakistani government and people in their struggle to preserve their independence and sovereignty and the peoples of Jammu and Kashmir in their struggle for the right of self-determination."[69]

The issue that proved most intractable was Taiwan. Differences were obviously too great to be papered over by a simple statement of opposite views. Since it directly concerned the Chinese and was the issue over which so much ink had been spilt and due to which Sino-American relations had remained hostile for so many years, they reneged upon their original understanding that each side could freely state its position. Whereas the Chinese proposed an unconditional American commitment to totally withdraw her troops from Taiwan, the US insisted on linking her withdrawal to the diminution of tension in the area. However, so firm was the common determination of the two countries not to allow—as far as this was possible—even this highly controversial issue to lead to a Sino-American impasse that a formula was finally agreed upon. Presumably one of the elements that led the Chinese to finally agree to a formula was the secret assurance given by Nixon of his intention to completely normalise relations with Beijing during his second term if he was re-elected in November 1972.[70] The relevant paragraph representing the American point of view read as follows:

> The United States acknowledges that all Chinese on either side of the Taiwan Strait maintain there is but one China and Taiwan is a part of China. The United States does not challenge this position. It reaffirms its interest in a peaceful settlement of the Taiwan question by the Chinese themselves. With this prospect in mind, it affirms the ultimate objective of the withdrawal of all US forces and military installations from Taiwan. In the meantime, it will progressively reduce its forces and military installations on Taiwan as the tension in the area diminishes.[71]

More important than the public airing of these bilateral differences was the meeting of minds between the two countries that all disputes should be settled peacefully, that all dangers of military conflict should be reduced, and that neither of them "should seek hegemony in the Asia-Pacific region" nor allow "any other country or group of countries to establish such hegemony."[72]

The communiqué also underlined the importance of developing bilateral relations. "To this end," it declared the accord of the two countries to develop relations in "such fields as science, technology, culture, sports and journalism, in which people-to-people contacts and exchanges would be mutually beneficial. Each side undertakes to facilitate the progressive development of trade relations between their two countries."[73]

Acceleration of Normalisation

In the immediate aftermath of Nixon's visit, relations between the two countries expanded rapidly. Regular contacts were established between Chinese and American embassies in Paris where discussions were opened on a variety of essentially bilateral issues. Kissinger personally averaged about two visits a year to Beijing to discuss broad international issues, though a wide array of pending bilateral problems were also raised.

Sino-American trade relations skyrocketed. From about $5 million in 1971 they increased to $934 million in 1974, making the United States China's second largest trading partner. The quantum of cultural exchanges also mushroomed during the same period. By late 1974 over 8,000 Americans had gone to the PRC. Though this was not reciprocated by an equal number of high-level delegations, about 500 Chinese visited the United States.[74]

Washington had equally taken some unilateral and friendly initiatives towards Taiwan. Its military forces in Taiwan were reduced from about 8,000-9,000 men to less than 4,000.[75] And in the fall of 1974, with the concurrence of the administration, the Senate repealed the 1955 Formosa Resolution which authorised the President to employ the armed forces "for the specified purpose of securing and protecting Formosa . . ."[76]

The most important development, however, was the accord of the two governments to establish "liaison offices" in each others' capitals in February 1973.[77] Each mission was headed by a senior diplomat: David Bruce represented the United States; Huang Zhen, central committee member of the CCP, represented China.

Since the People's Republic had so far consistently refused to establish diplomatic missions in countries which recognised Taiwan, this was clearly a major concession. Though the exchange of liaison officers fell short of full diplomatic relations, the creation of such a presence in the two capitals was nonetheless a major step.

By agreeing to the institutionalisation of bilateral relations, the Chinese leadership had opted for a policy of continuing the momentum of normalisation even before the resolution of the Taiwan issue. In the increasingly critical international situation of the early 1970s, this was presumably viewed as more vital for Chinese interests than the rapid acquisition of Taiwan. The Russian threat had increased. The international air was thick with rumours of a possible pre-emptive Soviet nuclear attack on China.

Parallel with these developments, tension regarding the United States was on the wane, especially after the Vietnam peace accords of January 1973 and the consequent withdrawal of US military forces from the Indo-Chinese peninsula. Though Taiwan was still an unresolved issue, it had lost much of its urgency since both the parties had agreed to de-escalate the tension, and, more particularly, since Nixon had, as stated above, given oral assurances to Zhou Enlai that he intended to fully normalise relations with

Beijing if he were elected for the second term.[78] For the Chinese, it was thus only a question of time.

The CCP leadership had therefore begun to adopt a low-key attitude on Taiwan. According to press reports, it made it a point of conveying to Americans visiting Beijing that Taiwan's integration was not urgent and that her incorporation into mainland China was to be envisaged in a long-term perspective.[79] The most authoritative exposition of this new line was Zhou Enlai's five-hour interview given to a group of overseas Chinese in August 1973 in which he declared that Taiwan was a complex matter and that the PRC was willing to negotiate with the existing regime.

At the same time and through a series of initiatives, the PRC sought to impress upon the people of Taiwan the advantages of their unification with the mainland and emphasised their role in their own "liberation".[80] A number of overseas Chinese of Taiwanese origin, especially from the United States and Japan, were invited to visit the mainland. The PRC stopped all attacks on the members of the Taiwan independence movement in the United States and Japan. The Kuomingtang Revolutionary Committee, which was composed of dignitaries who had rallied to the CCP in 1948 and which had become defunct, was revived; the department of the Central Committee of the party, which was in charge of establishing a common front with non-communist groups, was reactivated.[81]

Though the aim of this campaign was to convince the people of the island, it was also directed at the United States as a signal of their own flexibility on the question. It is noteworthy that many of these actions and initiatives were taken around the time of Kissinger's visit to China in 1973.

In November 1973, during Kissinger's sixth visit to Beijing, the Chinese agreed to be even more flexible and even more open on Taiwan. The joint communiqué issued at the end of the visit did not contain the categorical language which was used to explain the Chinese point of view in the Shanghai communiqué. Such expressions as "the Taiwan question is the crucial question obstructing the normalisation of relations" between the two countries or that "the liberation of Taiwan is China's internal matter" were conspicuously missing.[82]

Diplomatic Impasse in 1974

The US response to Chinese overtures was not that forthright or at least the Chinese did not perceive it that way. There was first of all the radical transformation of the American domestic situation, which did not lend itself to a continuation of the momentum to normalise of Sino-American relations. The unexpected developments pertaining to the Watergate crisis had so weakened Nixon's political position in the country that the process of normalisation from the American end came to a complete halt. Faced with a rising threat to his political career, Nixon did not wish to alienate the conservative members of the Congress who had been the strongest adherents of close US-Taiwan ties and who were his main supporters.

But this did not save him. He had to leave the Presidency in August 1974. His successor, Gerald Ford, had the opportunity to implement Nixon's plans, but he, too, for obviously domestic reasons, decided against pressing ahead with normalisation.

In fact, the uncertainities of American politics had pushed those who were at the helm of affairs to reinforce US ties with Taiwan. Instead of down-grading the Taibei diplomatic post, a senior American diplomat, Leonard Unger, was sent as the new Ambassador to Taibei. Two new Taiwanese consulates were opened in the United States and new American military equipment was sold on credit. The debate within the United States on the Taiwan issue perhaps confirmed Chinese fears of an American reluctance to extricate herself from the island. There were those who argued that the escalatory pattern of Sino-Soviet relations did not appear to leave much leverage for the Chinese in the formulation of their foreign policy except to continue the normalisation process with the United States. Besides, continued the argument, any attempt on the part of the US administration to abandon Taiwan would be opposed by American public opinion and would not fail to have repercussions on the stability of friendly regimes in Asia. There were others who argued that normalisation should be completed. Any attempt to rely on the Sino-Soviet dispute to force the Chinese hand would be counterproductive.

Though both these viewpoints were forcefully presented, the partisans of maintaining a status quo appeared to be more weighty in American politics.[83]

In any event, for the CCP, not used to the system of open debate, discordant voices emanating from the United States probably confirmed them in their view that US attitude was becoming even more ambivalent.

Chinese disappointment with the United States was further aggravated by Soviet-American détente, the most dramatic manifestation of which was the conclusion of the SALT-I agreement in 1974. Just as the Chinese appeared to be making concessions on Taiwan for the sake of seeking a global Sino-American entente, the Americans appeared to be focussing their attention on seeking out the Russians. This Kissingerian policy of tilting first to one side and then to the other with the two Communist giants to exploit Sino-Soviet animosity must have been one of the principal sources of Chinese annoyance with the US in 1975.

Compounded to all this was the existence of a disagreement between the two countries regarding the interpretation to be given to the Shanghai communiqué regarding the incorporation of Taiwan. Whereas the Chinese asserted that Taiwan was an internal matter and China could "liberate" the island in any manner she deemed appropriate, the US, on the other hand, appeared to insist that she would de-recognise Taiwan only if main-

84

land China pledged to limit herself to peaceful means to bring about reunification.[84]

To this basket of external explanations must be added the highly uncertain situation that was also developing in Chinese domestic politics. Disagreements within the party had become endemic. This was aggravated by the fading away of Zhou Enlai from the political scene due to illness. Mao himself had become less active. Vice-President Deng Xiaoping, who was in charge of the day-to-day affairs of the country, could not be certain of his position as Zhou had been. There was, moreover, evidence of a continuing debate within China over the policy towards both the Soviet Union and the United States.

All these elements undoubtedly constituted a major catalyst in pushing China to adopt a more firm attitude towards the United States, with effect from 1974. Negotiations on claims and assets, for example, were deadlocked. Despite being very close to the conclusion of an accord, Beijing decided to drag its feet as long as the normalisation process had not been completed. American correspondents were refused admission to reside in China as long as formal diplomatic relations were not established, though they were allowed to come in to cover official visits. Trade was slowed down. From a total turnover of $ 978.8 million in 1974, it declined to $ 461.9 million in 1975, and $ 336 million in 1976 (see Table 3.1). This was principally due to the Chinese decision to serverely curtail their imports. In late 1974, they reduced the quantities of farm products they had ordered, while contracts already firmed up were being stretched out. Though this was in part due to a succession of two good harvests in 1973 and 1974, it was also due to a deliberate decision to turn to other suppliers, particularly Australia and Canada.

Table 3.1. *US Trade with the People's Republic of China*
(in millions of US dollars)

Year	Exports	Imports
1971	– –	5.0
1972	63.5	32.4
1973	740.2	64.0
1974	820.5	114.7
1975	303.6	158.3
1976	135.0	201.0

Sources from 1971 to 1974: William Clarke and Martha Avery, "The Sino-American Commercial Relationship," in *China: A Reassessment of the Economy,* A Compendium of Papers Submitted to the Joint Economic Committe, 94th Congress 1st Session, 10 July 1975.

For 1975: see US Department of Commerce, Bureau of East-West Trade, *U.S. Trade Status with Socialist Countries, 15 June 1976.*

For 1976: see CIA Office of Economic Research.

Beijing also became critical of Washington. On 11 November 1974, Deng Xiaoping declared that the "so-called détente policy cooked up by the two superpowers was a trick."[85] When Kissinger visited Beijing in November 1974, he was not received by Mao Zedong—though Mao had seen less important foreign dignitries.[86] The terse, barely polite four-sentence communiqué compares very unfavourably with previous declarations.[87] Nothing was agreed upon.

Zhou Enlai personally noted in his report to the 4th National People's Congress in January 1975, the continuation of "fundamental differences" between China and the US. He also emphasized that for relations to improve further the principles of the Shanghai Communiqué would have to be "carried out in earnest."[88] During Kissinger's October 1975 visit the Chinese were even more critical. At the banquet given on the day of his arrival, Foreign Minister Qiao Guanhua criticised his American-Soviet détente policy. He said:

> The factors for both revolution and war are increasing. The stark reality is not that détente has developed to a new stage but that the danger of a new world war is mounting. We do not believe that there is any lasting peace. Things develop according to objective laws independent of man's will. The only way to deal with hegemonism is to wage a tit-for-tat struggle against it. To base oneself on illusions, to mistake hopes or wishes for reality and act accordingly, will only abet the ambitions of expansionism and lead to grave consequences. In this regard, the history of the Second World War provides a useful lesson. In the face of the growing danger of war, China's fundamental policy is to "dig tunnels deep, store grain everywhere, never seek hegemony," to persist in independence and self-reliance and make all necessary preparations. We are deeply convinced that whatever zigzags and reverses there may be in the development of history, the general development of the world is towards light and not darkness.[89]

Kissinger disagreed:

> The US will resist hegemony, as we have already stated in the Shanghai Communiqué (of 1972). But the US will also make every effort to avoid needless confrontation . . . In this policy we will be guided by action and reality and not rhetoric.[90]

President Ford's official visit to China in December 1975 was also not much of a success. Though he was correctly received, he was clearly informed of China's concern at the lack of progress on the Taiwan question and of her opposition to Soviet-American détente.[91] The level of discord can be gauged from the fact that the two countries could not even agree on a joint communiqué. Chinese discontent with official American policy can also be discerned in the invitation which was extended to Nixon to visit China in February 1976. The reception he received was warmer and more cordial than that Ford had received three months earlier. Hua Guofeng, who had been promoted to acting premiership and was serving as the ex-president's principal host, referred to his first visit as an "historic event" which had played a "major role" in improving and developing relations between the

US and China.[92] Mao met with Nixon for a "friendly conversation . . . on a wide range of subjects."[93]

The Carter Administration

During the first year of the Carter administration, Sino-American relations remained frozen. The Chinese continued to insist on *(a)* the severance of diplomatic ties with Taiwan; *(b)* the abrogation of the 1954 Mutual Security Treaty, and *(c)* the withdrawal of remaining American troops from Taiwan.[94] "If you want to normalise relations," declared a senior Chinese official to the *Washington Post* in April 1977, "you have to sever relations with Taiwan, withdraw your troops and abrogate the (defense) treaty."[95]

These three points were repeatedly and unambiguously underlined in almost all Chinese declarations pertaining to Sino-American relations, including the one made by Li Xiannian to Admiral Elmo Zunwalt, ex-chief of American naval operations, on 4 July 1977,[96] and another made by Hua Guofeng at the 11th Party Congress.[97]

Beijing, therefore, blocked all bilateral negotiations as long as it obtained no satisfaction on the Taiwan question. The bilateral negotiations on blocked assets, resumed in the spring of 1977, for example, were not allowed to reach a conclusive stage,[98] and the American invitation for the expansion of a scholarly and scientific exchange programme was declined.[99]

During the first year of the Carter Administration, the Chinese government consistently followed this line. Neither the intraparty struggle that followed Zhou's and Mao's deaths, nor the political struggle surrounding the liquidation of the "Gang of Four" really deterred them from the basic policy framework they had established regarding Taiwan.

The Carter administration, after an initial period of uncertainty, also settled on the previously established position of wanting to complete the normalisation process, but only after having obtained the appropriate assurances from Beijing that it would not use violence to incorporate Taiwan.

If the Chinese considered their position to be in accordance with the Shanghai Communiqué, the Americans insisted that their line was by no means a deviation from the same accord, since the US had made a point of including a sentence in the communiqué which reaffirmed American interest "in a peaceful settlement of the Taiwan question by the Chinese themselves".[100]

President Carter had publicly reaffirmed this by stating that the US was committed to the establishment of full diplomatic relations while still making sure that "the peaceful lives of the Taiwanese" were maintained.[101] The deadlock was apparently complete.

Secretary of State Vance's four-day visit to Beijing in August 1977 must have also provided an appropriate opportunity for reaffirming Washington's intentions of going ahead with the normalisation process, provided some assurances could be obtained on Taiwan. It is interesting to note that according to press reports, Vance discussed at some length the difficulties of the American domestic position and the opposition Carter would have to face if he did not wade carefully through the crisis. Vance, in his press conference, made a point of suggesting that "this was a useful discussion from (the Chinese) standpoint to hear first-hand what the views of the peoples of the United States are, of those who represent the people of the United States in the Congress."[102]

Secret Negotiations

Then suddenly in the spring of 1978 signs of some letting up became discernible. This first became evident on the American side. Pushed by a series of factors, including difficulties with the Russians on strategic talks, the United States took the decision to break the deadlock even if it involved making some concessions. Brzezinski's visit to Beijing in May 1978 gave the Carter administration the opportunity to inform the Chinese that "the US had made up its mind" to achieve full normalisation.[103] Soon afterwards, the head of American Liaison Office in Beijing, Leonard Woodcock, was given full authorization in the summer to negotiate with the Chinese. Meanwhile in Washington, Brzezinski met a dozen times with China's envoy—first Han Zu and later his successor Cai Zemin—in absolute secrecy.

The next key event was a meeting between President Carter and the head of China's Liaison Office. At this meeting the president is reported to have laid out his terms for normalisation. Beijing, he insisted, must allow US to keep her economic and cultural relations with Taiwan and must agree tacitly not to reunite Taiwan by force. This was followed by the October meeting between Carter and his advisers where it was agreed to set a target date of 1 January 1979 to complete the normalisation process.[104] Presumably the negotiations were fairly advanced to permit Carter to set the deadline.

When it became apparent that US policy was clearly moving in the direction of a *modus vivendi* and that it was only a question of time before the normalisation process would be completed, the Chinese began to respond. While still insisting publicly on American disengagement, the Chinese sent out a number of public signals. This became particularly evident in August 1978. First of all, while announcing the establishment of diplomatic relations with Libya, China did not insist on the formal breaking of relations between Libya and Taiwan. Though this may seem, on the face of it, a gratuitous concession, since Libya did not have any diplomats in Taibei. Nonetheless, the fact that she did not insist—as she had done in the past—on Libya making a formal declaration to break relations was a distinct change from her preceding position.[105] Secondly, Beijing did not object to the simultaneous presence of a Taiwan delegation in an international conference in Tokyo. Thirdly, the Chinese government agreed to the commencement of a Sino-American student exchange programme even before the establishment of diplomatic relations;[106] and fourthly, China began to show great interest in US equity financing. Before normalisation, major American companies were invited to make proposals in the fields of natural resource development, heavy industry construction, mining, and oil exploration.[107]

The interactions of all these elements set the stage for the final round of hard and detailed negotiations. Since the United States appeared to have reconciled herself to the idea of abandoning all hopes of obtaining some formal Chinese assurances regarding the non-use of military force, the major obstacle were removed.

In exchange, Washington sought and obtained three major concessions. Firstly the Chinese agreed that the US-Taiwan security treaty would not be scrapped overnight but would be allowed to run its natural course until its legal termination at the end of 1979. The acceptance of this proposal in effect created a two-China situation for the whole of 1979, since the US had established diplomatic relations with Beijing while the defense treaty with Taiwan was still in force. Secondly, China agreed that the United States could make a unilateral statement at the time of normalising relations, expressing the hope that the Taiwan question would be resolved peacefully, without a formal contradiction from the Chinese.

Finally, the real obstacle turned out to be the ticklish question of arms aid by Washington to Taibei. The US considered that for both domestic and international reasons it was not possible for her to cut off all military aid to Taibei. For the Chinese, on the other hand, this was unacceptable. Finally the two countries agreed to disagree. While the US could make an announcement of her plans to continue military assistance to Taibei, Beijing would publicly express its opposition, without in any way jeopardising the normalisation process. Washington, however, had to agree that it would not make any new commitments to sell arms in 1979, while the security treaty with Taiwan was still valid.[108]

Formal Establishment of Relations

With the removal of these major hurdles, the two countries moved towards the final stage of working on the language of the joint communiqué. After considerable exchanges, an agreement was reached. The communiqué, released simultaneously in Washington and Beijing on 16 December, was a brief and laconic document which announced the formal establishment of diplomatic relations between the two countries and which reaffirmed the points included in the Shanghai Communiqué. In addition, it contained two lines stipulating that the US "will maintain cultural, commercial, and other official relations with the people of Taiwan."[109]

The establishment of formal relations was undoubtedly a major watershed in Sino-American relations. They opened up possibilities for the expansion of non-political relations, about which the Chinese, until then, had been dragging their feet.

But there still remained the question of settling the Taiwan question in practical terms and of avoiding any steps, initiatives, or even declarations that could jeopardise the new and still fragile framework of Sino-American relations.

While having refused to give any formal assurances regarding the non-use of military force, the CCP began a two-pronged campaign: one aspect was directed at orienting public opinion within China to accept the idea that the incorporation of Taiwan would be a long-term affair. A document was prepared by the Central Commitee of the CCP in which was declared that it might well take generations before the rival Chinese regimes could be united, and in the meantime Taiwan would be permitted to retain its own economic and political system. This document, according to press reports, was widely circulated and was even read over loudspeakers at thousands of factories, offices, and communes.[110] After so many years of insistance that Taiwan was a part of China and that it had to be liberated, it was obviously considered vital to prepare public opinion to accept the idea that it was no longer necessary to incorporate Taiwan for the time being. The second part of the campaign, directed at other countries and particularly at the United States, was to assure them that China had no intention of invading Taiwan after the last American troops were withdrawn from the island.[111] Hua Guofeng declared on 16 December on Chinese television that China had no military designs on Taiwan.[112] He dropped all reference to "liberation" and instead spoke only of "reunification".[113] The editorial of the *People's Daily* on 17 December was even more conciliatory. "We are thinking," it declared, "of our Taiwan compatriots all the time, and the motherland, we know, is always in the minds of people of Taiwan ... We are firmly convinced that the day will definitely come when Taiwan will return to the embrace of the motherland and when our fellow countrymen there will be reunited with their kith and kin on the mainland."[114]

The CCP's conciliatory attitude was a recognition of reality. Though formally she had maintained her right to do what she wanted, in fact she did not appear to have any credible option other than to adopt the stand she did. For one thing, any attempt on her part to initiate military action would have inevitably brought her onto a collision course with the United States, where an important segment of public opinion had already expressed reservations over Carter's Taiwan policy. Under the existing configuration of international forces, this was viewed as being distinctly against her national interests. Moreover, it did not make sense to break down the whole new edifice of Sino-American relations, which had been established after so much effort and after so much hard bargaining. For another, the mainland lacked the appropriate military capability for undertaking a military invasion of Taiwan, and would not possess this ability for at least another five years.[115] For still another, any such attempt might push Taibei to seek an understanding with Moscow, some signs of which were already becoming discernible.[116]

For the United States, the task of seeking a framework for relations with Taiwan was even more difficult and delicate. The maintenance of too close a relationship with Taiwan could irritate Beijing and could even jeopardize all the efforts the administration had made to normalise Sino-American relations. On the other hand, any attempt to conspicuously downgrade US-Taibei ties could further provoke a severe domestic reaction, indications of which were already strong. Senator Barry Goldwater had, for example, denounced the new Sino-American entente as "a cowardly act" and Bill Brocker, Republican National Chairman, had accused President Carter of a "callous disregard for a fine friend and loyal ally."[117] Fifteen congressional members challenged the Sino-American agreement in a US district court on the legal grounds that the "advise and consent" of the Congress had not been sought by the executive before the termination of the defense pact with Taibei.[118]

The Carter administration thus moved cautiously in the establishment of a new framework. Immediately after the announcement of the normalisation of relations, the US administration, therefore, made a point of announcing (a) that almost all the existing agreements with Taiwan—about fifty of them—would be continued, with the exception of the defense treaty, [119] and (b) that it would continue to meet the defense needs of Taibei.[120]

A high-level US mission was immediately despatched to Taiwan to work out the modalities of a new relationship. The delegation was met by massive protest demonstration and by a government determined to conduct negotiations only on a government-to-government basis. President Jiang Jing-guo of Taiwan insisted that future ties between the two countries must rest on the five principles of "reality, continuity, security, legality, and governmentality."[121] But the Taiwan government was not in a position to resist American pressure to negotiate on the terms proposed by Washington; after about six to seven weeks of resistance, in the middle of February 1979, the Taiwanese finally accepted the proposition that future ties between the two countries would be handled by private organisations especially established for this purpose.[122]

This downgrading of official relations, however, has in no way caused US-Taiwan relations to deteriorate. Economic relations have improved. Taiwan has become the second largest trade partner, after Japan, with overall trade amounting to $ 7.9 billion in 1979[123] and with a 12 percent increase in US investment during the same year.[124] Three American banks have also opened new branch offices in the country.[125]

In mid-March 1979, the US Congress passed a bill which broadly stated that the use of force against Taiwan would be a threat to peace and stability in the western Pacific area.[126] At the same time, it criticised Carter for having abrogated the defense treaty without having sought the approval of the Congress.[127] Beijing showed some irritation over the bill, but it did not make an issue out of it, presumably because there was nothing much she could do short of rocking the Sino-American boat.[128]

With full normalisation, the last major obstacle to the expansion of relations was thus removed. The process of building up bilateral relations, which had lain dormant for so many years, was rapidly accelerated, and within a few months important ties were forged. American journalists, for example, were given permission to reside in China, and the quota of 20,000 Chinese tourist visas alloted for the whole year was exhausted within two months.[129] Assets and claims, blocked since 1949, were unblocked. Protocols or agreements on such diverse topics as atmospheric cooperation, marine and fishery cooperation, science and technology, and shipping were concluded. Even more important, a trade agreement was initialled in May and signed in July of the same year (see Table 3.2).

Table 3.2. *Agreements concluded between The United States and the PRC in 1979*

31 January 1979:	Agreement on High-energy Physics
	Consular Agreement
	Science and Technology Agreement
	Cultural Agreement
10 May 1979:	Agreement on Settlement of Claims on Assets
	Agreement on Trade Exhibitions
	Atmospheric Science and Technology Cooperation
	Marine and Fishery Cooperation
	Metrology and Standards Cooperation
	Cooperation in Science and Technology and Scientific and Technical Information
22 June 1979:	Agreement on Cooperation in Medicine and Public Health
7 July 1979:	Agreement on Trade Relations
28 August 1979:	Cultural Agreement
	Protocol on Hydroelectric Power Agreement and Related Water Resource Management

New Levels of Cooperation

On the political plane, a new and escalatory pattern of Sino-American understanding and even entente was established. Although some signs were already visible in the early 1970s, they became clearly evident only after full normalisation in December 1978. The first level of this understanding was characterised by the emergence of political, though unconcerted, convergence on a wide array of international issues in which Moscow was involved. Whether it was the Middle Eastern situation, or the Indochinese crisis, or Southern Africa or the Persian Gulf area, the two countries had

92

developed the same fears, though by no means the same solutions. The degree and form of these parallel views and fears has, however, varied on issues and areas involved. In some instances they were clear and explicit. In others, they were ambiguous and tacit.

The second level was characterised by politico-strategic rapprochement. Both countries arrived at the common conclusion that the maintenance of the independence of the other was vital to the security of each of them. If the Chinese implicitly considered the United States as a guarantee against Soviet expansionism, the United States had clearly expressed the view that the territorial integrity and independence of China was vital to American interests. Though some signs of this thinking had already appeared in the early 1970s, the official manifestation of the new line emanated from Vice-President Walter Mondale's visit to Beijing in September 1979. In a speech at Beijing University on 27 August, he declared that "any nation which seeks to weaken or isolate China in world affairs assumes a stance counter to American interests."[130]

The third level is more operational. It is reflected in attempts on the part of the two countries to consult and coordinate their activities to contain the Soviet threat. The Soviet intervention in Afghanistan in 1980 was the real catalyst in pushing the two countries to reach this operational level. During Defense Secretary Brown's visit to China in January 1980, the two countries moved towards the elaboration of a plan to contain the Soviet threat. The Americans appeared to favour a three-cornered arrangement to shore up Pakistan's defense capability. They envisaged selling China high technology capable of being switched to military use, and China in turn was expected to step up arms supply to Pakistan, followed by the supply of more sophisticated weapons by the US, either directly or bankrolled by a third country, probably Saudi Arabia.[131]

But this was not an *ad hoc* coordination limited only to Afghanistan. The Soviet advance beyond her own region had laid the basis for general Sino-American coordination in security matters. As Brown declared at the banquet on 7 January 1980 given by his Chinese counterpart:

> We both seek a peaceful international environment in which weak and small nations have no fear of military domination or invasion by outside powers in the name of "peace and friendship". With these considerations in mind, I have come to broaden security dialogue between our two governments and to exchange views on how we might facilitate wider cooperation on security matters in the future. We have begun to realise the benefits of contacts between our defense establishments. I am prepared to discuss arrangements for expanding such professional contacts and exchanges.[132]

Relations between China and the United States have thus come a long way since the Chinese Revolution. Within a period of three decades, they have evolved from a state of antagonism and confrontation to a state of mutual understanding, cooperation, and entente. That this new partnership of the 1980s between two ideological adversaries is indeed a major development is reflected in the fact that the central balance of international relations can no longer be viewed with the same perspective as before.

Conclusions

From the conclusion of the Treaty of Wangxia in 1844 until World War II, Sino-American relations were essentially uneventful, unequal, and antagonistic: uneventful in the sense that they did not have any major impact on the course of events in the Far East; unequal and antagonistic insofar as they were between a dominant industrial power and a weak semi-colonial country, and the relationship was one from which the United States reaped the most benefit.

After World War II, these relations evolved. They became more eventful, more equal, and more antagonistic. Having broken out of the previous roles of subordinate actors, the relations between these two nations became more impactful, not only on each other but also on other nations in Asia. No longer was it possible for any other nation to manage the rapidly changing Asian situation without taking into account the thinking and policies of the two countries. Also, they had become more equal. Having become strong and assertive, China was no longer prepared to accept such an unequal relationship. The determination of a nation not to accept a position of inequality often contributes to the final neutralisation of an asymmetrical position. But more striking than all this was the growing level of antagonism. For almost two decades after the Chinese Revolution, the two countries remained fixed in a confrontational position characterised by periodic increasing and diminishing tensions. The 1970s accelerated the momentum of change, resulting in a major qualitative transformation in the bilateral relationship, which became more eventful and even more equal as they became less antagonistic. Finally, in the last few years, they have taken a positive turn in the direction of cooperation and entente, to the point that the two nations have now linked their security interests.

Without going into the details of this realignment of forces, (dealt with elsewhere) suffice it to recall that the principal elements that have caused the development of this new relationship are the Sino-Soviet dispute and the burgeoning Soviet power in world politics. Both the US and China appear to perceive that the Soviet Union has become a major threat to the balance that had been established in the international system, and both of them appear to have introduced an element of coordination in their policies.

However, notwithstanding this growing convergence, American and Chinese interests are far from being identical regarding the Soviet Union. Serious differences continue to persist. The United States recognises that the Soviet Union has an important and legitimate role to play in international affairs and that the maintenance of the Soviet-American strategic military balance is a vital goal of highest priority—in fact higher than

Sino-American relations. Furthermore, she considers détente between the two superpowers crucial for international peace and stability.

The Chinese disagree. Though avoidance of a direct military conflict with Moscow is considered an understandable goal, they oppose Soviet-American détente, denounce all attempts at arms control, and criticise all signs of improvement in Soviet-American relations.

Divergent global perceptions are not the only factors that divide the two countries. There are a wide spectrum of other considerations, principally bilateral, that must also be taken into account.

First of all, distinct ideological frameworks separate the two societies. Their views and objectives regarding societal developments are not only contradictory, but they are also conflictual. For the time being, the two countries have been successful in sidetracking this dimension from their bilateral relationship. But can they continue to do so? Will these basic differences not affect the smooth functioning of their bilateral relations? Will they not inevitably create hurdles at some point in this apparently burgeoning relationship? Though all transnational relations are uncertain, are not the Sino-American relations—because of the ideological dimension—full of additional multitudes of imponderables?

Secondly, the more-than-normal rapprochement that the world is currently witnessing in Sino-American relations is principally based on the common perception of a Soviet threat, which for the Americans developed about four decades ago and for the Chinese only about two decades back. Can one say that two or three decades from now these common perceptions will persist, and that the Chinese will continue to view the Russians in the same light as before? Should there be a change in perception by either of the two countries, what would then happen to Sino-American relations, based as they are largely upon this perception of a threat?

Thirdly, the agreement over Taiwan is essentially provisional. The PRC has not abandoned its consistently declared objective of incorporating Taiwan into the mainland. For the sake of maintaining the present level in Sino-American relations, the Communist party leadership has expressed the hope of resolving the problem peacefully, without in any way abandoning the option of using force should it be deemed necessary. The United States, on the other hand, continues to expand her relations with Taiwan, including the maintenance of the commitment that she will continue to provide defensive arms. Though external strategic reasons are by no means absent from this policy, the US has been primarily moved by domestic considerations where public opinion, including the opinion of the majority of her legislators, though favouring ties with PRC, are against abandoning Taiwan. What if the Chinese come to the conclusion that peaceful incorporation is no longer possible, that indefinite co-existence with a rapidly developing Taiwan—representing a different socio-economic system—is a potential threat to their own system, and that consequently force must be used? What would happen to Sino-American relations then?

95

Fourthly, in the long run, China must export in order to import. What she can export—in addition to a limited amount of raw materials—are traditional items. Would the United States, influenced as she is by diverse pressure groups to protect the domestic market and saturated as she is becoming with goods coming from other countries, be able to accommodate burgeoning Chinese traditional exports? Consider in this connection the controversy surrounding the Chinese textile exports. As long as the Chinese Government did not agree to limit textile exports to the United States, Washington refused to accord most-favoured-nation status to China.

The balance that has been established between convergent and divergent aspects of Sino-American relations is a precarious one. Relations may continue on an even keel for decades, but, on the other hand, they could also easily degenerate should any one or more of the above factors again be given enough extra weight to tip the scales.

Notes

1. For details about Sino-American relations of the period, see A. Whitney Grisvold, *The Far Eastern Policy of the United States* (New York: Harcourt, Brace and Company, 1938); Warren I. Cohen, *America's Response to China: An Interpretative History of Sino-American Relations* (New York: John Wiley and Sons, 1971); Forster Rhea Dulles, *China and America: The Story of their Relations since 1789* (Princeton: Princeton University Press, 1941); Tyler Dennett, *Americans in Eastern Asia* (New York: Macmillan, 1922).

2. For details see Te-Kong Tong, *United States Diplomacy in China 1844-60* (Seattle: University of Washington Press, 1964).

3. A. Whitney Grisvold, op cit., p. 4.

4. Text in Henry L. Stimpson, *The Far Eastern Civilisation: Recollections and Observations* (New York: Harper, 1936), pp. 96-99.

5. F. D. Roosevelt, *Public Papers and Addresses* (London: Macmillan, 1941), Vol. VI.

6. See Hu Sheng, op cit.

7. A. Whitney Grisvold, op cit.

8. Department of State, *Papers Relating to the Foreign Relations of the United States 1922* (Washington: US Government Printing Press, 1938), Vol. II, p. 595.

9. Grisvold, op cit.

10. See John W. Esherick (ed.), *Lost Chance in China: World War II Despatches of John S. Service* (New York: Vintage, 1975).

11. Ibid.

12. David A. Barret, *The Dixie Mission: The United States Army Observer Group in Yenan 1944* (Berkeley: University of California Press, 1970).

13. After Ambassador Hurley had hammered out with the CCP a five-point plan for its participation in the coalition government in November and December 1944, Chiang Kai-shek rejected the plan.

14. See the Yalta agreement; for full text, see Aitchen K. Wu, op cit.

15. See Chapter 2.

16. See Lyman van Slyke (ed.), *Marshall's Mission to China* (Arlington VA: University Publications of America, 1976).

17. See Barbara W. Tuchman, *Notes from China* (New York: Collier Books, 1972).

18. Department of State, *United States Relations with China, with Special Reference to the Period 1944-1949* (Washington D.C.: US Government Printing Press, 1949).

19. *Pravda*, 15 August 1978.

20. See Department of State, *United States Relations with China*, op cit.

21. *Current Background*, 32 (1950).

22. Department of State, *American Foreign Policy 1950-55* (Washington D.C.: US Government Printing Office, 1957).

23. Ibid.

24. Ibid., Vol. II, p. 2468.

25. See K.M. Pannikar, *In Two Chinas: Memoirs of a Diplomat* (London: Allen and Unwin, 1955)

26. *New China News Agency*, 29 June 1960.

27. See Allen S. Whiting, *China Crosses the Yalu River* (New York: Macmillan, 1960).

28. *Khruschev Remembers*, Vol. I, op cit.

29. *Soviet Press Translations*, V (1950), p. 419.

30. Ibid., p. 590.

31. *New York Times*, 27 May 1954.

32. See Kenneth T. Young, *Negotiating with the Chinese Communists: The United States Experience, 1953-1967* (New York: McGraw-Hill, 1968).

33. *Important Documents Concerning the Question of Taiwan* (Peking: Foreign Languages Press, 1955), p. 182.

34. *People's China*, 10 (1955), Supplement, p. 6.

35. *Oppose the US Occupation of Taiwan and "Two China's" Plot: A Selection of Documents* (Peking: Foreign Languages Press, 1958).

36. *Extracts of China Mainland Magazines*, 92 (1956), p. 5.

37. Kenneth T. Young, op cit., p. 3.

38. *American Foreign Policy 1950-1955*, op cit., Vol. I, p. 995.

39. Ibid., Vol. II, p. 2486.

40. *Khruschev Remembers*, op cit.

41. Kenneth T. Young, op cit.

42. Ibid., p. 41.

43. Ibid.

44. Ibid.

45. *Peking Review*, 9 (1964).

46. From interview with Zhou Enlai given to the editor-in-chief of Middle East News Agency on 8 September 1965; text in *Peking Review*, 38 (1965), p. 9.

47. Zhou Enlai's speech on the 21st anniversary of Albania's liberation; text in ibid., 49 (1965), p. 5.

48. *People's Daily*, 27 November 1968.

49. Richard M. Nixon, "Asia after Vietnam," *Foreign Affairs*, 1 (1967).

50. Richard M. Nixon, *The Memoirs of Richard Nixon* (London: Arrow Books, 1979), p. 545.

51. Ibid.

52. *Department of State Bulletin*, 1575 (1969), p. 180.

53. Ibid., 1578 (1969).

54. For text see *The Memoirs of Richard Nixon*, op cit., p. 545.

55. See Henry Kissinger, *White House Years* (Boston: Little Brown and Company, 1979).

56. Ibid.

57. Ibid.

58. Kissinger, however, suggests that a few days later there were indications that the Chinese "preferred as yet to deal indirectly with us", ibid., p. 689.

59. For Mao Zedong's declaration of 20 May 1970, see *Peking Review*, Special Issue, 23 May 1970.

60. Both Nixon and Kissinger considered this an important sign of the Chinese intention to maintain contact with the United States; see *The Memoirs of Richard Nixon* and *White House Years*, op cit.

61. Edgar Snow, "China Will Talk from a Position of Strenght," *Life*, 30 July 1971, p. 24.

62. Kissinger, *White House Years*, op cit., p. 699.

63. Though the full text of Snow's interview was published much later in *Life* on 30 April 1971, Nixon read about the report only a few days later in a State Department report; see Kissinger, *White House Years*, op cit.

64. *New York Times*, 15 April 1971; for some details see *Peking Review*, 17 (1971).

65. *Memoirs of Richard Nixon*, op cit., p. 544.

66. Kissinger, op cit., p. 746.

67. Ibid., pp. 1078 and 1086.

68. Text in *Peking Review*, 9 (1972), p. 5.

69. Ibid.

70. Key officials in the Carter administration declared in April 1977 that they had discovered a top-secret document which recorded conversations between Nixon and Zhou Enlai, in which the former had clearly indicated his intention to normalise relations with Beijing during his second term if re-elected in November. See *International Herald Tribune*, 12 April 1977.

71. *Peking Review*, op cit., p. 5.

72. Ibid., 9 (1972), p. 5.

73. Ibid.

74. See National Committee on United States-China Relations, *Prospects for United States-China Relations* (Wingspread, Wisc: Johnson Foundation, 1975).

75. Joseph Lelyveld, "A 1½ —China Policy", *New York Times Magazine*, 6 April 1975.

76. *American Foreign Policy 1950-1965*, Vol. II. p. 2487.

77. *Department of State Bulletin* 1760 (1973).

78. See *International Herald Tribune*, 12 April 1977.

79. *New York Times*, 2 March 1973.

80. Jo Yung-Hwan (ed.), *Taiwan's Future* (Hongkong: Union Research Institute of Arizona State University, 1974).

81. *Le Monde*, 16 November 1973.

82. *Peking Review*, 46 (1973).

83. For details, see Committee on International Relations, *Normalisation of Relations with the People's Republic of China: Practical Implications*, Hearing before the Sub-committee on Asian and Pacific Affairs of the Committee on International Relations, Ninety-Fifth Congress, First Session (Washington: US Government Printing Office, 1977).

84. For details, see William F. Buckley Jr., "What did Nixon say to China?" *International Herald Tribune*, 26 April 1977.

85. *Le Monde*, 14 November 1974.

86. *International Herald Tribune*, 2 December 1974.

87. *Peking Review*, 49 (1974).

88. Zhou Enlai, "Report on the Work of the Government," *Documents of the First*

Session of the Fourth National People's Congress of the People's Republic of China (Peking: Foreign Languages Press, 1975), p. 58.
89. *New China News Agency*, 20 October 1975.
90. Ibid., p. 4.
91. *International Herald Tribune*, 4 December 1975.
92. *Peking Review*, 9 (1976), p. 4.
93. Ibid., p. 3.
94. Foreign Broadcasting Information Service, People's Republic of China, *Daily Report*, 5 July 1977.
95. *International Herald Tribune*, 29 April 1977.
96. *New China News Agency*, 5 July 1977.
97. *Peking Review*, 35 (1977).
98. *International Herald Tribune*, 3 May 1977.
99. Ibid., 29 June 1977.
100. *Peking Review*, 9 (1972), p. 5.
101. *International Herald Tribune*, 1 July 1977.
102. Ibid.
103. The American press, on the basis of different interviews with those who were directly involved in the negotiations, have been able to reconstruct the chronology of events; see *Time*, 25 December 1978.
104. *International Herald Tribune*, 19 December 1978.
105. *Le Monde*, 11 August 1978.
106. *International Herald Tribune*, 18 August 1978.
107. Ibid., 15 September 1978.
108. Ibid., 14 January 1979.
109. *Peking Review*, 51 (1978), p. 8.
110. *International Herald Tribune*, 18 December 1978.
111. Ibid.
112. *Le Monde*, 17-18 December 1978.
113. *International Herald Tribune*, 18 December 1978.
114. *People's Daily*, 17 December 1978.
115. *International Herald Tribune*, 18 December 1978.
116. See John W. Garver, "Taiwan's Russian Option: Image and Reality", *Asian Survey*, 7 (1978); also see *International Herald Tribune*, 18 December 1978.
117. Ibid.
118. Ibid., 29 December 1978.
119. Ibid., 19 December 1978.
120. *Daily Bulletin*, 21 December 1978.
121. *Free China Weekly*, 31 December 1978.
122. Ibid., 18 February 1979; also see *International Herald Tribune*, 14 February 1979.
123. *Free China Weekly*, 10 June 1979.
124. Ibid.
125. They were Seattle First National Bank, Rainier National Bank of Seattle, and the First National Bank of Boston; see ibid., 18 November 1979.
126. *International Herald Tribune*, 15 March 1979.
127. Ibid., 8 June 1979.
128. *New China News Agency*, 15 March 1979; *Le Monde*, 21 April 1979; *International Herald Tribune*, 21-22 April 1979.
129. *International Herald Tribune*, 22 February 1979.
130. *Daily Bulletin*, 30 August 1979.
131. *Dawn*, 8 January 1980.
132. *Daily Bulletin*, 8 January 1980.

Chapter 4

CHINA AND JAPAN

Process of Acculturation

The Chinese historical impact on Japan has indeed been monumental. Through a long process of imitation spanning over a thousand years, Japan acquired almost the totality of her conception of organised social life from China. Practically everything that goes under the name of culture and civilization in Japan stemmed from ancient China in the same way that much of Western culture is rooted in ancient Greece and Rome. Whether it was the writing system, religion, political concepts, forms of government, codes of law, music, architecture, dress, cooking, etc., it bore the conspicuous sinic imprint.

This long process of acculturation,[1] particularly intense during the 7th and 8th centuries, was not the result of military conquests—for Chinese armies had never set foot on Japanese soil. It was essentially caused by a sustained cultural spillover, a normal historical process between neighbouring nations. For centuries, Chinese as well as sinified Koreans had crossed over in considerable numbers to Japan and had settled down in the archipelago near the sea, bringing with them treasures of learning and religion. Also for centuries, large-scale Japanese expeditions had sailed to the Middle Kingdom, returning with zeal and determination to transform their customs and institutions to emulate those of the Tang empire.

However, regardless of this rampant sinification, the Japanese character remained essentially unchanged in its essence.[2] While evincing a remarkable capacity to extract the essence of Chinese culture, the Japanese developed an equally remarkable dexterity in retaining their own national personality. While demonstrating a critical expertise in understanding the empirical significance of all outward expressions, they neither betrayed their inner selves nor abandoned their own values. While assimilating the Chinese culture, for example, they refused tributary relations with the Chinese court on the ground that their belief in the divine origin of the Japanese monarchy was incompatible with the idea of subordination to an earthly ruler. While accepting the erudite nature of the Chinese language, a purely Japanese court poetry and literature was encouraged so that the national culture could be expressed without excessive dependence on a foreign tongue. While establishing a bureaucratic administration modelled on Tang China, the Chinese concept of the *carrière ouverte aux talents* was rejected, and in its stead a small circle of noble families ruled Japan along feudal lines. The shoguns of the Tokugawa family, who governed the country from the 17th to the 19th centuries, were patrons of Chinese scholarship and Confucian philosophy, but the political system they sustained, with its numerous hereditary fiefs, was far removed from mandarin China. And while accepting Buddhism from the Middle Kingdom, it was transformed to suit the Japanese temperament. The Japanese sect of Zen (meditation), which is a form of Buddhism and which has had an overwhelming influence on Japanese artists and warriors, was not used to advance self-realisation, but was employed essentially as a technique to increase the militarism of the nation's leading elements—the samurai.

The Japanese talent for giving national colour to alien civilizations and cultures was thus exceptional; but it is also noteworthy that the Chinese impact on Japan's culture and civilization was a permanent one; for despite the introduction of myriad indigenous modifications, it remained largely sinic, the signs of which are visible to this day.

However, these great and lasting influences did not result in the development of interaction in political and economic relations between the two countries. The Chinese were apparently content with having diffused their wisdom and culture and the insular Japanese with having received them. This was one of those peaceful historical processes of cultural diffusion spanning over centuries[3] without the parallel development of any organised inter-state communications. Therefore, apart from very rare and isolated military encounters—the 13th Century Mongol invasion, the 15th century pirate raids on China and 16th century confrontations between the Ming and the Japanese armies in Korea—relations right up to the 19th century were essentially restricted to Japanese learning missions to China, to travellers from and to the Buddhist temples, and to limited commercial relations established between traders from Fujian and southern Japan.

Antipodal Responses to the West

The forceful impact of the European industrial civilization on China and Japan in the 19th Century, however, transformed everything, including their power and their relations with one another. Their responses to Western intrusions were different, and their capacities to assimilate Western influences were dissimilar.

Shielded from any "strong incorporation"[4] into the world economy by other Asian states that had been reached previously by the West, the Japanese embarked upon a programme of autonomous industrialisation and militarisation in order "to meet Europe halfway and to remodel her national life upon Occidental lines."[5] It was like "the bursting of the dam" causing "the release of long pent-up forces."[6] As they had done a millenium

102

earlier, they radically changed their society by voluntarily borrowing not only Western technology, but also its political, legal, and economic institutions, demonstrating once again the remarkable Japanese capacity for and agility in assimilating external influences without compromising the integrity of their own social and cultural values.[7] But the reasons for reaching out, towards the West were different from those that had led them to turn to China: whereas they were convinced of the superiority of sinic culture and the importance of assimilating it, their decision to adopt Occidental technology and institutions was essentially shaped by the objective of acquiring the appropriate power to maintain their own political and economic independence.

The initial Chinese response, on the other hand, was different. In fact it was just the opposite. They were neither interested nor fearful of the Western world. They resisted change. The order and the system they had established through centuries of intellectual and physical effort was perceived to have made the Middle Kingdom the centre of civilization whose "majestic virtue has penetrated into every country under heaven by land and sea."[8] However, once the Western powers had forced their way into the country and had unilaterally embarked upon a nascent programme of industrialisation, the Chinese were left with no other option but to accept Western modernization. Following the footsteps of the Japanese, they therefore proceeded to move in the same direction in the hope of becoming strong enough to resist Western intrusion and to maintain their own values and ideas. But it was too late. Autonomous modernization à la japonaise was no longer possible. The Western powers were already installed on the mainland, the Chinese economy was already incorporated into the world economy, and imperial China was irreversibly locked into the ongoing process of territorial dismantlement. Instead of becoming a powerful modern state like Japan, the country had slid in the opposite direction—the direction of confusion, instability, and semi-colonialism, from which she did not recover until 1949.

The Rise of Japanese Imperialism

This converse process of development transformed the configuration of forces in the region. Whereas Japan had acquired the muscle necessary for power, China had lost everything, including her independence. Whereas Japan had successfully established a rapidly growing and dynamic socio-economic system to ward off any major Western intrusion, the "Celestial Empire," forcibly brought "into contact with the terrestrial world,"[9] had lost her own traditional, relatively well-balanced system and had inherited, also forcibly, the characteristics of a colonial economy. And whereas the two countries had hitherto had virtually no inter-state relations to speak of, the rapidly developing world economy in which both of them had become emmeshed, albeit in varying ways, inaugurated, for the first time, a process of intense and assymetrical relations, the dominant element in which was obviously Japan.

Driven by the inexorable logic of Western modernization, Japan became expansionist; and China, from whom she had learnt so much and for so long, became one of her principal victims. The most important milestones in this process were the establishment of Japanese control over the Ryukyus Islands in 1870, the annexation of Taiwan and the detachment of Korea in the aftermath of Sino-Japanese War of 1894, the acquisition of parts of Southern Manchuria, including the railways after the Russo-Japanese War of 1904-1905, and the pure and simple annexation of Korea in 1910.

This initial expansionism, spanning almost four decades, was essentially dictated by two factors. In the first place, the Western refusal to accept Japan as an equal power in the region had increasingly led the Japanese to consider that institutional modernization of their society was not enough to gain respect and to acquire a status equal to that of the West. Power still, they discovered, remained the principal means for commanding esteem, and unilateral expansion in neighbouring areas was the only way to force European imperialism to accept Japan as an equal power. Second, new doctrines began to influence Japan's strategic thinking in the latter part of the nineteenth century. It was roused by a sense of insecurity triggered by Western imperialist doctrines. Ably summed up by Aritono Yamagata in 1880, who argued that the best way to maintain national independence and a secure defense resided in protecting not simply Japan's home territories ("the line of sovereignty"), but also an outer perimeter of adjacent areas ("the line of interest") strategically vital to Japan. While, there was, in his view, little possibility that other powers would encroach on Japanese territory, there was great danger that they might obtain a foothold within the Japanese "line of interest".[10]

It is noteworthy that the idea of colonial expansion to secure new markets, raw materials, or overseas opportunities was still peripheral to Japanese thought. During the period in question, Japan scarcely had a major economic empire. Her own modern industries were still developing and her external economic interests and relations, especially in the region, were still marginal. Only a quarter of her trade went to the neighbouring region, in contrast to the much greater volume of trade with advanced countries of Europe and North America. The line of interest initially was thus primarily strategic rather than economic.

China's Attitude to Japan

The nature of China's interest in Japan was, however, different. For the first time in her long history she turned outwards for aid and inspiration. Concerned with problems of modernization, the Japanese model seemed to most Chinese more appropriate and more relevant to their conditions than the direct emulation of the European growth model.

In the writings of the leaders of the Chinese reform movement, for example, Japan was given the pride of place. Wang Tao, a pioneer advocate of reform, praised the selective nature of the Meiji Reformation by stressing that it did not represent indiscriminate use of imperial institutions. Huang Chunxian, who went to Japan in the suite of Chinese Minister Ho Ruichang in 1877 and remained there until 1882, commended, in one of his writings, the selective Japanese use of Western institutions, with particular emphasis on the merits of the drive for freedom and people's rights. Cheng Guanying, a comprador, praised in his reformist writings the Meiji government's intelligent attitude with regard to the protection of private entrepreneurs. Kang Youwei's communications to Emperor Guangxu contained a detailed analysis of the Meiji synthesis, with useful suggestions of what China could emulate;[11] and Liang Qichao, another important reformer, underlined the superiority of the Japanese. "Here is a land," he declared on his arrival in Japan to seek asylum from his country "of superior men. Its culture and people identical with ours . . . I come to ask for help and I am confident that a country so great will hear my request . . . I have studied Japanese history and I enjoy telling again the stories about Japan, where countless *shishi* sacrificed their lives for their country's cause."[12]

But Japan was not only perceived as a worthy developmental model by most Chinese; from the operational viewpoint, she was also considered to be a useful ally both by the Manchus for appropriate assistance in developing and reforming the country, and by the opposition, the Nationalist revolutionaries, in overthrowing the Manchus and expelling the Western intruders.

The Japanese were careful to react positively to all of them. Leading Chinese reformers were permitted to establish themselves in Japan after the collapse of the reform movement. Some of them were in fact even received by highly placed Japanese. Okuma, the Japanese Prime Minister, personally received Kang Youwei and maintained a correspondence with him for a number of years. Prince Konea Atsumara, the head of the House of Peers, organised Kang's trip to North America with a Foreign Office subsidy. During Huang Chunxian's five-year stay in Japan, the Chinese legation in Tokyo became the centre of attraction for Japanese Sinophiles. And Liang Qichao was encouraged to become the central figure in the selection of educational administrators for a Chinese school established in Japan.

To the Manchus, the Japanese offered their expertise on a wide array of problems faced by the dynasty. By the turn of the century, they had acquired a unique influence in the Chinese administration. Virtually every provincial army was staffed in part by officers who had studied abroad, particularly in Japan; in practically all the projected legal and administrative reforms, in all efforts to introduce a modern constitution, and in most of the attempts at industrial developments, not only did the Japanese model figure predominantly but Japanese participation, presence, and advice was also significant. The importance of Japan can be gauged by the rising number of Chinese students who went to Japan. In fact, it was the first truly large-scale modernisation-oriented migration of intellectuals in world history. In 1896, shortly after the Sino-Japanese War, the total number of students was only 18. By the end of 1905 estimates of Chinese students in Tokyo rose, indicating about 8,000, and by 1906, the peak year, the estimates ranged between 6,000 and 20,000.[13]

The Japanese were also careful to develop contacts with the Chinese Nationalist revolutionaries. The dangers of a Manchu collapse and the eventual partition of China was too great for them to ignore those who might one day be at the helm of affairs. Though no direct contacts were officially established with the revolutionaries, they were received with care and hospitality by high-ranking Japanese. Sun Yat-sen, who spent more time in Japan than in any other country, received extensive financial assistance, which came circuitously from the government and from business and private supporters.[14] During the period of his longest residency, 1897-1902, he developed strong sentiments of Pan-Asianism and anti-imperialism, seeing Japan as China's "natural ally". He could address himself to Japanese friends with a warmth and eloquence that he could never achieve with Westerners. Huang Xing, another notable opponent of the Manchus, was given appropriate facilities to meet Chinese students in Japan while he was living there, and to establish contact with Sun Yat-sen, the basic objective of which was to overthrow the Manchus and create a republican government.

In this connection, it is important to note that to most Chinese of the epoch, regardless of their political orientations, Japanese imperialism was not a major problem. Young Chinese, whose formative years had been dominated by Western imperialism and Manchu incompetence, perceived in Meiji Japan a nation that had resisted the former and humbled the latter. From Japanese friends they heard the language of Pan-Asianism, and it was indeed difficult for them to conceive of a thorough-going commitment to imperialism on the part of Japan as it was for many liberals in the 1930s to believe that the Soviet Union was increasingly sponsoring a new brand of imperialism. A confluence of interest was thus established between China and Japan in late 19th and early 20th centuries.

Conflict of Interests

All this, however, did not last long. The rapid transformation of the international configuration of forces, compounded with the evolving domestic situations in China as well as Japan, necessitated a change in mutual perceptions and policies. The confluence of interest became a conflict of interests. Having turned towards one another, they then turned against one another, finally heading onto a collision course which dominated the inter-war period.

World War I, first of all, diminished the power and interests of European imperialism in China. Germany, having lost the war, was removed from the list of European contenders. Imperial Russia, having became Bolshevik, disappeared as a real threat. Great Britain and France, heavily bogged down with reconstruction tasks at home, no longer possessed the surplus of investment capital that had hitherto drawn international bankers to development consortiums in China. With the exception of the United States, seemingly content with an open-door policy, Japan was the only major power left in the field of regional politics.

Domestic Japanese politics was also changing rapidly. With the end of the Meiji period in 1912, and after a brief transitional period during which contending political forces pulled and pushed the country's foreign policy into different directions,[15] the leadership finally, in the early 1930s, passed into the hands of younger, more vigorous, and more aggressive exponents of Japanese interests. Whereas the foreign policy goals of the preceding decision makers had centred around the development of Sino-Japanese relations in order to promote mutual interests and the practice of cooperative diplomacy with the Western powers, the new leadership viewed the collapse of the international system and the confusion created by the Chinese Revolution of 1911 as an excellent opportunity to strengthen Japan's own position on the mainland. Most of them, principally army leaders, were convinced that, strategically, Japan's position in Manchuria was momentous, and that the gains acquired by the Russians in Mongolia after the Manchu abdication had to be balanced by an equivalent Japanese advance in Northern Manchuria and Inner Mongolia.

Though strategic and political factors still influenced Japan's policy towards China, economic considerations clearly became more important, particularly after the Great Depression of 1929, when the Japanese realised that their new industrial economy was dangerously extended beyond what their small country could afford. Military expansion towards the mainland appeared to be the only solution.

The infamous Twenty-one Demands served on Yuan Shikai in 1915 was the first major milestone in the new policy. After a brief interruption in the aftermath of the Washington Conference of 1922, there followed a process of open and aggressive colonialism which began in 1931 in Manchuria. Thereafter, hardly a year went by without the Japanese making some inroads into the country, a process which reached its zenith in 1937 with the declaration of war on China.

During the same period the Chinese domestic scene also changed, though in ways very different from what had taken place in Japan. The Chinese Revolution of 1911 had driven from power the centralised authority of the Manchus and had replaced it by a form of political disintegration under which real authority had shifted to provincial warlords. Though the situation was partially amended by Chiang Kai-shek's "Northern Expedition" in 1925, the break-up of the Kuomingtang-Communist alliance in 1927 sent the country into an escalatory spiral of instability and civil war from which she did not recover until 1949.

However, notwithstanding the uncertainities of Chinese politics, the Chinese image of Japan underwent considerable permutations. No longer did the Chinese look to Japan as a friendly nation from whom they could learn or from whom they could solicit assistance: Japan was perceived as a major threat to Chinese security and national independence. Slowly and steadily everywhere in the country, anti-Japanese feeling was openly and increasingly voiced; [16] and for the first time a process of national integration really set in at grass-roots level. Japan was able to do for China what no other colonial power had done—awaken a ferocious nationalism. Initially, as is often the case with such movements, it was limited to intellectuals, as exemplified by the movement of 4 May 1919, but it was soon overwhelmed by other social groups, transforming Chinese nationalism into a vast, dynamic movement.[17] In fact, so deep was the discontent, so profound was the anti-Japanese sentiment, and so widespread was the urge to expel the intruders that the Nationalist movement rapidly passed from the hands of the hesitant and compromising Chiang Kai-shek into the control of the Communist party, which by its firm nationalist stand was able to success-fully project the image of being the only viable movement able to rally the population.[18]

The assymetrical elements in Sino-Japanese relations thus continued to operate during the inter-war period. By the late 1930s, Japan had become the predominant political factor in Chinese politics, to the exclusion of all the other imperialist powers. But within this wider framework, the relations had nonetheless evolved insofar as China, in contrast to what had been the case in the past, was neither prepared to look to Japan for inspiration nor was she any longer willing to accept Japanese domination.

Post-War Transformation

The allied victory in World War II transformed East Asia. The configu-ration of forces changed. The balance shifted. Once again the tables had turned; but this time they turned in favour of China. Whereas the newly-victorious revolutionary regime installed in Beijing in 1949 rapidly inte-grated the mainland, stabilised the degenerating economy, established a centralised control over the country, and generated a revolutionary dynam-ism, Japan, defeated and occupied, lay prostrate with no force to challenge or threaten anyone.

The rise of one nation and the fall of the other would not on its own have created a critical situation—China, despite her new dynamism, still had neither the real power nor the intention of either dominating or engaging in real relations with Japan; and the latter, after a terrible defeat, was in no position to effectively respond to any rhetoric emanating from the main-land. It was the overwhelming presence of the superpowers in the area with whom they had become willingly or unwillingly entangled that drew the two countries into the whirlpool of global politics, and through it into a web of bilateral relationships.

The occupation of Japan by the United States transformed the country into the main base of her power in Asia and, by the same token, gave her the role of the source from which all major US initiatives in the region emanated.

For revolutionary China, whose perception of the United States was that of an ideological adversary whose naval presence in the region had become more than evident, the new threatening situation was a major catalyst in focussing her attention on Japan. If the People's Republic had no reason to be fearful of the Japanese, she had every reason to be seriously concerned with the geostrategic reality of Japan.

Diplomatic and Revolutionary Initiatives

The principal weight of China's initial diplomatic and revolutionary initiatives was therefore directed against the United States and Japan. One of the first major decisions taken was to secure for herself a viable protection through the conclusion of a Treaty of Friendship, Alliance, and Mutual Assistance with Moscow soon after the revolution (14 February 1950).[19] That the main thrust of the treaty was directed against Japan and the US is evident from its main clause, which stipulated that the two countries would first of all take all "necessary measures" to prevent the "resumption of aggression and violation of peace on the part of Japan or any other state that may collaborate with Japan, directly or indirectly, in acts of agression."[20] However, should China and the Soviet Union fail in preventing the military resurgence of Japan, and should either one of them be attacked "by Japan or any state allied with her," the other party "shall immediately render military and other assistance by all means at her disposal."[21]

Parallel to this, and in line with the revolutionary euphoria that characterised the initial period, China also attempted to manipulate domestic Japanese politics by openly criticising the Japanese Communist Party (JCP) for having adopted a gradualist approach after World War II and by persuading it to opt for a more militant line against the newly-established Yoshida government and against the United States.[22] *The People's Daily* declared:

> Only by means of the stubborn revolutionary struggle against American imperialism and Japanese reactionary forces can the people of Japan secure an earlier end to American occupation to the domination of reaction and build a democratic Japan. Only by educating its people in the revolutionary spirit by rallying and constantly revolutionising the vanguard of the revolutionary Japanese people, can the Communist Party of Japan in reality achieve the aim of putting an end to the American occupation, of putting an end to reactionary domination and creating a democratic Japan. Here there is no other easier road.[23]

Although this line was part of a general revolutionary pattern dictated jointly by Moscow and Beijing, China was particularly forceful in pushing the JCP to adopt it, since it was much more in agreement with the general

Chinese perception of the period, in which the Yoshida government and the US presence in Japan were viewed as a much greater threat to China than any other country against which a similar policy had been designed.

The criticisms of the Soviet and Chinese parties had the desired effect. The JCP abandoned its gradualist approach and suddenly became violently anti-American.

The 19 January 1950 Takuda report, which embodied the new strategy, drew heavily from the Chinese experience. While carefully underlining the correctness of the general Soviet evaluation of the world situation, it represented a very close approximation of historic Chinese Communist tactics.[24] Comparisons were made between the Japanese and Chinese internal situations. The Yoshida cabinet was compared to the Kuomingtang government.[25] The conditions in old Shanghai were likened to that of post-war Japan insofar as in both the cases international monopoly capitalism had taken command, "making the people docile slaves of foreign capital and its agents."[26]

The programmatic document of the party published later, and also known as the 1951 thesis, was even more explicit in its Chinese orientations. It no longer used the term "bourgeois democratic revolution," preferring such terminology as "national liberation democratic revolution" and the "new liberation democratic government" to convey the idea of a combined nationalist democratic upsurge of the type that had occured in China.[27]

The implementation of the new line was indeed violent, easily comparable to similar communist tactics adopted in other Asian countries. In cities, numerous terrorist acts were carried out, including the bombing of police stations, the sabotaging of factories, and the assaulting of law enforcement officers. In the countryside the party, seeking to imitate its Chinese comrades, encouraged the creation of "activist units" in selected mountain villages, areas with a potential for defense that could be eventually developed into guerrilla bases.

Neither of the two policies, diplomatic or revolutionary, were really successful. During her first military encounter with the United States on the Korean peninsula, China had to fend for herself without the Soviet Union. Admittedly, the circumstances under which the Korean explosion had occurred could hardly be invoked by China to solicit Soviet assistance within the narrow framework of Article One of the Sino-Soviet treaty, but considering the stakes involved in the region, Soviet abstinence from the conflict was indeed revealing.

The JCP's attempts to implement China's militant strategy was also a catastrophic failure. Most of the young terrorists, those who did not manage to escape to China, were captured and sentenced to lengthy prison terms. Party membership dropped perceptibly. Election results spelled disaster. Not a single act undertaken during this period had any potential significance whatsoever, and not a single guerilla base lasted more than the briefest period.

110

The Japanese Response

The effect of all these pressures was considerable on US policy in Japan. Instead of continuing rapid institutional changes, the Supreme Commander for the Allied Powers shifted to the new politics of promoting social and economic stability, of restoring Japan's economic strength, and of converting her from a defeated enemy into a potential and useful ally. Although views appear to differ among observers regarding the approximate timing of this shift, a consensus nonetheless exists that, even if—as claimed by some—[28] it predated the Korean war, a real acceleration of the new US policy occurred only after 1949.

The new US intentions meshed neatly with the emerging postwar conservative leadership, led by Yoshida, which wished to regain Japan's independence and acquire some international status through economic strength. The government, whose deficit finance policy had hitherto exacerbated inflation, rapidly balanced its budget, rigidly curtailed expenditures, and deployed efforts to stabilise the yen. Using the Dodge Mission's recommendations,[29] which were proposed to Japan in 1949, as a weapon in the war against budget deficits and against the labour movement, the government dimissed as many as 260,000 government workers, many of whom were union activists.[30]

If Yoshida was prepared to go along with the US objectives of reinforcing Japan's political and economic position, he was initially reluctant to accept her recommendation to rearm, and even more hesitant to go along with Washington's increasingly belligerent China policy. In fact, he even went to the extent of suggesting in 1950 that he was prepared to send delegations to China as soon as the US would permit; and as late as 1951 expressed the view that geography and economics would eventually prevail over ideological differences in Sino-Japanese relations.[31]

Under the circumstances, however, Japan did not have much leverage. Her dependance on the United States was too great to permit a politics of independence; her anti-communist proclivities were too strong to allow any autonomous thinking in regard to her continental neighbour during the height of the cold war. Moreover, public opinion surveys demonstrated results too favourable to the US, which often came out on the top as the "best-liked" country,[32] to encourage the Japanese leadership to think in terms of an independent policy.

All these constraining elements could scarcely be ignored by any country, least of all by Japan, where a distinct correlation between domestic and foreign policies had been clearly established since the inauguration of the post-war political system.

Japan, therefore, took the only step that was reasonably possible—that of turning towards the West. Chinese and Soviet opposition notwithstanding, she signed the San Francisco Peace Treaty with the Western world and the Mutual Security Treaty (September 1951) with the United States. In accordance with the stipulation of the peace treaty, under which she was obliged to sign a separate treaty with China, she chose to conclude such a treaty with Taiwan in April 1952. In fact, so great was Japan's commitment to the West, and so firm was her orientation in favour of the United States, that Premier Yoshida, even before concluding the peace treaty, gave a written statement in August 1951 to John Forster Dulles to the effect that his government would not conclude a bilateral treaty with Beijing.[33] This was reiterated on 18 December,[34] and in a further letter to Dulles on the 24th of the same month, Yoshida went even further by clearly stating that his government "is prepared, as soon as legally possible, to conclude a peace treaty with Taiwan."[35]

That the US government exercised pressure on the Japanese government to obtain these written commitments is more than probable considering the initial Japanese reluctance to go along with Washington on the question. But it should nonetheless be an exaggeration to suggest that the pressure was inordinate, or that it was one of those important examples of arm-twisting in which the superpowers have often indulged. What else could defeated and prostrated Japan do when even victorious England had to reluctantly abandon, during Anglo-American consultations in April 1951, her own proposals favouring Beijing's participation at the San Francisco peace conference and the inclusion of a stipulation in the treaty that Taiwan was a part of the mainland.[36]

It is, however, interesting to note that Japan nonetheless attempted to hedge her bets by insisting in the notes accompanying the treaty with Taiwan that it applied only to territories "which are now or which may hereafter be under the control of the government in Taibei."[37] Yoshida reiterated this point in the House of Councillors and expressed the hope of concluding a treaty with "one total China" in the future.[38] But this did not make much difference to Sino-Japanese relations, since Zhou Enlai had already made it clear that the San Francisco Treaty was "absolutely unacceptable,"[39] that "the fact that Taiwan is part of China will remain unchanged forever,"[40] that Beijing was "irrevocably determined to liberate" it,[41] and that China would have no relations with any government which had established diplomatic relations with the island.

Hardly any relations therefore existed between China and Japan during the first two years after the revolution. In fact, it was a period of non-relations characterised by considerable demonstrations of contempt, opposition, and an ideologically-tainted revolutionary belligerence by China against Japan, and indifference by Japanese leaders towards China. Both the governments were locked up in their respective positions, and tied too closely to their superpower allies to permit any bilateral relationship.

New Diplomacy

As is often the case, however, international relations evolve, perceptions of nations change, and unexpected developments often intervene to modulate bilateral interstate relations. This appears to have occurred in 1952. For a number of reasons, dealt with elsewhere,[42] China's general foreign policy behaviour softened, and this resulted in a series of initiatives to improve bilateral relations with a number of countries, including Japan.

Since the prospects of forging any official ties with Japan still appeared remote, the Chinese government embarked upon a well-organised programme of establishing contact and relations with Japanese associations and organisations which were responsive to Chinese initiatives.

The first and obviously the most important component of this new policy was the left-wing parties (Communist[43] and Socialist parties[44]) which were at the time strong partisans of the People's Republic and as such constituted powerful pressure groups for the normalisation of relations. Secondly, Chinese non-governmental associations were encouraged to establish programmes of invitations to intellectuals, labour unions, trade and business associations, cultural and scientific groups, etc.[45] Thirdly, unofficial agreements were concluded on a wide range of subjects, including the £30 million (sterling) Trade Agreement of 1952 with Japanese Diet members,[46] the repatriation accord concerning Japanese prisoners of war of 1954 with the Japanese Red Cross, the Fishery Agreement of 1955 with the Japan-China Fishery Association, and the exchange of medical experience agreements, also of 1955, with the Japan Medical Association.[47]

Encouraged by some of these successes on the unofficial front, a well-planned campaign for the normalisation of Sino-Japanese relations was set off in 1953. The timing was well-chosen. For one thing, Japanese pressure groups favouring normalisation were beginning to have more impact; for another, the Yoshida government was slowly heading towards a political crisis. It was calculated that some proposals for forging political ties would have the effect of further accelerating the activities of the pressure groups and of pushing Yoshida into greater political difficulties.

The new strategy was therefore inaugurated. In an interview with Professor Iku Oyama, the Chairman of the Japanese National Peace Committee, Zhou Enlai declared the willingness of his government to restore normal relations with Japan.[48] This was reiterated in a long editorial in the *People's Daily* on October 30, 1953.[49]

The real acceleration of this new line, however, took place only in the autumn of 1954, when a series of political scandals severely rocked the stability of the Yoshida government.[50] In a meeting with members of the Diet on 11 October, Zhou Enlai proposed the conclusion of a non-aggression pact with "an independent and free democratic Japan."[51] The next day (12 October), in a joint declaration with Moscow, the Chinese government expressed its readiness to take steps to normalise relations with

113

Japan" and assured Tokyo that should the Japanese government reciprocate favourably, it would "meet with the full support of the People's Republic of China and the USSR as well as in all measures Japan undertakes to secure for its peaceful and independent development".[52]

After the resignation of Yoshida on 7 December 1954 and his replacement by Ichiro Hatoyama, who had indicated his intention to chart a new course in foreign policy, including opening Japan to China and the USSR,[53] the Chinese offers became more precise and less polemical. On 21 December 1954, Zhou Enlai expressed his readiness to take appropriate steps to restore official relations "if the Japanese government has the same desire and adopts corresponding measures".[54] At the Bandung Conference (April 1955), he took the initiative of assuring the head of the Japanese delegation, Tatsunosuke Takasaki, that Beijing recognised that the Hatoyama government was representative of the Japanese people and articulated the hope of restoring diplomatic relations with Japan within the framework of the Five Principles of Coexistence.[55] In July 1955, he expressed the hope that "artificial barriers" would be removed so as to increase trade.[56] On 17 August, the Chinese Consul General in Geneva, Shen Ping, went even further, formally proposing in a secret communication to his counterpart that, in the interests of promoting normalisation, the Japanese government send a delegation to Beijing to discuss trade, the status of overseas residents, and "other important problems of mutual interest."[57] On the same day the Chinese Prime Minister made a number of important concessions: he informed a group of Japanese journalists in Beijing that his government, though rejecting the idea of "two Chinas" did not object to Japan's maintaining relations with the nationalists and did not consider the San Francisco Treaty as an obstacle to the conclusion of a peace treaty between China and Japan.[58]

These are just a few examples of the initiatives taken by the Chinese Government. Numerous others could be cited, but this will not be done here since most of the declarations made or contacts established were repetitious or were only minor variations of the main Chinese theme of seeking out Japan.

Undeniably, some of the Chinese initiatives, particularly those taken after Yoshida's resignation, were major concessions; for example, by accepting normalisation of relations with Japan, which had already forged ties with the Kuomingtang government in Taibei, Beijing was setting up a dangerous precedent of accepting the "two-Chinas" idea. Also, by stating that the San Fransisco Treaty was no longer an obstacle to the conclusion of a peace treaty between China and Japan, she was implicitly accepting the validity of the agreement, which she had hitherto attacked on a number of occasions.

114

Japanese Prudence

For the Hatoyama government, despite initial pledges to improve relations, taking any new and bold initiatives in the direction of Beijing proved almost impossible. The new Prime Minister rapidly discovered that this was still too risky. US opposition was too great, and domestic constraints within the newly established Liberal-Democratic Party in November 1955 were too strong. Normalisation of relations with Moscow was one thing, but normalisation of relations with Beijing was quite another matter.

Thus, when the Chinese Consul General proposed to his counterpart in Geneva during discussions on the repatriation of Japanese prisoners of war that an official Japanese delegation be sent to Beijing to conduct negotiations for the normalization of relations, the Japanese never even replied to the proposals.[59] And when the Japanese Foreign Minister was criticised by a socialist member in the Diet for not replying to formal Chinese communications, he emphasised that the time was not ripe to restore official ties between the two countries.[60]

However, if the Hatoyama government and the short-lived Tanzan Ishibashi cabinet were prudent in establishing political relations, they were still prepared to improve the estranged atmosphere that existed between the two countries. This was done through the establishment of a clear distinction between economic and political relations. While conveying their growing interest in developing economic and cultural ties, they made more than clear their lack of interest in developing any political relations. Although on the face of it this constituted no real change, since this was a continuation of preceding policies, the Japanese government had clearly become more open towards China on economic relations than before. It had, for example, taken steps to facilitate trade with the mainland by relaxing embargoes, by seeking compromise formulas to settle the status of the proposed Chinese trade missions to Japan, and by concluding Sino-Japanese payments agreement.

A number of factors pushed the Japanese government to adopt this new attitude. Japanese public opinion was increasingly swinging in favour of developing relations with Beijing. According to a government-sponsored nation-wide poll announced on 3 April 1957, 63.7 per cent of the respondents favoured the further development of relations with China, 36.4 per cent wanted the Japanese government to restore official ties with Beijing, and only 2.1 per cent opposed trade relations with the mainland.[61] In another poll taken in January 1957 by the *Tokyo Shinbum* and the Public Opinion Science Association, a random sample of Tokyo's eligible voters were asked their opinions on a number of foreign policy issues. On trade with China, 73.8 per cent of 800 persons polled were in favour of its expansion, whereas only 10.4 per cent did not see any need for its development. On the issue of recognition of Communist China, 15.8 per cent wanted to continue the existing policy of recognizing Taibei rather than

Beijing, 40.2 per cent were in favour of the two-China formula and 22.5 per cent felt that Japan should recognize Communist China and "de-recognize" Nationalist China. On the question of the country with which Japan should have special relations, it is important to note China was a close rival of the United States (36 per cent).[62]

The rapidly growing Japanese economy was furthermore increasingly in need of securing the vast continental market. The House of Representatives had in fact unanimously passed a resolution on 12 December 1956 to promote Sino-Japanese Trade. A number of organisations, including the Dietman's League for the Promotion of China-Japan Trade and the Sino-Japanese Trade Association, had made themselves into powerful pressures groups which the Japanese government could no longer ignore. Even business groups were increasingly veering around to the idea of more trade with China. The results of a sample survey conducted in 1955 by the Osaka Public Opinion Poll, for example, bore this out for the city of Osaka. Of the 100 commercial and industrial firms questioned, about half planned to push trade with Beijing and 60 per cent wanted the Japanese government to promote such trade vigorously.[63]

The attitude of the United States regarding the establishment of contact and the conducting of negotiation on specific issues had also evolved slightly. In fact, on 25 July 1955, Beijing and Washington agreed to hold bilateral talks on the matter of repatriation of civilians and "to facilitate further discussions and settlements of certain other practical matters now at issue between the two countries."[64] Tokyo, though constrained by Washington on the issue of diplomatic relations, did not see any point in continuing the politics of maintaining a distant attitude towards Beijing on non-political matters.

Though unhappy over this distinction between economic and political relations, Beijing did not throw a spanner in the development of economic relations. Tokyo's determination not to proceed with any political relations was apparently too strong, and it would have been pointless to insist on their development.

The apparent pointlessness of a given policy has, of course, not stopped Beijing from pursuing it, if it was dictated by ideological or domestic reasons. But in the mid-1950s there were no apparent ideological or domestic imperatives for continuing to remain uncompromising vis-à-vis Tokyo. On the contrary and for a variety of reasons, the whole gamut of China's foreign relations had become open and flexible.[65]

By the mid-1950s nonpolitical relations between the two countries had begun to develop at an accelerated pace. The number of Japanese visiting China had steadily risen from about 800 in 1955 to more than 1,600 by the end of 1957; polemical propaganda from each side against the other had been reduced; agreements had been reached to mutually establish trade missions. By the end of 1957, the Chinese had signed roughly forty non-official agreements with various Japanese groups, and trade between the

116

two countries had risen from $ 34 million in 1955 to $ 150 million by 1956.[66]

The Great Leap Forward

The upbeat in Sino-Japanese relations was, however, in fact very brief; for by 1957 Chinese attitude once again changed and became rapidly belligerent and aggressive. No longer were they interested in accepting subtle solutions and in seeking amicable compromises. No more were they favourably disposed towards the Japanese formula of maintaining full diplomatic ties with Taiwan while expanding only economic relations with the mainland.

Polemical attacks against Japan therefore reappeared in the Chinese press. Official declarations once again became increasingly critical of the Japanese government's policies. The Kishi government, formed in February 1957, was dubbed "the most reactionary of all cabinets formed since the Japanese surrender in 1945."[67] The Premier was characterised as "a buffoon-like figure", who had come "forward from the latent Japanese imperialism,"[68] and was clearly informed that trade between China and Japan "can be considered only when the Kishi government abandons its hostility against China, stops obstructing the normalization of Sino-Japanese relations and ceases its plot to create two Chinas".[69]

From all these and other harsh invectives, it would seem that the Chinese objective was no longer limited to the goal of gaining recognition—for this they had come to realise was almost impossible as long as Kishi was in power; it had shifted to a new and larger objective of manipulating Kishi's political ouster and of obtaining the rejection of the revised security treaty under negotiation at the time.

A strategy was therefore designed to seek out political forces within the Japanese political system in the hope of generating a general consensus for some concerted action. The left-wing political parties obviously were their first choice. Japanese Communist Party delegations were, for example, received twice in Beijing in 1959 (March and October) where, after discussions with the top Chinese leadership, including Mao Zedong, it was agreed to do everything "to prevent the US imperialists and the Kishi Government from revising the Japan-US Security Treaty," and to do their utmost "to unite all patriotic democratic forces headed by the working class and to establish a united front including the Communist party and the Socialist party."[70] The Japanese Socialist Party (JSP), equally opposed to the Kishi government, was also invited to send a number of missions to Beijing, the most important of which were April 1957 and March 1959 visits of Inejiro Asanuma, the General Secretary of the party. On both these occasions joint statements were made. The first, issued on 22 April, while conceding to all the major international points sought by the hosts, declared that "the two sides fully agreed that the time has come for the governments of Japan and the People's Republic of China to restore diplomatic relations as soon as possible, formally and completely."[71] The second statement, published on 17 March 1959, comprised an even more sweeping JSP acceptance of Chinese positions.[72] What made Asanuma an overnight hero in China and a controversial figure in Japan was his famous comment in Beijing on 12 March that "American imperialism is the common enemy of China and Japan."[73]

These attempts at opposition diplomacy did not mean that contacts were limited only to the left-wing parties. The Chinese also established a strategy of cultivating LDP factions led by Tanzan Ishibashi and Kenzo Matsumura, both of whom had favoured the promotion of Sino-Japanese cooperation, and both of whom had publicly expressed their great discontent with Kishi's policies, especially with regard to the Security Treaty revision. Fully aware of the interfactional dynamics in the ruling party, Zhou Enlai invited Ishibashi (September 1959) and Matsumura (November 1959) to China, and some entente was sought on the development of Sino-Japanese relations. In many ways the establishment of contacts with political figures within the ruling party was viewed as even more important, since Kishi's effective removal from power in the Japanese political system was very much contingent on the level of discontent and opposition within the LDP. That this opposition diplomacy was by no means unrealistic strategy was evident from the rapid emergence of national tension after the conclusion of the Security Treaty, generating thereby the greatest crisis in Japanese politics since the end of the war. The opposition in the Diet made violent attempts to block its ratification. Huge well-organised demonstrations and strikes paralysed the effective functioning of the Japanese political system. In fact, the whole situation became so critical that President Eisenhower's trip to Japan had to be postponed by Kishi on the ground that he was unable to guarantee his safe reception. Kishi's arbitrary Diet tactics and his record as a pre-war nationalist made him even more vulnerable than most prime ministers to criticism from rivals within his own party.[74]

China therefore pushed her advantage further by taking a number of firm and concrete steps in the hope of toppling the Kishi regime. The two unofficial agreements—the Iron and Steel Accord and the Trade Pact—concluded in the months of February and March 1958, which provided for exchanges totalling more than China's trade with any other non-communist country, were abruptly cancelled.[75] All other accords, including economic transactions, cultural exchange programmes, and the ongoing negotiations for repatriation of Japanese nationals were suspended. Some fishermen presumably fishing in Chinese waters were seized. Japanese goods worth some $ 1.8 million on display at exhibitions in Wuhan and Kuangdong were brought back to Tokyo without being sold in China.

A number of events in Japan presumably contributed to the Chinese decision to abruptly adopt a belligerent line. In the first place, the Chinese flag was desecrated in a Nagasaki store. Though the culprit, a Japanese

118

rightist, was officially charged and punished for having destroyed furniture of the store, no mention was made of the desecration of the Chinese flag. Secondly, the Kishi government, presumably under pressure from Taiwan, refused permission to the prospective Chinese trade mission to fly the Chinese flag, which had been agreed upon in the unofficial trade agreement of March 1958. At the same time, it refused to permit the processing of financial transactions through the quasi-government bank in Tokyo. Thirdly, Kishi made the unpardonable mistake of visiting Taiwan in June 1957, of meeting Chiang Kai-shek "in an atmosphere of extreme cordiality,"[76] of declaring his agreement with Chiang Kai-shek's policies, and of giving his accord to the strengthening of Japan's economic and cultural cooperation with Taiwan. Fourthly, the revised US-Japanese Security Treaty of 1960, for which negotiations had begun in October 1958, was extended to the "Far East" without clearly indicating the area covered by it. That Japan, by conluding this agreement, had really gone very far in her military commitments can be gauged by the fact that a similar attempt in 1955 was blocked by an uproar in Japan. Finally, Kishi's declarations about China, Taiwan, communism, Japan's defense, etc., were far more blunt, direct, and aggressive than any statements made by any preceding Japanese premier since 1945. The Taiwan situation, for example, was not viewed as a civil war but "an international fight against communist aggression", Korea and Taiwan were considered essential for the security of Japan,[77] and "defensive" nuclear weapons were not considered to be "outside the realm of possibility for Japan to possess."[78]

All these elements must have contributed to the resurgence of Chinese concern about Japan and must have indeed played a role in the sudden hardening of the Chinese attitude. But can one say that the explanation for the change in Chinese policy can be found only in these incidents? Can one argue that it was due to the desecration of the Chinese flag, or due to the Japanese refusal to give diplomatic status to Chinese trade mission mutually agreed upon in the trade agreement, or because Kishi had visited Taiwan, or because he had made highly belligerent statement regarding the international situation? Undoubtedly all of them contributed to the levelling of harsh invectives against Japan, but they alone are not sufficient to explain the change—for the posture of animosity was not limited to Japan, but was rather a part of the general tightening up in China's foreign policy behaviour brought out by a host of factors, including the volatile domestic situation generated by the "Great Leap Forward".

New Chinese Initiatives

Only in the very early 1960s, after almost three years of non-relations, did the Chinese Government once again seek out Japan. While continuing to openly criticise the Japanese authorities and even the new Ikeda government that had succeeded Kishi's,[79] China adapted to the still immovable

Japanese policy of maintaining politico-economic relations with Taiwan and only economic relations with the mainland.

It is noteworthy that the initiatives to change, emanated from Beijing, where a number of interrelated factors catalysed Zhou Enlai on 27 August 1960 to hold out some hope for the resumption of economic relations. While still formally insisting on the establishment of government-to-government relations, he declared that "business can be done and private contracts can be concluded whenever conditions are mature."[80] Though some signs of change were visible soon after the declaration, they became clearly evident in 1962. By that year, China was eager to forge economic ties even if it meant the abandonment of her previous line that political and economic relations were inseparable, and even if it involved a retraction of the preceding position that Japan must break off all relations with Taiwan. In September of the same year, Kenzo Matsumura, adviser to the LDP and an important member of the lower house, arrived in Beijing to discuss different ways and means of improving relations.[81] Though he arrived in his private capacity, it was evident that the Matsumura mission enjoyed the whole-hearted endorsment of Prime Minister Ikeda, members of whose faction within the party were present in the delegation.

That this mission was indeed crucial for the development of relations is evident from the minutes of the talks, according to which Matsumura succeeded in persuading Zhou Enlai to accept the gradual and cumulative method for the normalisation of relations. At the same time he also appears to have succeeded in putting across to the Chinese the idea that Ikeda, unlike Kishi, had no hostile intentions against China.[82]

During the same year and after the visit of Tatsunosuke Takasaki, former Minister of International Trade and Industry, who had been invited by Zhou Enlai, an important memorandum was concluded to promote non-governmental trade between the two countries. The Takasaki memorandum provided for five years trade with an average yearly value of US $ 101 million, between the two countries,[83] making it possible for major Japanese firms to begin trade without any political pre-conditions. In fact, China now agreed—a virtual *volte-face* from her previous position—that trade "played an important role in promoting friendly relations between the two countries."[84]

Why this change? Why did Beijing once again make concessions? What were the reasons that led the Chinese leadership to jettison anew the repeatedly announced policy, designed only a few years earlier, of having no economic relations with Japan as long as political relations had not been normalised?

First of all Nobusuke Kishi, regarding whom Beijing had very serious reservations, had resigned in June 1960. Though this was essentially a product of the massive domestic opposition to the revised US—Japan Security Treaty, of which he was the main architect, and objections from the *zaikai*,[85] the large business interests which had lost faith in his policies,

China did play a role in his dethronement insofar as the litany of Chinese complaints against Kishi, publicly and rhetorically expressed, compounded with opposition diplomacy, contributed to the escalation of domestic discontent against him and his policies. Though his successor, Hayato Ikeda (also a product of *zaikai*), had designed a policy largely on the same lines as Kishi, he nonetheless appeared more independent of the US than Kishi, and he expressed an increased sense of confidence based upon Japan's resounding economic progress. China could not afford to ignore this change, for having thrown her entire diplomatic and rhetorical weight behind the rapidly growing opposition to Kishi, she could hardly afford to continue her preceding policy now that he had left the helm of affairs. It could be argued that since a certain momentum of change had set in in Japanese politics, China could have pushed her advantage even further by insisting on the establishment of political relations—but this would have been counterproductive. Japan's commitments to the US and Taiwan were still too great and her leverage in politics still too limited to permit any major modifications in Japan's foreign policy behaviour.

Secondly, by 1960, the Sino-Soviet dispute had set in. The sudden and unheralded withdrawal of Soviet technicians, beginning in July, signaled a drastic turn in the economic ties between the two countries. Trade shrank between them. Soviet aid was reduced to a trickle, causing incalculable damage to Chinese industry. An alternative source of economic support then became necessary. Japan, under the circumstances, was the only alternative that appeared credible, for Western Europe was still too mired in her own economic and political problems to get too involved in East Asian politics, and the United States was still too committed to anti-Beijing policies to envisage any change. One could perhaps ask the question whether the irreversibility of the Sino-Soviet dispute, established in the early 1960's, had not led China, already then, to perceive the potential importance of Japan in the configuration of new international forces; and whether she had not already at the time begun to consider the Soviet Union as a major potential threat to her own security. This would seem to be the case. Mao Zedong's talk with Japanese socialists, which was published in 1964, stresses this aspect, which the Chinese leadership hitherto had "only spoken about in whispers".[86] In this interview, in which the initial contours of a new framework of the international system was formulated, Japan was conceived as belonging to the "intermediate zone" which, in Mao's view, would inevitably disengage herself from the United States and would help China in many ways. "Politically," declared Mao on the occasion, "we must also support each other."[87] The orientation of Chinese policies towards Japan thus became increasingly evident even before the formal and repetitive presentation of the new three-world theory in the mid-1960s.

Thirdly to all this must be added the general changes introduced in China's foreign policy, which catalysed her new posture towards Japan. By

121

the 1960s—also a consequence of the Sino-Soviet dispute—Beijing was turning increasingly toward the Third World.[88]Though Japan was by no means viewed as a part of the Third World, her geographical location, compounded with the fact that her economic importance was becoming evident, contributed to the development of a benign attitude in Beijing towards Japan.

If China manifested a willingness to forge economic ties without insisting any longer on the normalisation of political relations, Japan, too, took some concrete steps in the direction of China, without making any major political concessions. The Japanese spokesman for the International Olympic Committee, for example, forbade the use of "Republic of China" by Taiwanese teams as their official title. [89] A member of a Chinese machine inspection delegation, Zhou Hongqing, who had sought asylum in the Soviet embassy, was handed over to the Japanese police and was not permitted to see Nationalist officials, as a result of which he returned to Beijing. A subsidy of 150 million yen was provided by the Government to open a Japanese industrial exhibition in Beijing in October 1963.[90] Chinese trade fairs were permitted in Osaka in April 1964.[91] Qualified approval was given to Beijing's proposal for the establishment of non-official trade delegations in Japan and China, and for the exchange of newspaper correspondents between the two countries.[92] The Japanese Foreign Minister, Masayoshi Ohira, even went to the extent of stating in February 1964 that Beijing's conduct in foreign relations was "very careful and realistic."[93] Perhaps the most notable sign of Japanese eagerness to develop relations with Beijing was the sale of a $ 20 million synthetics plant by the Kurashiki Rayon Company. Beijing was required to pay a quarter of this amount in cash and the rest in instalments spread over five years at 6 per cent interest. Since the Japanese government is required to approve all foreign sales on deferred payments terms, the government in effect sanctioned economic aid to Beijing.

Admittedly all these steps were not of major importance, but considering the overall situation at the time, including the Japanese overcommitment to the United States, the different actions taken were nonetheless significant insofar as they contributed to a breaking of the ice between the two countries.

Under the impact of all these initiatives, "a more relaxed mood came to pervade the relations" between China and Japan.[94] But even more significant than all this was the rapid development of trade relations between the two countries. The total turnover soared from $ 86.5 million in 1962 to $ 137 million in 1963, and to $ 310 million in 1964.[95] In 1965, it rose to $ 470 million with Japan replacing the Soviet Union as China's number one partner.[96] While the increase up to 1963 represented merely a recovery to levels previously attained in 1956 and 1957, the rapid expansion of trade in 1964 and 1965 clearly carried Sino-Japanese economic relations to new heights (see Table 4.1).

Table 4.1 *Trends in Sino Japanese Trade, 1950-67*
(in millions of dollars)

Year	Japanese exports	Japanese imports	Total volume	Annual change (percentage)	Percentage of China's total foreign trade
1950	19.6	39.3	58.9	—	4.8
1951	5.8	21.6	27.4	–53.5	1.4
1952	0.6	14.9	15.5	–43.5	0.8
1953	4.5	29.7	34.2	120.9	1.5
1954	19.1	40.8	59.9	74.9	2.5
1955	28.5	80.8	109.3	82.6	3.7
1956	67.3	83.6	150.9	38.1	4.5
1957	60.5	80.5	141.0	– 6.6	4.3
1958	50.6	54.4	105.0	–25.5	2.6
1959	3.6	18.9	22.5	–78.5	0.5
1960	2.7	20.7	23.4	3.9	0.5
1961	16.6	30.9	47.5	103.1	1.5
1962	38.5	46.0	84.5	77.7	2.8
1963	62.4	74.6	137.0	62.2	4.4
1964	152.7	157.8	310.5	126.2	9.6
1965	245.0	224.7	469.7	51.3	12.7
1966	315.2	306.2	621.4	31.3	14.1
1967	288.3	269.4	557.7	–10.2	14.4

Source: ChügokuYoran (China Almanac) (Tokyo: Jiji tsūshinsha, 1973).

While developing official or semi-official ties with the Japanese establishment, similar efforts were directed towards a wide array of different organisations, associations, and interest groups that were in a position to put pressures on the policy-makers. Some of them had even been created at the behest of Beijing. On the face of it, this may seem paradoxical, since relations had begun to develop on an even keel, but when one takes into account the Japanese political system, where a wide spectrum of pressure groups tend to have some voice in decision making, the Chinese policy of seeking them out to accelerate Sino-Japanese relations seems understandable.

China, however, did not limit herself to developing relations with economic and cultural groups; she also manifested particular interest in left-wing political parties whose influence in Japanese politics, though not weighty, was nonetheless significant, since they represented powerful and cohesive social groups and since their capacity for mobilisation, due to their tight organisational frameworks, was much higher than that of right-wing political groups.

The principal focus was on the JCP. Despite its marginality, obtaining its adhesion to the Chinese position in the Sino-Soviet dispute was viewed as vital. For one thing, signs of a pro-Beijing ideological orientation were already visible in 1961, and only a little additional effort was considered necessary to swing the party completely towards the Chinese camp; for another, winning over the Communist parties in general, even the most marginal ones, was given the highest priority as long as there was still some hope that this was possible.

Initially however, the JCP officially adopted a neutralist position. But with the exacerbation of the Sino-Soviet dispute this was no longer possible. The external pressures were too great to permit the party to maintain what could be called an equidistant attitude between Moscow and Beijing, and the internal factional tug-of-war became so strong that the issues, analogies, and even epithets within the party tended to become closely identified with the Sino-Soviet cleavage.

A delegation of the JCP diet members was therefore received with great pomp in June 1961, and during the course of its visit convergent views were expressed on a number of ideological issues.[97] The four-page communiqué, issued at the end of the visit by the two delegations, was conspicuously silent on the issue of Soviet leadership over the international Communist movement, an issue on which a ritual reference had always been made in the past.[98] At the 8th Party Congress of the JCP held in July, the new ideological line appeared even more clearly. The programme presented by Secretary General Kenji Miyamoto, for example, tended to define the Japanese revolution in Chinese terms.[99] In autumn 1962, after the Cuban missile and Sino-Indian crises, the party manifested an even stronger preference for the Chinese position; and by 1963, at the plenum of the Central Committee held between 15 and 18 October, the balance had tilted even more decisively in favour of Beijing.

To forestall a complete swing towards the Chinese, the Soviet party leaders suggested a bilateral meeting between the two parties. But the talks held between 2 and 11 March 1964 produced no agreement. If anything, they increased the differences, leading the Japanese party to refuse to sign a joint communiqué.[100]

The climactic effect of all this was the ousting of the two pro-Soviet leaders, Shiga and Suzuki, from the party, and Moscow's rapid decision to publicize and praise the actions of the two expelled leaders. *Pravda* and *Izvestia* treated the Shiga-Suzuki faction as the true upholders of Marxism-Leninism in Japan, and gave them prominent space in their columns. By the end of 1964, lines of communication between the Soviet and the Japanese parties had become tenuous indeed.

China did not focus her attention solely on the expansion of her influence in the JCP. Attempts were also made to forge ties with the JSP, which was equally critical of US policy in the Far East, and with which common ground had already been reached during Inejira Asanuma's two visits in 1957 and 1959.[101]

In the early 1960s, China was less successful with the JSP than with the JCP. Though the JSP delegation, led by Suzuki, was warmly received in Beijing in December 1961-January 1962, and though a joint communiqué reiterated the statement that American imperialism was the common enemy of China and Japan,[102] it was no longer in complete accord with the Chinese on a number of issues. China's pronouncements on the inevitability of war against "imperialism", her border conflict with India, her declared aim to go nuclear, and her denunciation of the nuclear test ban treaty alienated many Japanese socialists.[103]

The major issue of dissension, however, was neutralism. Whereas the JSP perceived Japanese neutrality essentially in terms of abolishing the Japan-US Security Treaty and maintaining Japan's unarmed status, the Chinese interpreted neutrality in the negative sense in terms of a complete end to Japan's American connection.

The appearance of differences did not imply that the JSP no longer viewed China favourably or that it had began to have second thoughts regarding the development of Sino-Japanese relations. On this, the Party position was clear and categorical. The joint statement issued in Beijing declared that:

> The Japanese Socialist Party delegation expresses its opposition to the policy of hostility towards China, declares its basic stand that there is only one China and will fight for Sino-Japanese friendship and restoration of normal relations between the two countries.[104]

Beijing had thus made some inroads into Japan during the period in question. But can one say that they were significant or that they gave a new dimension to Sino-Japanese relations, or that Beijing was able to exercise important influence on the political situation in the country? It would seem not. Gains were marginal and were often obtained either by making major concessions or by simple authoritarian methods. Sino-Japanese economic relations had undoubtedly improved, but this was possible only when China, deeply affected by the sharp deterioration of Sino-Soviet relations, came around to accepting the Japanese line of thinking that political and economic issue must be separated from each other, and that, under the existing circumstances, only economic relations could be fruitfully developed. The Chinese influence on the JCP had certainly become dominant, but this was made possible only after pro-Soviet elements had been expelled and only after the strength of the party had seriously eroded. Beijing did maintain some influence over the Japanese Socialist Party, but only after having damaged its power by unduly pressuring pro-Beijing elements within the party (The Heiwa Dashikai Faction: Association of Friends of Peace) to adopt positions that unquestionably hurt them and divided the radicals from the moderate.

The Cultural Revolution

By the middle 1960s, China once again downgraded her relations with Japan. This time they hit an all-time low, since her isolation was not only from the Japanese establishment but also from the opposition with which Beijing so far had managed to maintain a minimal relationship. Although some signs of this were already visible during the last year of Ikeda's rule, the real breaking point surfaced only after Sato became the Prime Minister in November 1964. Casting prudence to the winds, the Chinese press launched a vitriolic campaign against the new government. Japan, under Eisako Sato, declared *Peking Review* "is more deeply involved in the aggressive policies of US imperialism than ever"[105] and is "more reactionary than any previous Japanese Government".[106] An authoritative article in the *People's Daily*, written in January 1965 by "Observer" clearly stated that Sato "has gone further than his predecessor in toeing the US line."[107] As the months went by, the attacks against Sato became more and more ferocious,[108] and by autumn they reached a peak, with the Chinese declaration that a "military bloc" of Japan, South Korea, and Taiwan, "masterminded by US imperialism from beginning to the end has in fact come into being."[109]

Critical comments against Japan were not limited only to the latter's subservience to Washington; by 1966 her "collusion" and alignment with Moscow were also highlighted,[110] with adverse comments on practically all forms of cooperation between the two countries.[111] The Soviet-Japanese negotiations of December 1968 regarding the joint development of natural resources in Siberia were characterised as a "collusion" between Soviet "revisionist clique" and the "Japanese reactionary lackeys of imperialism" and was perceived as a plot to encircle China.[112] Japanese Foreign Minister Shiina's visit to the Soviet Union in January 1966 and Gromyko's return visit to Japan in July 1966 was considered as " a new counter-revolutionary 'holy alliance' of the United States, Japan, and the Soviet Union".[113] Even the relatively innocuous Soviet-Japanese aviation agreement permitting Japan to fly over Siberia[114] on Tokyo/London flights was compared to a territorial invasion.

The operationalisation of the new Chinese perception was vigorous. Since political ties hardly existed between the two countries, they struck where they could strike. When the Liao-Takasaki trade agreement, signed in 1962, came up for renewal at the end of 1967, the Chinese refused to conclude a long-term agreemend, as originally stipulated, and agreed to sign an accord for one year only.[115] And this was done on the condition that political statements denouncing the LDP's separation of politics and economics would be inserted in the agreement. The Japanese industrial exhibition, which closed on schedule on 11 April 1969, was not allowed to reopen in Shanghai on 15 April as previously planned. Several Japanese citizens residing in Beijing were summarily arrested,[116] and three of the nine

Japanese journalists stationed in Beijing were expelled for having "positively cooperated with the Sato government" which is "committing a criminal act of antagonism against communism, China and the Chinese people."[117] By September 1979, the number of Japanese correspondents residing in Beijing was reduced to one. Trade also suffered. Japanese exports decreased from 3.2 per cent of total exports in 1966 to 2.8 per cent in 1967 and to 2.5 per cent in 1968. Similarly, imports from China took a downward spiral. From 3.2 per cent in 1966, they declined to 2.3 per cent in 1967 and to 1.7 percent in 1968.[118]

Relations with JCP also eroded. The Chinese party did not react favourably to the new developments that were taking place within the JCP. Despite the latter's generally pro-Chinese bias on a wide array of ideological issues, some nationalist trends were increasingly becoming discernible in late 1965.

Firstly, by that year a clear recognition had emerged within the JCP that neither the Chinese model of national liberation nor its developmental framework were relevant for a developed country like Japan. The changed circumstances of the 1960s and the highly uneven levels of economic development between the two countries excluded all rational possibilities of emulating the Chinese model. Secondly, the debacle of the pro-Beijing Indonesian Communist Party (PKI) in the autumn of 1965, as a result of which the PKI had been totally decimated, led many party members to wonder whether the national liberation doctrine advanced by Beijing ought not to be re-examined in the light of that abortive revolt. Perhaps even more of an eyeopener and a source of considerable bemusement was Beijing's inability to come to the rescue of its Indonesian comrades.[119]

It was perhaps this realization that led the majority of JCP leaders to reconsider the party's posture vis-à-vis the Sino-Soviet dispute and to conclude that, given the existing configuration of international forces, any real communist success in Asia would, after all, have to rely on Soviet support. In the larger interest of communism in general and Vietnam communism in particular, it was therefore necessary to call a temporary truce with regard to Sino-Soviet polemics and to deploy efforts to rebuild the unity of the socialist camp.

The 7 December 1965 editorial in the JCP paper, *Akahata,* clearly took this line. Specifically directed against China, the editorial urged Chinese leaders to reconsider their policy towards the Soviet Union and publicly urged them to form a joint front with Moscow at least as far as Vietnam was concerned.[120] The Chinese rejected all these argumentations. Instead of permitting the JCP to seek its own national path or allowing it to feel autonomous enough to express discordant voices on specific issues within an overall pro-Chinese ideological framework, the Chinese leaders reacted sharply and promptly to the new JCP thinking. They insisted that the Chinese model was the best and the most appropriate for the Asian countries, and they maintained that the Indonesian set-back was not due to the inappropriateness of the Chinese national liberation doctrine but was caused by the betrayal by the Indonesian bourgeoisie.

The most vigorous reaction, however, was against the new JCP view that the highly explosive Vietnam situation needed a united front strategy between China and the Soviet Union in Asia. How would this be possible, countered the Chinese, when the Soviet Union was in fact collaborating with the United States; when she had reached a tacit agreement with the latter in Europe to permit the transfer of US troops to Asia; and when Moscow was in the process of striking a "political deal" in South Vietnam?[121] The Chinese made it clear that they would "never take any united action with the new leaders of the CPSU as long as they refused to abandon the Khruschev revisionist line of Soviet-US collaboration and did not abolish the Soviet-US-Indian-Japanese alliance."[122]

Polemical attacks against the Japanese party began to appear in the Chinese press. Following the usual Chinese pattern, they were initially directed against "the Soviet revisionists and their assortment of followers" who were "wrecking the friendship and cooperation between the Chinese and Japanese people";[123] but with the exacerbation of relations and the growing focus on the Cultural Revolution, the Miyamoto-Nosaka leadership of the Japanese party was directly attacked for having "degenerated into a group of traitors prostrate at the feet of imperialism."[124]

The JCP reacted to these polemical assaults only after the spring of 1967 when the excesses of the Cultural Revolution led to physical assaults on JCP representatives in Beijing and to open attempts by the pro-CCP faction within the Japanese party, as well as within the front organizations, to either control them or, failing that, to split the party. The response from the JCP was sharp and prompt. While making it clear at the 10th Party Congress in October that the JCP was determined to maintain its "stand of independence and self-determination," a systematic expulsion of pro-Beijing elements was begun by the end of 1967, which included some 43 residents in Beijing who had been broadcasting anti-JCP propaganda since November 1966. The nadir of relations was reached in the autumn of 1967 when the JCP released a scathing analysis of Maoist foreign policy which contained the following caustic summation of the Cultural Revolution:

> It is an anti-socialist, anti-Marxist-Leninist "scheme" which is aimed solely at allowing the Maoist faction to establish and strengthen an absolute dictatorial system based on the morbid deification of Mao Zedong. As a result, the order and discipline of the party have been impaired, the achievements of the Chinese revolution . . . have been nullified and the CCP and the State structures of China have been virtually dissolved.[125]

Relations with Japan's Socialist Party also suffered seriously during the Cultural Revolution. Despite its Marxist orientation and its generally pro-Chinese stance, the highly belligerent mood of the Chinese leaders during this turbulent period, compounded with their intervention in the internal affairs of the party, pushed the JSP further from the Chinese orbit. At the

29th National Congress, the pro-Beijing chairman had to resign, and after the party's disastrous performance in the House of Councillors elections in 1968, the leadership fell in the hands of leaders such as Tomoni Narita (Chairman) and Saburo Eda (Secretary-General) who refused to ally themselves with either Beijing or with Moscow and who downgraded the Chinese question from the list of priorities established by the party. Thereafter, the JSP—at least during the Cultural Revolution—was unable to spearhead a popular movement for Sino-Japanese diplomatic normalisation or to exert concerted pressure upon the LDP government's China policy.

Sino-Japanese relations had thus reached a total impasse; ties between all the major components of the relationship had been snapped by the late 1960s. Even the private trading companies, through which most of the trade between the two countries was channelled, were completely disorganised as a result of Chinese pressures. The Japan-China Trade Promotion Association, for example, was forced to fire three of its top pro-JCP executives, and a new International Trade Promotion Association was finally established which included only pro-Chinese elements from the Socialist and Liberal Democratic Parties. Maoist control over the new association was demonstrated several months later when a joint statement signed with the new association, was issued, dealing principally with political subjects such as "China's Great Proletarian Cultural Revolution, the great thought of Mao Zedong, and the excellent world situation."[126]

The new tensions in Sino-Japanese relations were once again the result of a complex mixture of specific and general factors. Firstly, by the middle 1960s, the political balance within the LDP had clearly shifted in favour of Taiwan. The active promoters of Sino-Japanese relations among the Diet members had been reduced to a handful. According to one of them, they were no more than five or six in number by the mid-1960s.[127] Though this was partly due to the death in August 1965 of Ikeda, who was generally in favour of a more open policy towards China, the real catalytic agent in this decisive shift within the LDP was the harsh invectives levelled not only against the Sato government but also against the Japanese ruling elite for anti-Chinese activities, arms expansion, economic aggression, foreign military ambitions, etc. The issue on which the Chinese press particularly focussed its attention was the revival of Japanese militarism. The total amount of space, for example, devoted to these two issues in Chinese newspapers had increased considerably during the Cultural Revolution much to the chagrin of LDP members, even those who were favourably inclined towards China (see Table 4.2). Furthermore, the Chinese insistence on including highly critical remarks against the Japanese regime in the trade agreements also became a source of irritation for many. The incorporation, for example, of the "three political principles"[128] in the 1968 trade agreement "caused a commotion inside the party,"[129] and led to vitriolic attacks on those members of the LDP who were in the Japanese negotiating team and who had accepted the Chinese conditions.[130] The Furui-Liu joint communiqué issued in April 1970 on memorandum trade, which contained a series of polemical attacks on Sato, resulted in a counterattack by the Executive Council of the LDP on 28 April 1970. While regretting China's "unilateral criticism and attack", the LDP statement condemned the Chinese denunciation of Japanese militarism as a "vicious slander" to the Japanese people who were "seeking to build a peaceful society."[131]

Secondly, the Japanese government had partially gone back on its self-proclaimed objective of developing non-political relations with its continental neighbour. Presumably under pressure from the pro-Taiwan lobby in the ruling party, in March 1965 Prime Minister Sato endorsed an unofficial statement made by Yoshida Shigeru in May 1964 to Taiwan that Japan would not give any official financial support for the exportation of Japanese plants to China, including the $ 26.5 million vinylon plant about which an agreement had already been concluded by the Nichibo Trading Company. Such a decision was tantamount to applying the brakes to the expansion of economic relations at a time when China was showing some signs of opening up.[132] Also, presumably under pressure from the pro-Taiwan lobby within the party, in September 1964 the Japanese government decided against the operation of "unscheduled flights" between the two countries which were under negotiation between the Chinese and Japanese airlines.[133]

Thirdly, the official Japanese attitude towards China had become even less friendly than before. Despite De Gaulle's recognition of Beijing in January 1964, which had generated, a consensus in favour of her recognition among Japanese intellectual circles,[134] the Japanese government refused any political normalisation with the mainland. Prime Minister Ikeda declared in March 1964 that relations between Tokyo and Beijing would be normalised only after the Chinese leaders had agreed (a) to recognise the Japan-US Security Treaty; (b) to respect the treaty between Japan and Taiwan; (c) to renounce any reparation claims against Japan; and (d) to pledge not to interfere in Japan's internal affairs.[135] That this endorsement of a rigid line by the relatively moderate Ikeda was a setback to Sino-Japanese relations can be gauged from the fact that his predecessors had carefully avoided taking any clear position on the question. His successor, Sato, however, was even more categorical in his anti-Beijing stance. In a speech delivered to the House of Councillors in November 1964, he not only condemned China for having gone nuclear—which was perhaps understandable—but expressed the view that China had the "intention to dominate through the use of force."[136]

Fourthly, also in the mid-1960s, the Japanese government began to show some signs of using the Soviet card. Anastas Mikoyan's goodwill mission to Japan in June 1964 was used to reach an agreement on the expansion of trade and the establishment of an air service between Moscow and Tokyo.

Table 4.2. *People's Daily* Reports on Japan, 1967-70

	1967 IV	1968 I	II	III	IV	1969 I	II	III	IV	1970 I	II	III	Total
Total number[a] of paragraphs on Japanese rulling elite	172	164	234	280	183	297	193	330	343	267	267	307	3,037
(%)[b]	46.9	49.4	50.6	58.7	42.9	60.9	63.9	70.2	73.3	60.7	67.1	86.5	60.9
Aggressiveness	51	53	69	62	26	59	48	85	129	110	160	184	1,036
(%)	29.7	32.3	29.5	22.1	14.2	19.9	24.8	25.8	37.6	41.2	59.9	59.9	34.1
Arms expansion	2	20	20	27	12	10	11	53	47	65	27	34	328
(%)	1.2	12.1	8.5	9.6	6.6	3.4	5.7	16.1	13.7	24.3	10.1	11.1	10.8
Foreign military dispatch	4	0	0	2	3	1	0	12	29	31	27	11	120
(%)	2.3	0	0	0.7	1.6	0.3	0	3.6	8.5	11.6	10.1	3.6	4.0
Economic aggression	6	1	30	27	15	14	19	39	48	44	28	46	317
(%)	3.5	0.6	12.8	9.6	8.2	4.7	9.8	11.8	14.0	16.5	10.5	15.0	10.4
Militaristic propaganda	0	8	2	11	3	1	8	14	3	16	9	35	110
(%)	0	4.9	0.9	3.9	1.7	0.3	4.1	4.2	0.9	6.0	3.4	11.4	3.6
Anti-China activities	72	13	30	52	30	35	37	78	67	69	50	71	604
(%)	41.9	7.9	12.8	18.6	16.4	11.8	19.2	23.6	19.5	25.8	18.7	23.1	19.9

Source: Tatsumi Okabe, *Gendai Chūgoku no taigai seisaku* (Modern Chinese Foreign Policy) Tokyo: Tokyo daikaku shuppankai, 1971) p. 33.

a   References to the Japanese ruling elite include "Japanese reactionaries," "Japanese government," "Sato government," "Japanese militarists," and "Japanese monopoly capitalists."

b   Percent of total paragraphs on Japan

131

Though negotiations on the Kurile Islands were deadlocked, Japan was at the time careful to play down the whole problem. The most conspicuous sign of this new orientation was the unusually complimentary remarks Sato made about the Soviet Union. In the same speech in which he attacked China, he made a point of flattering Moscow by declaring that "although the Soviet Union possessed nuclear weapons, we do not quite feel any menace" because she "pursued the line of peaceful coexistence."[137] The Japanese Foreign Ministry at the same time announced that Sato was planning to visit the Soviet Union in June 1966, a visit for which arrangements were already being made.[138]

Fifthly, the successful conclusion of the Japan-South Korean Normalisation Treaty in June 1965, under which South Korea was recognised as the sole legal government and under which possibilities were opened up for the establishment of a Japanese political and economic foothold near China's borders, was perceived as an inimical act. The treaty was considered as part of an attempt by the US and Japan to encircle China by creating a system of alliances between hostile powers.[139] In a number of articles, the spectre of war was invoked,[140] the theme of the "anti-China" nature of the treaty was repeatedly voiced,[141] and the dangers involved in Japanese militarism were loudly proclaimed.[142]

Sixthly, the Johnson Administration, having escalated the Vietnam conflict, pressured the Sato Government in 1967 to stop rewarding an aggressive enemy like China and to take up part of the burden of containing Chinese communism.[143] While resisting US pressures to break with Beijing completely, Sato did, however, make an important concession by agreeing with Washington, during his visit there, on the necessity of prior consultation with the US regarding his policy towards China, and he accepted at the same time the charge that Japan gradually assume greater responsibilities for the defense of the area.

Compounded to all these specific reasons for an increasingly tense relationship between Japan and China was of course the general diplomatic isolation China had inflicted upon herself in 1966 as a result of the Cultural Revolution. Her relations with practically all states had taken a downward turn. Revolutionary euphoria in the country was too rampant, the government's preoccupation with the domestic situation was too great, and the contempt for classical diplomacy had become too widespread to permit the decision-makers in the Foreign Ministry to cultivate other states or to allow party leaders to maintain a normal relationship with any Communist party which displayed some neutrality in the Sino-Soviet dispute.

The problem of distinguishing the dominant from the contributory factors complicating Sino-Japanese relations during the entire period of the Cultural Revolution is by no means easy. The specific elements analysed above were certainly important. But so, too, was the influence of the new Cultural Revolution itself, on the perception of the Chinese leaders. One could, in fact, validly ask whether Sino-Japanese relations would have

132

taken the turn they did in the late 1960s had China not experienced the convulsions of the Cultural Revolution.

Inauguration of Normalisation

After the brief and turbulent period of the Cultural Revolution, a new process of normalisation and rapprochement was set in motion in the early 1970s. This time the two countries were finally able to break down the barriers that had hitherto obstructed normalisation of their relations, and they were able to overcome the obstacles that had so far prevented them from cobbling together a wide array of agreements.

The factors contributing to the inauguration of this process and its acceleration were momentous. A series of multi-dimensional developments had transformed the configuration of forces and had significantly changed the perceptions of China and Japan, thereby facilitating the appropriate bilateral connection.

By the late 1960s, it had become increasingly evident that the centrepiece of Japanse diplomacy—the United States—was manifesting serious signs of fatigue. The excessive embroilment in Vietnam and the resulting domestic convulsions in the US had led Washington to inaugurate a unilateral process of withdrawal from East Asia and to design a new policy, exemplified in the so-called Nixon Doctrine of 1969, of reducing the US military commitment in the region. That this was indeed a major development can be gauged from the fact that it constituted a significant shift away from the internationalist principles on which American diplomacy had been based since 1945.

But these symptoms of fatigue were not only military. They were also economic. Serious signs of erosion had become evident in her economic power, the most important manifestations of which were the Nixon initiatives to alter the post-war international monetary system and to devalue the dollar.

One of the major consequences of the new situation was the US decision to unilaterally initiate a series of steps to normalise her relations with the PRC. Nixon's visit to China in July 1971 was the most dramatic sign of this new process.[144]

For Japan, dependent as she was on the United States for both her security and for trade, the new situation undoubtedly merited a new evaluation. It is noteworthy that the annual report of the Ministry of Foreign Affairs did not hesitate to highlight this state of affairs by stating that "a shadow has been cast over the economic strength of the United States,"[145] and by suggesting that the "relative importance" of her senior partner in world politics "has been diminishing and its military role in Asia is tending to decrease."[146]

The new developments in Sino-American relations proved to be a traumatic experience (the "Nixon shock", as it is known in Japan). Having shaped their own China policy to conform to that of Washington for two decades, the Japanese felt a sense of betrayal in not being consulted before the US made her approach to China. If Washington could take initiatives, it was argued, why couldn't Japan? If her senior partner no longer considered China to be her principal adversary, why should Japan?

The first major impact was on the LDP. The new US initiatives towards Beijing resulted in the rapid diminution of influence of those who had favoured Tokyo's basic policy of *seikei bunri* (separation of political and economic relations) and the decisive tilting of the balance in favour of those who had been advocating normalisation of Sino-Japanese relations. Their numbers increased from 19 to 77 in the Diet, and their pressure became particularly intense after the LDP critics of the government joined hands with the opposition to form the Dietman's League for the Normalisation of Japanese-Chinese Relations.

To this was added the pressure exerted by Japanese business groups who had also begun to change their orientations. The economic recession faced by the country, compounded with growing resistance to Japan's export drive in the developed world, resulted in the emergence of pressure groups favouring a reversal of Japan's policy towards the mainland. This was further accelerated by a growing fear that if rapid steps were not taken with regard to the vast Chinese market, the US and the West European countries might obtain major economic concessions from China, to the exclusion of Japan. Though pressure from the chemical and steel industries, which had already established footholds in the Chinese market, were important,[147] what proved most decisive in tilting the balance in favour of the mainland was the decision of 17 July 1971 by New Japan Steel's Chairman Nagano Shigeo and President Inayama Yoshiro (also vice-chairman of the Federation of Economic Organisations)—hitherto partisans of Taiwan—to desist from participating in the meetings of the Committees on Japan-(South) Korea Cooperation and on Japan-(Nationalist) China Cooperation.[148]

At the same time, the Chinese domestic situation had also evolved. The Cultural Revolution was over. The Chinese decision-makers had taken firm control of the volatile internal situation, and Zhou Enlai had launched a vast campaign of rapprochement with the trilateral world.

The stage seemed set for the normalisation of Sino-Japanese relations. All major external and internal constraints that had kept Japan from seeking out her continental neighbour for more than twenty years had at last been removed.

There still remained one constraining factor, however. Notwithstanding the new developments, the Chinese refused to develop government-to-government relations as long as Sato remained the prime minister. In their eyes he was too hostile to China,[149] too friendly to Taiwan,[150] and too tied up with the United States to pursue an independent line.[151] His removal from office was a *sine qua non* before any major diplomatic initiatives could be taken.

Sato's departure from the government finally occurred in July 1972. Though the elements that caused this important change can be traced principally to the myriad interacting and highly complex internal developments in Japan, the Chinese refusal to deal with Sato must have contributed to his downfall. The Japanese response to the kaleidoscopic developments in the international system was considered too vital for Japanese interests to be left in the hands of a politician in whom China, one of the principal actors, had lost all confidence.

His successor, Kakuei Tanaka, created the appropriate climate for the reopening of a Sino-Japanese dialogue. The new Japanese Prime Minister made clear in one of his initial declarations the determination of his government to "expedite the normalisation of diplomatic relations with the PRC,"[152] for which "a concrete plan was being worked out."[153] His Foreign Minister, Ohira, went even further: he suggested that "the days are over for Japan to follow in the footsteps of the United States" and made it clear that the Japan-Taiwan peace treaty would be discontinued after the normalisation of Japanese-Chinese diplomatic relations.[154]

Reciprocating the new Japanese attitude, Zhou Enlai publicly welcomed the new Japanese diplomacy[155] and extended an informal invitation to Tanaka to visit Beijing "on an early date to discuss the problems of normalisation of relations between the two countries."[156]

Once the Japanese response was positive, events moved rapidly, including the involvement of a spate of go-betweens in finalising the details of the Sino-Japanese meeting before the arrival of the Japanese delegation.

The historic journey of Tanaka to Beijing on 25 September 1972 undoubtedly opened "a new page in the annals of relations between the two countries."[157] After a series of top-level meetings, Zhou and Tanaka concluded a joint statement on 29 September under which "the abnormal state of affairs" between the two countries was terminated, the PRC was recognised as the sole legal government, with Taiwan depicted as an integral part of China, and opposition was voiced against "the efforts by any other country or groups of countries to establish" any global hegemony. An accord was also reached to hold negotiations to conclude a peace treaty.

One of the first problems that the Tanaka government then had to face was how to maintain a relationship with Taiwan after diplomatic relations were broken off and after the embassy was withdrawn on 28 November 1972. That this was viewed as a problem both urgent and vital to Japanese interests can be seen in the time and effort that went into seeking a solution to this vexing question. For one thing, Japan's trade with Taiwan in 1973 ($ 2,354 million) exceeded the total amount of trade with Beijing during the same period ($ 2,015 million).[158] For another, the pro-Taiwan lobby within the LDP, composed of such powerful conservative leaders as former Prime Ministers Kishi and Sato and former Foreign Minister Fukuda, insisted on the maintenance of some ties with Taibei. Developing relations with Beijing was one thing, but breaking off all ties with Taibei, in their view, was another matter.

The Japanese government found an ingenious solution. The Japanese embassy in Taiwan was replaced by the Japan-China Exchange Association on 1 December 1972. On the Taiwan side, a private group called the East Asia Relations Associations was organized the following day to perform functions similar to those of its counterpart (e.g., issuing visas, trade licences, and attending to other consular functions). The overseas branches of both associations were staffed by diplomats and government functionaries carefully designated as "on temporary leave".

The importance of this first solution to this ticklish problem lies not only in its ingenuity, but also in the fact that both Taiwan and Beijing implicity acquiesced to the new arrangement: Taibei by permitting the establishment of the private association to do the work of the diplomatic mission, and Beijing by shutting her eyes to such arrangements.[159]

Interaction between Japan and the People's Republic took a great leap forward. It seemed as if after Tanaka's historic journey to Beijing the dam of constraint had been opened, flooding the two countries with a stream of visitors and goods. According to one report, as many as 10,000 Japanese visited China in 1973 and about 15,000 in 1974.[160] In a technological age, this may not seem much, but when compared with preceding figures, it is not unimpressive.

In the fields of trade and economic relations progress was even more striking. As many as 28 Japanese economic and trade missions visited China during the first year following the rapprochement, including the Yasuhira Nakasone mission in January 1973 and the important delegation of the Kokubosuka (the Association for Promotion of International Trade). In addition, numerous representatives of Japanese firms and banks (Mitsui, Mitsubishi, etc.) also visited China during the same period (see Table 4.3). In return, the PRC despatched nearly 30 Chinese economic delegations, including the high-powered economic mission led by Liu Xiwen in September 1973.[161]

The rapid increase in exchanges was paralleled by a significant increase in Sino-Japanese trade. Tokyo's trade increased from $ 900 million in 1971 to $ 2,015 million in 1973, to $ 3,293 billion in 1974.

Table 4.3 *Major Japanese Economic Delegations to China from September 1971 to August 1972*

Name of delegation	Number of members	Status of leader(s)	Month of departure
1971			
Kansai Businessmen's Delegation	20	Saeki[a]	September
Participants at Canton Fair	2,200	–	October
New Japan Steel	8	Vice-president	November
Tokyo Businessmen's Delegation	15	Shoji[b]	November
1972			
Itochu Shoji	7	President	March
Nippon Yusen Kaisha	3	President	March
Fertilizer Manufacturers' Group	11	Suzuki[c]	April
Sumitomo Shoji	7	Board Chairman	April
Participants at Canton Fair	2,272	–	April
Sumitomo Bank	5	President	June
Domen Co.	7	President	June
Sanwa Bank	5	President	June
Marine Transportation Group	25	Sanwa[d]	June
Marubeni-Iida	8	President	June
Nichiro Fisheries Co.	14	President	July
Hitachi Shipbuilding and Eng.Co.	6	Board Chairman	July
Taisei Construction Co.	10	President	July
Nagoya Businessmen's Delegation	16	Ishii[e]	July
Bank of Tokyo	6	President	August
Mitsubishi Group	7	Tajitsu[f]	August
Japan Air Lines/All-Nippon Air Line	12	President	August
Japan Economists' Delegation	13	Inayama[g]	August

Source: *Shukan Asahi*, September 22, 1972 p. 130
Notes: [a] Chairman of Osaka Chamber of Commerce
 [b] Ex-president of Nihon Aeroplane Manufacturing Co.
 [c] President of Showa Electrical Engineering Co.
 [d] President of Shinwa Marine Transportation Co.
 [e] Vice-chairman of Nagoya Chamber of Commerce
 [f] Board chairman of Mitsubishi Bank
 [g] President of New Japan Steel

Hurdles in Negotiations

In contrast to the impressive breakthrough in cultural and economic relations, little progress was made in rapidly working out the other administrative agreements stipulated in the 1972 communiqué. This was principally due to Japan's existing relations with Taiwan. The ingenious solution mentioned above functioned well as long as Tokyo and Beijing were not faced with the task of having to work out practical and administrative details which, however indirect, also concerned Taiwan, An example can be found in negotiations pertaining to a civil aviation pact. When they opened in November 1972, difficulties immediately surfaced. The Beijing Government, for example, opposed the so-called "coexistence" of the two flags (representing the Beijing and Taibei governments) at Tokyo's Haneda airport on the grounds that this was against the spirit of the 1972 Sino-Japanese joint communiqué. As negotiations advanced to break the deadlock, it became increasingly apparent that China was adamantly insisting that Japan should recognize both in principle and in practice that Taiwan was a province of the PRC. The Chinese contended that since the termination of Japan's Peace Treaty with Taibei on 29 September 1972, all government-to-government relations between the two countries had ceased to exist, including the air services agreement. The Japanese government should therefore either cancel the Japan-Taiwan air route operated by Japan Air Lines (JAL) and China Airlines (CAL) or re-route CAL flights to another Japanese airport where the mainland planes were not expected to land. Beijing further demanded that the Taiwan aircrafts should, in any event, be stripped of their Republic of China markings and that Taiwan must drop the name China from its airlines. In Beijing's view, it was unacceptable for a Chinese plane to use, side-by-side with a Taiwanese carrier, the same Japanese airport, since this would be an implicit recognition of two Chinas.

The Tanaka government was not prepared to meet the Chinese demands. In the first place, Taiwan simply refused to accept any arrangements that would restrict the existing rights of CAL serving the Taiwan-Tokyo route. Since as many as 448,000 Japanese tourists had either used JAL or CAL in 1973 to visit Taiwan, the closure of such a line would have involved the loss of a very lucrative operation. Secondly, accepting the Chinese arguments would give them the legal right to raise similar objections in regard to other agreements, particularly in regard to shipping, thereby disrupting the booming Japan-Taiwan trade which amounted to $ 2,534 million. And finally, the powerful pro-Taiwan lobby, led by former Prime Ministers Kishi and Sato, argued against making any further concessions to Beijing at the expense of Taiwan as long as the PRC was incapable of enforcing her authority on Taiwan. In addition, they countered the Chinese argument by saying that as representatives of China and Taiwan could coexist in Washington, it was indeed "absurd" that their planes could not park side-by-side at the Japanese airport. Since the pro-Taiwan lobby of LDP was still powerful, and since 66 of its members, having visited Taiwan in 1973 to apologize for Tanaka's diplomatic turnabout, threatened to block any civil aviation agreement that included Beijing's demand, the Tokyo government was unable to proceed any further with Sino-Japanese negotiations.[162] Finally, in order to break the deadlock on this question, which was considered vital for the maintenance of the momentum of normalisation, Foreign Minister Ohira personally visited Beijing in early January 1974. During the course of the negotiations, he discovered that the Chinese, equally concerned about the political consequences of a prolonged deadlock, were prepared to accept a compromise solution under which Japan could maintain her air services with Taiwan even after the conclusion of the Sino-Japanese accord, provided Japan would replace JAL with a separate company and provided that the names and the emblem of Taiwan would be regarded as private markings. Encouraged, Ohira returned to Tokyo and drafted the basis of a new Japanese proposal to be presented at the final negotiations. By 14 January 1974, a "six-point guideline," reflecting many of these points was finally delineated in cooperation with the Transport Ministry.

The six-point proposal, however, did not get the support of the LDP, nor was it received favourably by Taibei. It seemed as if the compromise solution reached at the foreign ministers' level would be dashed to the ground by LDP opposition. But the Japanese government appeared determined to conclude the pact before the end of the then current session of the Diet in April 1974. On 17 March 1974, Tanaka therefore declared that his government hoped to present the pending civil aviation agreement for ratification by the Diet during the current session.[163] The Japanese Prime Minister's apparent determination to conclude the accord can be attributed partly to his objective to improve the sagging popularity of his government and partly to avoid any complications in Sino-Japanese relations due to the political turmoil that was developing around anti-Lin Biao and anti-Confucius campaigns. The final round of negotiations commenced on 24 March 1974 and a civil aviation agreement was concluded on 20 April.[164]

Under the agreement, JAL secured the right to fly to Beijing and Shanghai, while the Chinese Civil Aviation Administration was accorded the right to serve Tokyo and Osaka. Both countries also gave each other the right of through-flights, China securing the right to fly to Japan and on to Canada, the United States and Latin America; and Japan obtaining the transit rights through China to the Middle East and Western Europe.[165]

Despite Taibei's threats to break off civil aviation relations with Japan and despite determined opposition from the pro-Taiwan lobby, the Tanaka government sought immediate ratification. The decision was finally endorsed by the LDP's executive committee after three days of heated debate on 26 April, and it was ratified unanimously by the House of Representatives on 7 May, with many pro-Taiwan members boycotting the session.

A major stumbling block was thus removed. The prospects for concluding other administrative accords became brighter. The Maritime Transport Agreement, also delayed due to the Taiwan problem, was concluded on 13 November, though with a vague formula specifying that this intractable issue be resolved "in accordance with the spirit of the Sino-Japanese communiqué of 29 September 1972."[166]

Negotiations on fisheries, however, did not run that smoothly. The Japanese delegation raised serious objections to the Chinese enforcement of restrictions on shipping and fishing in certain unilaterally defined military and conservation zones along the coast. It was particularly critical of the Chinese "military warning lines". In mid-1974 negotiations were suspended and existing private arrangements were extended for one year. The negotiations were resumed later in the year, and finally in August 1975 an accord was concluded.[167] Although it, like other agreements, was the result of a compromise between the two positions, the Japanese appeared to have ceded more by accepting numerous restricted zones.

The conclusion, by 1974, of the three administrative agreements considerably improved the relations between the two countries[168]—so much so that they agreed to hold preliminary discussions in November 1974 on the peace treaty even before the final conclusion of the fisheries agreement. With the accelerated momentum that was maintained in different negotiations, the two countries had every reason to be optimistic about a rapid concord on even such a ticklish issue as the peace treaty, for at the preliminary talks substantive agreement was reached regarding the basic framework as well as the contents of the proposed peace treaty. Both sides, for example, had agreed to shelve such intractable issues as the disputed ownership of the Senkaku islands[169] from the discussions, and both sides furthermore had concurred on drafting the proposed treaty on the basis of the principles propounded in the 1972 Sino-Japanese communiqué.

However, soon after preliminary discussions were initiated on some of the general principles, serious difficulties surfaced regarding the incorporation of the hegemony clause into the treaty. The PRC had made it her fixed diplomatic objective to obtain the inclusion of such a clause in the proposed agreement. As this had been made part of her broader global policy and had been incorporated into her new constitution as well as into diverse communiqués concluded with different countries, the Chinese negotiators did not see why it should be abandoned in the negotiations with the Japanese. In fact, so clear was the Chinese position that even before the commencement of the formal negotiations, they had clearly expressed such a hope to the Chairman of Komeito (Clean Government Party), Takeiri Yoshikatsu, who had gone to China to prepare the ground for the reopening of Sino-Japanese talks.[170]

When the discussions, however, moved from preliminary talks to actual negotiations in April 1975, it became more than evident that differences on the hegemony clause were considerable, and that this would become the crucial and perhaps the most controversial point in the negotiations.

The Japanese were reluctant to include such a clause in the treaty. They feared that the inclusion of such a provision might seriously jeopardize the parallel and long overdue negotiations they had initiated with the Soviet Union. Their prudent utilisation of the Chinese card to obtain Soviet concessions in their demand for the return of the northern islands was one thing, but a wholehearted acceptance of the Chinese position on hegemony was another matter, since it was felt that this might harden the Soviet negotiating position even further. Moreover, acceptance of the Chinese proposals would give the LDP pro-Taiwan lobby—which was already opposed to the treaty—an additional tool which could be useful in obstructing Sino-Japanese negotiations. Though this group no longer constituted a majority, its capacity to obstruct was still significant, especially after the formation of the Miki government which included such pro-Taiwan partisans as Fukuda.

For the Chinese, on the other hand, inclusion of the hegemony clause was a *sine qua non*. The absence of such a clause in the proposed treaty, in their view, would constitute a step backward, as a paragraph to this effect had already been included in the 1972 Sino-Japanese joint communiqué; moreover, the inclusion of such a provision in their calculation would help to exacerbate difficulties in Soviet-Japanese relations and would thereby diminish the possibility of any amelioration of relations between those two countries.

In the face of Chinese intransigence, Japan modified her position and advanced a compromise formula in May 1975 which incorporated the proposed clause into the preamble of the treaty but did not direct it against any specific country. The Chinese rejected this proposal and made it clear on the occasion of a meeting between the Japanese and Chinese Foreign Ministers on 24 September 1975 that they would rather prefer the joint statement of 1972 to an ambiguous treaty. The deadlock was total and negotiations were suspended amid mutual recriminations.

It was only in the beginning of 1978, almost two years after the suspension of negotiations, that the Japanese government once again began to show signs of interest in reopening the negotiations. In a statement to the Diet in the beginning of 1978, even the new conservative Prime Minister Fukuda, indicated that the "time is getting ripe" for the conclusion of the treaty[171] and instructed his ambassador in Beijing to iron out the remaining differences on the hegemony clause with a view to resuming formal negotiations. The Japanese government became even more receptive to the idea of reopening negotiations after the Secretary General of Komeito, Yano, returned in the middle of March from Beijing with a new four-point Chinese statement containing some moderate proposals. Stripped of its diplomatic verbiage, the statement indicated that there was a slight shift in the Chinese position on the hegemony clause. The statement attempted to assure the Japanese that should the threat of hegemony arise, Japan was not bound to China in taking joint action against any other country, and that the two nations would have the right to pursue their own diplomatic policies.[172] After visiting Beijing, the Chairman of the Socialist Party, Ichio Asukuta, also confirmed the earlier impression that the Chinese were eager to seek a way out of the deadlocked situation through high-level political negotiations.[173]

Having thus assured himself of the new Chinese conciliatory position, Fukuda tried to work out an intra-party consensus—an essential, but by no means easy, task—before taking any major initiatives.[174] His efforts were briefly marred by incidents between the Chinese and Japanese fishing fleets near the disputed Senkaku islands, but this problem was finally overcome by an understanding between the two countries, a reaffirmation of the Zhou-Tanaka truce, that they would avoid touching on the issue.[175]

Formal negotiations finally opened on 21 July 1978, and the agreement was concluded on 12 August. That the treaty was a compromise was evident from the wording of the controversial clause in the agreement. The Japanese accepted the Chinese clause on hegemony under the terms of which both pledged not to seek hegemony and expressed their opposition to such efforts by "any other country or a group of countries to establish such hegemony."[176] The Chinese, on their side, accepted the Japanese proposal that the treaty would not effect the position of either nation with regard to its relations with third countries.[177]

An analysis of the previous position on the question would seem to point to a greater concession by the Chinese government than by the Japanese, for it was the Chinese who were adamantly insisting, throughout the negotiations and until 1975, on the inclusion of a clear anti-hegemony clause specifically directed against the Soviet Union; whereas the Japanese, though willing to sign a general clause, were not prepared to specify a country. However, what is indeed striking in the text is that the Japanese concession (the general hegemony clause) in Article 2 is separate from the Chinese concession in Article 4 (that no specific country be mentioned) by an article covering cultural and economic relations, when it would perhaps have been more logical to place them together. In the opinion of a Japanese observer, the result of such an organizational framework was "that the effectiveness of Japan's third-country provision has been further watered-down, in addition to its lukewarm wording."[178] Without questioning the veracity of such an observation, it would seem that once the Chinese had made the concession of no longer insisting on a precise anti-hegemony clause specifically directed against the Soviet Union, it was perfectly normal that in the last stage of detailed negotiations the Japanese felt it necessary to reciprocate. Presumably the diluted nature of the provision regarding third countries and the separation of the two clauses was the Japanese concession to the Chinese.

But why did the Chinese make the concession in 1978 when they had systematically refused to do so until 1975? What led them to become conciliatory; and why did they take the initiative to break the deadlock? What was the need?

142

First of all, Soviet pressures to dissuade the Japanese from concluding such a treaty were accelerated. On 20 February 1978, the Soviet ambassador to Tokyo, Polyanski, clearly warned Japanese Chief Cabinet Secretary Shintaro Abe that the Soviet Union would take retaliatory action, including a ban on Japanese fishing in the Soviet 200-mile fishing zone, should Japan proceed with a treaty which included a hegemony clause.[179] Three days later (23 February) Moscow unilaterally published a draft text of a Russian proposal for a Soviet-Japanese good neighbour and cooperation treaty. Presumably this initiative was taken to mobilize pressure groups in Japan against the treaty.[180] And on 19 June 1978, before the commencement of the Sino-Japanese negotiations, Moscow despatched a formal note to the Japanese Foreign Minister warning him that should Japan conclude a treaty against the Soviet Union "the Soviet side would be compelled to draw certain conclusions and introduce certain correctives in its policy towards Japan."[181]

A campaign against the treaty was also unleashed by the Soviet press. Michael Demchenko, a Tass commentator, repeated the Soviet warning that Moscow "will be compelled to take appropriate measures to protect its interests."[182] Another Soviet correspondent, S. Levchenko, highlighted the domestic Japanese opposition to the conclusion of the treaty in one of his despatches from Tokyo.

In the face of this intense Soviet pressure, the Chinese presumably realized that Japan would not, under any circumstances, accept the conclusion of a treaty directed against the Soviet Union, and that it was probably futile on their part to insist on such a provision. Any further insistance on this issue might indeed prove counterproductive insofar as it might force embattled, hesitant and conservative Fukuda to cede to the pressures of the pro-Taiwan lobby and to accept the joint recommendations of his Vice Foreign Minister, Keisuke Arita, and his ambassadors to Beijing and Moscow in December 1977 not "to hurry about concluding the Sino-Japanese peace treaty."[183]

Secondly, notwithstanding the post-Mao turbulence in Chinese politics, by 1978, the balance in China had clearly tilted in favour of Deng Xiaoping, who was a firm partisan of an open foreign policy and who had clearly opted for a politics of accelerated modernization in cooperation with developed countries. Japan was naturally viewed as an important partner in reaching this objective.

Japan, too, had reasons to move in the direction of seeking an understanding with Beijing. Firstly, if the Chinese perception was apprehensive regarding a Soviet-Japanese entente, the Japanese were increasingly coming to the conclusion[184] that their hesitation and even opposition regarding the anti-hegemony clause had not paid any dividends in terms of obtaining the return of the four northern islands from the Soviet Union. Secondly, the United States, pillar of Japan's foreign policy, had endorsed the renewal of talks between China and Japan. The Japanese press suggested that, in his conversations with Fukuda in May 1978, Carter had made it known that he had no misgivings about the hegemony clause.[185] Finally, it would seem that Fukuda, whose popularity was declining and who was preparing himself for the forthcoming electoral contest within the party in December 1976 needed some dramatic development to reassert his own position in Japanese politics.[186]

Normalisation of Relations

The final conclusion of the Sino-Japanese treaty in August 1978 removed all major obstacles to the normalisation of relations between the two countries. Though all facets of the new relationship were given a major impetus, the stress laid on the economic componant was the most obvious. That this was natural is clear from the different natures of the two economies, and from their imperative need to acquire a new major economic partner. In the first place, the economies are complementary. China is essentially a developing country with abundant natural resources, and Japan, a highly industrialized nation, is in perpetual need of external markets and increasing quantities of raw materials. Secondly, they are geographically proximate. Only a narrow strip of water separates them. Transportation costs, an essential component in setting prices, is low. Thirdly, the Chinese are increasingly attracted by the Japanese growth model. Reminiscent of the latter part of the 19th and the early part of the 20th centuries, China has embarked on a policy of learning from the "great industrious, heroic and wise Japanese people."[187] Of all existing examples, the Japanese model appears most appropriate because (a) Japanese efficiency and enterprise are not tainted by the rugged individualism the Chinese find so distasteful in Western models; (b) the model of Japan suggests a way of industrialising without losing too much of the traditional way of life; (c) Japanese society offers economic vitality without major economic differences or social schisms; and (d) Japan insists on the respect for elderly leaders, a philosophy that sits well with China's current gerontocracy. So great is China's interest in the Japanese model that a wall poster appeared on 23 January 1977 in Beijing, presumably inspired by the authorities, that pronounced an open envy for Japan. The poster declared:

> In 1957, Japan produced about 10 million tons of steel, approximately the same amount as China. But in 1972, Japan's steel production was more than 100 million tons while ours was only 29 million tons . . . Does it mean that the Chinese people are less intelligent than the Japanese, that we are less diligent? Does it mean that Chinese natural resources are inferior to those of Japan or that our social system is somehow lacking?[188]

No, concluded the poster. The envy of Japan was obvious.

Economic relations, already accelerated by the February 1978 Sino-Japanese trade agreement, took one of those significant leaps after the

144

conclusion of the peace treaty making China one of Japan's major trading partners.[189] A number of Chinese economic and technical delegations successively visited Japan to study the role of the state in Japanese economy, to acquaint themselves with modern management methods, to participate in seminars held especially for them, to familiarize themselves with Japanese economic phenomena, and to seek collaboration with their Japanese counterparts in the field of scientific research and in the development of joint industrial ventures.

In 1978, the two-way trade totalled $5 billion, almost 45 per cent more than in 1977.[190] In 1979 before September, it already hit a record of $4,092 million, up 44.7 per cent from the same period in 1978.[191] According to JETRO (Japan's External Trade Organisation) forecasts the 1979 overall trade is expected to reach $7,000-7,200 million dollars, almost 40 per cent above the previous year[192] (see Table 4.4).

Table 4.4 *Sino-Japanese Two-Way Trade*

1975	$3,792.65 million
1976	$3,033.48 million
1977	$3,485.09 million
1978	$5,008.08 million
1979 (January-September)	$4,092.00 million

The multi-dimensional importance of Sino-Japanese trade can also be gauged from the fact that in 1977 it was greater than that with the Soviet Union and the European Economic Community,[193] and the eight-year 1978 trade agreement—extended in 1979 to 1990—is expected to expand the two-way volume initially targeted at $20 billion to almost $60 billion.[194]

China has also sought technical and financial collaboration with Japan for the development of some of the major industrial projects involving investments of over $6 billion. One noteworthy project is the agreement of November 1978 concluded between the partly state-owned Japan National Oil Corporation and China, under which the Japanese have been assigned the entire responsibility of financing the project and of extracting offshore oil in Pohai Bay in a zone of 20,000 square kilometres, including the construction of pipelines to transport oil and the setting up of terminal points to receive it.[195] Also noteworthy is the agreement assigning Japan the task of constructing $3 billion worth of a modern high-performance Paoshan steel complex in Shanghai which was concluded in December 1978.[196] It is likewise interesting to consider the help sought by the Chinese from Japan for (a) the construction of world's largest and most modern steelworks in the Chitong region (near the eastern port of Hebei) for the extraction of coal and the development of electrical energy;[197] and (b) the construction of three giant integrated lead-zinc production plants combine at three places;[198] (c) the setting up of facilities for the production of ethylene, the basic petro-chemical material developed from crude oil;[199] and (d) the joint development of jet aircraft engines, which is expected to become "one of the pillars" of scientific and technical cooperation.[200]

To facilitate collaboration in the industrial field, China is now authorising Japanese companies to open offices in Beijing and allowing the Chinese companies to do the same in Tokyo.[201] Furthermore, beginning in 1979, China, according to some reports, has given Japanese businessmen one-year instead of short-term visas.[202]

By far the most important developments that promise to accelerate the process of Sino-Japanese collaboration are two recent Chinese decisions: the first concerns external credits. The Chinese leadership has finally taken the decision to seek external financial assistance for China's economic development. Currently, a series of loans are being negotiated with Japanese banks and official agencies for more than $15 billion at very favourable rates, including a short-term loan or refinancing facility of $6 billion, a five- to six-year loan of $2 billion with a consortium of twenty-two Japanese banks; about $2 billion from the Japanese Import-Export bank, a $1 billion dollar with Sanwai Bank,[203] and a $5.5 billion official loan from the Japanese Government.[204] The second decision, equally unprecedented, is to allow foreign companies to make direct investments in joint ventures so long as the majority of the capital remains in Chinese hands.[205]

The third component of economic relations between the two countries is the training of a large number of Chinese cadres in various areas, ranging from initiation in factories to education in Japanese universities. According to different agreements, degree holders from Chinese universities would be permitted to join Japanese universities for periods from six months to a year to improve their knowledge in their own field of specialisation. Initially, 400 to 500 students will be admitted, but the figure is expected to reach the 10,000 mark eventually.[206]

The Chinese government has also shown some interest in developing military relations with Japan. Having arrived at the conclusion that a military threat to China emanates principally, if not exclusively, from the Soviet Union, China appears to be considering Japan as one of her potential partners in the Pacific region. Some of the recent Chinese initiatives appear to confirm this new orientation. Firstly, presumably to allay any Japanese fears regarding the continuation of the Sino-Soviet military alliance of 1950 against Japan, the Chinese leaders have made it clear that they intend to abrogate the treaty in April 1980. The treaty, declared Deng Xiaoping to Japanese journalists, "no longer exists in substance."[207] Secondly, he has also declared that he is "in favour of Japan having her own defense capacity"[208] and that both China as well as Japan must prepare themselves "against common threat."[209] Thirdly, the Chinese have expressed an interest in buying armaments from Japan;[210] and fourthly, China has proposed the establishment of military contacts between the two countries.[211] The

Chinese general Chang Caichien, Deputy Chief of Staff visited Japan for a six-day stop-over on his way to Mexico. During this visit, he made the unprecedented proposal to General Takashina, Chairman of the Council of Self-Defense Forces, that both countries should promote contacts not only between civilian officials but also between military personnel in order to increase mutual understanding.[212] The Chinese government has already taken the initiative by inviting military specialists in the field of tank development who are employed in the private sector.[213]

Resurgence of Difficulties

As is often the case with bilateral relations, however, problems and difficulties have also begun to surface between the two countries, and there is a great likelihood that they may develop further with the expansion of Sino-Japanese relations.

First of all, with her ambitious developmental plans, China is expected to face serious balance-of-payment difficulties. A trend in this area appears to exist where relations between developing and developed countries are concerned and it is hard to believe that China will not face the same problems, even with her recently reduced developmental plans. Temporary relief could, of course, be obtained by deferring payments, as China is currently attemping to do, but in the long run she would have to balance her imports by attempting to export not only raw materials but also non-traditional items. There are already indications that China is no longer satisfied with the role of raw material supplier, and that she has therefore begun to insist that Japan must also buy finished commodities from China. In negotiations, China is reported to have already warned Japan that she will turn elsewhere to buy her plants and equipment should Japan remain adamant on the question.[214]

China has also begun to demand preferential treatment for her goods. So far Japan has balked, pointing to the need to study various related matters, including the possible effect on Japanese industry and on the developing countries already receiving such treatment.[215] On this issue Japan is indeed faced with a difficult dilemma. If she remains evasive for too long, she may have to face the prospects of China turning to the United States or Western Europe, her major competitors. On the other hand, if she agrees to the Chinese demands, she may have to face the indignation of other developing countries, particularly her Southeast Asian neighbours, whose exports to Japan would inevitably be affected by the Chinese competition, which, more often than not, underprices export items.

Difficulties have also surfaced with regard to Chinese primary commodities. The problems involved in importing Chinese oil provide a good example. Japanese oil companies have begun to balk at importing Chinese oil on the grounds that it is poorer in quality than light crude oil and is more expensive than Arabian light crude oil, and, moreover, that they have neither the refining nor the storage facilities to handle large quantities of Chinese oil. Differences have developed on the question between the Japanese government and the oil companies, since the government is eager to increase oil imports for political reasons, and since the oil companies would like to reduce even the quantity of oil originally agreed upon in the original Sino-Japanese accord.[216] If the Japanese government is not successfull in persuading the oil companies to use more Chinese oil, the Chinese balance of trade with Japan would become even more unfavourable, since one of the items with which the Chinese are hoping to pay for their burgeoning Japanese imports would be removed from the list of exports.

Furthermore, Japanese industrialists and bankers have begun to wonder whether China's relatively backward economy will be able to handle the amount of credit she is asking for; whether the size of her development plans, even though these have been reduced,[217] are not still too ambitious; whether she has the appropriate management skills to oversee her big projects; and whether, within the generally highly bureaucratic Chinese system, one hand really knows what the other is doing. One JETRO study has argued that if the Chinese recent past is any help in understanding the present and the future, one can only be pessimistic, since each of the three earlier attempts at industrialisation in the 1950s, early 1960s, and 1970s have been scuttled by domestic political turmoils.[218] JETRO concluded:

> All of these political conflicts clearly indicate that China's introduction of overseas technology and industrial plants was always subjected to a series of political struggles involving confrontation between those favouring such introduction and those against it.[219]

Even more than this, one could validly ask whether the rapidly changing situation in the Pacific region might not threaten Japanese security, and whether this in turn would not have an important bearing on Sino-Japanese relations. The recent Soviet military build-up in the area, including the deployment of aircraft carrier "Minsk" at Vladivostok, the guided missile cruisers "Petropovlovsk" and "Ivan Rogov", and the "backfire" bombers equipped with nuclear warheads, is clearly tilting the military balance in favour of the Soviet Union.[220] Concerned about these developments, the Japanese have already begun to take some steps. They have publicly warned Vietnam of economic retaliation in the event of a Soviet military build-up in the country,[221] they have decided to improve their own defenses,[222] and they have established for the first time (in November 1978) a series of "guidelines" for joint military contingency planning with Washington.[223]

What bearing could all this have on Sino-Japanese relations? In the face of this new situation, is it not likely that Japan could be faced after all with the prospect of invoking the anti-hegemony clause of her treaty with China? And might she not have to envisage the prospects of developing some military relations with China—a prospect she has so far refused to consider, at least officially? In any event, Japan's role has become crucial. Her actions as well as her inaction are bound to have some repercussions on her relations with China. If Japan perceives the Soviet threat to be real, she may well have to continue developing her ties with China, along with reinforcing ties with the United States in which case the risk of her becoming embroiled in any conflicting internatinal situation would become considerable. On the other hand, if Japan decides to make less than full use of her Chinese connection, she may well have to face the prospect of her continental neighbour turning more and more towards Washington and less and less towards Tokyo.

Conclusion

Before their final normalisation in 1978, Sino-Japanese relations had ceaselessly undergone a metronomic vacillation between the extremes of belligerence and cautious friendliness. Though these movements were indeed a result of complex and interacting processes, the Chinese role and initiatives in this bilateral relationship appeared to be more important than those of Japan. Each phase or fluctuation was preceded by a visible new development in Chinese internal or external policies. The revolutionary militancy of the late 1940s, the peaceful coexistence, followed by the Great Leap Forward of the 1950s, the Sino-Soviet dispute and the Cultural Revolution of the 1960s, and finally the internal political turmoil leading to the disappearance of the so-called "gang of four" of the 1970s, appeared to have been far more determinant in giving direction to Sino-Japanese relations than the myriad interacting processes, that are commonly witnessed in most bilateral relations.

The Chinese initiatives can be principally attributed to three basic factors. Firstly, the Chinese system lends itself more easily to more dramatic and clear-cut decisions than the complex Japanese pluralistic political system in which the domestic pressures exerted by numerous groups with conflicting interests have a tendency to slow down the whole process. Secondly, China manifested a far greater interest in seeking out Japan than vice versa: whereas the history of three decades of Sino-Japanese relations has been replete with friendly diplomatic initiatives, threats, retaliatory pressures, etc. from China to push Japan into forging normal political ties, it is literally void of any major Japanese initiatives. Once they had obtained implicit Chinese acceptance of developing economic relations with Beijing and the maintenance of politico-economic relations with Taiwan in the mid-1950s, the entire Japanese objective thereafter, until 1974, was to maintain this situation. Thirdly, China had a much greater political leverage and much greater political autonomy than Japan, whose military and commercial dependence on Washington was considerable and whose capacity therefore for independent action in the field of international affairs was severely limited.

The basic determinants of China's foreign policy behaviour towards Japan were a mix of ideological objectives, security considerations, and modernisation goals. All of these three elements were present to varying degrees in the formulation of bilateral relations with Japan, though, during each of the phases analysed in this chapter, some were more important than the others. Ideology and the US security threat, for example, were weighty in the 1950s. To these was added the new Chinese perception of Soviet threat in the 1960s, intensified in the 1970s by an even greater fear of the Soviet Union and by the internal goal of rapid modernisation of Chinese society.

Notes

1. For details, see Ryusaki Tsunoda, William Theodore de Barry, Donald Keene, *Sources of Japanese Tradition* (New York and London: Columbia University Press, 1971); Edwin O. Reischauer and John K. Fairbank, *East Asia: The Great Tradition* (New York: Houghton Mifflin, 1958).
2. See Raymond Dawson (ed.), *The Legacy of China* (Oxford: University Press, 1964); also see Amaury de Riencourt, *The Soul of China: An Interpretation of Chinese History*, Revised edition (New York: Harper and Row Publishers, 1965).
3. For some details on this phenomenon, see Robert G. Wesson, *The Imperial Order* (Berkeley and Los Angeles: University of California Press, 1967).
4. Expression used by Frances V. Moulder, *Japan, China and The Western World Economy* (London: Cambridge University Press, 1977), p. 199.
5. G. B. Sansom, *The Western World and Japan: A Study in the Interaction of European and Asiatic Cultures* (New York: Alfred A. Knopf, 1950), p. VI.
6. W. W. Lockwood, *The Economic Development of Japan* (Princeton: Princeton University Press, 1954), p. 5.
7. Peter Duus, *The Rise of Modern Japan* (Boston: Houghton Mifflin Company, 1976).
8. From the decree of the Qian Lung Emperor; text in Harley Farnsworth Macnair, *Modern Chinese History: Selected Readings* (Shanghai: Commercial Press Limited, 1923).
9. K. Marx and F. Engels, *On Colonialism* (Moscow: Foreign Languages Publishing House, n.d.).
10. For details, see Marius Jensen's contribution in Robert E. Ward (ed.), *Political Development of Modern Japan* (Princeton: Princeton University Press, 1968).
11. For details of the reform movement, see Ssu-yü Teng and John K. Fairbank, *China's Response to the West: A Documentary Survey 1839-1923* (Cambridge, Mass: Harvard University Press, 1954).
12. Cited in Marius B. Jensen, *Japan and China: From War to Peace 1894-1972* (Chicago: McNally College Publishing Company 1978), p. 137.
13. Ibid.
14. Marius B. Jansen, *The Japanese and Sun Yat-Sen* (Cambridge, Mass: Harvard University Press, 1954); also see C. Martin Wilbur, *Sun Yat-Sen: Frustrated Patriot* (New York: Columbia University Press, 1976).
15. For details, see Nobuya Bamba, *Japanese Diplomacy in a Dilemna: New Light on Japan's China Policy 1924-29* (Vancouver: University of British Columbia Press, 1972).

16.   Within a few months between 1931-32, Japanese exports to China fell by half and reached their low 1908 level.

17.   See Lucien Bianco, *Les origines de la révolution chinoise* (Paris: Editions Gallimard, 1967).

18.   See Chalmers A. Johnson, *Peasant Nationalism and Communist Power: The Emergence of Revolutionary China 1937-1945* (Stanford: Stanford University Press, 1962).

19.   Full text in *Oppose the Revival of Japanese Imperialism. A Selection of Documents and Commentaries* (Peking: Foreign Languages Press, 1960).

20.   Ibid., p. 2.

21.   Ibid., p. 2.

22.   For details about the party, see Robert A. Scalapino, *The Japanese Communist Movement 1920-1966* (Berkeley and Los Angeles: University of California Press, 1967); Rodger A. Swearington and Paul F. Langer, *Red Flag in Japan: International Communism in Action 1919-1951* (Cambridge Mass.: Harvard University Press, 1952); Toshio G. Tsukahiro, *The Postwar Evolution of Communist Strategy in Japan* (Cambridge, Mass.: Center for International Studies, MIT, 1954).

23.   *People's Daily,* 17 January 1950.

24.   Text in *For a Lasting Peace, For a People's Democracy,* 14 April 1950.

25.   Ibid., p. 2.

26.   Ibid.

27.   Ibid., 23 November 1951, p. 3.

28.   Jon Halliday and Govan McCormark, *Japanese Imperialism Today: Coprosperity in Greater East Asia* (London: Penguin Books, 1973).

29.   Joseph Dodge, a conservative Detroit banker, had recommended a harsh programme of deflation and budget cutting.

30.   For details, see Shigeru Yoshida, *The Yoshida Memoirs: The Story of Japan in Crisis* (Westport, Conn.: Greenwood Press Publishers, 1973).

31.   Shigeru Yoshida, "Japan and the Crisis in Asia", *Foreign Affairs,* 2 (1951).

32.   See D. H. Mendel, *The Japanese People and Foreign Policy* (Berkeley: University of California Press, 1961).

33.   Department of State, *Foreign Relations of the United States 1951* (Washington DC: US Government Printing Office, 1978).

34.   Ibid.

35.   Ibid.

36.   *Le Monde,* 3 May 1951, and 15-16 April 1951.

37.   Denise Folliot, *Selected and Edited Documents on International Affairs, 1951* (London: Oxford University Press, 1955).

38.   See Yoshida's testimany of 26 June 1952; cited in Choe-Jin Lee, *Japan Faces China: Political and Economic Relations in the Postwar Era* (Baltimore and London: The Johns Hopkins University Press, 1976).

39.   *Oppose the Revival of Japanese Imperialism,* op cit., p. 15.

40.   *Important Documents Concerning the Question of Taiwan* (Peking: Foreign Languages Press, 1955), p. 14.

41.   Ibid., p. 20.

42.   For details, see other chapters.

43.   See Robert A. Scalapino, op cit.

44.   Allan B. Cole, George O. Totten, and Cecil H. Uyehara, *Socialist Parties in Postwar Japan* (New Haven, Conn.: Yale University Press, 1966).

45.   Richard L. Walker, "Guided Tourism in China", *Problems of Communism,* 5 (1957).

46.   Full text in *People's China,* 16 June 1952.

47. For details about these agreements, see Shao Chuan Leng, *Japan and Communist China*, (Kyoto: Doshisha University Press, 1958).

48. *New China News Agency*, 9 October 1953.

49. *People's Daily*, 30 October 1953.

50. *Keesing's Contemporary Archives*, 22-29 January 1955.

51. Cited in Coral Bell, *Survey of International Affairs, 1954* (London: Oxford University Press, 1957), p. 266.

52. *Oppose the Revival of Japanese Imperialism*, op cit., p. 26.

53. *Keesing's Contemporary Archives*, 22-29 January 1955.

54. Cited in Coral Bell, op cit., p. 266.

55. George Kahin, *The Afro-Asian Conference* (New York, Itacha: Cornell University Press, 1956).

56. *People's China*, 16 August 1955, p. 5.

57. Full text in ibid., Supplement, 16 February 1956.

58. *New China News Agency*, 17 August 1955.

59. Supplement to *People's China*, 16 February 1956.

60. *Kyodo*, 16 February 1956.

61. Shao Chuan Leng, op cit.

62. Ibid.

63. Ibid.

64. Paul E. Zinner (ed.), *Documents on American Foreign Relations, 1955* (Harper for the Council on Foreign Relations, 1956), p. 310.

65. See supra.

66. *Yearbook of International Trade Statistics, 1956* (New York: United Nations, 1958).

67. *Oppose the Revival of Japanese Imperialism*, op cit., p. 41.

68. Ibid., p. 42

69. Ibid.

70. See the joint statement of the two parties of 22 October 1959; full text: ibid., p. 85-86.

71. *New China News Agency*, 22 April 1957.

72. *Oppose the Revival of Japanese Imperialism*, op cit.

73. *Peking Review*, 11 (1959), p. 20.

74. See George E. Packard, *Protest in Tokyo: The Security Treaty Crisis of 1960* (Princeton: Princeton University Press, 1966).

75. *Peking Review*, 2 (1958).

76. See *Keesing's Contemporary Archives*, 13-20 July 1957.

77. Interview given to NBC correspondent on 14 October 1958.

78. Quoted by Wolf Mendl, "Japan's Defence Problems", *Yearbook of World Affairs*, 1968, p. 155.

79. *People's Daily*, 11 October 1960.

80. See Zhou Enlai's declaration of 27 August 1960 to Kazuo Susuki, Director of the Japan-China Trade Promotion Council; full text in *China Today*, 24 September 1960, p. 7.

81. *Survey of China's Mainland Press*, 2890 (1963).

82. Chae-Jin Lee, op cit.

83. *Survey of China's Mainland Press*, 2860 (1962).

84. A protocol was signed between the Chairman of the China Council for the Promotion of International Trade and the Director General of Japan-China Trade Promotion Association; full text in ibid., 2890 (1963).

85. See Chitoshi Yanaga, *Big Business in Japanese Politics* (New Haven, Conn.: Yale University Press, 1968).

86.   From editorial in the *Pravda,* 2 September 1964.

87.   Ibid.

88.   For details, see Chapter 6.

89.   *Far Eastern Economic Review,* 53 (1964).

90.   *Peking Review,* 41 (1963).

91.   *Far Eastern Economic Review,* 69 (1964).

92.   Ibid., 61 (1964).

93.   Ibid., 59 (1964).

94.   Seiichi Togowa, "Don't forget the Well-Diggers", *Japan Quarterly,* 1 (1979).

95.   *Yearbook of International Trade Statistics 1964* (New York: United Nations, 1966), p. 411.

96.   *An Economic Profile of Mainland China,* op cit.

97.   *Survey of China's Mainland Press,* 2522 (1961).

98.   Ibid., 2523 (1961).

99.   Ibid.

100.   For texts of Chinese replies to the Soviet Party, see *Letters of the JCP in Reply to the CC of the CPSU* (Peking: Foreign Languages Press, 1965).

101.   See supra.

102.   *Survey of China's Mainland Press,* 2661 (1961).

103.   See J. A. A. Stockwin, *The Japanese Socialist Party and Neutralism: A Study of a Political Party and its Foreign Policy* (Melbourne: Melbourne University Press, 1968).

104.   See Allan B. Cole, et al, op cit.

105.   *Peking Review,* 4 (1965).

106.   Ibid., 39 (1967), p. 29.

107.   Ibid., 5 (1965).

108.   Ibid., 9 and 18 (1965).

109.   *Survey of China's Mainland Press,* 19 November 1965.

110.   *Peking Review,* 5 (1966).

111.   *New China News Agency,* 13 December 1968.

112.   Ibid.

113.   *Peking Review,* 31 (1966).

114.   Ibid., 17 (1968).

115.   *Peking Review,* 13 (1968).

116.   *White Papers of Japan: Annual Abstracts of Official Reports and Statistics of the Japanese governments, 1969-1970* (Tokyo: Japan Institute of International Affairs, 1971).

117.   *Peking Review,* 39 (1967), p. 29.

118.   *Japanese White Papers,* op cit.

119.   *Far Eastern Economic Review,* 184 (1966).

120.   *Akahata,* 7 December 1975.

121.   *Peking Review,* 7 (1966).

122.   Ibid., p. 11.

123.   *People's Daily,* 22 September 1966.

124.   *New China News Agency,* 10 October and 10 November 1967.

125.   *Akahata,* 10 October 1967,

126.   Seiichi Togowa, loc cit.

127.   Ibid.

128.   The three principles were (a) not to carry out policies antagonistic to China; (b) not to take part in plots to create two Chinas; (c) not to put obstacles in the way of normalisation of Sino-Japanese Diplomatic Relations.

129.   Seiichi Togowa, loc cit., p. 31.

130.   Ibid.

131. *Asahi Shimbun,* 27 April 1970.
132. *Peking Review,* 8 (1965).
133. *Far Eastern Economic Review,* 91 (1964).
134. See Yoshimi Takeuchi, "A return to the Sino-Japanese Problem", *Journal of Social and Political Ideas in Japan,* August 1965.
135. *Far Eastern Economic Review,* 64 (1964).
136. *New China News Agency,* 30 November 1965.
137. Ibid.
138. Ibid.
139. *Peking Review,* 37 (1965).
140. Text in *New China News Agency,* 18 November 1965.
141. Ibid., 15 November 1965.
142. *Peking Review,* 49 (1965).
143. See William P. Bundy, "Japan and the United States: The Essentials of Partnership", *Department of State Bulletin,* 1377 (1965).
144. See Chapter 2.
145. *White Papers of Japan, 1972-1973,* Annual Abstracts of Official Reports and Statistics of the Japanese Government (Tokyo: Japan Institute of International Affairs, 1974), p. 62.
146. Ibid.
147. In 1970, for example, 61.7 per cent of foreign sales of the chemical fertiliser industry and 8.3 per cent of all steel sales were to China.
148. Interestingly, the announcement was made on the very day Nixon's visit to China was announced; *Asahi Shimbun,* 17 July 1971.
149. *Peking Review,* 9 (1972).
150. Ibid., 7-8 (1972).
151. Ibid., 4 (1972).
152. Ibid.
153. Ibid., 30 (1972).
154. *Asahi Shimbun,* 8 July 1972.
155. He welcomed the change in his speech at the banquet held on 9 July in Beijing for the delegation of the People's Republic of Yemen, *Peking Review,* 28 (1972).
156. *Le Monde,* 25 July 1972.
157. *Peking Review,* 40 (1972).
158. *The Japan Economic Review,* 15 March 1974.
159. *Asahi Shimbun,* 1 October 1972.
160. Ibid., 2 October 1973.
161. "Second stage of Sino-Japanese Relations", *Japan Quarterly,* 1 (1974).
162. *The Japan Times Weekly,* 14 October 1973.
163. Ibid., 23 March 1974.
164. Full text in *Japan Review,* April 1974.
165. *Peking Review,* 16 (1974).
166. Ibid., 47 (1974).
167. *New China News Agency,* 2 March 1975.
168. In 1977 the two countries worked out two other administrative agreements. One was the Japan-China Trademark Agreement concerning trademark protection between the two countries; the other was the Japan-China Service Agreement on the establishment of Meteorological Circuits, which provides for an exchange of weather information, see *White Papers of Japan, 1977-1978,* op cit.
169. *The Japan Times Weekly,* 8 February 1975.
170. *Asahi Evening News,* 30 July 1975.
171. *The Japan Times Weekly,* 11 February 1978.

172. Ibid., 23 March 1978.
173. Ibid.
174. Ibid.
175. Ibid., 20 May 1978.
176. *Peking Review,* 33 (1978), p. 8.
177. Ibid.
178. *The Japan Times Weekly,* 26 August 1978.
179. Ibid., 25 February 1978.
180. Ibid., 4 March 1978.
181. *Soviet News,* 27 June 1978.
182. Ibid., 18 July 1978.
183. *The Japan Times Weekly,* 18 February 1978.
184. In Tokyo in January 1976, negotiations between Andrei A. Gromyko, the Soviet Foreign Minister and Kiichi Miyazowa, the Japanese Foreign Minister, failed; ibid., 17 January 1976.
185. *Le Monde,* 30 May 1978.
186. Ibid.
187. *Peking Review,* 16 (1979).
188. Cited in *International Herald Tribune,* 30 October 1978.
189. Philippe Pons, "Peking et Tokyo au rendez-vous historique, le coopération économique", *Le Monde,* 27 October 1978.
190. *Quarterly Economic Review of China, Hongkong, North Korea,* 2nd quarter, 1979.
191. *The Japan Times Weekly,* 3 November 1979.
192. Ibid.
193. Ibid., 4 November 1978.
194. *Quarterly Economic Review of China, Hongkong, North Korea,* 3rd quarter, 1979.
195. *Le Monde,* 10 November 1978.
196. *The Japan Times Weekly,* 9 December 1978.
197. *Le Monde,* 20 October 1978.
198. *The Japan Times Weekly,* 16 December 1978.
199. *The Japan Economic Review,* 15 August 1978.
200. Ibid., 21 October 1978.
201. *International Herald Tribune,* 5 December 1978.
202. Ibid.
203. This loan agreement, the first of its kind, to finance petroleum and coal development projects, was concluded in May 1979; *The Japan Times Weekly,* 2 June 1979; for other details, see *Le Monde,* 27 October 1978; *The Japan Economic Review,* 15 August 1978.
204. *The Japan Times Weekly,* 25 August 1979.
205. *International Herald Tribune,* 28 November 1978 and 16 May 1979.
206. *Le Monde,* 29 November 1978.
207. *The Japan Times Weekly,* 16 September 1978.
208. Ibid.
209. Ibid.
210. Ibid.
211. Ibid.
212. Ibid.
213. They were General Okawara, employed by Nippon Electric and General Tanaka, adviser to Nissan Motor; *International Herald Tribune,* 27 September 1978.

214. Ibid.

215. Ibid.

216. *International Herald Tribune,* 9-10 December 1978.

217. As many as 32 contracts already concluded have been temporarily suspended; see *The Japan Times Weekly,* 10 March 1979.

218. JETRO notes that there were three earlier attempts at industrialisation: in 1953-57, when China imported plants from the Soviet Union and Eastern Europe; in 1963-65 when China bought more than twenty industrial plants from Western Europe and Japan; and in 1972-74, when China bought another 170 plants again from Japan, Western Europe, and the United States; see Alan Lun, "China's Trade 'Going East' Through New Agreements", *International Herald Tribune,* A Special Report, September 1978.

219. Ibid.

220. See *Defense Bulletin,* 2 (1979).

221. *International Herald Tribune,* 21-22 April 1979.

222. See Ohira's interview of 19 April 1979, ibid.

223. The "guidelines" consist of three points: (*a*) position for containing aggression; (*b*) actions in response to an armed attack against Japan; and (*c*) Japan-US cooperation in case of situations in the Far East outside of Japan which would have an important influence on the security of Japan. See *Defense Bulletin* 2 (1979).

Chapter 5

CHINA AND EUROPE

Unequal Relationship

The relations between China and Europe have seen a great deal of history. They can be traced back to the 16th century, when unruly and adventurous Portuguese traders, driven by the hopes of making big profits, arrived on the shores of China after the long trip around the Cape of Good Hope, across the Indian Ocean and through the straits of Malacca and the South China Sea. For four centuries these relations continued to expand, affecting almost all aspects of a traditionally self-enclosed civilization.

The nature of this long relationship has been essentially one-sided and unequal. With the exceptions perhaps of the wave of Jesuit missionaries in the 17th century who attempted syncretism through a fusion of Confucianist ethics and Roman Catholicism and the European intellectuals of the 18th century who were influenced by Chinese thought, the entire spectrum of Sino-European relations were conducted so as to be beneficial to the Europeans.[1] Each wave of European influence, which forced its way to the shores of the Middle Kingdom, whether it brought Catholic or Protestant missionaries, traders or European armies, also brought deep humiliation to the Chinese people.

This penetration of China was calamitous, particularly after the European industrial revolution, since it set in motion a vicious circle of economic instability which destroyed the balanced Chinese socio-economic structures, of unequal commercial treaties which established a permanent disadvantage for the Chinese in the balance of trade, and of the massive efflux of silver which resulted in tight financial conditions for the state. The only exception perhaps to this general process of impoverishment was the emergence of new social groups, including a trading community and a middle class, which grew rich in their dealings with the Europeans. But the beneficial effects of even this development were more apparent than real—for the modernisation and affluence of the new Europeanised class, who were located mainly in the treaty ports of the south, set off a process of social, cultural and economic disequilibrium between the north and the south, generating an unprecedented gap between peoples within this same civilisation.

A consensus appears to exist regarding the widespread impoverishment this prolonged Western intrusion caused the Chinese people, but views seem to diverge concerning the exact nature of the sociological impact industrialised Europe had on pre-industrial Chinese civilisation. While some consider that the "meeting of East and West" were genuine additions to the enrichment (aesthetically, economically, and religiously) of the traditionally incomplete culture of the two civilisations,"[2] others viewed this as a phenomenon that had smashed "the delicate and refined civilisation which had taken thousand of years to build."[3] Still others, more concerned with dynamics of socio-economic change, seemed to adopt a middle position. While accepting that this phenomenon may have caused the Chinese people multi-dimensional suffering, the objective consequences were viewed as beneficial insofar as they catalysed "the only social revolution ever heard of in Asia"[4] which "brought out in the open air a hermetically sealed coffin."[5]

The Chinese Response

Whatever the exact nature of the impact may have been, one thing was certain: Chinese society entered into a transitory stage; China was deeply disturbed by the crumbling of some of her traditional structures and uncertain about how and with what to replace them. The self-assurance of the emperor, for example, was destroyed; the new social groups, particularly the middle class, propelled by the Western impact, had become alienated from their cultural roots; and members of the civil service, the backbone of China's socio-economic structures, discovered that all their education and their administrative skills, relevant for so long and usefully utilised for so many centuries, suddenly seemed unrelated to the problems of the day. Inevitably, as is often the case in such circumstances, a process of "introspective revolution" emerged at the turn of the century regarding the manner in which China should meet the disturbing challenge from the West.

There was, first of all, a highly conservative group which showed a marked repugnance to anything European. Led by Dowager Empress Cixi (1835-1908) and her close adviser, YongLu, they were of the view that any attempt to introduce Western technology would inevitably undermine Confucian values, since one was closely linked to the other, and it was therefore pure illusion to think that it was possible to separate knowledge from values. If Western science and technology were accepted as a new framework for Chinese education, it would, they were convinced, set off a process of doubt regarding the validity of Confucian values.

Others like Kang Youwei, loyal to the dynasty, insisted that traditional patterns of life and thought were superior to all others. If the Chinese found themselves in difficulty, it was not because of their inherent conservatism, but because they had not attempted to fit modernization into the traditional Confucian system by continuously reforming it and by reinterpreting

158

the Confucian texts in the light of modern conditions.[6] While belonging to this group, there were still others who wished to take over Western techniques without disturbing accepted beliefs and values. Students of modern Chinese history are familiar with Zhang Zhidong's (1837-1909) slogan "Chinese learning for substance, Western learning for function", which exemplified his thought and which became for a generation the main theme of an extensive debate on the future of China.[7]

A third group came to the conclusion that China's entire traditional patterns of political, social, and economic organizations were completely unsuited to the world of today. The only salvation lay in not only borrowing Western technology, but also accepting Western thought and institutions. Like the conservatives, they argued that the one was not possible without the other. "As we gradually thought back in our disappointment," wrote Liang Qichao in 1920, "we have realized that a social culture is a whole unit, and as such it definitely cannot make use of new institutions with an old psychology. By degrees there has grown up a demand for reawakening of the whole psychology".[8]

Of the three intellectual currents that swept across China, the one that finally prevailed was the Westernization thesis. The futility of undertaking haphazard renovation within the Confucian framework was clearly exposed by the ill-fated Hundred Days Reforms of 1898, which culminated in the execution of several reformers, and the obsolescence of conservative attempts to cling to the traditional Confucian world view was clearly demonstrated by the failure of the Boxer Rebellion (1900) which was directed against the foreigners, their churches, and their railways.

The dismal failure of all the anti-modernisation attempts encouraged an increasing number of Chinese to think of the need for major institutional changes. An important impact of breaking away from the Confucian model can be gauged from the spectacular rise in the number of students studying in Westernised schools as soon as the examination system was changed. In 1905 there were more than 100,000 students in these schools. By 1907, the number had increased tenfold; and at the time of the 1911 revolution they had reached the peak of more than 1.5 million students. But an even more decisive element that favoured modernisation was the rapid change in the economic life of China. Under internal and external pressures, Chinese society had already moved in the direction of Westernization with the rapid rise of foreign investments, with the establishment of industries and railways, and with the growth of urbanization, from which there was no going back. Foreign investments increased rapidly. From $788 million in 1902 they reached the impressive figure of $1.6 billion by 1914. Between 1903 and 1908 as many as 127 Chinese industrial concerns, with a capital of $32,199,800, were registered at the Ministry of Agriculture, Industry and Commerce, and through foreign loans and contracts, the country also completed 9,618 kilometres of railway construction.[9]

What were the implications of this intellectual option? Did it have any concrete effect on the ongoing Nationalist movement? Where was all this leading to at the turn of the century?

The final acceptance of modernisation inaugurated an unprecedented process of Chinese dissatisfaction with their traditional ways, setting the stage for a profound sociocultural and political revolution. Instead of rejecting Western civilization as inferior and barbaric, they began to see great merits in it.[10] Instead of adopting a xenophobic defense of their own existing order, the Chinese swung in the direction of "an uncritical self-humiliation and acceptance" of Western superiority.[11] Instead of seeking their own solutions to their problems, they sought inspiration from Western liberal systems. Instead of maintaining loyalty to the Chinese culture with its universal pretensions as they had done since time immemorial, they focussed their attention on transforming China into a nation based on the Western model and projected themselves into the role of continuing the historic struggle of the French and American peoples for republican institutions.[12]

The English language, rejected in the 19th century, became the second language of schools, and by 1910 many more Chinese could read and speak it than there were Europeans who could speak Chinese. A growing number of Chinese intellectuals went abroad to study Western political economy, political theory and science. The old fabric of Chinese institutions was torn down. The Manchu monarchy was dethroned in 1911, Confucius was demoted, classical examinations for the civil service were abandoned, and with it the whole traditional system of education was abolished.[13]

If the Chinese intellectuals finally reconciled themselves to the dynamics of Western civilization and realized the vital necessity of learning from the West, of even reconstructing their own culture so as to make it suitable for modernization, the political presence of the Europeans in China was, however, totally unacceptable. In fact, since the failure of the Boxer Rebellion—the last major attempt to reject all things European—the basic objective behind this process of emulating the West was to acquire the necessary level of power to confront the European and to ensure his departure.

The emergence of Chinese nationalism in the late 19th and early 20th centuries was thus a challenging response to European rapaciousness; at the same time, it was inspired and given the necessary intellectual content by liberal and nationalistic ideas emanating from Europe.

This phenomenon of "Anti-Western Westernization",[14] however, proved inadequate to the needs of the rapidly changing political situation. The republic that was established in 1911 and was expected to epitomise some of these ideas was a failure, for China could neither obtain the departure of the European powers nor could she develop herself into a fully democratic state based on the Western liberal system. To attain the first objective, she needed the political and military strength which she did not possess and was unable to acquire, and to secure the second objective she needed time, which history did not grant. On the contrary, the number of imperialist nations scrambling for concessions increased with Japan's determination to take over Germany's place after World War I; authoritarianism became more authoritarian, corruption more corrupt, and the country more fragmented with the proliferation of warlordism in the aftermath of 1911 revolution.

Unavoidably, the Chinese became "completely disillusioned with the false gods imported from the West".[15] Influenced by the May 1919 movement of students of the National University in Beijing, nationalism showed signs of becoming increasingly aggressive and increasingly violent. Even more than this, nationalism manifested a secular trend by turning to the left. After his initial disillusionment with the West, Sun Yat-sen personally began to orient his movement towards more Marxist directions by seeking agreements with Bolsheviks, by adopting the Soviet party system, and by admitting into the Kuomingtang fold members of the CCP. However, before this trend could become irreversible, Sun Yat-sen died in 1925. His successor, Chiang Kai-shek, whose anti-Marxist proclivities were well-known, took a number of sudden and rapid initiatives to block any further left-wing evolution, the most dramatic of which was the decimation of the CCP. The political forces behind the Chinese Revolution were thus placed in a state of confusion, discord, and even regression.

The real acceleration and the real ideological orientation came only after World War I, and particularly in the 1930s, when Japan—having put other foreign powers on the defensive—systematically pursued an expansionist policy by taking over Manchuria in 1931, by extending her influence over Rehe province in 1933, over Hebei and Chahaer in 1935 and finally by initiating the war that lasted until 1945.

Everywhere in the country nationalism took the Great Leap Forward, creating widespread hostile public sentiments against the Japanese presence and achieving the goal—perhaps for the first time—of integrating China into one nation.

Like most nationalist movements, it was initially identified with student protests, which took the lead by generating, through a series of massive demonstrations, the appropriate climate for resistance. Soon, however, it was overwhelmed by an influx of other social groups, including the peasants, thereby transforming Chinese nationalism into a vast movement of violent upheaval against Japanese imperialism.[16]

It is interesting to note that unlike the preceding phase of Chinese nationalism where the intellectual framework for the movement was provided by European imperialist powers, Japan did not furnish the necessary intellectual inspiration. In fact, she had nothing to offer in terms of an ideological framework, for she had none; and whatever attraction she had held for the Chinese nationalists at the turn of the century was destroyed by the brutality of Japanese imperialism. An intellectual impulse was provided by the Bolshevik Revolution, which had pushed to the helm of Russian affairs leaders who had denounced imperialism, unilaterally abolishing unequal treaties and relinquishing all privileges obtained by Tsarist Russia, including extraterritoriality, as well as their share of Boxer indemnities.

For a country like China which had been a victim of Tsarist imperialism for so long, the effect of this reversal of fortune was indeed immense. In the universities, among the intellectuals, and even among a number of politicians, all translated literature concerning revolutionary Russia was eagerly read. There was hardly a Chinese novel or a piece of literature or political tract that was not inspired by this new wave, and few that did not express hostility to the capitalist system or proclaim contempt of the liberal political system which the former generation had so ardently admired.

But why this orientation towards Marxism? What were the elements in this essentially European framework which served to inspire China? And how did Marxism arrive on the shores of the country?

The Chinese intellectuals were obviously impressed by the changes introduced in Russia in the aftermath of the Bolshevik Revolution. Having been victims of Tsarist imperialism for so long, they were deeply influenced by the fact that Soviet leaders had unilaterally renounced their imperialist privileges, not only in China but also elsewhere.[17] Any ideology which could introduce such multi-dimensional transformations in the foreign policy behaviour of a state could not but serve as an inspiration for those who had been its victims.[18]

Marxism, furthermore, is essentially a product of Western industrialization. It is, therefore, an effective tool by which "anti-Western Western man and society can criticize Western methods while simultaneously adopting them."[19] For a nation pushed to a state of "cultural despair" and "alienation" by Western intrusion, Marxism thus offered considerable psychological security and satisfaction.

Marxist ideology, lastly, permitted Chinese intellectuals to make the much-needed reinterpretation of their own history. Instead of totally rejecting their past, they could, through the instrumentality of this new dialectical framework based on conflict and revolution, give a new perspective to the actions of their ancestors.

The two developments—Japanese imperialism and Marxism—thus transformed the very nature of Chinese nationalism. In the face of unprecedented Japanese violence, it became more violent, and spurred by Marxist ideas, it attracted new social groups into its fold, finally gathering enough momentum to push the Chinese Communist Party into power in 1949, thereby marking the end of Japanese imperialism.

The Decline of Europe

The defeat of Japanese imperialism and the resurgence of China coincided with the general decline of Europe as the dominant power centre of the international system. Having lost much of their economic power and some of their colonies in this ongoing process of nationalism—a process that had also developed in other countries of Asia and Africa—the European states were no longer able to influence effectively the working of the international system and were no longer in a position to orient international politics in a given direction.

This was caused by the following developments. First of all, this distant continent at the hands of which China had suffered considerable humiliation and exploitation for more than a century no longer constituted a serious threat to her national security. This was not because the hitherto European patterns instituted from afar by dominating peoples and nations had undergone sudden and profound transformations; it was simply because the slow process of historical decline—already begun in the 1920s—compounded with the terrible ravages of World War II, had deprived the Europeans of the power necessary to sway the world. In its place, there now appeared a weak, dependant, partitioned and uncertain Europe completely sucked into the orbits of one or the other of two powerful extra-European nations, the USA and the USSR, each of which represented a magnitude of power never before possessed by any one national unit. For the CCP, influenced as it was by a rigid ideological framework and accepting as it did—rather unquestioningly—the Soviet global perception at the time, its interest in Europe could only be marginal; for the area, in its view, was composed of a group of socialist nations and a cluster of US-dominated capitalist countries, in regard to which the principal responsibility for operational diplomacy and revolutionary activity could only be that of the Soviet Union—the leader of Socialist bloc.

Secondly, the Chinese leadership was preoccupied with other problems—problems which were perceived to be far more important than Europe, and which were within her immediate environment. There was the military involvement in the Korean War in 1950 which tied China's hands considerably. There was the unfinished national task of integrating Tibet and Taiwan with the mainland. There was the European colonial presence on the periphery—the French in Indo-China, the British in Hongkong, and the Portuguese in Macao. But more important and much more threatening than all this, in the Chinese perception, was the US military encirclement of the mainland and her presence in the proximate strategic points formerly controlled and effectively used by Japan against Chinese interests.[20] For China, whose recent history had been studded with incidents of British, French, Russian, and Japanese imperialism, the overwhelming presence of the United States was viewed as highly theatening, necessitating the direction of most of her attention into the field of foreign affairs.

Thirdly, the domestic tasks of national reconstruction, social transformation, and political stabilization of a ravaged country were indeed stupendous. They scarcely left much time for dealing with international affairs. Admittedly, domestic preoccupations need not necessarily restrain nations from active embroilment in external affairs; in some cases they have

163

even impelled the decision makers to become unusually involved in international affairs to divert the attention of the population from more pressing domestic problems. But this diversion, if and when it has occurred, has invariably been focussed on issues of direct concern and not on those that were peripheral. For China, engrossed with pressing national and regional problems, distant, weak and non-threatening Europe, under the circumstances, could hardly be considered an important target for Chinese diplomacy.

Fourthly, China had implicitly accepted a geographical division of responsibility with her senior partner. While the principal onus of responsibility for revolutionary activity in the developed world was considered to fall on the shoulders of the Soviet Union, the task of inspiring and accelerating revolutionary processes in the Third World—and particularly in Asia—were considered by the Chinese leaders to have devolved on them since the 1949 revolution. With this implicit division of labour, China was careful to abstain from designing an independent and active policy on European issues and appeared to be content to play second fiddle to the Soviet Union in the hope and the expectation that the latter in return would reciprocate in Asia.

Fifthly, for a developing China, whose level of dependence on the Soviet Union was high, whose economic power at the time was unimportant, whose ideological influence outside of her own frontiers was still relatively insignificant, and whose military strength was tenuous, it was hardly feasible to put into operation a policy, even if she wanted to do so, related to a faraway continent.

It was thus scarcely possible for China to take an active interest in Europe or to design even the outlines of a policy towards a continent which had hardly anything to offer. With Western Europe, relations were further circumscribed by disagreements regarding the status of Taiwan[21] and by the imposition of an extensive embargo by a special China Committee (CHICOM) composed of Western nations[22] which severely hindered the development of normal trade partnership. Therefore, with the exception of indifferent diplomatic relations with a few willing capitalist countries,[23] of some cultural exchanges, and of the periodic publication of highly rhetorical statements against Western European governments, capitalist Europe was essentially a closed book.

Relations with Eastern Europe, however, were more intense. By 1953, in addition to the establishment of diplomatic relations, China had concluded a series of agreements on trade, cultural, scientific, technical and telecommunication cooperation with all East European countries except Albania and Yugoslavia.[24] The Chinese press, furthermore, was full of complimentary articles and news items regarding developments in Eastern Europe and regarding the socialist character of the regimes. However, notwithstanding this general display of warmth and solidarity, the socialist countries of Eastern Europe, during the first few years after the revolution, remained at

164

the low rung of the Chinese diplomatic ladder with hardly any conceptualised and independent goals. China obviously considered that her role in the region was essentially marginal since Moscow had the principal responsibility of giving the lead in the area, and of maintaining the integrity of the Socialist bloc. The measure of Chinese willingness to accept such a subordinate position can be gauged from her attitude towards Yugoslavia. The fluctuations in Moscow's Yugoslav policy were closely followed. When the Soviet-Yugoslav dispute blew up in 1948, the CCP denounced Tito as a Fascist and compared him to Chiang Kai-shek[25] and in the aftermath of Stalin's death in 1953 when the Soviet Union began to revise her policy towards Belgrade, the Chinese did the same by establishing diplomatic relations and by rapidly injecting an element of warmth in their attitude towards Yugoslavia.[26]

Involvement in Eastern Europe

The rumblings of discontent in Hungary and Poland in 1956, however, impelled the Chinese to focus attention on the area. The news coverage from Eastern Europe increased, exchanges became more frequent, and the general level of Chinese concern over some of the developments rose conspicuously. This new interest was neither dictated by geo-political considerations—for China's diplomatic and political activity was still essentially limited to her area—nor was it the result of considerable and concerted pondering on the part of the decision makers, for there were other and more immediate areas of concern which required Chinese scrutiny. It was one of those fluctuating and explosive situations in which the Chinese could not possibly afford to remain silent; they had to react, for any dereliction on their part to respond to critical situations within their own ideological orbit would have been tantamount to abandoning their publicly proclaimed objectives of consolidating the unity of the Socialist camp. Furthermore, it would have meant virtually shying away from forging ties with Communist nations which were seeking viable counterbalances to Soviet hegemonial influences within the bloc after Stalin's death, and which looked with great laudation at the "Hundred Flowers Movement" launched in China in May 1956, presumably in the hope that it could have a spillover effect in Eastern Europe.[27] On 31 October 1956 Beijing therefore took a public position on the highly explosive situations that had developed in Hungary and Poland.[28] This first major attempt to intervene diplomatically in Europe (which was in prompt reply to a Soviet declaration of the same day) permitted the Chinese leaders to publicly explain their own position on the developments in the area. While applauding the new Soviet moderation, evident in the declaration, in the development of which they had presumably played a discreet role, the Chinese seized the opportunity to criticize the Russians for having neglected "the principle of equality among nations in their mutual relations",[29] to underline the vital importance of the Five

Principles of Peaceful Coexistence[30] in the determination of relations between the Socialist countries, and to openly reiterate their support of the Hungarian and Polish demands "for the strengthening of democracy, for independence and equality, and for an elevation of the standards of living as a result of the development of production."[31] The publication of this important declaration contributed to the enhancement of China's image among a number of intellectuals in Eastern Europe, who, having already welcomed the liberalising trend of the "Hundred Flowers Movement", viewed the statement as a possible precursor to the eventual creation of an autonomous Yugoslav-Hungarian-Polish-Chinese national Communist grouping within the Soviet orbit.[32] This development elicited general euphoria in China. Mao's pronouncements on "nonantagonistic contradictions" between the masses and the leaders were published extensively in the Polish press where, according to an observer, "since the time of physiocrats, no European country had displayed so much interest in Chinese affairs,"[33] and in Hungary, Chinese revisionism appeared to have strengthened the hands of anti-Stalinist intellectuals "more than any other single influence."[34]

The development of these relations was, however, marred by the sudden deterioration of the Hungarian political situation. Paradoxically, this happened on the same day (30 October) the Soviets moderated their attitude towards Eastern Europe, and the Chinese extended their support to Hungarian and Polish demands for liberalization and greater autonomy. Carried away by popular grass-roots pressures, Imre Nagy abolished one-party rule in Hungary, formed a coalition with some of the other parties, and proclaimed the neutrality of his country by denouncing all obligations emanating from the Warsaw Pact.[35]

For Beijing, this was a dangerous and unacceptable development. Liberalizing regimes and seeking autonomy from Moscow was one thing, but opting out of the Socialist bloc was another matter. The Chinese evaluation of the East European situation therefore underwent a rapid change; a distinction between the Polish and the Hungarian situations was made. The two events were now considered "different in character".[36] While maintaining support of the Polish party's attempts to attain a certain degree of autonomy within the Socialist system, it denounced Imre Nagy's decision to extricate Hungary from the Socialist fold. "The Polish and Hungarian events are following different paths," declared a Chinese publication; "in Poland the mass movement since the beginning is under the firm control of the Party, the Government and the revolutionary people. The imperialist conspiracy and counter-revolutionary elements cannot therefore manifest themselves. In Hungary they could find an opportunity to stage a counter-revolutionary *coup d'état*".[37]

In line with this new evaluation, the Chinese, according to their subsequent declaration of 6 September 1963, took a series of informal diplomatic initiatives to dissuade the Russians from committing "the error of great power chauvinism"[38] of intervening in Poland, and to persuade them to take all "necessary measures to smash the counterrevolutionary rebellion in Hungary".[39]

This is what took place: The principal Soviet leaders who were on the verge of intervening in Poland and who had flown to the Polish capital on 19 October to warn the dissident leaders from taking any anti-Soviet steps, decided to abandon all plans of intervening militarily. In Hungary, however, where they initially appeared divided and hesitant,[40] the revolution was brutally suppressed on 4 November by Soviet troops.

But were these actions, the Soviet non-intervention in Poland and her intervention in Hungary, really the result of their firmness and behind-the-scene pressures as the Chinese claimed? Was it really through their efforts that "the prestige of the CPSU,"[41] which appeared to be wobbling during the Hungarian and Polish crisis, was finally safeguarded? Or was it—as Soviet writers suggested—that during the events in Hungary, the Chinese too were hesitant,[42] or that they "gambled on the difficulties within the international Communist movement . . . in an effort to undermine the prestige of the CPSU and portray themselves as guardians of revolutionary traditions".[43]

From the mountain of complex official writings that appeared after the Sino-Soviet dispute, in which severe polemics were exchanged by the two parties, it is not possible to seek out even the approximate truth; the multitude of explanations given by each side regarding their mutual relations are too numerous and too contradictory to permit an objective evaluation of the total situation. However, some of the writings that have appeared in the Western world concerning the events in Eastern Europe seem to confirm the existence of a growing Chinese involvement in some of the major decisions taken by the Soviet Union, at least regarding the Polish crisis. For example, it has been suggested that the Chinese supported Polish efforts to obtain autonomy,[44] restrained the Soviet leaders from militarily intervening in Poland,[45] and persuaded them to accept the liberalisation of the Polish party.[46]

Whatever the nature and effectiveness of behind-the-scene pressures may have been, the indisputable fact remains that the 1956 events impelled the Chinese to appear on the European scene, and to play, for the first time, a role in East European affairs. One could even venture to suggest that this role, which was by no means insignificant, probably encouraged the Party leadership to envision even a greater participation in European affairs. The editorial published in *People's Daily* on 29 December 1956 represented the first major example of the Chinese intention to ideologically intervene in the European Communist movement after the 20th Party Congress and in the aftermath of Hungarian and Polish revolts. In this balanced and moderate declaration, an attempt was made to defend Stalin without forgetting his mistakes, to stretch out a friendly hand to the Yugoslavs without accepting their innovated ideas, to appeal to the international Communist movement "to strengthen international proletarian solidarity with the Soviet Union as its centre,"[47] without forgetting to advise the Russians "to respect the national interest and sentiments of other Socialist countries".[48]

Zhou Enlai's visit to Moscow, Warsaw, and Budapest in January 1957 was the second major manifestation of the growing Chinese interest in Europe. While stressing in Moscow the importance of "international proletarianism" and the meritorious role the Russians played in Hungary,[49] the Chinese Prime Minister made a point of stressing in Warsaw that the relations between Socialist countries "must be founded on the principle of respect for their sovereignty, non-interference in their internal affairs, equality, and mutual benefit."[50] In Hungary, while condemning the reactionary imperialist forces and counterrevolutionary elements "who had exploited the Hungarian situation," he took account of the "legitimate discontent of the working masses and of the Hungarian youth due to the serious mistakes of the former leaders."[51] However, if China made a point of underlining the need for the continuation of the ongoing process of autonomisation in Eastern Europe, she balanced this objective by insisting that the international Communist movement must, at the same time, continue to strengthen international proletarian solidarity "with the Soviet Union as its core."[52] The development of the one, she emphasized, must not be at cost of the other. While arguing this point, the editorial department of the *People's Daily* wrote on 29 December 1956:

> Marxism-Leninism had always insisted upon combining proletarian internationalism with the patriotism of the people of each country. Each Communist party must educate its members and the people in a spirit of internationalism, because the true interests of all peoples call for friendly cooperation among nations. On the other hand, each Communist party must represent the legitimate national interests and sentiments of its own people. Communists have always been true patriots, and they understand that it is only when they correctly represent the interests and sentiments of their nation that they can really enjoy the trust and love of the broad masses of their own people, effectively educate them in internationalism and harmonize the national sentiments and interests of the people of different countries.[53]

It was the maintenance of this balanced view that made it possible for Beijing to develop close and friendly relations with Eastern Europe without offending the Russians. It was this position that permitted the Chinese to assume the role of arbitrators in Eastern Europe. By pressuring the Russians to respect the national sovereignty of Socialist states, they were able to project themselves as champions of small nations. By making it clear to East European countries that international solidarity must be maintained under Soviet leadership, they were at the same time able to gain the confidence of Moscow.

This delicate balance did not last, however. A number of developments in Eastern Europe and in China led the Chinese decision makers to reconsider their policy. First, bolstered by the general waning of Stalinism, revisionism became more pronounced within the ruling parties in Eastern

Europe. Internal party discipline became lax, demands for greater autonomy from Moscow became rampant, and a lively exchange of views took place among Marxist intellectuals in Eastern Europe, in the course of which many of the tenets of Marxism-Leninism were questioned. For example, Leszek Kolakowski, a former Stalinist ideologue and a gifted young scholar of philosophy, attacked the dogmatization of Marxism and demanded that the party abstain from interfering in scientific and intellectual pursuits. Wolfgang Harich, a philosopher in East Germany, expressed concern over the inability of Marxism to adjust to peculiar national conditions.[54] Secondly, the Soviet leaders, to some extent carried away by the process of de-Stalinization, had begun to reconcile themselves to the idea of liberalization and to the introduction of some degree of autonomy with a greater reliance and emphasis on the community of economic relations in order to maintain unity within the Socialist bloc. Leading members of the orthodox "anti-party" group were removed in the Soviet Union, contacts were reestablished with "revisionist" Yugoslavia, and a status of full equality was accorded to her despite her refusal to integrate within the Socialist camp. Thirdly, the rapidly changing internal situation in China had become disquietening. The "Blooming and Contending Movement", launched in 1956, had generated such a multi-dimensional process of criticism of Chinese leaders that the whole political situation within the country was perceived to have become highly explosive.

The combination of all these elements led the Chinese to review their liberal policy and to introduce a number of changes. Internally the "Blooming and Contending Movement" was abruptly ended, and the dissident elements both within as well as outside the party who had generated the explosive situation were not only severely reprimanded in the party press but were also deprived of their positions. Externally, the delicate balance that had been established between the support for the autonomy of Socialist countries and the collateral maintainance of Socialist bloc unity under Soviet leadership was abandoned.

A vigorous campaign was then launched in favour of a firm maintenance of international proletarian solidarity, discreet pressure was exerted on the Soviet leaders to assume the leadership of the Socialist bloc, Gomulka was repeatedly criticised for being "too weak" on revisionism,[55] and the Yugoslav "revisionists" were publicly denounced in a series of widely publicised articles for having refused to sign the 1957 declaration of the representatives of Communist and Workers parties of Socialist countries in Moscow, for "following the imperialist reactionaries," and for "venomously" attacking "the proletarian dictatorship in the Soviet Union and other Socialist countries".[56]

But all this did not appear to have any effect either on Eastern Europe or the Soviet Union. The situation had changed. Whereas, the 1956 Chinese call for greater diversity and greater equality responded to the aspirations of small Socialist countries, the 1957 and 1958 declarations favouring a general tightening up of the Socialist bloc were not only tantamount to abandoning the process of increasing autonomy already commenced in Eastern Europe, but were in contradiction with the objectives of the Socialist states implicitly acknowledged by the Soviet Union.

China was thus swimming against the tide; and as she possessed neither the military power nor the appropriate economic clout to neutralise the disadvantages of preaching generally unpopular causes, the goodwill she had been able to build up in Eastern Europe in 1956 was seriously eroded by 1958.

Albania was the only exception to this general rule of eroded relations. Having already developed reservations regarding Soviet "revisionism", Albania became clearly alarmed at the new rapprochement between Moscow and Belgrade. As Tirana's attitude towards other nations is invariably conditioned by their attitude towards Yugoslavia, China appeared to be the only friendly voice, since she had become the principal and most ferocious opponent of Yugoslav "revisionism". But it would be an exaggeration to suggest that relations between the two countries had suddenly become warm or that a mutual understanding had been reached on a wide spectrum of issues. The process of rapprochement had only begun; the real acceleration took place a few years later with the explosion of the Sino-Soviet dispute.

The Great Schism and European Communism

It was only after the real commencement of the Sino-Soviet rift in the early 1960s that China once again returned to the European scene. This return, however, was neither simply reactive nor as pragmatic as in 1956; it appeared to possess all the characteristics of a policy that had been designed to operationally integrate with other strands of China's foreign policy. The initial manifestations of this new approach to Europe were principally ideological, with a focus on the European Communist movement, which to the Chinese appeared to be the only acceptable political force on the continent. How could it be otherwise when revolutionary euphoria, during the late 1950s or early 1960s, was still rampant in China, when Marxist dialectics were considered the only acceptable form of communication among the Communist parties, and when most non-Communist governments of Europe were not even marginally interested in forging ties with Beijing.

Without delving into the substantive or chronological details of the dispute (this has been dealt with elsewhere),[57] it is important to note that after it became evident that the dispute had reached an irreversible point, the Chinese leaders arrived at the conclusion that without flinging an open challenge to their opponents, the revisionist ideas unilaterally introduced by the CPSU at its 20th Party Congress would hopelessly and irrevocably engulf the whole international Communist movement and bring it into some sort of confusion.

170

It was perhaps this fear that led Beijing to open a polemical offensive against the Soviet leaders. The publication of the important article, "Long Live Leninism," in the party's theoretical journal, *Red Flag*, on 16 April 1960 was the first major manifestation of this campaign.[58] Every opportunity was thereafter seized to point out the relevance of the Chinese line of thinking and the magnitude of Soviet deviation from original Marxist thought. The highly critical declarations made in the general council of the World Federation of Trade Unions in 1961, at the World Peace Council during the same year, and at the November 1960 meeting of 81 Communist parties in Moscow demonstrated this policy, as did the Chinese declarations at the Congress of the Bulgarian, Italian, Hungarian, Czechoslovak Communist parties in 1962, and that of East Germany in 1963.[59] On all these occasions the Chinese point of view was patiently explained and the Russians were impatiently attacked for their attempts to give a revisionist orientation to the entire international Communist movement.

While the Chinese leadership received some support from the Communist parties of a number of Third World countries in their dispute with the Soviet Union, the attitude of their European counterparts was on the whole negative. For them, with the exception of Albania, the revised Soviet outlook appeared to represent a more effective and more relevant response to the rapidly changing situation in Europe. The Khruschevian thesis favouring liberalizing Communist regimes and accepting different roads to socialism, and underlining the fundamental necessity of improving the living standards of Socialist societies was more in tune with the aspirations of European Communists than was the rather highly intransigent Chinese line of thinking which the European Communists had unsuccessfully followed in the past and which, in the light of the evolved situation on the continent, they were only too eager to cast aside. Similarly, on a wide spectrum of international issues, the West European Communists were closer to Moscow than Beijing. They appeared to agree with the Soviet evaluation of the international situation, the vital importance of peaceful coexistence, the development of East-West relations, the necessity of détente, etc. Even more important was the disagreement regarding the configuration of forces in the international system. Notwithstanding the emergence of the Third World, which was stressed by the Chinese, the European continent, along with North America, still remained for the European Communists the focal point of international politics. As Jacques Arnault of the French Communist party declared:

> Whether this pleases them or not, the global future of the world during the next historical period will essentially depend not on Asia, Africa or Latin America, but on what will happen in Europe and North America. For it is here that there is a concentration of the means of destruction of humanity as well as the most important means of its development. It is here that the most advanced science exists and will exist for a long period of time. Incantation will not change anything"[60] (translated).

It was therefore not surprising that at all the Communist party congresses held in Europe in the early 1960s, the Chinese or Albanian points of views were criticized and clear options were taken in favour of innovative Soviet ideas on the international situation and on a series of theoretical and practical issues facing the capitalist and socialist societies.

Emergence of Eurocommunism

Notwithstanding this decision to side ideologically with the Soviet Union, however, the objective situation generated by the Sino-Soviet dispute nonetheless generated a parallel process of diversification within the European Communist Movement which is still continuing and which has in recent years become rampant.[61] For the first time, the party leadership of European parties began to show signs of bemusement, hesitation, and uncertainty; and for the first time a process of autonomous decision-making slowly began to develop, giving a new momentum to an impressive array of revisionist ideas within a number of parties.

In Eastern Europe, new concepts were brought out into the open which significantly contributed to the extension of liberalism in Hungary and Poland, the assertion of economic nationalism in Rumania, and the implementation of new economic experiments in Yugoslavia. Dissident voices for greater liberalization, for freer ideological discussions, and for greater political autonomy became increasingly strident. In foreign affairs, a degree of autonomous behaviour or even diversity became apparent. Yugoslavia continued her politics of non-alignment, Albania defied Moscow, and Rumania adopted a noncommital posture on even such a sensitive issue as the Sino-Soviet dispute. But these changes, although important, were nonetheless limited in scope either by the overwhelming obtrusiveness of the Soviet Union in the area or by the inherent hesitancy of the ruling parties to initiate any major changes that could jeopardize their own power.

More important than all this was the widespread incidence of dissidence that developed among a number of West European Communist parties. While implicitly acknowledging Beijing's contribution to the development of a polycentric situation within the international Communist movement—thereby giving them more room for manoeuvre—most of them, deeply influenced by the 20th Soviet Party congress and tumultuous de-Stalinization in Eastern Europe, made it abundantly clear in countless declarations and speeches in the mid-1960s that conditions in Europe had undergone a sea change; that the constellation of socio-economic forces within their own societies had evolved; that power could no longer be seized violently; that understandings with other left-wing forces (hitherto castigated as reactionary) had become necessary in order to give a decisive orientation to capitalistic societies; and that pluralism, an integral part of their societal systems, could no longer be rejected as irrelevant. The Italian Communist party, for example, long influenced by Antonio Gramsci's idea of a "national collective will" that could ignite socialism, invoked in 1965 "the possibility of a peaceful road of access to socialism" and "the possibility of the conquest of positions of power by the working class within a state that has not changed its character as a bourgeois state."[62] In 1973 it broke new ground by proposing " a new historical compromise between the forces that rally and represent the great majority of the Italian people," including those who belonged to the right-wing Christian Democratic Party.[63] The French Communist party—though later than the Italian Communists—accepted the need for a multi-party system not only during the transitional phase but also after the establishment of the socialist system,[64] and the Spanish party, evolving in the same direction after the death of Franco,[65] underlined the vital importance of avoiding the development of a left-wing front which "would polarize the country when it needs harmony to consolidate the fragile democratic system."[66]

But this response to the new political environment in Europe was not confined to internal issues. A series of factors—including the dynamics of the situation, the need to project a new image, the Soviet occupation of Czechoslovakia in 1968—catalysed the three parties to adopt an independent line on a wide spectrum of international issues. They accepted the reality of military alliance systems, agreed to operate within the European Economic Community, and supported the autonomic process in Eastern Europe. While most European Communist parties kept themselves at a distance from Moscow, some of them became outspoken on the oppressive nature of the Soviet system.[67] Even on the question of the Sino-Soviet dispute, in which they had originally sided with the Soviet Union, the new Eurocommunist trend was to disengage and become increasingly non-aligned. The French, Spanish, and Italian parties in fact stymied Soviet attempts to include polemical comments against Beijing in the joint declarations signed by European Communists in Karlovy Vary in 1967 and in Berlin in 1976 and appeared to have even attempted on their own to renew contacts with the Chinese party.[68]

This phenomena of evolutionary change was, however, not confined to the big Communist parties of southern Europe, though these were undoubtedly the principal catalysts. Impelled by the winds of "revisionism" that were creating an increasing intellectual impact among left-wing circles, the British, Belgian, Swiss, and Scandinavian parties also moved in the same direction.[69]

The Chinese Response

If West European parties were showing signs of increasing autonomy from Soviet control, the Chinese party was becoming more occlusive and more inflexible. It appeared to focus its attention more on the "revisionist" character of the change than on the growing political disengagement of Eurocommunist parties from Moscow. After an initial attempt at a polite polemical exchange with "Comrades" Thorez and Togliatti in 1963,[70] the Chinese leaders arrived at the conclusion that most of the European parties had become "new types of Social Democratic parties,"[71] and the "main bulwark of revisionism of the most rabid type".[72]

The ideological gap, in the Chinese view, had indeed become unbridge-able, making it futile to deploy any further efforts to seek an understanding on a number of issues. To them, this had become clear at the Moscow Consultative Conference of March 1965 where, despite Chinese opposition, nineteen Communist parties had assembled to discuss the international situation;[73] and it had become glaringly evident at the Karlovy Vary Conference of European Communist parties in April 1967,[74] where the Soviet global perception was adhered to.

Casting their general prudence to the winds, the Chinese now came out openly against the European Communists. As the "Observer" in *People's Daily* wrote:

> The Karlovy Vary Conference was a meeting serving US interests . . . The meeting usurped the name of the Communist and Workers Parties in Europe. What kind of Communists are they? The participants: the Brezhnev Kosygin crowd from the Soviet Union, the Ulbricht crowd from East Germany, the Gomulka crowd from Poland, the Novotny crowd from Czechoslovakia, the Zhukov crowd from Bulgaria, the Kadar Janos crowd from Hungary, the Rochet crowd from France, the Longo crowd from Italy, the Gollan crowd from Britain, the Ibarruri crowd from Spain, etc. . . . all are renegades to Marxism-Leninism, working class scabs and the enemies of the revolutionary Communist parties. The meeting at Karlovy Vary was a meeting of representatives of the privileged bourgeois stratum of the Soviet Union and East European countries and the agents of the bourgeoisie of some capitalist countries in Europe. It was a meeting at which new Social Democratic parties took a further step in colluding with the old Social Democratic parties. The new Social Democratic parties and the old Social Democratic parties have become a "maintenance club" to keep all reactionary rule, reactionary system and reactionary forces going a bit longer.[75]

It should be noted that these open attacks were launched at a time when the European Communist parties were themselves changing. If the nineteen parties had agreed to meet in Moscow—much against the Chinese wishes—they were already seriously divided between those who were partisans of the Soviet line of thinking and those who were eager to adopt an autonomous position. The Italian party, for example, made it clear through the Togliatti memorandum that the Chinese line, though erroneous, must not deter all Communists from uniting. "The unity of all socialist forces in a common action," declared the memorandum, "going also beyond ideological differences against the most reactionary imperialist groups, is an indispensable necessity. One cannot imagine that China could be excluded from this unity."[76] Similarly, at the Karlovy Vary Conference of European parties in April 1967, where all of the parties were not present,[77] a common declaration was signed, but a number of them refused to include any critical reference to China in the joint declaration.[78]

Why did the Chinese rhetorical attacks on the European parties become more belligerent, more resounding and more venomous just at a time when these parties were clearly showing signs of some independence from Moscow? Why did the Chinese fail to exploit this situation? Why did they ignore the opportunity to accelerate this trend towards greater autonomy by cultivating the European parties and by supporting them? Was it not in their interest?

The paucity of documentation on these events permits the advancement of only tentative and plausible explanations of the Chinese behaviour. First of all the appearance of signs of change among a number of European parties coincided with the radicalization of Chinese politics. The Cultural Revolution, which, among other things, aimed at the maintenance of ideological purity, was in full swing by the time the European Communists met in Karlovy Vary in April 1967. Under the circumstances, it was hardly possible for the Chinese decision makers to seek an understanding with the European revisionists.

Secondly, even more than the question of Soviet hegemony over West European parties, China was fearful of the deleterious influence that revisionism might have on the international Communist movement. Any effort to exploit the contradictory situation that was developing in the European Communist movement would have in effect meant giving Beijing's stamp of approval to the new theoretical changes. The adverse consequences resulting from such an action, in China's view, might override the short-term political advantages that she might gain by indulging in the game of power politics.

Uncertainties of European Politics

If "revisionism" had impelled the Chinese to maintain a supercilious attitude towards European Communism, the congealed state of European diplomacy did not seem to permit taking any major European initiatives which might rock the boat of existing alliance systems. The European governments were still too tied and still too dependent on the two superpowers. There were of course such exceptions as Yugoslavia, Albania, and Rumania in Eastern Europe which had successfully disengaged themselves from the tight Soviet grip; but the Chinese leaders could scarcely square their ideologically-oriented diatribes against Yugoslav "revisionism" with forging ties with her;[79] they could hardly use isolated Albania to advance their interests, as her outspoken anti-Soviet attitude had rendered her ineffective in the region,[80] and they could barely rely upon Rumania, which, though neutral in the escalating Sino-Soviet dispute, could not really break away from the Soviet orbit.[81] They did not of course ignore these new trends, but their capacity for creating ripples in the seemingly calm waters of Eastern Europe of the mid-1960s was relatively inconsequential.

In Western Europe, France was beginning to display some signs of independence from Washington. In the context of a new world view, as repeatedly expressed by De Gaulle after 1958,[82] she had established diplomatic relations with China in January 1964, much to the consternation of her allies; this development, however, though considered important,[83] was still not viewed as significant enough by the Chinese to merit any dramatic initiatives. De Gaulle's France was perceived as lacking any real capacity for independent behaviour and was considered at the time to be principally concerned with developing closer relations with Moscow and its client states of Eastern Europe.

There were also some visible signs of an independent attitude by the Federal Republic of Germany, which was influenced by the French recognition of Beijing and German economic pressure groups and which had opened negotiations with China in 1964 in Berne.[84] But this also proved to be chimerical: under heavy pressure from the United States, the Erhardt government not only called off negotiations,[85] but also unilaterally cancelled an agreement in 1966 to construct a $150 million steel plant in China.[86]

Most of the other West European countries were even more restrained in their relations with Beijing. The US pressure against any form of normalisation was much too great to permit them to follow France. The majority of them, in fact, continued to vote with Washington against the admission of the People's Republic to the United Nations.

China thus did not make much headway in the mid-1960s. A diplomatic break-through in Europe still appeared difficult, and the marked escalation of the Sino-Soviet dispute, compounded with the explosion of the Cultural Revolution, had resulted in a complete snapping of ties with most of the European Communist parties.

The Search for "Revolutionary" Europe

It was this generally unfavourable situation in Europe that encouraged China, on the one hand, to turn increasingly to the Third World,[87] and, on the other, to focus her attention, perhaps as a subsidiary matter, to the task of establishing secessionist parties or party-like organisations that ranged behind Beijing. The signal for promoting this type of factionalism—and eventually schisms—among Communist parties was given in 1963 when the Chinese party in its first formal polemical assault on its Soviet counterpart clearly warned the latter that "if the leading group in any party adopts a non-revolutionary line and converts it into a reformist party, then Marxist-Leninists inside and outside the party will replace them and lead the people in making revolution."[88]

This Chinese posture of demonstrative independence from and open defiance of Moscow gave the necessary impetus to their ideological friends in Europe, who were already rumbling with discontent at the varying degrees of pro-Soviet partisanship represented by the established Communist parties. Dissident parties or associations were therefore established practically everywhere in Western Europe (see Table 5.1).

Most of these splinter groups presented a scene of great diversity in their origins.[89] While some used legalistic processes to justify the split, the others simply broke with the established party in the name of Marxism-Leninism and announced the formation of a rival body. While some of them were founded through local initiatives, others received the necessary impetus from outside.[90] In all cases, however, one thing appeared to be certain: either before or after the establishment of Maoist groups, Chinese or Albanian moral and, in some cases, financial support was forthcoming. In fact, their existence was often first proclaimed in the Chinese press, where propaganda coverage regarding their activities was completely out of proportion to their real strength.

This interest in "revolutionary Europe" increased markedly during the student revolts of May 1968. At the height of the Cultural Revolution, it was claimed that it was this interest that had "speeded up the spreading of Mao Zedong thought in West Europe and North America where the number of students carrying copies of Chairman Mao's works and *Quotations from Chairman Mao* had been growing steadily."[91] Mass meetings were

Table 5.1. *List of Pro-Chinese Parties or Groups[a]*

Country	Name	Year
Austria	Communist party (Marxist-Leninist)	1967
Belgium	Communist party	1963
Denmark	Communist Study Circle	unknown
Finland	Helsinki Marxist-Leninist Group	1969
Federal Republic of Germany	German Marxist-Leninist party	1965
France	Marxist-Leninist Communist party	1967
Great Britain	Communist party (Marxist-Leninist)	1967
Greece	Communist party (Marxist-Leninist)	1966
Italy	Communist party (Marxist-Leninist)	1966
Luxemburg	Luxemburg-China Society	unknown
Norway	Young Socialist League (Marxist-Leninist)	unknown
Netherlands	Marxist-Leninist League of Holland	1966
Portugal	Marxist-Leninist Committee	1965
Spain	Communist party of Spain	1964
Sweden	Marxist-Leninist League of Communists	1967
Switzerland	Swiss Communist party (Lenin Centre) Organization of Communists (Marxist-Leninist)	1963

a   Only the year of the formal creation of the party or organization are given. Many of them were preceded by different groups concerning which complete information is unavailable.

organised in a number of cities where support was extended to "the revolutionary struggle of French workers and students",[92] and for fourteen consecutive weeks the Chinese press, particularly the *Peking Review,* carried articles on the subject.[93]

Chinese interest in student upheavals in Western Europe was essentially due to the mounting instability these movements generated in West European politics. In a country like France, for example, where discontent was widespread, the established system of authority indeed became wobbly during the student-initiated revolt of 1968, leading many to think that revolutions in affluent societies were after all not that remote. It would seem that interest in this process of destabilization could be the only plausible explanation for the development of Beijing's interest in "revolutionary Europe"—as the "new left" student movement represented a pattern of ideas and a system of values which were antagonistic to the existing Chinese thinking and which were inspired by leaders (Che Guevera and Regis Debray) whose ideological beliefs and political behaviour had been seriously challenged by the CCP. Furthermore, the ideas the "new left" represented in Western Europe were fairly close to the ultra-leftist group, Sheng-wu-lien, ("Hunan Provincial Proletarian Revolutionary Great Alliance Committee"), which was founded in the autumn of 1967 and which the Chinese authorities had been seriously trying to suppress.[94]

In any event, none of these efforts were much of a success, for none of the pro-Beijing Communist groups or parties managed to acquire any sizable degree of influence in any of the West European countries,[95] and the rumblings of discontent among a section of the European student community—essentially a European and North American phenomena and which had very little real linkage with the Maoist movement—rapidly dissipated.

The failure of such a policy was more than evident. But the Chinese at the time did not seem to care. The euphoria of the Cultural Revolution had generated such confidence in the nation and had inculcated such faith in the future of revolutions that the leaders felt an exaggerated optimism regarding their prospects—even in regions where there were none. If revolutionary upheavals were not in the cards today, they felt, it did not matter; the Chinese were convinced that they would inevitably come tomorrow or the day after.

The New Diplomacy

The overly optimistic Chinese perception of the revolutionary potential in Western Europe was, however, not due only to the euphoria caused by the Cultural Revolution; it was also a result of the absence of any real external threat which could have perhaps modulated Chinese political behaviour by impelling them to focus their attention on more immediate and concrete issues. None of their real or perceived enemies were able or willing to

178

challenge them in the mid-1960s. India, bemused and weakened by a humiliating defeat in the Sino-Indian war of 1962, had neither the capacity nor the desire to initiate any conflict with Beijing. Taiwan did not possess any credible capacity for crossing the narrow waters that separated her from the mainland. The United States, despite a significant presence in Vietnam, had no intention of attacking China or of coming up to her borders;[96] and the dispute with the Soviet Union, limited so far to polemical exchanges, was not considered a serious threat to China's security and was not viewed with any unusual concern, despite the tense activity along the Sino-Soviet border.

The situation changed in the late 1960s. The Chinese suddenly began to perceive the emergence of a real threat from the north and began to consider the Soviet Union "as our principal and most dangerous enemy."[97] Thenceforward, the dispute was no longer viewed as a simple matter of polemical exchanges, but something more real and something which could seriously undermine their security.

This new perception was influenced by a series of developments. There was, first of all, the firm and rather brutal Soviet armed intervention in Czeckoslovakia in August 1968, which was a clear warning to the socialist countries of the risks they were likely to run in the event of any major transgression of the political guidelines and the foreign policy framework established by the Soviet Union. There was the proclamation of the Brezhnev doctrine, also in 1968, under which the Soviet Union arrogated to herself the right to intervene in socialist countries "when internal and external forces, hostile to socialism, seek to reverse the development of any socialist country whatsoever in the direction of the restoration of the capitalist order . . .".[98] There was the important reinforcement of the Soviet military presence along the Chinese border in 1969, the explosion of actual border conflicts in the spring and summer of the same year,[99] and the existence of vague rumours of a possible pre-emptive Soviet attack on China.[100] There was also the Brezhnev proposal, made at the International Conference of Communist and Workers' parties in June 1969, for the establishment of "a system of collective security in Asia"[101] which, at least in Chinese eyes, was "another unbridled step taken by Soviet revisionism in its collusion with US imperialism in recent years to rig up an anti-China ring of encirclement and to make war clamours and threats of aggression against China."[102] The situation had thus changed; for the first time since the Korean War, the Chinese felt seriously threatened—and by a major land power with a large frontier with China.[103]

It was probably this new and threatening situation that stimulated a re-examination of the basic guidelines of China's foreign policy. Repeated proclamations of her adherance to revolutionary goals were no longer considered adequate, although they were not abandoned. Revolutionary friends, isolated and scattered all over the world, were no longer viewed as viable competitors of the established pro-Soviet Communist movements,

179

though they were by no means disowned. In the eyes of the Chinese leaders, something more palpable, more pragmatic, and more national was needed to meet the rapidly changing international situation.[104]

Internally, the Cultural Revolution, which had generated considerable dissension and instability in the country, was seemingly abandoned at the 9th Congress of the party in 1969, and efforts were made to bring under control a rapidly degenerating domestic situation. The role of the party, which had suffered erosion, was reasserted, and diverse political elements which had caused ripples of dissent by revolting against part of the leadership were curbed.

Important defense measures were also taken. These included accelerated evacuation of urban areas, air raid practices, strengthening the militia, encouraging the population to dig bomb shelters everywhere in the country, and spreading a real war psychosis.

It was perhaps in the field of foreign affairs that China, concerned as she was about Soviet intentions and uncertain of her own capacity to effectively meet the challenge, began to design a new pattern of diplomatic behaviour which was similar to the one that states have traditionally adopted to safeguard their own security and to undermine that of their real or perceived enemies. That is to say, they sought out and cultivated relations with other powers equally concerned by and preoccupied with the intentions and behaviour of the same adversaries.

Within this general framework in which the power equation was the crucial element, the Third World countries, hitherto a focal point of Chinese operational diplomacy, was relegated to a secondary position, since none of them possessed a measure of economic, political, or military power great enough to be useful in meeting the Soviet challenge. There were of course myriad declarations that still underlined the importance of the Third World in the Chinese global perception, but these were more an expression of Chinese confidence in the potential importance of the area rather than a reflection of any real capacity to effectively manage the crisis. Fearful as China was of the Soviet Union and needing as she did some credible counterbalances against her northern neighbour, the developed countries, equally concerned with rising Soviet power and equally distrustful of her intentions, appeared to her to be the only viable partners in the great power game.

The Growing Importance of Europe

One of the first countries to become the object of this new diplomatic posture was the United States, towards which a policy of normalisation was initiated in November 1968 with a proposal for the conclusion of a treaty based on the "Five Principles of Peaceful Coexistence". Although this particular suggestion did not meet with US approval, the area of understanding between the two countries (dealt elsewhere in this study)[105] was

180

considerably enlarged. A number of problems still persist, but it is indeed remarkable that Beijing-Washington relations have come such a long way in such a short time, since a few years ago the two countries hardly communicated with each other.

The European continent was the other important object of Chinese diplomacy. Having been varyingly characterized as the "second intermediary zone,"[106] or "the Second World",[107] or as one of the five major power centres of the international system,[108] Europe began to occupy an even more important position in the Chinese perception than the United States did.[109]

First of all, China no longer perceived a real conflict of interest with Europe. There were no major issues that remained outstanding and no major controversies that needed to be resolved. With Asian and African decolonization, the ex-colonial powers of Europe had no imperial interests to defend, no discernible ambitions to economically dominate the Third World, and no apparent capacity or inclination to assert themselves in the international system. In fact, like the Third World, Europe was viewed as having become a victim of superpower contention and a potential partner with which considerable scope of dialogue, understanding, and even joint action was possible. "These countries too," wrote a Chinese observer, "were subjected to the control, intervention and bullying of the two overlords to varying degrees, and the contradictions between these countries and the two superpowers are daily developing".[110]

Secondly, Europe had indeed evolved from the days of the "Cold War". Many of the nations which had hitherto constituted an integral but subservient part of the bipolar system had begun to assert themselves by the late 1960s. In the economic and political domains they were no longer prepared to completely accept the views and objectives of the superpowers; and they were no longer willing to subscribe unconditionally to the foreign policy frameworks designed by their senior partner. Admittedly, there were a number of political, military, and economic imperatives—more in Eastern than in Western Europe—that constituted major constraints for the countries involved in cutting themselves off from Moscow or Washington, but the fact remains that the alliance systems were no longer the same.

The Chinese leaders, preoccupied as they were with the continuous escalation of the Sino-Soviet dispute, viewed this as an important development within the international system. In most of the writings and declarations that emanated from Beijing, in which a general evaluation was made of the constellation of forces in international politics, Europe, as an independent phenomon, was given a prominent place. The editorial department of the *People's Daily* declared that:

> The establishment of the Common Market in Western Europe, the independent policies pursued by France under de Gaulle, the passive and critical attitude taken by the West European countries towards the US war of aggression in Vietnam, Cambodia and Laos, the collapse of the dollar-centred monetary system in the capitalist world and the sharpening trade and currency wars between Western

Europe on the one hand and the United States on the other—all these facts mark the disintegration of the former imperialist camp headed by the United States.[111]

At the same time, the Chinese also underlined the development of contradictions with the Soviet bloc. Moscow, according to them, was "sitting on the volcano of the resistance of the people of the East European countries."[112] "Uneasiness," in their view, was "growing among the East European people, and the struggle to defend their independence, security and equal rights is gathering momentum."[113]

Thirdly, most of the European nations have continuously viewed Russian policies, behaviour and intentions with considerable alarm. In the 19th century, when alliances had been forged by some of them with the Tsarist empire to face other threats or to balance the international power equation, Russian objectives and designs did not fail to haunt a number of European countries. After the Bolshevik revolution, the level of mistrust in Soviet intentions rose; and with Russia's acquisition of superpower status and the Sovietization of Eastern Europe in the aftermath of World War II, European apprehension regarding Soviet intentions reached new heights which even the recent atmosphere of détente has not been able to obliterate. It should be recalled that with the escalation of the Sino-Soviet dispute, some similarity had indeed appeared in Chinese and European perceptions insofar as the former have ceased to make any distinction between the old Tsars and the "new Tsars in the Kremlin".[114] A Chinese commentator wrote:

> Two dynasties—the Romanov dynasty and the Khruschev-Brezhnev dynasty—are linked by a black line, that is the aggressive and expansionist nature of great Russian chauvinism and imperialism. The only difference is that the latter dons a cloak of "socialism" and is "social imperialism" in the true sense of the word.[115]

Fourthly, for a nation like China, which is in the throes of economic development, Europe was perceived as an important economic partner. With the abandonment of the autarkical policy of the 1960s and the launching of a very ambitious developmental programme in late 1972 involving the importation of complete factories and power plants, Europe with its remarkably developed base in aerospace, communications, transportation, shipping, etc., was viewed as an area from which China could obtain important economic benefits. In fact, Europe appeared to offer the only sensible and viable option. Curiously enough, the Japanese were regarded in some sectors as technologically inferior to the Europeans, and the United States was viewed as politically unattractive as suppliers of capital goods.[116] Already in 1974, next to Japan, Europe had become China's biggest trading partner,[117] and according to information that has appeared in the European press, trade prospects have become even greater with the emergence of new Chinese wealth in oil and natural gas.[118]

Finally, in the military field, Europe—already China's biggest supplier—could replace obsolescent elements of her armed forces. Dwindling air power through obsolescence is China's most critical military problem. Her 3,000 Soviet-built MIG-17s, MIG-19s and 200 MIG-21s cannot match Soviet aircraft. Despite relative success in building missiles and atomic warheads,[119] the Chinese have been unable to develop on their own the difficult metal technology and high-altitude test chambers to make high-performance jet engines.[120] But obsolescence is not only limited to air power. China's ground force and naval equipment is also based largely on the technology of the 1950s. Only seven of the 156 Chinese divisions are armoured and their equipment is much inferior to modern Soviet designs. China's navy, though the world's third largest, is about twenty years out of date in anti-submarine warfare and other underwater sensing devices.[121] China, therefore, is manifesting great interest in European military technology. The conclusion of a $160 million contract with Great Britain (December 1975) under which Rolls Royce jet engines and technology had been provided to Beijing for their manufacture,[122] the agreement to buy military engine Atar-9 K-50 which powers the latest French Mirages,[123] and the keen interest China has shown in purchasing large numbers of Harrier jump jets are some of the important examples of Europe's attractions.

But what about Europe? Are the European nations also interested in developing relations with China? Do they consider that Beijing could be helpful in advancing European objectives and interests?

Evidently all the European nations do not consider that the development of close relations with Beijing are vital. There are, for instance, a number of East European nations who are unable or unwilling to go beyond a simple normalisation of relations. Either the Soviet constraints are too severe or the ideological differences with Beijing are too basic. But the majority of them—principally in Western Europe but some in Eastern Europe—seem to have realized the vital importance of Beijing for the advancement of their own interests. All the government delegations exchanged between Europe—Eastern, as well as Western Europe—and China, the visits made by executives of Western companies to China, the trade exhibitions held to explain and sell European merchandise,[124] the extraordinary Chinese buying spree in the European markets, and the quantum of contracts that have been concluded in recent years under which European nations have set up a wide spectrum of complete plants in China are all examples of this growing interest. Undoubtedly, China is viewed as the "next growth market" for the European nations.[125]

But this evidently is not the only reason. The Europeans also consider China a significant counterbalance to Soviet power. The NATO countries have "now decided that it is in their interest to help China keep up its military strength,"[126] and a growing number of exceptions are therefore being made to the general ban that was imposed after 1949 on the export of strategic goods to China.[127]

If, however, considerable convergence is discernible between European and Chinese thinking, there are areas of disagreement, the most important of which is the Chinese insistence on the evaluations European nations ought to make of Soviet behaviour and the policies they should adopt towards Moscow. Since 1970 China has consistently attacked the whole gamut of international negotiations and agreements in which the Soviet Union has been directly involved and which have resulted in an improvement of the international political atmosphere. For the Chinese, this is a smoke screen for ultimate Soviet domination; whether it was disarmament negotiations or SALT or MBFR or even simply East-West economic relations, they have spared no effort and no media to scathingly attack Soviet motivations. To cite just a few examples, the Soviet-West German Treaty of 1970 was characterised as "a betrayal of interests of the German people, of the Soviet people, and of all the peoples of Europe";[128] and the European Security Conference was viewed as a Soviet attempt to "preserve the status quo in Europe."[129]

Almost all the European leaders who streamed through Beijing were informed with disconcerting repetition that Europe was the focus of superpower contention, that it was "still in a state of aggravating armed confrontation,"[130] and that the objectives of Soviet diplomacy were nothing more than a concerted attempt to dominate the entire world. To encourage the Europeans to adopt an anti-Soviet stance, the Chinese even abandoned their own repeatedly proclaimed view that their country was Moscow's principal target[131] and replaced it with a new line which stressed that "Soviet Union's strategic offensive" was "spearheaded in the first place against the West."[132] Two-thirds of the Soviet armed forces, the Europeans were warned, were concentrated along the Soviet Union's western frontiers and were all set to establish "a military hegemony on the continent."[133]

The European reaction to the "era of negotiations" (with the exception of Albania) was generally as follows: we grant, they argued, that the Soviet Union should be regarded with some mistrust, and we admit that there often does exist a wide gap between Soviet declarations and real Soviet intentions; the European nations, therefore, should be on their guard. But what, they insisted, are the alternatives to a policy of negotiations and détente? In their view, there were none.

However, notwithstanding all these pressures and even warnings,[134] the Chinese were nonetheless realistic and flexible enough not to permit these differences to interfere with their policy of seeking a rapprochement with Europe—for within the framework of the existing international situation and the changing constellation of international forces an understanding with Europe had become a vital necessity for China's national and security interests. Therefore, with a throughness that was impressive and a perception that was remarkably free from rigid ideological preconceptions, a new framework of foreign policy was designed for Eastern as well as Western Europe.

184

Eastern Europe

The first signs of change in the Chinese attitude towards Eastern Europe were visible soon after the Soviet intervention in Czechoslovakia. Most of the region, heretofore considered hopelessly tied to the Soviet orbit, was perceived after 1968 to be showing varying signs of autonomous behaviour on an impressive array of issues: East European disenchantment with the Soviet Union had increased, disappointment with Western Europe's abstentious attitude during the Czechoslovak crisis had become wide-spread, and the envious fascination with the successful Chinese defiance of Moscow had swelled to include ever-larger segments of the East European population.[135]

Even more significant in the Chinese view was that the continuously expanding Soviet "colonialist economic control" over Eastern Europe[136] had increased the level of discontent and had given an impetus to the "separatist tendency among the exploited nations."[137] The most important signs of this new trend were the increasing determination of Council of Mutual Economic Assistance (CMEA) nations to tap their own energies and to develop economic relations with Western European as well as Third World countries.[138]

It was perhaps this new evaluation, compounded with the perception of a Soviet threat to their own security, that served as a major catalyst to the Chinese activation of their hitherto dormant policy towards the area as a whole. This does not mean that the Chinese suddenly began to have visions of possessing any great capacity for rocking the Soviet boat in Eastern Europe or of having developed a military capability strong enough to come promptly to the assistance of small nations who were threatened by their powerful neighbour. Far from it. They were too conscious of their own limitations;[139] however, new conclusions were arrived at and the rapidly evolving situation in Eastern Europe was perceived to require a new response—even if this could not be backed by a credible military policy in the area.

One of the first visible signs of change was the extension of radio trans-missions (so far limited to Russian and Serbo-Croatian) to include the Czech, Slovak, Polish, and Rumanian languages. To emphasize the impor-tance Beijing attached to these broadcasts, they were relayed by Albanian radio transmitters during the peak hours of the evening to provide clearer reception in the target areas and to reach a wide number of listeners.[140] The contents of the broadcasts were carefully selected to respond to the aspi-rations of the area. Having realized the ineffectiveness of ideologically oriented transmissions, the main Chinese propaganda thrust was on denouncing Moscow, on comparing the Soviet invasion of Czechoslovakia with US actions in Vietnam, and on underlining the details of Soviet "colonialist" plunder of the region.[141]

China also initiated a campaign to normalise inter-state relations which had seriously deteriorated with the escalation of the Sino-Soviet dispute. Ambassadors were once again despatched to the whole of Eastern Europe,[142] different economic and cultural agreements were concluded, and the level of criticism directed at East European leaders was carefully lowered. One of the most important manifestations of this process of normalisation was the two-fold increase in trade with CMEA countries between 1970 and 1976[143] (see Table 5.2). It is noteworthy that within this general framework, the Chinese attempted to design a two-pronged policy: the one broad enough to encompass even the non-Communist countries of the Balkan peninsula, the other narrowly focussed on the three Communist dissidents states of the area.

Broad Balkan Cooperation

The broad and wide-ranging Balkan policy was designed to respond to developments in the area. The perception of a mounting Soviet threat resulting from an egregious increment of Russian global power and the waning of US influence accruing from her hesitation to intervene actively in conflictual situations led to the manifestation of an autonomous geopolitical approach by the nations which constitute the Balkans. Notwithstanding the numerous issues that divide them, a two-phase process of drawing closer appears to have been set off which may eventually have important repercussions in Europe.[144] The first phase was characterised by greater bilateral interaction. Beginning around 1970, this has already resulted in the re-establishment of diplomatic relations among the Balkan nations, in the development of economic ties, and in the exchange of high-level political visits, often culminating in joint declarations upholding the familiar principles of respect of sovereignty, territorial integrity, and non-interference in the internal affairs of each other.

The second phase, which began in 1975, was characterized by multilateral consultations, and in January 1976 a conference was held, attended by Bulgaria, Greece, Rumania, Turkey and Yugoslavia, where common non-political problems were discussed.[145] That such a conference ended without even making the decision regarding where and when to hold the next meeting is less surprising and less important than that such a conference was held at all; for when one takes into account the fact that the Balkans—often characterized in the past as the "powder keg of Europe"—is still a geopolitical potpourri where client states of the United States, the Soviet Union, and China coexist in an area slightly larger than New England, the conference was certainly an important development.

In China's constant search for counterweights to balance the expanding Soviet influence, the new developments in the Balkans did not go unnoticed by the Chinese. Bilateral relations with all the states of the area, including Greece and Turkey, were therefore established.[146] And, at the same time, she realized the potential importance of multilateral Balkan cooperation,

Table 5.2. *Trade with Socialist Countries*
(*in millions of dollars*)

	1972		1973		1974		1975		1976	
	Imports to China	Exports from China	Imports to China	Exports from China	Imports to China	Exports from China	Imports to China	Exports from China	Imports to China	Exports from China
USSR	120	135	135	135	145	140	130	150	200	200
Eastern Europe (excl. Yugoslavia and Albania)	265	230	300	305	360	405	505	480	550	525

and welcomed it even before it was convened. As an article in the Chinese press emphasized:

> The Balkan Peninsula belongs to the Balkan people, and the Balkan problem should be solved by the people of the Balkan countries themselves. No outside force whatsoever has the right to interfere in Balkan affairs or encroach upon the Balkan countries' sovereignty and independence . . . The Balkan countries are daily strenghtening their relations and are taking effective measures to safeguard their national independence and State sovereignty . . ."[147]

Recently, the Chinese have reiterated their interest in this development. During his visit to Athens in September 1978, the Chinese Foreign Minister expressed the hope that Balkan cooperation would be activated.[148]

The Three Dissidents

For a number of obvious reasons, the main thrust of China's policy in Eastern Europe, however, was directed towards Albania, Yugoslavia, and Rumania. In the first place, the three Balkan nations had acquired varying degrees of independence from the Soviet Union. The Albanians had successfully defied Moscow and were carrying out an intense polemical campaign against Soviet "revisionists"; the Yugoslavs had, since 1948, resisted all Soviet attempts to make them toe the line, and Yugoslavia had become a leading member of the non-aligned world with which China had already established close relations; and the Rumanians had assumed an independent posture on a wide array of international issues, including the Sino-Soviet dispute. All these independent voices functioned to erode Soviet influence in the area—an area in which the Soviet Union had hitherto exercised considerable authority. Secondly, the projection of a nationalist image by the defiant Communist states had given to the three governments a level of legitimacy and popularity which was far more deep-rooted and far more widespread than that of other East European governments. And lastly, after 1969 the three countries had turned to each other, creating thereby an autonomous web of interaction within the wider European socialist system. This process began with the forging of ties between Rumania and Yugoslavia, including regular consultations at the highest levels and joint economic collaboration on a few economic projects.[149] Each country furthermore tended to view threats to the other as threats to their own security, a fact that was clearly exemplified by the sharp Yugoslav reaction to the Soviet campaign against Rumania after Ceausescu's return from Beijing in the summer of 1971. In addition to the bond caused by their common fear of the Soviet Union, this "deepest and most fertile collaboration"[150] was made possible by the fact that the two countries had a history of unclouded friendship and by the geopolitical constant that while Rumania separates Yugoslavia from Russia, Yugoslavia is for Rumania the only neighbouring country which is not a member of the Warsaw Pact, and she thereby forms a bridge with the Mediterranean and the West.

The process of normalisation had also included Albania. Since the invasion of Czechoslovakia and the commencement of the Sino-US rapprochement, this inward-looking and isolated nation has been forced to widen her contacts with the outside world. Her relations with Rumania have steadily improved, particularly in the economic field. Ties with Yugoslavia have also been forged. Particularly after the Czechoslovakian crisis, Albania began to regard greater Balkan cooperation as vital and went so far as to pledge assistance to Yugoslavia in case of Soviet attack.[151] The gradual improvement of relations began with the formal re-establishment of diplomatic relations between the two countries and with the conclusion of a five-year trade agreement in 1971. That this was an important milestone can be gauged by the fact that the two countries had been in a continuous conflictual state for a number of years, and still regard each other with considerable misgivings and distrust.

China proceeded to systematically develop relations with Rumania and Yugoslavia and forged even closer ties with Albania. In fact, it soon became evident that a new pattern of relationships had slowly emerged.

One of the first manifestations of this pattern was the despatching of ambassadors to the three capitals: in May 1969 to Tirana, in June to Bucarest, and in November to Belgrade. Party delegations were exchanged on a regular basis with Rumania and Albania. With Yugoslavia, however, Beijing scrupulously abstained from such relationships until 1976. The establishment of this distinction until that year can be principally attributed to the basic guidelines that China had established during the Maoist period in regard to her relations with the outside world. Whereas she had increasingly practised a remarkable flexibility in developing inter-state relations with all countries irrespective of their socio-economic structures, she has shown an equally remarkable degree of consistent inflexibility in abstaining from establishing inter-party ties with "revisionist" parties, even if they had defied Moscow. Regarding office-holding parties, however, this policy was gradually cast to the winds after the death of Mao Zedong in 1976; and in line with growing pragmatism increasingly discernible in Chinese diplomatic behaviour, party relations have begun to improve. The most dramatic and climactic demonstration of this important development was made by Hua Guofeng on the occasion of his official visit to Yugoslavia, when he clearly stated that relations between the two parties "are based on Marxism-Leninism."[152]

China had also sent high-powered military delegations to the three defiant states, an honour which she bestowed on very few countries. The exchange of such delegations with Albania and Rumania had resulted in the disbursing of important military aid and the issuing of sharp declarations that the Chinese would assist their friends in any way they could.[153] Although the exchange of military delegations between Yugoslavia and China does not appear to have resulted in any concrete assistance to the former, the visits were used to underline the importance of cooperation between the armies of the two nations. Lieutenant-General Branislav Joksic, leader of the Yugoslav military delegation to Beijing, publicly expressed the belief in October 1974 that his visit would serve to enhance cooperation between the armies of Yugoslavia and China.[154]

Trade relations with the three countries were also rapidly developed. With Rumania, the total trade turnover increased from $ 66 million in 1966 to $ 300 million in 1974[155] and to about $ 650 million in 1977, making her China's fourth largest trade partner.[156] With Yugoslavia, it increased from about $ 2.1 million in 1966 to about $ 140 million in 1974,[157] but decreased to $ 100 million in 1977.[158] And with Albania it increased from $ 120 million in 1966 to a much higher level in the early 1970s—a level which accounted for more than 50 per cent of the total trade.[159]

The area also received economic assistance from Beijing. To the Albanians, China has already disbursed the sum of about $ 5.500 billion since 1954. Of the 142 industrial projects for which credits were committed, 91 have already been completed, 23 substantially completed or well underway, and only 17 are still at the design stage following survey. The industries covered by this programme were iron and steel, chemical fertilizers, caustic soda, production of acids, glass, paper and plastics, copper processing, and armament manufacture (all new to Albania), and major additions to the nation's capacity in electricity generation, coal, petroleum, machine tools, light industry, textile, building materials, communication, and broadcasting.[160] To the Rumanians, a $ 245 million interest-free loan was given to permit them to buy equipment and to obtain assistance for the installation of complete projects.[161] Additional agreements for long-term interest-free loans and technical assistance were signed on 28 October 1971,[162] on 30 September 1974,[163] and on 3 July 1975.[164] No loans have so far been given to Yugoslavia, but the Chinese have been chartering an increasing number of Yugoslav ships for transportation to China of not only Yugoslav goods but also those of Hungary and Austria.[165] Furthermore, Beijing has also indicated that it is prepared to buy ships, ship equipment, trucks, and locomotives from Yugoslavia, even if prices are not competitive.[166]

But all these attempts to make a dent in the area have met with only limited success—for neither the countries of the Balkan Peninsula nor the three Communist dissident states were prepared to take any major steps or initiatives in the direction of Beijing that would chafe Moscow. The geopolitical constraints are too great to permit them to adopt policies that would be perceived by the Soviet leaders as inimical to their national interests. Establishment of normal and even friendly relations was something to which Moscow really could not object, but injecting an unusual warmth into relations with Beijing might indeed have been viewed as an inadmissible provocation which, under the circumstances, might have proven dangerous to their own interests. Greece and Turkey were too tied to the Western world, and were, at the same time, too eager to establish a friendship with Moscow for the sake of their respective national interests to

190

indulge in close relations with faraway China; and non-aligned Yugoslavia and autonomous Rumania were too involved in establishing equilibrated relations with most of the countries to go further than they already had where China was concerned.

Even China's closest ally in Eastern Europe, Albania, attempted to limit her relations with Beijing, though by no means for the same reasons as Rumania and Yugoslavia. Already concerned by the normalisation of Sino-American relations and the declining role of ideology in post-Maoist domestic and foreign policy formulations, she became visibly alarmed at the extraordinary interest that the new Chinese leaders had begun to focus on Yugoslavia, a traditional enemy of Albania. The quantum of articles and press coverage on Yugoslavia had clearly increased, whereas those concerning Albania had considerably declined (see Table 5.3). The exchange of high-level delegations between the two countries had also significantly increased,[167] and these were crowned by Tito's visit to China in August/September in 1977 and Hua Guofeng's visit to Belgrade in August 1978.

For Albania, China had indeed gone beyond the acceptable level of normalisation. The ties between the two began to weaken. A process of deterioration has in fact set in, the most important signs of which are the passing of anti-Chinese tracts in European capitals, the withdrawal of Chinese aid to Albania, and the Albanian denunciation on 29 July 1978 of China's policies.[168]

Table 5.3. *Chinese Press Attention to Yugoslavia and Albania 1969-1977*

Year	Albania articles (number)	Yugoslavia articles (number)
1969	136	5
1970	155	20
1971	264	76
1972	300	69
1973	187	54
1974	163	55
1975	145	81
1976	91	58
1977 (to mid-Aug.)	33	71

Sources: American Consulate General, Hong Kong, *Survey of China Mainland Press and Survey of People's Republic of China Press Indices,* 1969-1977.

Western Europe

China's policy towards Western Europe also underwent a sea change. Patterned after the framework already established for the socialist countries of Eastern Europe, it sought to focus attention on seeking another and—hopefully more viable—counterweight to the expanding influence of the Soviet Union.

This new interest, increasingly evident in the early 1970s, was circumstantially and qualitatively different from that shown in the early 1960s for the following reasons. Firstly, whereas a decade earlier, ideological elements were still discernible in Chinese policies,[169] they had disappeared by the early 1970s, and had been replaced by the more palpable inducements of national security and modernisation. The significance of this major transformation does not reside so much in the up-grading of national interest—for this had occurred before—but in the fact that so soon after the termination of the ideologically saturated Cultural Revolution, ideological considerations had been jettisoned.

Secondly, whereas in the 1960s,[170] China's attitude towards Western Europe was circumscribed by her interests in the Third World, the roles of the two areas had reversed in the 1970s. Europe had increasingly become the focal point of Chinese attention, and the Third World—at least in operational terms—had been apportioned a secondary position.

Thirdly, unlike in the 1960s, a decade later Western Europe had acquired a political and economic personality of her own and had begun to show visible signs of wanting to play an autonomous role within the international system. The Gaullist policy of national independence, culminating in the French withdrawal from NATO, and the building-up of the *Force de Frappe tous azimuts* (multidirectional nuclear strategy) was fairly advanced. The problem of Britain's oscillation between the Commonwealth, the United States, and Europe was resolved in favour of her European partners with her entry into the Common Market in January 1973. For the Federal Republic of Germany, a choice between a Bonn-Washington axis and her European partners had become even more problematic. Italy, drawn more deeply into the domestic whirlpool of instability and of rising communism, was no longer able to voice openly and clearly her Atlantic loyalties. And the process of democratisation, in full swing in Spain and Portugal, had brought to the fore political forces which appeared to be more interested in seeking close ties with Western Europe than with the United States.

Fourthly, the early 1970s also witnessed intense activity aimed at strengthening the European Economic Community as a distinct unit. A series of measures were agreed upon at the Hague summit meeting in December 1969, intended to intensify political cooperation among its members, to take appropriate steps for the eventual establishment of a European economic and monetary union, to set off the process of enlarging the Community, and to extend the budgetary powers of the European Parliament. Further, Western Europe had become—and was recognised as such by the Chinese—an important technological centre whose assistance could be of considerable value to China in acquiring a modernised economy and up-to-date military weapons.[171]

The first major initiative taken to seek out the area was the establishment

192

of diplomatic relations with all the countries of the region irrespective of their socio-economic systems and irrespective of their political orientations. This process was inaugurated with the establishment of relations with Italy in 1970 and was completed with the forging of similar ties with Portugal in 1979 (see Table 5.4).

The only issue on which China insisted in her negotiations for recognition was the unconditional acceptance that Taiwan was an integral part of the mainland. Different formulas, however, were used in the joint communiqués that announced the establishment of relations. Those countries which had no ties with Taiwan issued statements containing either a bland announcement on the establishment of relations (the Federal Republic of Germany) or containing a brief statement to the effect that the government in Beijing was "the sole legal government of China" (Austria and Luxembourg).[172] For those countries which had diplomatic relations with Taiwan or which had indicated in the past their preference for a "two-Chinas" formula, the Chinese insisted on the inclusion of a paragraph which not only reaffirmed Beijing's declared policy that Taiwan was "an inalienable part of the territory of the People's Republic of China" but also contained a sentence that clearly indicated that the European government concerned took "note of the statement of the Chinese government".[173]

For the Europeans accepting the Chinese formula on Taiwan this did not really constitute a major problem, since virtually none of them maintained any viable relations with the island from which they could not extricate themselves. What really constituted the major hurdle for them was the US opposition to any recognition of Beijing. This, however, had been removed by the American decision to commence her own process of bilateral normalisation in 1971. Moreover, the international pressures for recognition were indeed mounting within the United Nations system, as was evidenced by Beijing's formal admission to the United Nations in 1971.

Table 5.4. *West European Countries Having Relations with the People's Republic of China since 1970*

Austria	May 1971
Belgium	October 1971
German Federal Republic	October 1972
Greece	June 1972
Iceland	December 1971
Italy	November 1970
Luxembourg	November 1972
Spain	March 1973
Portugal	February 1979
Turkey	August 1971

The establishment of diplomatic relations was, however, considered to be only a first step, for soon thereafter China commenced a systematic campaign of establishing meaningful contact by receiving a host of West European public figures. In 1972, Beijing received Maurice Schuman in July, Walter Scheel in mid-October, Sir Alec Douglas-Home in October-November. In 1973 President Pompidou was given the red carpet treatment. In 1974, Edward Heath arrived in Beijing. In 1975 it was the turn of Chancellor Schmidt, Dom Mintoff, Franz Josef Strauss, Max van der Stoel, Sauvargnes, and Leo Tindemans. In 1976 there arrived in Beijing Anthony Crosland and Margaret Thatcher; and in 1977 Raymond Barre was received with great fanfare, followed by Juan Carlos in 1978, Gaston Thorn in 1979 and Giscard d'Estaing in 1980. From reports that appeared in the European press and from statements made by Chinese leaders on the occasions of these visits, it would seem that the Chinese seized practically all these opportunities to define in fairly precise terms their views on Western Europe, their evaluation of the international situation, and their apprehensions of Soviet global designs. Nowhere else in the world were the West European leaders given such a warm and enthusiastic reception as in China; and nowhere in the world did they hear such profuse language underlining the past suffering of the European people, the present importance of the continent, and the future key role it could play. For example, while personally receiving the French Foreign Minister, Maurice Schuman in July 1972, Mao Zedong paid an unprecedented homage to France. He said, "I cannot receive Foreign Ministers who visit China, but only Heads of State. But you, Mr. Schuman, are not the same thing. You are not only Foreign Minister. You are a minister of France."[174]

Return visits were also made by Chinese dignitories. These were systematic and well-organised and as enthusiastic as the ones made by the Europeans to China. Some of the European countries received Qiao Guanhua (Deputy Foreign Minister) in 1972, Ji Pengfei (Foreign Minister) and Bai Xiangguo (Minister of Trade) in 1973, Deng Xiaoping (Deputy Prime Minister) in 1974, Huang Hua (Foreign Minister) Gu Mu (Deputy Prime Minister) in 1978, and Hua Guofeng in 1979. The politics of this regular and almost continuous exchange of visits since 1972 has certainly served a useful purpose, for it has not only given the Europeans and the Chinese decision makers the opportunity to personally evaluate each other (undoubtedly a vital element in the game of diplomacy) but it has also made it possible for them to clearly define the limits beyond which they are not prepared to take any political and military risks. Although it could be argued that the Chinese did not need to come to Europe or the Europeans to go to Beijing to comprehend the clear reluctance of the West Europeans to rock the boat of détente, the occasions of these visits and talks have nonetheless permitted the Chinese leaders to grasp the degree of this reluctance and to understand the general West European political atmosphere, which does not lend itself to any confrontation with the Russians.

To underline the importance that China assigns to Western Europe, she has also systematically forged economic relations with the area and has begun a systematic programme of buying machinery and advanced technology from a number of nations. From the Federal Republic of Germany, for example, China agreed to buy, among other items, rolled ferrous metals, chemical products and heavy machinery. With France, she has concluded agreements to acquire complete equipment for a hydroelectric power station and for a twenty-one enterprise petro-chemical complex. And from Great Britain, she has ordered machinery, Trident aircraft, means of transport, etc. (see Table 5.5.)

But how is China going to pay for this vast programme of technological expansion, which, according to some sources,[175] may cost as much as $40 to $43 billion in the course of the eight years of the plan (1978/85)? Does she have the appropriate financial resources? Alternatively, should this not be possible, does she have the capacity to mobilise sufficiently large quantities of exportable resources to cover such a heavy bill for technological importation?

At the time of the inauguration of her economic modernisation plans, the Chinese leadership seemed determined to rely upon China's own resources to reach her targeted economic goals. This was in line with and in continuation of two decades of Maoist thinking that self-reliance was the only dignified path of growth, though some modifications had nonetheless been introduced in the concept in that the party leadership had accepted the role of commercial relations in the modernisation process.

When the quantum of international economic agreements was increased under the post-Maoist leadership, however, it became increasingly evident that the economy of even an advanced developing country such as China was far from adequate to financially and commercially cover the heavy bill for imports of turnkey projects. Either the Chinese leaders had to revert to their original Maoist politics of self-reliance or they had to go ahead with their new policy by introducing some modifications and improvements. To meet the difficult situation, they decided to opt for the latter course, undertaking a series of realistic steps which took them even further from their original and very rigid socialist framework. Firstly, the overextended development targets were moderated to make them realistically achievable. Secondly, a number of major economic orders, falling within the heavy industry sector, were either delayed or suspended; and thirdly, a series of steps were taken (a) to obtain credits from European State and private sectors,[176] (b) to adopt politics of "compensatory trade",[177] and (c) to establish mixed companies with China possessing 51 per cent of equity holdings.

Table 5.5. *List of Important Industrial Projects Valued in Excess of US $ 50 Million concluded with Principal West European Countries*

Year	Name	Item	Amount
A. Federal Republic of Germany			
1972	Demag A.G.	Ball bearing factory	$80 million
1974	Demag A.G.	Steel complex	$198 million
1974	Demag A.G.	Cast steel moulded	$58 million
1979	Zimmer A.G.	Polyester polycondensation plant	$218 million
1979	Lurgi and Metallgesell-schaft	Petro-chemicals	$300 million
1979	Lurgi and Metallgesell-schaft	Plastic and fibres industry	$546 million
B. Italy			
1973	Gruppo Electro mechnichi per impianti all estero	Power houses	$86.2 million
C. France			
1972	Petro-chemical Complex	Technipand Speichim	1200 million francs
1974	Heutrey	Fertilizers	620 million francs
D. Great Britain			
1973	Hawker Siddeley Aviation	15 planes	£50 million
1975	Rolls Royce	Supply of "Spey" engines and equipment for the production of motors in China	£80 million
1978	John Brown Ltd.	High density polyethylane plant	£26 million

The intensification of exchange visits and the establishment of diplomatic and industrial ties were not the only elements of the new bilateral Chinese diplomacy. The West European countries were also viewed as crucial in supplying arms. For one thing, a number of them, particularly France, West Germany, and Great Britain, had greatly excelled even the United States in the field of conventional weaponry; for another, they were

196

the only developed countries which were prepared to meet the Chinese needs, since both Japan and the United States were still reluctant to become involved in any arms deal with Beijing.[178] In fact, with US concurrence, they had already begun to send off signals to Beijing indicating their willingness to consider such requests by formally lifting the embargo on arms sale to China.[179]

From the different military missions sent to the region, particularly in the summer of 1978, it would seem that Beijing had made up an impressive shopping list of sophisticated items. From the British they were interested in buying Harrier jump jets, Chieftan tanks, and Rolls Royce aero engines; from the French they were eager to obtain anti-tank and anti-aircraft missiles and the French Mirage fighters 2000; and from the West Germans they were interested in acquiring electronic equipment like intertial guidance platforms and range finders, the highly effective Leopard tank, and some anti-tank mobile artillery.

When the dimensions of the Chinese list became evident, however, the West European countries, though obviously attracted by the prospects of reaping economic benefits, nonetheless began to show varying signs of hesitation. The West Germans declined to conclude any major deal; the French reportedly put off the completion of the $350 million agreement and have delayed giving the go-ahead to the manufacturers of the Mirage 2000 (Dassault) to negotiate an accord. Even the British, less inhibited than the others to strike an arms agreement, hesitated for more than seven years before announcing their readiness in January 1979 to open negotiations concerning the sale of Harrier jets.[180]

These general signs of vacillation were principally due to intense Soviet pressures against the conclusion of such agreements with China. Brezhnev threatened James Callaghan, the Prime Minister, of serious consequences for Anglo-Soviet relations if Britain went ahead with the Harrier sales.[181] Gromyko reportedly pressured the French to sell only defensive weapons to China.[182]

While the West European governments have formally resisted all external pressures and have invoked their sovereign right to take any decisions that accorded with their national interests, it was evident that pressures emanating from Moscow did have some impact in dissuading them—at least for the time being—from concluding any major arms deals with China.

Even more striking than all these bilateral ties was the support extended by the Chinese to the unification of Western Europe. Originally in 1970 when China for the first time became a partisan of political and military integration of the area, she had expected that it would be achieved by the West Europeans themselves, independently of the United States. Only through the autonomous attainment of this goal, the argument ran, would they be able to project themselves as an independent factor within the international system.

However, not more than a year later China went even further: instead of continuing to proclaim the crucial necessity for autonomous integration, she began to support West European integration within the wider NATO framework; instead of demanding the departure of US troops, she now favoured their continued presence; and instead of considering the whole NATO military potential as a threat to world peace she now viewed it as "meeting the interests not only of the defence of independence and security of these countries but the interests of the peoples of all the countries of the world."[183]

This process of change went through two phases: the first, lasting until 1976, was discreet and diplomatic, and the second, beginning in that year, was strident and rhetorical. For the first time, during the second half of 1972, the change became visible, particularly on the occasion of Walter Scheel's visit to Beijing in the autumn of that year. Thereafter on a number different occasions they gave their approval to the US military presence in Western Europe.[184] It was, however, on the occasion of Tindeman's visit to Beijing in 1975 that the Chinese attitude became more than apparent on the question. Since the West Europeans, they argued, were unable to unite, "it was better for them to continue their support to NATO in the face of Soviet political and military pressures."[185] During Helmut Schmidt's visit in October-November 1975, they made it clear that they were satisfied with the close defence collaboration between the United States and Europe. In fact, the German Chancellor stated in a press conference that he had "not heard one negative remark about the United States."[186]

The strident and rhetorical phase began in the mid-1970s, particularly after the death of Mao Zedong, with the publication of a series of declarations underlining the Soviet threat to Europe,[187], stressing the importance of unity,[188] appealing to the West "to strengthen Western defences to oppose the Soviet threat,"[189] and even suggesting that China was "the Eastern NATO."[190]

Why this change? Why was China, critical of the United States as late as January 1970,[191] now prepared to go so far as to not only favour the continuation of her military presence in Western Europe but also her reinforcement? How could she explain this *volte face* to the militants within China herself and their friends outside? How could she square this new attitude with her own Marxist framework in which the United States, together with the Soviet Union, were denounced as the two superpowers out to dominate the world.

A number of elements led to this major shift. First of all, the Chinese rapidly realised that Western Europe was unable to create an independent and viable deterrent system on her own. The whole area was politically too divided to develop an integrated defence system; moreover, this would have required a gigantic financial effort from the West European governments, which they were either unable or unwilling to make in view of their deep immersion in economic affairs. Furthermore, by 1973, China had come to

198

the conclusion that the focal point of "the Soviet Union's strategic offensive" had shifted from the Sino-Soviet border to that of the West,[192] where through a well-organised carrot-and-stick policy she was aiming to drive a wedge between the West Europeans and the Americans in order to "disintegrate Western Europe and dominate the whole of Europe."[193]

Since the succesful freezing of the Soviet western flank would inevitably lead to serious repercussions on the international balance of power and would permit the Soviet Union to once again turn threateningly to China, European military integration, under effective US leadership, had become crucial to Chinese security.

The European Economic Community

If reconciliation with the US military presence in Europe was viewed as essential, the Chinese, on the other hand, perceived Western Europe as being sufficiently strong to become an independent economic and political power centre. In fact, argued China, Washington was exercising considerable pressure on Western Europe "to sacrifice their economic interests, to support the ever-weakening dollar, and to maintain its privileged status as the reserve currency of the capitalist world."[194] Support of the European Community was thus in line with the new Chinese thinking. "We support" declared Deng Xiaoping in 1975, "the Union of Western Europe and we want to create a powerful Western Europe."[195]

Chinese interest in the European Community[196] first became discernible in the summer of 1971 with the publication in the press of a series of news items on its development.[197] On the occasion of the Pompidou-Heath talks in May 1971 regarding British admission to the Community, a Chinese weekly declared that the "trend of these countries getting united to challenge contention by US imperialism and social imperialism is developing further."[198] During Ceaucescu's visit to Beijing in June 1971, Zhou Enlai, while welcoming the trend of independence among medium and small countries, stated that a "new development has also taken place in the multifarious struggle of many European countries which are uniting to resist the aggression, control, and interference of big powers."[199] And on the successful conclusion of British-Common Market negotiations in June 1971, the Chinese press became even more categorical. It declared:

> With the relative strengthening of the Common Market and the weakening of US imperialism the trend has become increasingly evident in which these countries strengthen their union politically so as to jointly oppose the power politics of US imperialism and domination and control of Europe by two overlords—the United States and the Soviet Union.[200]

It is not without significance that in all these initial declarations, the Chinese highlighted what they considered to be the anti-American aspects of West European integration. Reviewing the Pompidou-Heath conversations, *Beijing Review* expressed the view that Britain's participation in the

Common Market "will cause further disintegration of the imperialist camp and put US imperialism in a more isolated and difficult position".[201] For them, at least until 1973, the development of the Common Market was more a setback to US imperialism than an effective countervailing power against the "social imperialists".[202] Only a few years later did they decide to focus their attention on the importance of the Community in the containment of "Soviet hegemonism", and to make only ritual reference to US "imperialism".

The change in Chinese attitude was also coincidental with the development of pro-Europeanism in British policies. In most of the Chinese analyses of the Common Market in 1971, the British decision to join the Community was given the pride of place. In fact, Zhou Enlai in one of his 1971 interviews abundantly quoted from Edward Heath's pro-European speeches, and explicitly pointed out that Britain's entry into the Community was an element in promoting China's interest in the Community.[203]

Strengthening the European Community thus became the lynchpin of Chinese diplomacy in Western Europe. And the whole weight of its rhetoric was focused upon (a) impressing upon the European leaders the vital importance of maintaining the US military presence in Europe; (b) paradoxically encouraging them to dissociate themselves politically and economically from the United States; (c) persuading them to accelerate their process of integration; and (d) attempting to convince them that the principal danger to them emanated from the Soviet Union.

In line with promoting the strength of the European Community, the Chinese, it should be noted, perceived of a closer collaboration between the "Second" and the "Third" Worlds, both of which, in their view, had the common goal of disengaging themselves from the control or the influence of the "First" World. In numerous declarations on this issue, the Chinese government therefore welcomed the Euro-Arab dialogue in the summer of 1974, [204] affixed its stamp of approval to the Lomé convention,[205] approved the negotiations between the EEC and the five-nation Central American Common Market countries, and congratulated West European countries for reaching some preliminary agreement with the developing countries in October 1975 in Paris.[206]

Chinese activities were, however, not limited to rhetorical declarations where the European Economic Community was concerned. They were also operational. With the opening of the Chinese embassy in Belgium in 1972, informal contacts were established between the embassy and the European Commission in order to permit Chinese officials to acquaint themselves with the work of the Community;[207] in 1973 correspondents of the China News Agency were accredited to the European Commission;[208] and with the expiry of all bilateral treaties between China and the members of the Community towards the end of 1974, all technical obstacles were removed to the establishment of official relations between them. Accordingly, in

November 1974, the Community forwarded to China a memorandum accompanied by an outline agreement laying down broad provisions for the conclusion of a possible trade agreement between the two parties.[209] This was followed, in the beginning of 1975, by an invitation from the Chinese Institute of External Relations to Sir Christopher Soames, then Vice-President of the Commission, to visit China.

During this trip, which lasted from 4 to 11 May, the Chinese authorities made known their decision to establish official relations with the Community as such and to send an ambassador to Brussels. At the same time, they communicated their intention to give favourable consideration to the Community's proposal for negotiations of an appropriate trade agreement between the two parties to replace the bilateral agreements.

Not much headway, however, was made in the ensuing exploratory talks. In fact, the eruption of turbulence in Chinese political life following Mao's death in 1976 shelved all contacts between China and the European Commission. Presumably this was caused by the development of disagreements within the party leadership on a wide array of basic issues pertaining to China's external economic relations. What should be, for example the nature and scope of China's economic relations with the outside world? Should they be minimal as was the case during most of the Maoist period, or should an extra effort be made in this field in order to accelerate the process of modernisation?

The controversy was finally resolved with the political elimination of the "Gang of Four", advocates of self-reliance and partisans of maintaining only minimal relations with the outside world. That these domestic convulsions were indeed a major obstacle to the development of Sino-EEC relations is evident from the fact that the subsequent Chinese initiatives to resume talks in 1977[210] coincided with the consolidation of political power of those who argued that "for the sake of furthering the cause of socialism, it is necessary to pay attention to production"[211] and to develop foreign trade.[212]

The first major sign of changed attitude appeared in June when Pu Ming, leader of a Bank of China delegation touring Europe, remarked in the course of his talks with François Ortoli, Vice President of the Commission, that China was interested in a long-term agreement to stabilise her growing trade with Europe. He also expressed confidence that the rapidly expanding Sino-European trade would exceed the trade level between China and Japan through such an agreement[213] (see Table 5.6.).

Seizing the opportunity represented by the offer, the EEC deputized in July a high-level team to begin talks with the Minister of Trade in Beijing. During the course of these talks, it became evident that the delegations were divided on two major issues: firstly, the Chinese resisted the inclusion of a safeguard clause to reimpose quotas—a standard feature of EEC agreements—in the event of a sudden influx of imports in sensitive areas or at prices far below the market median; and secondly, they wanted guarantees

Table 5.6. Trade between the Community of Nine and China (million EUA)[a]

	1958	1960	1963	1966	1967	1968	1969	1970	1971	1972	1973	1974	1975	1976	1977	1978	1979
Imports	163	235	165	357	315	318	370	348	362	418	544	722	667	858	860	940	1324
Exports	384	331	153	417	521	444	432	461	397	369	607	807	1153	1175	794	1489	2101
Balance	+221	+ 96	− 12	+ 60	+206	+126	+ 62	+113	+ 5	− 49	+ 63	+ 85	+486	+317	− 66	+ 549	+ 777[b]

Sources: SOEC Special Issue 1958-1976 and SOEC Monthly Bulletin 4/78

a   One European Unit of Account (EUA) is approximatively US $ 1.40.
b   During the first nine months.

for the balancing of trade with the EEC, which the Community's delegation could not give since this was beyond their power.[214]

Finally a five-year non-preferential trade agreement was initialled on 3 February 1978 and was formally signed two months later.[215] Without making any palpable concessions on the two points, the EEC agreed "to introduce measures extending the list of products for which imports from China had been liberalised,"[216] and accorded, under the agreement, the most-favoured-nation treatment to China—an important innovation insofar as the latter was the first state trading country for which such a concession was made.[217] The Chinese, for their part, agreed to give particularly favourable consideration to imports coming from EEC and undertook not to send low-cost items to the Community.[218]

A few months after the agreement came into force (June), the EEC authorities made a few significant concessionary gestures in the direction of Beijing. The potential capacity of the vast Chinese market to absorb Common Market exports was so large that making some demonstrative initiatives and responses was considered judicious. They introduced, with effect from 1 January 1979, new regulations to allow China to export to the Community twenty more products than were permitted under the previous restrictive regulations applicable to state trading countries, including China;[219] and they readily agreed to draw up a programme for the training of managerial staff and students. At about the same time, the Community accepted the suggestion to open negotiations (December 1978) on the ticklish problem of trade in textiles, a source of major export earnings for China. In fact, the agreement that was finally concluded appears to give to China much better terms than to any other Asian Country. Despite objections from the French—who were concerned about their own textile industry—the European Commission virtually doubled the quantity of sensitive textile products which China could export to the EEC. Quotas for 1979, for example, were set at some 40,000 tons, which would put China in fifth place among the Asian suppliers.[220]

The External Economic Relations Commission of the European Parliament went even further. It expressed the hope that the Common Market would give preferential treatment to Chinese imports[221] as against the imports emanating from countries which had not recognised the Community. Additionally, it recommended that the European Investment Bank should give loans at a favourable rate of interest and that the Community's budget should bear the burden of the *"bonification d'intérêt"*.[222]

All these initiatives have indeed resulted in the significant expansion of trade ($2.5 billion during first nine months of 1978) and in the conclusion of important economic cooperation agreements with France of $13.6 billion in December 1968 and with Great Britain of £7 billion in March 1979, including the allocation of loans[223] (see Table 5.7).

But what about the future? Can one say that there is still considerable scope for the further development of Sino-EEC relations? Is the Chinese market still big enough to continuously absorb an increasing amount of Common Market exports?

Much will of course depend on whether the Chinese, who have temporarily accepted living with deficits are prepared to renounce their politics of balancing their trade with other countries, and whether the Community in turn is prepared to refrain from applying too strictly the safeguard clauses in the event of sudden influx of Chinese imports in sensitive areas or at prices far below the market median.

From some recent developments, it would seem that the future—at least in economic terms—may not seem all that bright. The Common Market countries have increasingly become sceptical of the Chinese capacity to pay back and the Chinese have increasingly become irritated by the difficulties they have begun to face, in return for their imports, in supplying exports to a market which is becoming saturated and which is facing structural problems of unemployment. In any event, whatever the future of Sino-EEC commercial relations may be, one thing appears to be certain: the conclusion of the trade agreement between China and the EEC was an important political milestone[224] in the relations between the two new centres of power whose voices in the international system were hardly audible until recently.

Focal Point: West Germany

Within this general framework of bilateral and multilateral diplomacy, China has also sought out a focal point in the area with which some sort of a special relationship could be established—as she did in Eastern Europe. Great Britain and France were her initial choices: Great Britain because the newly elected Conservative government in 1970 had adopted a firm attitude towards the Soviet Union and had entered the European Economic Community in 1973;[225] and France because of her policy of disengagement from the United States. However, about a year or two later, when it became increasingly evident that the newly elected British Labour government in February 1974 showed signs of hesitation in using the Chinese card against Moscow, as they did in February 1974, or in merging with the European stream, and that the imperatives of the power equation had led France to seek out the Soviet Union, China increasingly turned her sights towards the Federal Republic of Germany. This does not mean that Beijing had decided to ignore France and Great Britain or minimise her relations with them. Far from it—for there appears to exist an ongoing trend towards forging ties with the two countries, the most important and dramatic manifestation of which was Hua Guofeng's visit to the two countries in October 1979. It simply means that in their evaluation of the overall situation in Western Europe, the Chinese had presumably come to the conclusion that it was perhaps in their interest to make an extra effort to cultivate Bonn.[226]

But why the Federal Republic? What are the factors that appear to have

Table 5.7. *Loan Agreements Contracted or Initialed by China* (Reported up to June 1979)

Country/institution	Amount (US$million)	Interest	Period (maturity)	Type of credit/purpose
Britain				
Ten-bank consortium, including Midland, US $400 million; National Westminster, US$300 million	1,200	7¼% standard ECGD preferential rated for two to years cr.	not announced (n.a.)	Deposit facilities financing ordinary capital goods export contracts, covering 85% of contract value
Lloyds Bank International	100	½%/LIBOR	5 years	Commercial Eurodollar credits, not tied to specific projects but may be used partly in payment for British exports
National Westminster Group	100	Probably ½% LIBOR	about 5 years	Commercial credit for import of British capital goods
Midland	100	½%/LIBOR	n.a. possibly 5 years	Commercial credits, not tied to, but may be used partly for, British exports
Standard and Chartered	100	n.a. most probably ½%/LIBOR	n.a. possibly 5 years	Commercial credits, not tied to contracts
A consortium of British, Canadian, and Australian banks	175	½%/LIBOR	5 years	Commercial credits, not tied to contracts
France				
Syndicate of more than 20 Arab and non-Arab banks led by Paris-based Union de Banques Arabes & Françaises (UBAF)	500	½%/LIBOR	3½%	United Eurodollar Loan
Italy				
Italian State Credit (IMI)	1,000	7¼% (originally offered	Terms not disclosed	Official credits, initial agreement, for Italian exports

influenced the Chinese decision? And why do they consider the Federal Republic "one of the more powerful forces of this divided continent, both in economic and political terms"?[227]

In the first place, for over two decades, West Germany has gradually and unobtrusively built the best West European conventional army comprised of a 495,000 man force and equipped with some of the most sophisticated conventional weapons.[228] Admittedly, a conventional army of this size is no match for the Russians, but then none of the armies of Western Europe, alone or together, would be able to contain a massive Soviet attack without US support. What the new *Bundeswehr* can do—and this is important—is to make a purely conventional attack increasingly costly for the Soviet Union. The precise West German mission within overall NATO strategy is to prolong the fighting long enough to permit both sides to decide whether they are prepared to commit themselves to the terrible uncertainties of nuclear war.

Secondly, as a highly industrialized nation[229] with an estimated GNP. of US$634.2 billion,[230] and possessing a sophisticated technology, West Germany was probably considered to be capable of making a far more significant contribution to China's modernisation than any other single nation of Western Europe.[231] Already the Federal Republic, as noted above, has become China's biggest European trade partner, with a total turnover of $894 million dollars in 1976;[232] and from the comments that have appeared in the press in the aftermath of an important West German industrial exhibition held in Beijing in September 1975, trade relations between the two countries are expected to become even more important[233] (see Table 5.8).

Thirdly, among the big nations of Western Europe, the Federal Republic was perhaps the most important supporter of European unification. Not only has Bonn continued to insist that integration of European nations must remain an important objective of all involved in this endeavour, but also that the Common Market must first of all set budget priorities for those projects that really enhance European unity.[234]

More than all this, however, the Federal Republic is the most dissatisfied nation of Europe because the German nation remains divided. Notwithstanding the facts that she was one of the important initiators of détente, and that an element of indifference—at least among the younger generation—seems to exist on the issue of reunification, there is perhaps no country in Europe where the number of people having reservations about détente is as high as in the Federal Republic.[235] Consider the attitude of Christian Democratic Union (CDU)/Christian Social Union (CSU) to the *Ostpolitik* initiated by Willy Brandt. While shying away from formal denunciations of such a policy, most leaders expressed serious reservations on the grounds that all principal concessions in the name of relaxation of tension were made by West Germany—with the Soviet Union reaping all the fruits. But this feeling of unease and reservation is not limited to the CDU/CSU, for there are indications that many within the Social Democratic Party (SDP)/ Free Democratic Party (FDP) coalition also feel frustrated and even cheated on some of the political concessions that have been made. They had hoped that the series of treaties concluded with East European countries, plus the four-power agreement on Berlin, would be followed by a break-through in cooperation with the East and by Moscow's acceptance of Bonn's right to represent West Berlin internationally. But all this was not forthcoming.

Table 5.8. *Total Two-Way Trade Between China and The Federal Republic* (US$)

1973	$487 million
1974	$650 million
1975	$750 million

The growing Chinese interest in the Federal Republic appears to have coincided with the removal of the major impediments that had hitherto thwarted the relations between the two countries. The United States, which had in the past exercised a restraining influence on the development of relations between the two countries, no longer constituted an obstacle. Having herself taken a series of dramatic initiatives towards normalisation of her own relations, she could hardly hold back the Federal Republic from doing the same. The East German obstacle was also removed insofar as a process of mutual recognition had begun between the two German states. If the East German state could engage in a process of normalisation, there was no reason why China could not do the same.

The most important element that contributed to the abandonment of the hesitations still discernible in China's policy towards West Germany was the East German attitude to the Sino-Soviet dispute. The unequivocal support extended by the East German state to Moscow in the Sino-Soviet dispute was perhaps the decisive element. Despite China's firm condemnation of the Soviet-West German Treaty of August 1970,[236] the conclusion of which was also received unfavourably by East Germany, the East German government and press continued to unequivocally support the Soviet Union in the Sino-Soviet dispute.

In fact, in a six-column commentary on Chinese attacks on the Soviet Union regarding the treaty, *Neues Deutschland,* the official organ of the East German Party, analysed the motivation behind these attacks as an attempt to drive a wedge between the USSR and East Germany, and the article concluded with an assertion that the latter was firmly anchored in the Socialist community and that she had in the Soviet Union her best friend and ally.[237]

For China it became increasingly evident that all efforts on her part to woo East Germany would not reap any diplomatic benefits, since the latter was too woefully tied to and dependent upon the Soviet Union.

With the removal of these impediments, a process of normalisation was initiated between the Federal Republic and China. In the summer of 1972, after almost three months of negotiations in Bonn, an agreement was concluded in September to establish diplomatic relations between the two countries. These were formally established on 11 October 1972 on the occasion of West German Foreign Minister Walter Scheel's, visit to Beijing.[238]

Nevertheless, despite this important opening between the two countries, Willy Brandt, who had indeed adopted a flexible attitude towards China in 1968,[239] became careful in not overplaying this card after he assumed the office of the Chancellor of the Federal Republic in the fall of 1969. He did not wish to jeopardize his newly-established policy of seeking an understanding with the Soviet Union or of slowing down the process of normalisation with Eastern Europe. The *"Ostpolitik"* of the new Social Democratic-Liberal coalition was considered too vital for West German interests and too important for the general process of détente to be abandoned for the sake of bringing about a pronounced rapprochement with China, which, apart from some diplomatic leverage and a limited economic market, did not appear to have much to offer.

China was understandably disappointed that the establishment of diplomatic relations with Bonn did not have the desired effect of forestalling the development of Soviet-West German relations. In fact, it seemed—since the Federal Republic had fallen in line with the other members of the Common Market by recognizing Beijing—that she had adopted an even more prudent attitude in order to avoid anything that might jeopardize her *"Ostpolitik"*. The state of her relations with Beijing thus improved or stagnated in inverse proportion to her relations with Moscow: the more smooth they became with Moscow the more careful they became with Beijing.

Under the existing circumstances in which China's diplomatic leverage was indeed very limited and her options considerably reduced, she did what seemed most appropriate: in addition to forging significant economic ties with West Germany (more than with any other European country) for which there did not appear to exist any major political hurdle, the principal thrust of her initial policy was focussed on developing closer relations with the CDU/CSU, the opposition party. The open adoption of such a political option can be attributed to the fact that the opposition leaders appeared to have serious reservations regarding Soviet intentions, and had repeatedly made clear their hostility to the *"Ostpolitik"* initiated by Willy Brandt "because it encourages the Soviet Union to pursue an aggressive policy."[240]

Most of the important German visits to China were thus essentially limited to political leaders belonging to the opposition: in June 1972 Gerhard Schröder, ex-CDU Foreign Minister, visited Beijing, where he was received by Zhou Enlai for an exchange of views and was allowed to make a trip to a military unit, an honour which had not previously been conferred on any foreign visitor;[241] in October 1974, R. Jaeger, Bundestag Vice-President and one of the important leaders of the CSU, was publicly informed in Beijing of China's "resolute opposition to a permanent split of the German nation";[242] in January and September 1975, Franz Joseph Strauss, the leader of the CSU, whose anti-Soviet views have made him popular in China,[243] was given a welcome that is normally reserved for heads of states[244], including meetings with Mao Zedong and Zhou Enlai;[245] and in February 1976, Alfred Dregger, President of the CDU of the state of Hess was received with great honour, including a meeting with Hua Guo-feng.[246]

These visits were by no means simple courtesy calls; they were calculatingly used to attain certain goals. Schröder's visit was a precurser to the establishment of diplomatic relations between the two countries; Jaeger's and Strauss' visits led to the expansion of trade relations; and Dregger's presence in Beijing was used not only for making offers to exchange military attachés and nuclear scientists,[247] but to inform West Germany of Chinese support for German re-unification even under a capitalist system.[248]

By focussing their attention principally on the CDU/CSU, the Chinese were taking a calculated risk[249]—but it was hardly an unrealistic one, since the Christian Democrats had governed West Germany for more than fifteen years, and they appeared to possess every chance of being once again at the helm of affairs.

This one-sided Chinese focus, however, did not last long; for this "highly sensitive" Central European state "whose international position is still special as compared to other Western countries"[250] began to show prudent but nonetheless visible signs of some disenchantment with its own "Ostpolitik". The benefits reaped by the Federal Republic from such a policy did not appear to be that great. Bonn's right to represent West Berlin internationally continued to be challenged by the Soviet Union; the original West German hope of making far-reaching headway in Eastern Europe, an area of traditional influence, did not materialize; and the Soviet military presence in Eastern Europe, instead of declining in the aftermath of détente, had become so overwhelming and so menacing that it caused West German Foreign Minister Genscher to declare that "we face a highly equipped military system in the East," and led West German Defence Minister Leber to publicly state that "the threat from the Warsaw pact and the stepped-up armaments efforts in the East have made it impossible for us to slacken our defense efforts."[251]

The development of this new awareness in official West German circles, compounded with the dramatic departure of Willy Brandt in 1974 and the arrival of Helmut Schmidt—in Chinese eyes, by no means a partisan of détente[252]—created a new situation which in the Chinese eyes merited fresh attention. Those who were at the helm of affairs in the Federal Republic were then no longer ignored and were no longer viewed with the disconcerting irritation that the Chinese had often displayed in the past.

While continuing to maintain and even develop ties with the CDU/CSU, Beijing now also began to seek out the leaders of the Social Democratic-Liberal coalition. The first occasion that presented itself for this process of normalisation was the official visit of Qiao Guanhua, Chinese Foreign Minister, to Bonn in October 1974, when he was received by Chancellor Schmidt and Foreign Minister Genscher.[253] The Chancellor's subsequent visit to China in October 1975, the reception he was given—including a meeting with Mao—and the series of agreements that were concluded[254] opened up significant possibilities for forging of state-to-state ties.

The breaking down of these governmental barriers has opened new avenues. Within a period of not more than four years, the Sino-West German relations have indeed taken the Great Leap Forward, making Bonn Beijing's principal economic partner in Europe. It is significant to note that in the last two years West Germany had already concluded industrial contracts worth $ 1,064 million[255] and has pushed her two-way trade also to more than $ 1 billion.[256]

Increasing evidence now also appears to be available on the expansion of cooperation in the military field. Chinese military delegations, for instance, visited Messerschmidt-Bolkov-Blohm ammunition factories, showed an interest in buying German arms, and invited in the autumn of 1977 retired army officers, including the ex-Commander-in-Chief of NATO's Central European sector, Count Kielmannsegg, to Beijing.[257] Agreements were also reached to exchange military attachés and know-how on training military units and on civil defense.[258] And significantly, while Brezhnev was being officially welcomed in the Federal Republic in 1978, the Chinese invited three more retired military officers to Beijing, where they were received by the Chinese Minister of Defense.[259]

Sino-West German relations have thus taken a significant turn. The increasing linkage of their own security with that of Western Europe had led the Chinese to seek out the Federal Republic, whose strategic location on the periphery of Soviet-dominated areas has made her the key element in the Atlantic defense system. And the Federal Republic, more autonomous in foreign policy than before and more concerned with the mounting Soviet military presence in Eastern Europe than in the past, has probably begun to perceive the importance of China—without of course wanting to jeopardize her relations with Moscow, the improvement of which still remains her principal objective in Europe. A balance has thus been established in German relations with China and the Soviet Union. The Federal Republic is no longer restraining herself from establishing close relations with Beijing out of fear of the Russians, but at the same time, she is no longer—at least under the SPD/FDP—prepared to play the Chinese card against the Soviet Union.

210

Conclusions

Within a span of about three decades, China's perception of Europe has noticeably evolved. During the first fifteen years after the revolution, the Chinese image of Europe was that of a distant land that had lost its identity and capacity to play an independent role within the international system; Europe was an area which was no longer considered to be in the mainstream of international politics, but rather a cluster of small and disunited nations which had been thrown into the dustbin of history and replaced by other areas, more dynamic and more assertive.

This perception was cast into an ideological mold according to which principal responsibility for policy formulations towards socialist and capitalist Europe was readily left in the hands of the Soviet Union. There were brief periods when the Chinese leaders were impelled to play an autonomous role in Eastern Europe, such as in 1956, when they persuaded the Russians to intervene in Hungary and dissuaded them from taking such action in Poland. But this was essentially a role limited in time as well as in space which was abandoned with the pacification of the situation in the area.

In the aftermath of the Sino-Soviet dispute, the Chinese perception of Europe changed. It was then seen as a continent which was non-belligerent, a continent which had cast aside its colonial past, which had once again acquired a frontal position in the international system, and which had slowly begun to acquire an identity separate from that of the superpowers.

During this period, China began to design an independent policy. While officially maintaining a battery of polemical assaults highlighting Soviet "revisionism", they formulated, at the same time, an outright pragmatic diplomacy based on forging ties with European governments, irrespective of their socio-economic options. This marked dilution of the ideological factor in Chinese operational diplomacy towards Europe could be explained until about 1975 by the Chinese need to seek a countervailing power against the Soviet Union. Though this explanation is still valid, it is apparently not sufficient to comprehend new diplomacy. To it has been added the newly designed Chinese domestic objective of accelerated but non-autarkic modernization in which the European connection is viewed as equally important.

That this confluence of external and internal goals has already led to the establishment of close relations between Europe and China is evident; that they will probably develop even more intensely in due course is clear from the myriad declarations that have been made by both the sides underlining the mutuality of interests.

But the area where the Europeans generally appear to part company with the Chinese concerns the policies they ought to adopt to meet the commonly perceived danger of Soviet threat. Whereas, with the probable exception of Great Britain, the European governments, have veered around to the idea that détente is the only rational solution and that patient negotiations with the Russians on all the intractable issues is the only sane choice that is left to them; the Chinese, however, do not seem to think along these lines. To them, détente is a myth; East-West negotiations are a Machiavellian attempt to lull the Europeans to a false sense of security; and the only viable solution that is left is the continuous build-up of appropriate power to counter Soviet expansionism. In fact, in their obsessive, but perhaps understandable, concern about the Soviet threat they have gone to the lengths of disregarding any serious Marxist analysis of European socie-ties and of seeking entente with any country, any socio-economic group, or any political party that is clearly anti-Soviet.

Thus an agreement exists concerning the sources of the threat, but views diverge regarding the way it should be met. It is therefore unlikely that the Chinese would succeed in persuading their new friends to adopt the same level of rhetorical and operational belligerence as they have done vis-à-vis the Soviet Union. The war-weary Europeans, though perhaps equally eager to seek sufficient countervailing power to obtain consessions from Moscow, are nonetheless reluctant to push their advantage too far in view of the overwhelming Soviet capacity to rock the boat of détente and peace—an objective to which the Europeans appear to give utmost priority.

Notes

1. Joseph Needham, *Science and Civilization* Vols. I and II (Cambridge University Press, 1954-56); also see Etiemble, *Connaissons-nous la Chine?* (Paris: Editions Galli-mard, 1964); Raymond Dawson (ed.), *The Legacy of China* (Oxford: Oxford University Press, 1971); Isabelle and Jean-Louis Vissière (Chronologie, introduction, notices, et notes) *Lettres édifiantes et curieuses de Chine par des missionnaires jésuites 1702-1776* (Paris: Garnier-Flammarion, 1979).

2. F. S. C. Northhop, *The Meeting of East and West: An Enquiry concerning World Understanding* (New York: Macmillan, 1946), p. 376.

3. Amaury de Riencourt, *The Soul of China*, Revised edition (New York: Harper and Row, 1965), p. 153.

4. K. Marx and F. Engels, *On Colonialism* (Moscow: Foreign Languages Publishing House, n.d.), p. 36.

5. Ibid., p. 87.

6. See Ssu-yu Teng and John K. Fairbank, *China's Response to the West. A Documentary Survey 1839-1923* (Cambridge: Harvard University Press, 1954).

7. Ibid.

8. Ibid., p. 271; for analysis of intellectual currents, see H. G. Creel, *From Confucius to Mao Tse-tung* (New York: The New American Library, 1960).

9. J. Chesneaux and M. Bastid, *La Chine*, 2 Vols. (Paris: Hatier Université, 1972); also see *An Outline History of China* (Peking: Foreign Languages Press, 1958).

10.   Ishwer C. Ojha, *Chinese Foreign Policy in an Age of Transition: The Diplomacy of Cultural Despair* (Boston: Beacon Press, 1969), p. 12.

11.   Rupert Emerson, *From Empire to Nation: The Rise to Self-Assertion of Asian and African Peoples* (Boston: Beacon Press, 1966), p. 10.

12.   Ssu-yu Teng and John K. Fairbank, op cit.

13.   Lucien Bianco, *Les origines de la révolution chinoise, 1915-1949* (Paris: Editions Gallimard, 1967).

14.   Ishwer C. Ojha, op cit., p. 8.

15.   C. P. Fitzgerald, *The Birth of Communist China* (London: Penguin Books, 1964), p. 53.

16.   Lucien Bianco, op cit.

17.   According to Mao Zedong, "the salvoes of the October Revolution brought us Marxism-Leninism", *Selected Works,* op cit., Vol. IV p. 413.

18.   For details see Chapter 1.

19.   Ishwer C. Ojha, op cit., pp. 14-15.

20.   Underlining this point, Mao Zedong said in 1946: "In the Pacific the US now controls areas larger than all the former British spheres of influence there put together; it controls Japan, that part of China under Kuomingtang rule, half of Korea and the South Pacific." *Selected Works,* Vol. IV op cit., p. 99.

21.   Most of European countries maintained diplomatic relations with the Chiang Kai-shek government in Taiwan. China refused to accept any solution other than the total integration of Taiwan into China.

22.   Towards the end of the Korea War, the embargo list for China was almost twice as long as the prohibited list for the Soviet Union and Eastern Europe; see A. M. Halpern, (ed.), *Policies Toward China: Views From Six Continents* (New York: McGraw-Hill, 1965).

23.   For details, see Ibid.

24.   Klaus H. Pringsheim, "New Dimensions in China's Foreign Policy", *The China Quarterly,* 4 (1960).

25.   H. Arthur Steiner, "Mainsprings of Chinese Communist Foreign Policy", *American Journal of International Law,* 1 (1950).

26.   In the current Sino-Soviet dispute, the Chinese declared that in 1954 it was Khruschev who proposed that they improve relations with Yugoslavia "for the purpose of winning it back to the path of socialism." China did so, although "we did not entertain very much hope for the Tito clique even then"; *People's Daily,* 26 September, 1963.

27.   The editor-in-chief of *Tribuna Ludu,* Stanislaw Brodzski, underlined on 8 October 1956 the importance given to democratic principles in the new statues adopted by the 8th Congress of the Chinese Party and the need for the Polish Party to emulate it. In an article in the October issue of the monthly journal of the party, *Zycre Partii,* Polish economist Oscar Lange highlighted the Chinese Party's tolerance of different ideological and cultural currents and considered that this example could "help many fraternal parties of Eastern Europe to resolve many of their problems." See *La Documentation Française: Notes et études documentaires,* No. 3238 (1965). Also see Tamas Aczel, "Hungary: Glad Tidings from Nanking", and Leopold Labedz, "Poland the Small Leap Sideways", *China Quarterly,* 3 (1960).

28.   *People's Daily,* 1 November, 1956.

29.   Ibid.

30.   These principles are (*a*) mutual respect for each other's territorial integrity; (*b*) mutual non-aggression; (*c*) mutual non-interference in each other's internal affairs; (*d*) equality and mutual benefit; (*e*) peaceful coexistence. These principles were first

enunciated in 1954 in a statement made by the prime ministers of India and China.

31. *People's Daily*, 1 November, 1956.
32. Tamas Aczel, loc cit.
33. Leopold Labedz, loc cit., p. 98.
34. Tamas Aczel, loc cit., p. 94.
35. Paul Zinner, *National Communism and Popular Revolt in Eastern Europe: a Selection of Documents on Events in Poland and Hungary Feb.-Nov. 1956* (New York: Columbia University Press, 1957).
36. "The origin and development of the differences between the leadership of the CPSU and ourselves", *in Polemic on the General Line of the International Communist Movement* (Peking: Foreign Languages Press, 1965), p. 69.
37. *Shih Chih Shin*, 30 November 1956. English translation published in *Extracts of China Mainland Magazine*, No. 64 (1956).
38. *Polemic on the General Line of the International Communist Movement*, op cit., p. 69.
39. Ibid.
40. In a speech on 2 December 1959 given in Budapest, Khruschev admitted that while discussing the question of Soviet intervention in Hungary, the question cropped up "among our comrades whether the Hungarian comrades would take our assistance in the right spirit"; N. S. Khruschev, *World With Our Arms, Without War*, Book 2 (Moscow: Foreign Languages Publishing House, n.d.), p. 459.
41. *Polemic on the General Line of the International Communist movement*, op cit., p. 69.
42. Khruschev suggests in his memoirs that Liu Shaoqi, with whom the Soviet leaders had dicussions on the Hungarian crisis, appeared as hesitant as the Soviet leaders; N. S. Khruschev, *Khruschev Remembers* (New York: Bantam, 1971).
43. O. B. Borisov and B. T. Koloslov, *Sino-Soviet Relations 1945-1973: A Brief History* (Moscow: Progress Publishers, 1975), p. 71.
44. Zbigniew K. Brzezinski, *The Soviet Bloc*, Revised edition (New York: Frederick A. Praeger, 1961); K. S. Karol, *Visa pour la Pologne* (Paris: Gallimard, 1958).
45. Flora Lewis, *A Case History of Hope: The Story of Poland's Peaceful Revolutions* (New York: Doubleday, 1958); Jacques Lévesque, *Le conflit sino-soviétique et l'Europe de l'Est: Ses incidences sur les conflits soviéto-polonais et soviéto-roumain* (Montréal: Les Presses de l'Université de Montréal, 1970).
46. Flora Lewis, op cit.
47. *More on the Historical Experience of the Dictatorship of the Proletariat* (Peking: Foreign Languages Press, 1957), p. 35.
48. Ibid., p. 37.
49. See Sino-Soviet Joint Communiqué, *Izvestia*, 19 January 1957.
50. See Joint Communiqué of 16 January 1957, *La Documentation Française. Articles et Documents d'actualité mondiale, 458 (1957), p. 5.*
51. Ibid., *Notes et Documents*, 2395 (1957), p. 15; Zhou Enlai repeatedly, but without success, attempted to obtain official Polish assent to a statement of Soviet primacy in the Socialist bloc; see Zbigniew K. Brzezinski, *The Soviet Bloc* op cit.
52. *More on the Historical Experience*, op cit., p. 35.
53. Ibid., pp. 36-37.
54. For details, see Zbigniew K. Brzezinski, The Soviet Bloc, op cit.
55. *New York Times*, 8 May 1958.
56. *In Refutation of Modern Revisionism* (Peking: Foreign Languages Press, 1958), p. 45; for Yugoslav defense of its thesis, see Edvard Kardelj, *Socialism and War: A Survey*

of Chinese Criticism of the Policy of Coexistence (London: Methuen and Co., 1961).

57. For details, see Chapter 1.

58. *Long Live Leninism* (Peking: Foreign Languages Press, 1960).

59. See William E. Griffith (ed.), *Communism in Europe: Continuity, Change and the Sino-Soviet Dispute,* 2 vols. (Cambridge, Mass.: MIT Press, 1966).

60. "Chine où vas-tu", *La Nouvelle Critique,* 150 (1963), p. 72. For a detailed analysis of the Chinese situation by the French Communist Party, see Jean-Emile Vidal, *Où va la Chine* (Paris: Editions Sociales, 1967).

61. For details see Neil McInnes, *The Communist Parties of Western Europe* (London: Oxford University Press, 1975); Marcelle Padovani, *La Longue Marche: Le PC Italien* (Paris: Calmann-Levy, 1976); Annie Kriegel, *Un Autre Communisme* (Paris: Hachette, 1977); Harish Kapur and Miklos Molnar (eds.), *Le "Nouveau Communisme": Etude sur l'eurocommunisme et l'Europe de l'Est* (Geneva: Institut Universitaire de Hautes Etudes Internationales, 1978); Santiago Carrillo, *Eurocommunisme et Etat* (Paris: Flammarion, 1977); Donald Blackmer, *Unity in Diversity: Italian Communism and the Communist World* (Cambridge Mass.: M.I.T. Press, 1968).

62. "Memorandum of Comrade Togliatti", August 1964; for complete text, see *Global Digest,* 4 (1965).

63. *Rinascita,* 40 (1973).

64. Parti Communiste Français, *Le Socialisme pour la France* (Paris: Editions Sociales, 1976).

65. Santiago Carrillo, op cit.

66. C. L. Sulzberger, "A Very Shrewd and Quiet Man", *International Herald Tribune,* 22 June 1977.

67. See Santiago Carrillo, op cit.; also see Jean Ellenstein, "Ellenstein répond à Marchais", *Paris Match,* 25 August 1978.

68. See letters of condolence sent on the occasion of Mao Zedong's death.

69. West German, Portuguese, and to some extent Dutch parties resisted the Eurocommunist trends.

70. See "Les divergences entre le camarade Togliatti et nous"; "Encore une fois, sur les divergences entre le camarade Togliatti et nous", and "D'où proviennent les divergences? Réponse à Maurice Thorez et d'autres camarades"; in *Prolétaires de tous les pays unissons-nous contre l'ennemi commun* (Peking: Foreign Languages Press, 1963).

71. Remark made by Mao Zedong to André Malraux; see André Malraux, *Antimémoires* (Paris: Gallimard, 1967), p. 543.

72. Editorial of *Zeri i Popullit,* 6 January 1965, published in *Peking Review,* 6 (1965).

73. Editorial comments on the meeting in *People's Daily* and *Red Flag,* English translation in *Peking Review,* 13 (1965).

74. For complete text of the communiqué, see *World Marxist Review,* 6 (1967).

75. "Observer", "Bankruptcy of Europe's New Scabs", *People's Daily,* 4 May 1967, English translation in *Peking Review,* 20 (1967).

76. "Memorandum of Togliatti on Questions of the International Working Class Movement and its Unity," *Foreign Bulletin,* 4 September 1964. After Togliatti's death, the Italian Communists, according to a report, made the publication of the memorandum in the Soviet press a *sine qua non* to Italian participation in the meeting convened in Moscow on 15 December 1964 to prepare the Moscow Consultative Conference of Communist Parties; *L'Express,* 26 October 1964. The full text was published in *Pravda,* 10 September 1964.

77. Seven parties were absent: Dutch, Norwegian, Swedish, Icelandic, Yugoslav, Albanian, and Rumanian.

78. For complete text of the declaration, see *World Marxist Review*, 4 (1967).

79. See *In Refutation of Modern Revisionism*, op cit.

80. William E. Griffith, *Albania and the Sino-Soviet Rift* (Cambridge, Mass.: The MIT Presss, 1963).

81. For some details; see Robert L. Farlow, "Romanian Foreign Policy: A Case of Partial Alignment", *Problems of Communism*, 6 (1971).

82. W. W. Kulski, *De Gaulle and the World: The European Foreign Policy of the Fifth French Republic* (New York: Syracuse University Press, 1966); also see James M. Gavin, "On dealing with de Gaulle", *The Atlantic*, June 1965.

83. Hsin-win, "Franco-American Antagonism Deepens", *Peking Review*, 5 (1966); Chung Ho, "De Gaulle's New Challenge", ibid., 13 (1966).

84. In February 1964, a German industrialist on his return from China urged the Federal Republic to examine the possibilities of establishing a trade mission in Beijing. The Director of Demag—also after a visit to China during the same period—added his voice to the call for improvements in relations and also stated that other nations were a step ahead of West Germany in exploiting the Chinese market; for details, see *Far Eastern Economic Review*, 60 and 61 (1964).

85. Between the first and second meetings in Berne, Chancellor Erhardt visited the United States, where under pressure from the US, he declared that no substantial moves towards the People's Republic of China would be made before the end of the year, and that neither diplomatic recognition nor a formal trade agreement with that state were being considered, *New York Times*, 14 June 1964.

86. Roger Morgan, *The United States and West Germany 1945-1973: A Study in Alliance Politics* (London: Oxford University Press, 1974); also see Arthur A. Stankhe, *China's Trade with the West: A Political and Economic Analysis* (New York: Praeger, 1972).

87. For details, see Chapter 6.

88. *The Polemic on the General Line of the International Communist Movement*, op cit., p. 23.

89. For some details, see "Liste générale des partis et mouvements pro-chinois dans le monde", *La Documentation Française (Problèmes politiques et sociaux)*, 13 (1970); also see, "Les groupes et partis communistes pro-chinois en l'Europe", *Est et Ouest*, 543 and 549 (1975); Chung-Mao Hsia, "Maoist-oriented Communist parties and their splinter organizations: an instrument of revolution", *Issues and Studies*, 4 (1977).

90. Kevin Devlin, "Schism and Secession", *Survey* 54 (1965); Eric Willen and Pio Uliassi, "Western Europe", ibid.

91. *Pekin Information*, 21 (1968).

92. Ibid., 24 May 1968.

93. See Klaus Mehnert, *Peking and the New Left: At Home and Abroad* (Berkeley: University of California, 1969).

94. Ibid.

95. Perhaps the only exception was the Belgium Party.

96. In an interview with Edgar Snow in January 1965, Mao Zedong predicted that the United States would not invade North Vietnam, and that after a year or two would "lose interest"; for details, see "Interview with Mao", *The New Republic*, 9 (1965).

97. Speech by Fu Sheng, Chairman of the Provincial Revolutionary Committee of Helungjiang, Harbin Radio, 6 August 1969; cited in *Comparitive Communism. An Inter-disciplinary Journal*, 3 and 4 (1969), p. 149.

98. Brezhnev's speech to the 5th Polish Party Congress on 12 November 1968, *Pravda*, 13 November 1968.

99. Harrison E. Salisbury, *The Coming War Between Russia and China* (London: Pan Books, 1969).

100. Ibid.

101. *Pravda*, 8 June 1969.

102. *New China News Agency*, 28 June 1969.

103. For details, see Chapter 2.

104. For different views on this new policy, see *Problems of Communism*, 6 (1971).

105. See Chapter 2.

106. In January 1964, in an editorial commenting on Mao's statement on the just struggle of Panama against the United States, the *People's Daily* included only the capitalist countries of Western Europe, Oceania and Canada in the "Second Intermediary Zone".

107. See Deng Xiaoping's speech at the 6th Special Session of the UN General Assembly in April 1974. The expression, "Second World", was used in a broader sense, which included the developed countries that existed between the Soviet Union and the USA.

108. "La république populaire de Chine et les 'cinq centres'", *Annuaire du Tiers Monde*, 1975.

109. At the end of 1972, the Chinese Foreign Affairs Ministry set up a separate division to deal with European affairs which had been previously dealt with by a department which was also concerned with Oceania and America.

110. Shih Chun, "On Studying Some history of the National Liberation Movement", *Peking Review*, 45 (1972), p. 8.

111. Editorial in *People's Daily* "Chairman Mao's Theory of the Differentiation of the Three Worlds is a Major Contribution to Marxism-Leninism", *Peking Review*, 45 (1977).

112. *Ibid.* 11 (1969).

113. Ibid.

114. "The New Tsars and the Degeneration of the CPSU", *New China News Agency*, 16 May 1969.

115. "A Black Line Running Through Two Dynasties", *Peking Review*, 36 (1973), p. 42.

116. Out of approximately 100 complete plants purchased by the Chinese between 1972 and mid-1975, only eight are American. For details see Alexander Eckstein, "China's Trade Policy", *Foreign Affairs*, 1 (1975).

117. "China's Foreign Trade", *Current Scene*, 9 (1975).

118. Clyde H. Farnsworth, "China with Energy Potential Seeks Goods, Arms in Europe", *International Herald Tribune*, 12 November 1975.

119. The Director of the Defense Intelligence Agency of the Pentagon has in fact suggested that China's programme to redeploy ICBMs was called off in mid-1973; ibid., 26 February 1976.

120. For details about China's air power see: The International Institute for Strategic Studies, *Military Balance 1975-1976* (1975).

121. Ibid.

122. *International Herald Tribune*, 19 December 1975.

123. K. P. Broadbent, "China and the EEC: the Politics of New Trade Relationship", *The World Outlook*, 5 (1976).

124. British and West German in 1975.

125. *Financial Times*, 18 April 1972.

126. *New York Times*, 19 December 1975.

127. The British Under-Secretary for Trade, for example, clearly indicated that the Labour Government made "no limitations whatsoever on the sale of aircraft and aerospace equipment to China and that no representations were made to Britain by her

NATO allies to ban sales to China of computers and other sophisticated equipment", see *News Review on China, Mongolia and the Koreas*, April 1975, p. 248.

128   *People's Daily*, 13 September 1970. In an article that appeared in *People's Daily* on 22 December 1969, Brandt's *Ost-Politik* was characterized as a "dirty affair".

129.   Ibid.

130.   Deng Xiaoping's speech at banquet for Helmut Schmidt in November 1975; *Peking Review*, 45 (1975), p. 7.

131.   *Washington Post*, 27 May 1973.

132.   *People's Daily*, 7 November 1973.

133.   Ibid., 20 December 1973.

134.   According to a Soviet publication, Zhou Enlai threatened West European countries that they "should not count on maintaining equally good relations both with China and with the Soviet Union". I. Alexeyer., "Peking's European Policy", *International Affairs*, 1 (1976), p. 61.

135.   For some details, see Jerzy Lukaszewski, "La Chine et l'Europe de l'Est"; *Le Monde*, 24 February 1972; also see articles on China and Eastern Europe in *La Nouvelle Chine*, 8 (1972).

136.   *Peking Review*, 11 (1969).

137.   Ibid., 51 (1975).

138.   Ibid.

139.   In an interview to a Yugoslav editor, Zhou Enlai said "we are far away from Europe and as you know one of our popular proverbs says 'distant waters cannot quench fire'"; cited in Joseph O. Kun, "China and Eastern Europe", *Radio Free Europe Research*, 10 (1970).

140.   *International Herald Tribune*, 28-29 September 1968.

141.   Jerzy Lukaszewski, loc cit.

142.   Prague was the last East European capital to receive a new ambassador from China after the Cultural Revolution. He presented his credentials to President Svoboda on 2 Juni 1971.

143.   See Y. Avesenev, L. Karshinov, E. Potymkina, "China's Foreign Trade", *Far Eastern Affairs*, 4 (1975).

144.   For background information on this development, see Paul Lendras, "The Taboos are Breaking", *Financial Times*, 24 June 1971; also see Dan Morgan, "The Balkans, Geopolitical Potpourri", *International Herald Tribune*, 30 August 1971.

145.   *Le Figaro*, 27 January 1976; *Le Monde*, 6 February 1976.

146.   See *Peking Review*, 20 (1971) and 23 (1972).

147.   Jen Ku-Ping, "Sovereignty and Independence of Balkan Countries Brook No Encroachment", ibid., 43 (1974), p. 19.

148.   *Le Monde*, 27 September 1978; for some details of his visit of Athens, see *New China News Agency*, 22 September 1978; *Ta Kung Pao*, 28 September 1978.

149.   The two countries are also collaborating in the construction of small military planes.

150.   Ghita Ionescu, *The Break-up of the Soviet Empire in Eastern Europe* (London: Penguin Books, 1965), p. 140.

151.   F. Stephen Larrabee, *Balkan Security. Adelphi Papers* (London: International Institute of Strategic Studies, 1977).

152.   *New China News Agency*, 24 August 1978.

153.   For some details regarding Chinese military assistance to Albania, see note of Chinese Ministry of Foreign Affairs to Albanian Embassy in Peking on 7 July 1978, ibid., 7 July 1978.

154.   *Peking Review*, 44 (1974).

155. Rumania displaced the USSR as China's biggest Socialist bloc trading partner.

156. *China Trade and Economic Newsletter,* 222 (1974).

157. *Current Scene,* 9 (1975). The trade between the two countries, however, declined to $ 30 million in 1975 and 1976; *Le Monde,* 16 August 1977.

158. *International Herald Tribune,* 22 August 1978.

159. Figures for 1974 and 1977 were not available; for some details, see *China Trade and Economic Newsletter,* 237 (1975).

160. From the note of 7 July 1978 of the Chinese Ministry of Foreign Affairs; *New China News Agency,* 20 July 1978.

161. *Radio Free Europe Research,* 0939 (1971).

162. *New China News Agency,* 28 October 1971.

163. *China Trade and Economic Newsletter,* 228 (1974).

164. *New China News Agency,* 3 July 1975.

165. Slobodan Stankovic, "A Survey of Yugoslav-Chinese Relations", *Radio Free Europe Research,* 1442 (1972).

166. Slobodan Stankovic, "Croatians Economic Relations with China", ibid., 1466 (1972).

167. More than 100 delegations were exchanged between the two countries in 1977, *International Herald Tribune,* 22 August 1978.

168. *Le Figaro,* 22-23 July 1978; *Le Monde,* 1 August 1978.

169. See supra.

170. See Chapter 4.

171. It should be noted that China took some time to arrive at this conclusion. During the Maoist period, though economic relations were established with Western countries, the main stress was laid on the principles of self-reliance. Only after Mao's death and the political elimination of the "Gang of Four" in October 1976 (who were opposed to such a policy), did China begin to stress the importance of trade and of importing technology.

172. *Peking Review,* 23 (1971), p. 11.

173. Ibid., 11 (1973), p. 3.

174. *Le Monde,* 12 July 1972.

175. See V. Akimov and V. Potapov, "Four Modernisations: Outlines and the Reality", *Far Eastern Affairs,* 3 (1979).

176. *Le Monde,* 3 May 1978.

177. "Compensatory trade" means that China, for example, will use its products to pay for equipment and technology. For example, the construction of oil fields will be paid with oil and the construction of coal mines, will be paid with coal.

178. *International Herald Tribune,* 8 November 1978 and 9-10 December 1978.

179. Ibid., 8 November 1978.

180. The Labour Government, obviously under great domestic pressure, agreed to allow defence sales, but only as part of an overall package deal which would include exports of industrial equipment. This reservation seems to have been dropped; *Financial Times,* 2 November 1979.

181. Ibid., 24 November 1978.

182. Ibid.

183. From Foreign Minister Huang Hua's speech to the 33rd session of the UN General Assembly; *People's Daily,* 10 October 1978.

184. Reporting on the Nixon-Heath talks of February 1973, the *Peking Review,* for example, quoted both leaders' statements that "economic rivalry between the US and the Common Market must not be allowed to weaken Atlantic solidarity on the eve of major East-West negotiations"; *Peking Review,* 6 (1973). For similar declarations to US

Congressional leaders in July 1972, see L. Bartalits and Jan H. Groenen, "The People's Republic of China and Western Europe", in F. von Geusau Alting, *The External Relations of the European Community: Perspectives, Policies and Responses* (Farnborough Hants: Saxon House, 1974).

185. Cited from an article from *Le Monde,* 22 April 1975.

186. *International Herald Tribune,* 1-2 November 1975.

187. See Li Xiannian's interview with French journalists in October 1976.

188. Hua Guofeng declared to Neil Cameron, British Chief of Staff: "One finger is a small force, but fingers clenched into a fist make up a great force, and then you will be strong", *People's Daily,* 1 May 1978.

189. Ibid., 10 October 1978.

190. Deng Xiaoping's interview with Japanese journalists on 19 May 1978; *Akhata,* 23 May 1978.

191. Joint editorial of *People's Daily, Red Flag, Liberation Army Daily;* text in *People's Daily,* 1 January 1970.

192. Ibid., 7 November 1973.

193. From the speech of Qiao Guanhua, head of the Chinese Delegation to the 28th Session of the UN General Assembly on 2 October 1973; *Peking Review,* 40 (1973), p. 12.

194. Cited in *European Community,* March 1972; also see "New Monetary Crisis in Capitalist World", *Peking Review,* 7 (1973); "Euro-Dollar and the Dollar Crisis", ibid., 11 (1973).

195. From a speech given at the United Nations, ibid., (1975).

196. For background informations, see Agnès Hubert, "Le sens du rapprochement CEE-Chine: Pragmatisme commercial et alliance stratégique", *Revue du Marché Commun,* 211 (1977); W. B. Findorff, "China and the European Community, New Development in China's International Theory", *The Round Table,* 251 (1973); Dick Wilson, "China and the European Community", *The China Quarterly,* 55 (1973); "The People's Republic of China and the European Community", *Europe Information,* 17 (1979).

197. According to British sources, by March 1971, the Chinese had discreetly expressed the desire to establish relations with the Common Market; M. J. de Saint-Blanquat, "La République populaire de Chine face à l'Europe", *Revue du Marché Commun,* 155 (1972).

198. *Peking Review,* 23 (1971), p. 23.

199. Ibid., 24 (1971), p. 15; according to an article in a Soviet publication, in 1971, Zhou Enlai characterized the Common Market as a "first step towards independence;" V. Pavlov, "Europe in Peking's Plans", *International Affairs,* 3 (1972).

200. *Peking Review,* 27 (1971), p. 36.

201. Ibid., 23 (1971).

202. Zhou Enlai's interview to Neville Maxwell, *Sunday Times* 5 December 1971.

203. Denis Healey, the British Labour Party leader, concluded from his visit to Peking in 1972 that "China's enthusiasm for Britain's entry into the EEC is based not only on Russia's hostility to the project but also on the belief that the economic contradictions between a United Europe and North America will reduce the international influence of the United States"; *The Times,* 1 December 1972.

204. *Peking Review,* 29 (1974).

205. Agreement between the Community and 46 countries in Africa, the Carribean, and the Pacific, signed in February 1975.

206. United States was attacked as the main obstructor in the Paris talks between the developing and developed countries; see *Peking Review,* 51 (1975).

207. *European Communities*, 5 (1977).

208. "La République populaire de la Chine et la Communauté européenne," *Information*, 168 (1978).

209. *China and Economic Trade View*, 2 (1975).

210. *European Communities*, Working Document, May 1977.

211. Chen Yen, "Why Did the 'Gang of Four' Wield the Big Stick of the 'Theory of Productive Forces'?", *Peking Review*, 26 (1977).

212. See the proceedings of the National Foreign Trade Conference held in Peking in July 1977; ibid. 31 (1977). China signed more trade agreements and contracts with foreign concerns in the first half of 1978 than in the corresponding 1977 period; *International Herald Tribune*, 8 September 1978.

213. *The China Business Review*, 9 and 10 (1977).

214. Ibid.

215. "The People's Republic of China and the European Community", *Europe Information*, 17 (1979).

216. Ibid.

217. Ibid., pp. 7-8.

218. Ibid.

219. Ibid.

220. *Far Eastern Economic Review*, 31 (1979).

221. *Communautés Européennes*, 23 (1978).

222. Ibid.

223. *Quarterly Economic Review of China, Hongkong, North Korea*, 1st Quarter, 1979.

224. On the occasion of the formal signing of the Trade Agreement, both the delegations underlined the political aspects of the relationship, *International Herald Tribune*, 4 April 1978.

225. A. Larin, "Britain in China's Foreign Policy", *Far Eastern Affairs*, 3 (1979).

226. For details about Sino-West German relations, see A. I. Stephanov, *FRG i Kitaii* (Moscow: Izdatelsvo Mezadunaronie Otnoishnia, 1974); Ernest Majonica, *Bonn-Peking. Die Beziehungen der Bundesrepublik Deutschland zur Volksrepublik China* (Stuttgart: W. Kohlhammer, 1971); "Les relations entre Bonn et Peking, Documents", *Revue des Questions Allemandes* November-December 1971; Ernest Henri, "German Revanchists and Peking. Essays and Reminisences", *Far Eastern Review*, 2 (1975); Hans Myron Henning Vent, "The Bonn-Peking Connection: Overview of the Trade and Treaty Relations", *Issues and Studies*, 12 (1975); Bernhard Grossman, "Peking-Bonn: Substantial Non-Relations," *Pacific Community*, 1 (1970); Vladimir Reisky De Dubnic, "Germany and China: The Intermediate Zone Theory and the Moscow Treaty", *Asia Quarterly*, 4 (1971).

227. *Frankfurter Allgemeine Zeitung*, 31 July 1972.

228. See *The Military Balance 1979-1980*. (Published annually by the International Institute for Strategic Studies, London.)

229. Ibid.

230. The GNP of West Germany is higher than those of Great Britain ($302 billion) and France ($463 billion).

231. It is interesting to note that China and Japan have begun to use the West German mark as a means of payment in their trade relations. It became known on 20 February 1975 that a leading Japanese trade firm, Nichimen Jitsugyo, recently concluded an important agreement with China worth 40 million yen, the settlement for which was to be in West German marks. See *News Review on China, Mongolia and Koreas*, March 1975.

232. *Dossier R. P. de Chine* (Paris: Centre Français du Commerce Extérieur, 1977).

233. The West German exhibition covered a floor space of 22,000 square meters and exhibited such products as machine tools, machinery, iron and steel, aviation, textile, chemical, and optical products. For details, see *To Kang Pao,* 11 September 1975. Nearly 300 firms participated in the exhibition; *China Economic and Trade Review,* 5 (1975).

234. This point is stressed in a 60-page report presented to the government after a top-level review of Bonn's fundamental European policy; for details see *International Herald Tribune,* 1 December 1975.

235. In a recent article by a Xinhua correspondent in Bonn, the reservations that West Germany has about détente are underlined. "The people living on the banks of the Rhine," he wrote, "are seeing through the détente smokescreen spread by the Soviet Union. They are raising their vigilance against the spectre of war now haunting Europe. The call for reinforcing defence, strengthening unity in Western Europe, and opposing aggression and expansion by the social imperialists is growing louder"; *Peking Review,* 1 (1976).

236. Ibid., 18 September 1970.

237. *Neues Deutschland,* 22 September 1970.

238. *Peking Review,* 42 (1972).

239. He declared in 1968: "China is far away, but nevertheless in the political game Germany can hold the Chinese card, which should not be put aside or ignored"; quoted in *Izvestia,* 29 March 1968.

240. Declaration by Rainer Barzel, Chairman of the CDU/CSU to Washington correspondent of *Die Welt,* 17-18 April 1971.

241. *Peking Review,* 30 (1972).

242. Speech made at a banquest in honour of Jaeger, by Vice-Chairman of the Standing Committee of the Chinese National People's Congress on 14 October, ibid., 43 (1974).

243. *Frankfurter Allgemeine Zeitung,* 18 September 1975.

244. On the occasion of Strauss' visit in September 1975, the Chinese ambassador to Bonn returned to Beijing—an indication of the importance attached to the visit; ibid., 6 November 1975.

245. *Peking Review,* 4 (1975); according to a poll taken after Strauss' visit, more than 70 per cent of the German population sympathized with China; *Die Welt,* 30 December 1975.

246. Ibid., 21 February 1976.

247. Ibid.

248. *Süddeutsche Zeitung,* 26 April 1976.

249. The warm reception given to Strauss in January 1975 irritated the Bonn governement, and there were rumours that Schmidt might postpone his visit to China, which was due to take place in October-November, *The Guardian,* 19 January 1975.

250. From a report made by the Chinese journalistic delegation after their visit to the Federal Republic in 1973, *Peking Review,* 32 (1973), p. 10.

251. Both these declarations were carried by the *New China News Agency,* 21 December 1974.

252. *Frankfurter Allgemeine Zeitung,* 28 October 1975.

253. *New China News Agency,* 10 and 12 October 1974.

254. Three agreements were concluded: the Maritime Transport Agreement, the Civil Transport Agreement, and an agreement on the establishment of a Mixed

Commission for the Promotion of Mutual Economic Relations. For details, see ibid., 29 October and 2 November 1975.

255.   *China Trade and Economic Newsletter,* 279 (1979).

256.   Ibid.

257.   The others were ex-chief of intelligence of NATO, Rear-Admiral Poser, retired Inspector General Trettner, and the ex-chief of NATO's military committee; *Der Spiegel,* 15 May 1978.

258.   *Die Welt,* 21 and 27 February 1976.

259.   They were ex-Inspector General Maiziere, ex-Vice Admiral Meentzen and ex-Lieutenant General of Aviation Vogel; *Der Spiegel,* 15 May 1978.

Chapter 6

CHINA AND THE THIRD WORLD

Historically, China has had very little impactful experience of what is currently known as the Third World. Having developed through centuries of autonomic effort into a self-contained, self-satisfied, and essentially land-based civilisation, the world beyond was either perceived as "an endless ocean fading into space and marking the end of the world"[1] or as containing inferior civilisations from which China had nothing to learn.

The only exceptions to this generalised perception were the "moonlight satellites,"[2] such as Korea, Vietnam, and Japan. Having acquired the essence of the Chinese cultural and institutional frameworks either through a long process of diffusion (as was the case with Japan) or through a long period of occupation (as with Korea and Vietnam), these countries were recognised by the Chinese as the co-heirs to a common Far Eastern civilisation of which China was the focal element.

But this does not, of course, mean that China did not have any contacts with "countries beyond the horizon";[3] for her history—like that of most culture-civilisations—is studded with examples of expeditions, of prolonged presence of foreigners in her southern ports, of extensive commercial exchanges,[4] of abiding cultural relations,[5] and of occasional emigrations; it only means that there was little in these relations which made any striking impression on China or shook from her the conviction of her own superiority.

It was the common colonial experience of the 19th and 20th centuries that generated the appropriate psychological conditions for the establishment of more sustained political relations between China and other Asian countries which had also become victims of Western imperialism. Examples of such contacts abound, but are particularly numerous in the 20th century when an increasingly expansive technological revolution, compounded with increasing international political activity[6] has pushed China to establish relations with other colonised countries. In his pursuit of revolution, Sun Yat-sen, for example, spent more time in Japan (1897-1902) than in any other foreign country.[7] Chiang Kai-shek maintained regular contact with other nationalist movements.[8] Even the CCP, despite physical isolation from the outside world during the Yenan years, maintained a continuous interest in coordinating its struggle with that of other Asian countries.[9] Nevertheless, it would be an exaggeration to suggest that the Chinese nationalism that emerged in the country during this period eventually became transnational, that its contacts with Asia became frequent and meaningful, that its history was replete with such examples, and that these essentially emotional relations were, in due course, solidified into something more ideological, more political, and more institutional. China's nationalist experience was essentially national. Like all Asian nationalism of the period, it was principally inspired by internal factors. The ideological influences that marked Chinese nationalism emanated, paradoxically, from the Western world. Sun Yat-sen was influenced by Western ideas, and thereafter in the early 1920s by the Bolshevik Revolution.[10] Chiang Kai-shek, preoccupied as he was with domestic convulsions and subsequently by Japanese invasion, was primarily concerned with the power game, for which he too had to turn to the West. His interest in nationalist movements in other countries was essentially marginal, and whatever relations he established were fragmentary and episodic.[11] Mao Zedong's partisanship for Marxist theory, to take another example, had led him to seek guidance and inspiration from ideas emanating from Soviet Russia.[12]

Revolutionary Interest in Asia

Only in the aftermath of the 1949 revolution did an interest in the developing world become conspicuously evident. The principal focus, however, was not so much on the Third World, which at the time was still a sentimental abstraction; it was more specifically directed towards the neighbouring countries of the Asian continent where burgeoning nationalism was pushing some of the colonial countries to abandon power.

But the heady wine of victory, combined with ideological militancy—so characteristic of periods immediately after revolutions—did not favour a benign attitude towards the emerging new states. In fact, so virulent and unremitingly hostile was China's deportment to all things non-communist, so deep was her commitment to Marxist ideology at the time, and so new was her experience with the outside world, that she found it virtually impossible to objectively evaluate the important process of de-colonisation that swept through the Asian continent in the aftermath of World War II. The Chinese leaders, for example, considered it hardly possible for any colonial country to acquire genuine independence under a non-communist leadership. In arriving at such a conclusion, they were obviously influenced by the experience of their country, which, under the leadership of Chiang Kai-shek, had escalated from one crisis to another, finally culminating in a state of helplessness and dependence on the West. For any empirical observer of the Chinese political scene, such a traumatic experience would have constituted a convincing proof of the poverty of Chinese nationalist leadership; for the new Chinese leaders, with their long and rigid Marxist training, it was much more: it was the living example of the poverty of all non-Communist leaderships.

226

Thus, the entire historic process of de-colonisation, in full swing under non-Communist leaderships in Asia, was considered nothing more than simple formality, not even remotely connected with real independence. The peaceful transfer of power by the British in Burma, India, Pakistan, and Sri Lanka was anathema to Chinese Communist leaders, a behaviour which contradicted their own experience as well as their ideological convictions. Even the violent nationalist revolution in Indonesia was not viewed favourably, simply because the Communist party was not leading it.

Already encouraged by Moscow to raise the flag of revolt, the Asian Communist parties received an accelerated impetus from developments in China and from the ready flow of open communications that emanated from the area. In fact, even before the successful culmination of the Chinese Revolution, the CCP was advocating the relevance of its violent revolutionary model to the colonial countries. In his important work *"New Democracy"* published in 1940, Mao Zedong argued that since neither the bourgeois dictatorship of the Western world nor the dictatorship of the proletariat of the Soviet Union were suitable to the developing countries, they should adopt the Chinese model, the viability of which had been proved in China.[13] Liu Shaoqi went even further and unambiguously declared in 1946 that the Chinese revolutionary model, as formulated by Mao, "charts a way not only for the Chinese people but for the billion folk who live in the colonial countries of Southeast Asia."[14]

While implicitly challenging the universality of the Soviet revolutionary system, the Chinese leaders attempted to project the relevance of their model to the colonial countries on the grounds that the socio-economic structures there were similar to those in China. They did not leave open the possibility of the Asian revolutionary leaders discovering their own model, seeking their own path, and adapting the broad Marxist-Leninist framework to their own specific conditions. What was relevant to China apparently appeared to them to be relevant to other colonial countries.

Such views continued after the revolution. In fact, they were even more clearly and even more forcefully expressed. At a conference of Asian and Australasian Trade Unions convened in Beijing in November-December 1949, Liu Shaoqi openly recommended that the Asian countries follow China's example.[15] Another Chinese spokesman at the conference went even further, frankly stating that the Chinese people would give "moral and material support to the national liberation fighters in Malaya, Burma, Indo-China, Indonesia, and the Philippines."[16] Mao Zedong personally sent a cable to the Indian Communists giving them his full support in their struggle against the Nehru government, and expressing the hope that the day was not far off when India, like China, would "one day emerge in the Socialist and People's Democratic family; that day will end the imperialist reactionary rule in the history of mankind."[17]

But did the Chinese leadership go beyond these rhetorical declarations? Did they actually attempt to establish contact with Asian Communists?

And did they give real material assistance to those who had raised the flag of revolt against the newly established nationalist governments?

To this day, it is indeed difficult to state with any degree of assertiveness that assistance was given and that attempts were made to help Asian Communists to attain power or to intensify their revolutionary activities.

If, however, this particular issue is still shrouded in darkness, it is more than evident that their revolutionary stance did effect their diplomatic behaviour insofar as they did not appear to attach any major importance to the establishment of friendly relations with the newly independent Asian states. In his first report to the Chinese People's Congress, Zhou Enlai underlined the importance of Beijing's ties with Socialist countries but made almost no mention of China's relations with the non-communist countries of Asia.[18] In fact, *People's China* presented the editorial view that if the Asian countries had established relations with China, it was because they were "left with no other alternative."[19]

It would nonetheless be an oversimplification to suggest that the Chinese behaviour towards Asia was exclusively determined by revolutionary objectives, that the whole range of her policies and relations were focussed only on the goal of bringing about radical changes in Asia; for no nation, whatever her economic and social structures may be, whatever her perception of the international system may be, can afford to ignore the national security dimension—least of all a country like China, which had been for centuries a victim of international aggressions, and which, in the immediate aftermath of the Chinese Revolution, was threatened by the United States, whose military power was present at all the strategic points formerly controlled by Japan. In addition, US air and sea power was far more effective and far more menacing than that of Japan and Britain in the early days. The Chinese remembered that such power in the hands of their adversaries was invariably the first cause of their frequent and severe humiliations before actual invasions.

The second major goal of Chinese diplomacy was therefore to extrude US military power in the Far East and to exclude her naval power from the adjoining seas.

This, however, was easier said than done—for what could China do to eliminate this threat? How could she, with minimal naval or air power, challenge the might of the United States? Obviously, she could do little. Furthermore, it was apparent that she could not even rely on her senior partner to attain this objective. The balance between the two blocs at the time was too assymetrical to permit any credible action on the part of the Soviet Union. Moreover, Moscow had other geographical priorities and other pressing diplomatic goals that needed more urgent scrutiny than that demanded by the US presence in the Far East.

Verbal and vicious attacks against US imperialism were thus the only weapon that existed in the Chinese armoury; and this, as is apparent from the documentation of the period, was used liberally.

228

If China was helpless to dethrone US power from the area, she was nonetheless determined not to permit the United States to come closer to her frontiers. Her response to the Korean war is a case in point. When the escalation of the war brought General MacArthur's troops close to the Yalu River, China intervened and drove US troops back beyond Seoul. Her intervention in Korea was obviously an hazardous action insofar as she could not foresee the consequences that might result from such an action. For the Chinese leaders, notwithstanding the possibility for rational analysis, could not really know how the United States would respond to their action. What appeared vital to them was safeguarding the security of the Chinese state, even if this embroiled them in an escalated and terrifying conflict with a powerful nation such as the United States.

The third Chinese objective in Asia was the integration of all areas considered to be an integral part of the Middle Kingdom. Within a short period after the revolution, the Chinese leaders asserted their power in Xinjiang and Inner Mongolia; and parallel to China's involvment in Korea, proceeded to forcibly integrate the Tibetan region. The Chinese publicly manifested their determination to integrate Taiwan into the mainland as well, making it clear on numerous occasions that no other solution would be acceptable. Yet almost no concrete action was taken to attain this objective. But this was not due so much to any lack of determination as to the fact that the Chinese did not have a naval power credible enough to encounter the presence of the US 7th Fleet that had been interposed into the area.

The different Chinese responses to Tibet and Taiwan thus were not so much due to any inconsistency in Chinese claims, but rather to the assymetry of forces.

The three basic goals of Chinese diplomacy in Asia met with varied success. While they successfully kept US troops at bay in Korea, they could not obtain the withdrawal of the American naval presence around China. While they succeeded in integrating Tibet, Xinjiang, and Inner Mongolia to the mainland, they were unable to occupy Taiwan.

The Failure of the Revolutionary Policy

If China's policy to attain the goals of security and national integration were neither a success nor a failure, her aim to introduce radical changes in Asia foundered completely. Not only did she fail in restructuring Asia after her own image, but her isolation from the mainstream of Asian politics came to be further accentuated. Wherever the Asian Communist parties rose in revolt, they were promptly suppressed. In some countries, rebels were exterminated, while in others they suffered serious set-backs. In Burma, for example, after the Communist guerillas had gained control over broad sections of the country and were quite near the capital, the government gradually restored its authority, leaving the insurgents in a state of confusion and without support. In Indonesia, the Party ceased to have any substantial hold in the country after the Madiun revolt of September 1948. In the Philippines, after a brief period of struggle, it was on the run with its military power completely broken. In Malaysia it failed to establish authority over any area large enough to provide it with a secure base. And in India, where the party had through the years established impressive footholds among workers, peasants, and intellectuals, the feckless revolts engineered under the leadership of B.T. Ranadive and Rajeswar Rao—the one centring around the workers, the other around the peasants—caused party membership to plummet to an all-time low, declining from an estimated 89,263 to 20,000.[20]

This set-back can be principally attributed to the pronounced inability of Asian Communist parties to comprehend the true nature of the political situation in Asia. Carried away by the euphoria of the Soviet victory in World War II and heartened by the rapid advancement of the Chinese Revolution in the late 1940s, they simply ignored the true configuration of forces in their respective countries. While exaggerating their power to shape their own societies, they underestimated the strength of their adversaries.

The failure of these upheavals was also due to the fact that they became victims of conflicting Soviet and Chinese pressures regarding the relevance of their respective revolutionary models. While the Chinese were openly recommending that the peasant-oriented Chinese path "should be taken by the peoples of various colonial and semi-colonial countries,"[21] the Soviet Union was insisting upon the universal applicability of her own model, in which the working class constituted the hard core of the revolutionary forces.[22]

The emergence of these substantive Sino-Soviet differences were a source of considerable bemusement and even internal discords within the Asian parties—for, having been accustomed through the years, until the Chinese Revolution, to the comfortable situation of total allegiance to Moscow, they were disturbed by the new predicament of having to make a choice between two different revolutionary options. Inevitably, this tug-of-war between the two centres of power generated factional dissension within the Asian parties, thereby making it difficult for them to arrive at a consensual strategy to be followed by all of them. The fluctuating and rapid shifts in strategy and tactics, to which they now fell victim, greatly weakened their capacity to influence the politics in their respective countries.

For China as well as the Soviet Union, this was a serious set-back. Their capacity to exercise influence over most of Asia declined significantly. Even the well-established image of friendliness towards nationalism, so sedulously projected for many years, was tarnished.

On the other hand, responding to the groundswell of nationalism, the non-Communist Asian leaders experienced a meteoric rise in prestige and popularity. Undoubtedly their influence on the people of their countries was too strong and too deep-rooted to be overthrown by artificially created revolutionary upheavals. Furthermore, many of the Asian nationalist leaders, influenced by the Soviet revolution, had proclaimed their intention to attain a much more far-reaching socialistic pattern of society than the non-Communist leaders of many European countries. Obviously, this was a new development which merited objective analysis instead of being contemptuously and thoughtlessly identified with capitalism. The Chinese attitude showed the magnitude of Chinese dogmatism and exposed a lack of intellectual sophistication which was needed to understand new trends and new thoughts.

Perhaps even more significant was the fact that the confluence of events and circumstances resulting from Moscow and Beijing's belligerent line did not leave much leverage for the newly independent countries in the actual designing of their foreign policies. How could these nations, having just gained their independence, implement the non-aligned policies to which they had only recently adhered and develop meaningful relations with all nations—irrespective of political and ideological orientations—when the Communist states, highly vitriolic in their attacks, were not prepared to go beyond the simple establishment of diplomatic relations? The real success of the politics of non-alignment is contingent upon its acceptance or toleration by other nations.[23]

Therefore, notwithstanding their repeatedly announced intentions to remain non-aligned, many of these countries found themselves moving closer to the United States and Western Europe, which, significantly enough, appeared to be more tolerant towards their policies. Almost the entire economic and military assistance to Burma, faced as she was with Karen and Communist insurrections, emanated from the Commonwealth countries and the United States and most of her treaties and trade agreements were concluded with non-Communist nations. Indonesia, under Prime Ministers Hatta and Natsir, was decidedly pro-Western, receiving economic assistance mainly from the Netherlands and the United States; and India's relations with the outside world were principally limited to non-Communist nations and her economic assistance emanated principally from the West.

If many of these nations were operationally left with no choice but to turn to the West for economic and military assistance, they nonetheless adopted an independent rhetoric on a number of international issues. In fact, it was quite often in contradiction to the policy proposed by the West. Many of them demanded the admission of the new China to the United Nations, insisted on the return of Taiwan to the mainland, refused to label China an aggressor in the Korean war, and declined to go to San Francisco to sign the Japanese Peace Treaty on the grounds that Communist China, a major victim of Japanese aggression during World War II, had rejected the US draft treaty.

This dichotomous situation between having close relations with, and at the same time, showing rhetorical opposition to, the West was possible since the European and American pluralistic political systems permitted autonomy and allowed dissent. Towards the Socialist bloc, as it was then constituted, it would have been impossible to adopt such an attitude since its monolithic character neither allowed autonomy nor tolerated any dissent from its allies or friends.

Peaceful Co-existence

The failure of Beijing's revolutionary policy, compounded with the realisation that Asian countries were after all not that subservient to the West, resulted in the abandonment of its militant line. As is often the case with mobilised regimes, the process of change was set off slowly, signalled by a few discreet signs before it became conspicuous and accelerated.

The first signs became apparent during the Korean war. The Chinese attitude towards India, for example, changed when it became increasingly apparent that Nehru's attitude towards the Korean conflict was by no means identical to that of Western countries. Zhou Enlai paid tribute to Nehru for his contribution in ending the war.[24] Mao Zedong, who personally proposed a friendly toast at the Indian embassy's first anniversary celebrations of the Republic, spoke to the ambassador in warm terms about the Indian Prime Minister, and expressed the hope of meeting him soon thereafter in Beijing. He also underlined the importance of developing cultural and educational exchanges between the two countries.[25] India's refusal to sign the Japanese Peace Treaty was warmly received by the Chinese Press. *The People's Daily* editorially welcomed the decision and expressed the view that such an action proved "that the age is past when imperialist governments can do whatever they please.[26]" The big change, however, became evident with the six-week visit of a high-level unofficial Indian goodwill mission to China in April 1951 and a return visit in September of the same year of a Chinese cultural delegation.[27]

Similarly, the Chinese attitude towards Burma also shifted. Contacts with the Rangoon government were re-established, the level and quality of Sino-Burmese relations were upgraded, and the Burmese leaders were praised for having refused to sign the Japanese Peace Treaty proposed by the United States.[28]

The first and perhaps the most important sign of a general change, however, appeared in 1952 when Beijing developed its "people's diplomacy". At a well-attended meeting of Asian and African peoples in Beijing in October of that year, the Chinese proclaimed their new line of peaceful coexistence. Instead of enunciating a revolutionary line, they highlighted the importance of concluding a peace treaty with Japan, stressed the vital necessity of reaching an agreement between the five big powers, and emphasized the importance of expanding trade.[29] The seven-point message the conference addressed to the United Nations recommended steps to end the conflict in Vietnam, Malaysia, and other countries and further recommended bringing about "a just and reasonable settlement through negotiations."[30] The message also underlined the new Chinese view that "countries with different social systems and ways of life can coexist peacefully.[31]

If Chinese declarations at the Beijing conference were encouraging signs of change, the Chinese role at the Geneva conference of 1954 was undoubtedly a definite proof of its new intentions—for it was at this occasion that Zhou Enlai's search for peaceful solutions led him to persuade the Vietminhs to withdraw their troops from Laos and Cambodia, and he further pushed them to abandon their demands that the governments set up by pro-Beijing Khmer Issorak and Pathet Lao forces must participate in the conference. According to some reports, it was also Zhou that induced the reluctant Vietminhs to accept the unfavourable dividing line along Vietnam's narrow waistline at the 17th parallel.[32] Undoubtedly the new peace offensive left a significant impact on many Asian countries. Not only did it contribute to the partial breaking down of barriers between Beijing and non-Communist Asia, but it also helped considerably in the development of new lines of communications between them. It was perhaps this new atmosphere of friendliness and credibility that led the Colombo powers to take the major diplomatic step of inviting China to participate in the Afro-Asian conference in Bandung in 1955.

Zhou Enlai's friendly and remarkably moderate attitude at Bandung quelled whatever lingering suspicions many of the Asian countries might still have had about Chinese intentions. He assured the conference that his desire was to be conciliatory and to "seek common ground".[33] Side-stepping frontal attacks from pro-Western delegates who condemned Communist imperialism, he worked patiently to gain confidence, to extend the area of contact with each of the participating states and to inspire trust in China's peaceful intentions. Even on the intractable issue of Taiwan, the Chinese Prime Minister declared his readiness to enter into bilateral negotiations;[34] and before leaving Bandung, he invited Cambodian and Thai delegates to send representatives to China to make an on-the spot check and thus assure for themselves that there were no preparations to subvert their governments.[35]

To allay any fears of subversion, Zhou Enlai furthermore took the unprecedented step—consistently refused by preceding Chinese governments—of concluding a dual nationality treaty with Indonesia which stipulated that the 3 million Chinese residents of that country would be required to decide within two years whether they wanted Chinese or Indonesian nationality.[36] At the same time he announced his readiness to conclude similar agreements with other states which were faced with such a problem and which recognized China.[37]

The remarkably sober performance of Chinese leaders at the multilateral conferences thus greatly contributed to breaking down diplomatic barriers and to developing some mutual understanding on a number of international issues with many of the Asian countries.

To gain more appeal and credibility, the Chinese also engaged in a sustained and massive programme of cultural diplomacy, utilising information, ideas, people, and culture as a systematic and integral part of their foreign policy. That China was equally successful in this domain was evident from the growing numbers of visitors who travelled to China. In 1955, there were approximately 4,760 visitors from 63 countries. In 1956, there were 5,200 from 75 countries.[38] The composition of delegations varied from year to year, depending on political developments. When the *Panch Sheel* declaration was made by India and China in 1954, the rising curve of Indian visitors reached a peak. When the tensions in the Middle East escalated, particularly during the Suez Crisis of 1956, the number of Arab visitors increased markedly. And when political turbulence became more rampant in Africa and Latin America, the number of visitors from these areas rose steeply.

Parallel to her multilateral diplomacy, China also proceeded to systematically cultivate those countries which had opted for a policy of non-alignment. Bilateral agreements were concluded with some of them setting forth the so-called "Five Principles of Co-existence" which were to have so much vogue in Asia and which were subsequently embodied in many treaties and international policy statements made by Asian states in the middle 1950s.[39] Visits were undertaken to and encouraged from these countries with the specific object of giving verbal assurances of China's peaceful intentions.

The new Chinese policy reaped good results: not too long after its adoption, the non-aligned nations which had of neccessity turned to the West responded favourably to Beijing's initiatives. Every opportunity, in fact, was thereafter seized to reciprocate Beijing's initiatives, and diverse efforts were deployed to seek common ground on many issues of international affairs.

If the sights of non-aligned countries had turned towards Beijing, they evidenced less interest in further developing relations with the West. Some of them showed signs of partially disengaging from a position of excessive dependence on the West, thereby establishing a greater equilibrium and flexibility in their foreign policies.

The most striking consequence of the new situation was the crumbling of US efforts to create a military alliance system under her leadership. Many of the Asian states openly denounced such efforts and expressed the view that the establishment of such an alliance would only serve to aggravate tensions in the area. U. Nu of Burma proclaimed that the formation of regional military organisations "increases the chances of World War III",[40] making it clear that his government would not be a party to the proposed military alliance. Kampuchea declined SEATO protection.[41] Indonesia became so antagonistic to SEATO that she proposed the formal creation of

234

a neutralist bloc professing friendship with China.[42] And Nehru considered the formation of military alliances as having only "added to the tension and the fear of the situation."[43]

In the face of such mounting opposition from non-aligned countries, US plans to set up a viable military alliance system in the area could not meet with much success. Pakistan, the Philippines, and Thailand were the only Asian countries to adhere to SEATO; and even among them, the motivating elements that influenced their decision did not necessarily coincide with those of their principal partner, the United States. In the case of Thailand, an inherent fear of her northern neighbour led her to join SEATO, but her concern over developments "east of Laos" was equally important. In any event, Thailand was eager to avoid a major involvment in issues not directly related to her own security. Since the commencement of informal Sino-US discussions in 1955 in Geneva, she was increasingly veering around to the idea that accommodation with China might be the best form of security.[44]

Pakistan adhered to SEATO not because her leaders had any special reason to fear Communism or because they had any major difficulties with any of the Communist states; for her, mounting differences with India were far more important and far more real than the relatively nonexistent danger of Communism.[45] Similarly, the Philippines, despite SEATO membership, appeared to be principally concerned with the tasks of limiting the US military presence in the country, of using the alliance system to suppress Huk guerillas, and of obtaining the support of her allies against any threat from Indonesia.[46]

The consequences of this formal adherence to the alliance system were severe. All three countries ran into serious domestic difficulties insofar as this course of action generated not only rancorous debates on alliance systems, but also exacerbated internal tension among different political forces, thereby revealing the full spectrum of the internal contradictions plaguing them. Unlike the politics of non-alignment which cushioned domestic shocks and which provided an acceptable framework for a broad consensus, the alliance systems, particularly with the Western world, proved great de-stablisers of domestic situations.

China's moderate policy was thus remarkably successful; it not only suceeded in stymieing US plans of creating a viable military alliance system, but it also actually led to a diminution of the feeling of insecurity that generally pervaded the area in the aftermath of the Communist Revolution of 1949. More and more, Asian nations were prepared to seek common ground with Beijing, and an increasing number of them were now favourably disposed towards the idea of developing economic and cultural relations with China.

All this, however, did not endure; for hardly had China's policy of peaceful coexistence been put into full swing, and hardly had it begun to bear fruit in Asia, when it was abandoned. As previously,[47] the shift in

235

Chinese policy was rapid and prompt. By the end of 1957 some signs of change had appeared on the political horizon, and by the autumn of 1958 the new hard line had already been operationalised.

The Great Leap Forward

Internally, the "Blooming and Contending" movement, launched in May 1957 to generate free discussion, was abruptly ended in the summer of 1958. A vigorous programme of political education and a kind of Cromwellian conformity were initiated to eradicate doubts and "erroneous" thoughts that were on the ascendent among Chinese intellectuals. Top positions in higher educational institutions were alloted to party officials to ensure political and ideological orthodoxy, and a number of senior Communists who had sympathised with liberal ideas were summarily dismissed from their posts and expelled from the party.[48] In a *People's Daily* editorial, the "rightist-inclined opportunists" were vigorously attacked for conspiring to overthrow the party and the proletariat. "Their threats," underlined the paper, "are a warning to us that the class struggle is still going on and that we must adopt the class struggle point of view and review the present-day phenomenon and matters and thus arrive at correct conclusions."[49]

In the economic field, the policy of the "Great Leap Forward" was launched with great panache. The carefully planned economic targets announced at the 8th Party Congress in 1956 were set aside for more fancifully ambitious goals which were to be achieved by a maximum mobilisation of the masses through a combination of ideological exhortation and efficient party leadership at the grass-roots level.[50] The five-year targets set for 1962 were now to be accomplished in one year. In place of doubling industrial production, it was to be multiplied six-and-a-half times. Instead of increasing agricultural output by 35 per cent, it was to be augmented by 250 per cent. Steel output of $5^{1}/_{2}$ million tons was to be doubled in 1958. The country was to surpass Britain as an industrial power in ten years.[51] And Communism was no longer perceived as a distant dream, but something which was rapidly becoming a reality with the introduction of People's Communes.[52]

Externally, more and more emphasis was laid on the decisive shift in the international balance of power in favour of the socialist countries, on the imperialistic character of US policies,[53] and on the relevance of "uninterrupted revolutions" in the developing countries.[54] Perhaps the most striking development was the manifestation of growing disappointment with the whole phenomenon of nationalist revolutions in the Third World. The leadership seemed to fear that time was not necessarily on its side, and that the newly independent governments established by non-Communist political figures might stabilise and eventually gravitate back into the Western fold. Writing in the anniversary issue of the *Red Flag,* Wang Qiuxiang, a secretary of the Chinese Party, voiced impatience with nationalist leaders, warning that they might slide back into the "imperialist" camp. He wrote:

> The bourgeoisie which is in power in these countries (Asia and Africa) has played to a certain degree an historically progressive role . . . It may to a greater or lesser degree go part of the way in opposing imperialism and feudalism. But after all, the bourgeoisie is a bourgeoisie. When in power it does not follow resolutely revolutionary lines. It oscillates and compromises. Therefore, it is out of the question for these countries to pass to socialism, nor is it possible for them to accomplish in full the tasks of national democratic revolutions. What is more, even the national independence they have achieved will not be secure . . . There may emerge bureaucratic capitalism which gang up with imperialism and feudalism. Thus in the final analysis they cannot escape the control and clutches of imperialism.[55]

Apparently, the simple establishment of diplomatic relations and the forging of economic and cultural ties with the existing non-Communist governments were no longer considered sufficient to satisfy the resuscitated revolutionary zeal of the increasingly left-wing-oriented Chinese leadership. In fact, an immoderate development of such links was considered counterproductive insofar as it could be interpreted as an implicit stamp of Communist approval of the bourgeois Asian governments, thereby rendering the goal of revolutions even more unattainable. Therefore, while maintaining minimum diplomatic relations, the Chinse veered around to the idea of opening up collateral non-governmental channels through which they could attack the West, seek meaningful relations with revolutionary forces in the Third World, and implicitly expose the conservative nature of nationalist leaders.

Such an opportunity presented itself with the establishment of the Afro-Asian Solidarity Organization, which held its first conference in Cairo from 28 December 1957 to 1 January 1958. For China—besides the accretion of bilateral ties to Asian Communist parties—this was undoubtedly an important international forum which merited more than casual interest.[56] It was the first major non-governmental meeting of the peoples of Asia and Africa, representing 45 countries, since the Brussels conference of 1927 whose purpose was by no means to voice the views of those who happened to be in power. Many of the organizers were either Communists or alternatively subscribed to left-wing views.[57] In fact, many of the participants to the conference were more representative of Afro-Asian political trends and popular interests[58] than those who had attended the Bandung conference. Beijing therefore actively participated in the conference and considered it an excellent opportunity to establish direct contact with prominent figures of national liberation movements who happened to be in Cairo on this occasion. The Chinese role, thought not prominent, was nonetheless significant. They were assigned the role of making the principal report on the promotion of cultural exchange between African and Asian nations. The report's main thrust concerned the "vitality of Eastern civilization" and the considerable harm that was inflicted on it by the encroachment of colonialism. Warning against the danger of "imperialistic cultural influence", the Chinese delegate said, "We must be on guard against such invasion so that the vigorous younger generation will not be misled, spoiled, and drugged by the corrupting and poisonous influence of imperialist culture".[59]

That China was able to exercise, at least during the first two to three years, weighty influence on the organization is evident from the records of different meetings. That she attached considerable importance to the organization is clear from the efforts that were deployed to make it into a viable movement embracing the whole of Asia and Africa.[60]

While China's interest in revolutionary movements was thus rising, her faith in the policy of peaceful coexistence was waning. While on the one hand, she increasingly participated in the militant activities of the Afro-Asian Solidarity and other organizations,[61] she, on the other, adopted an unfriendly attitude towards practically all nations. By 1959 it seemed as if Beijing was at loggerheads with most of the Third World states.

First of all, a carefully prepared campaign was put into action against the United States, whose intervention in Taiwan Straits and the Middle East was denounced in strong terms. On 17 July 1958, half a million people were mobilised and brought out into the streets of the capital to demonstrate against US military intervention in Lebanon. On 28 August, a massive bombardment of Jinmen was begun as a probing operation, presumably designed to test the strength of the nationalists on the island and the will of the United States to aid them. Mao Zedong personally delivered a polemical assault. In a speech before the Supreme State Conference on 8 September, he attacked the United States' presence in Taiwan and Lebanon and called attention to hundreds of US bases located in the socialist countries, comparing them to "nooses tied around the neck of US imperialism".[62]

The pro-Western countries of Asia were also made targets of Beijing's vitriolic attacks. In the case of some of them, harassing tactics were used. In Laos, the Pathet Lao was emboldened in the summer of 1958 to begin an armed insurrection against the right-wing Sananikone. The confused and uncertain situation in the country was assuming, in Beijing's eyes, the pattern of an anti-colonial struggle, with the growing American influence in the role of the colonialist power. On 12 August 1959, a spokesman of the Chinese Foreign Ministry warned Washington and the Laotian authorities against creating tension in Indo-China "and further menacing the security of China" as this "will certainly face the firm opposition of the Chinese government and people."[63] With Japan all relations were broken. The two unofficial agreements, the iron and steel accord and the trade pact, which had been concluded in the beginning of 1958 and which provided for commercial exchanges totalling more than China's trade with any other non-Communist country, were abruptly cancelled. The politics of maintaining normal relations with Pakistan were abandoned. The new government, set up after the military *coup d'état* in October 1958, was castigated for having concluded a bilateral defence agreement with Washington and for having proposed a joint defence pact with New Delhi. The unexpected arrival in Karachi of a Moslem mission from Taiwan, which was actually on its way to Mecca, led Beijing to denounce "the vicious role played by Pakistan's ruling clique" in Asia.[64]

Attitudes towards the non-aligned countries also hardened. The first country to be condemned was Egypt. Nasser was criticised for having embarked on a policy of persecuting Communists, and for having manifested serious reservations regarding pro-Communist orientations of the Kassem regime in Iraq. He and his collaborators were furthermore accused of having abandoned the struggle against imperialism and were warned that people may have to "form a new judgement of them in the light of new facts".[65] Khaled Bagdash, the Syrian Communist who was visiting Beijing in 1959 was permitted by Chinese leaders to publicly characterise Nasser's government as terroristic and dictatorial,[66] and, according to Egyptian sources, the UAR embassy in Beijing was placed under close watch.[67] Indonesia was bitterly attacked for curbing the economic activities of overseas Chinese in many parts of the country and was publicly warned that Beijing would not "simply look on while their compatriots are being subjected to unjustified discrimination and persecution abroad".[68] India, too, was made a target of Chinese hostility. The Nehru government was accused of fomenting the Tibetan revolt of March 1959; and, for the first time, the entire boundary alignment between the two countries was formally questioned. In September of the same year, the dispute was further escalated when the Chinese claimed 50,000 square miles of what the Indians considered to be part of India.[69] With Burma, considerable difficulties were raised concerning the exact alignment of the border between the two countries. The package deal personally proposed by Zhou Enlai in 1956,[70] and accepted by the Burmese was retracted in the summer of 1957 and new demands were put forward. All the efforts of the Burmese government, which was prepared to go to great lengths within the new set of Chinese terms to settle the differences, were rebuffed.[71]

What were the reasons for the adoption of such a hard line? Why did the Chinese leadership abandon the slow but nonetheless steady pace of economic development planned by experienced economists for fanciful projects conceived by ideologists? What led them to cast aside the apparently successful policy of peaceful coexistence and to introduce one characterised by an inordinate number of diatribes against the Third World? Was this new orientation towards militancy a result of the effective assertion of left-wing forces in Chinese politics,[72] or was it really "a synthetic solution worked out collectively" after prolonged debate within the party?[73]

Considering the paucity of archival documentation, it is indeed difficult to advance any assertive explanations of this conundrum. Only tentative hypotheses can be put forward.

In the first place, the developments within the Communist bloc appeared to have contributed to the general tightening up of the political situation in China. The process of increasing autonomy in East European politics, the upheavals of 1956 in Poland and Hungary, the partial de-Stalinization in the Soviet Union, the presentation of a new theoretical framework at the 20th Soviet Party Congress, etc., had generated an atmosphere of bemusement, of ideological dissonance, and of an unprecedented lack of discipline among Communists everywhere. In China, for example, the "Blooming and Contending" movement, originally launched under the influence of developments in Eastern Europe, unharnessed astonishingly forceful and bitter attacks from different sources on Communist Party policy and generated a high degree of instability. This resulted in the wholesale defection of peasants from collective farms in some provinces, in the assertion of some independence by trade unions, and in the open manifestation of discontent among students.[74] Unaccustomed to any challenges to the established system, the flood of unexpected criticism impelled the shocked Communist leadership to shift to the left, to rapidly clamp down on the "Hundred Flowers" movement, and to re-introduce, with considerable brutality and determination, the rigid conformism of the earlier period.

Second, the internal economic situation also became bleak in the summer of 1957. Reports of cutbacks in development plans all along the line and of serious reductions in cloth and pork rations cropped up in the press. Natural calamities shook the country, and the failure of collectivization to produce the expected agricultural expansion became evident. Compounded to all this was the fact that the principal supply of external aid, which came from the Soviet Union, was rapidly drying up due to economic and political reasons. For China, there appeared to exist virtually no other solution but to rely on her "own strength as far as possible",[75] and to advocate a breakneck pace of economic development as the only way out.

Third, the non-aligned nations were not showing any visible signs of swinging further in the direction of the Socialist bloc. Having succesfully established an equilibrium in their relations with the Socialist and Western blocs, many were reluctant to formally line themselves up with one against the other. The domestic benefits, the economic advantages, and the political leverage accruing from this middle-of-the-road option were obviously too important to be abandoned for the dangerous game of bloc politics. For China in the late 1950s, any open approbation of non-alignment by Socialist bloc countries was tantamount to a perpetuation of existing non-revolutionary regimes, when the Chinese felt that the Communist objective should be "the firm grasping of hegemony in the democratic revolution by the proletariat."[76] Moreover, an endorsement of non-alignment only rendered the Asian Communist task of coming into power even more difficult—for why should the Communists be supported by political forces within their countries when their own ideological allies, the socialist nations, appeared to be satisfied with existing non-aligned regimes? Such a situation, in the eyes of the Chinese, had in fact already developed in many Asian countries where the Communist adoption of a benign attitude towards the national bourgeoisie had considerably diminished their chances of gaining power.

Fourth, important developments in Soviet weaponry by the fall of 1957[77] led the Chinese to conclude that the international situation had "reached a new turning point" where the "East Wind" was prevailing over the "West Wind" and where the socialist forces were "overwhelmingly superior to the imperialist forces."[78] It was thus now possible for the Socialist bloc to seize the advantage of the new strategic equation by formulating bolder policies of confrontation against the "imperialists" and by accelerating activities to promote national liberation wars in the Third World.

Explanations for the new Chinese firmness were thus multiple. They were neither exclusively domestic nor only external, but were rather a combination of a number of interacting elements. The rapidly deteriorating domestic situation certainly had repercussions where foreign policy was concerned; but then the rapidly changing external situation (the drying up of Soviet aid, political upheavals in Eastern Europe) also had a considerable impact on internal conditions.

From this, however, one should not conclude that Beijing, influenced by the "Great Leap Forward," was determined to artificially create problems that did not exist. All the difficulties and tensions concerning India, Burma, Indonesia, etc., analysed above were indeed real and were based on genuine disagreements traceable back to decades before the installation of Communist power in China. The only difference was that during the peaceful coexistence phase, when China was seeking common ground with other Third World countries, she considered it expedient to remain uncommunicative on these issues, while during 1958-59, when signs of belligerence and radicalism were becoming increasingly evident, she allowed these differences to bubble to the surface.

Just as this was happening, just as China was adopting a hard line against the United States and many Asian countries, differences also began to surface with Moscow. At first, they appeared insignificant, but soon it became apparent that they were serious and covered a wide range of issues relating to Marxist theory and practice, to the assessment of the international situation, and to the nature of strategy and tactics that ought to be adopted to face the existing international situation. By the early 1960s it became evident that the differences had developed into a real and serious dispute, spreading in all directions, and by the late 1960s, the dispute had clearly escalated into a real confrontation with absolutely no hope of any reconciliation.[79]

241

Re-examination of Policy

China was thus placed in the most unenviable situation, for not only was she faced with a bleak internal situation but she was also now isolated from practically everyone, including her allies and friends. The development of such a situation would be viewed as serious for any major power. For developing China, it was simply disastrous, since she had at the time neither the military clout nor the necessary economic strength to stand on her feet—an essential precondition for any nation that wishes to pursue an independent and defiant policy.

For the Chinese leaders, it had therefore become necessary to once again re-examine their policies in the light of the new situation created by the "Great Leap Forward" and to attempt to breakthrough this dangerous situation of encirclement by political or ideological adversaries. In many ways the difficult position of simultaneous confrontation with different political adversaries that they had themselves created was contrary to the Maoist strategy of wiping out "the enemy forces one by one"[80] and of avoiding the necessity "to strike everywhere without enough strength anywhere".[81]

Internally, the bewildered government took courageous and energetic measures to meet the difficult situation. A period of recovery and readjustment was inaugurated which marked a change in economic priorities and in the style of management. Priority was placed on the restoration of food production, on the designing of simplified economic planning, and on the control of the rapidly expanding population. The People's Communes, for example, were dissolved in effect though not in name, and agriculture resumed the pattern characteristic of the old collective farms. The peasants were allowed to cultivate their garden plots again and raise a few of their own chickens or a pig or two. Perhaps the most vital Chinese response to the degenerating internal situation was the decision to wrap itself in the flag of patriotism and "self-reliance". When the Soviet Union suddenly withdrew her experts from China in the summer of 1960, causing considerable chaos in the country, increasing stress was laid on the vital importance of becoming economically independent and of relying principally on the genius of the Chinese nation to develop militarily and economically.

Externally, however, what could China do to make the situation more favourable? To whom could she turn to in order to breakthrough the high wall of isolation, without of course sacrificing some of the basic principles?

An understanding with the United States was deemed impossible. In the first place, the US was an "imperialistic" nation which had manifested a determination to weaken if not destroy China. Second, she had stymied all Chinese efforts to seize Taiwan by interposing her naval power in the straits of the area. Third, Washington had taken upon itself the responsibility for containing Chinese expansion in the area where the latter had traditionally exercised influence.

242

The maintenance of an entente with Moscow was equally impossible. The rapidly escalating Sino-Soviet dispute involved issues on which a retreat from the Chinese side seemed out of question. Some of the fundamental tenets of Marxist theory had been substantially and unilaterally altered by the post-Stalinist leadership. For example, war was no longer considered as an instrument of social change; peaceful transition to socialism was considered possible; and the state in a socialist society was no longer viewed as an institution representing the interest of the working people alone but that of the entire people.[82]

In the Chinese perception, the Third World was the only region with which there was some hope of reaching an understanding, despite their "bourgeois" orientations and despite the existing leadership's tendency to avoid seeking revolutionary solutions to their basic socio-economic problems—for their continuing economic poverty, political instability, and mounting Western capitalistic exploitation would inevitably push them to seek revolutionary solutions. Therefore, in the existing configuration of international forces, the increasingly marginalised Third World was the only potential ally left for China.

China turns to The Third World 1960-1965

While the original ideas of Marxist theory in this new orientation were continually used to denounce Soviet "revisionism,"[83] the Chinese party, interestingly enough, displayed remarkable flexibility in its assessment of the Third World. Many arguments used were not even remotely connected with Marxism. For instance, the issue of European domination was constantly stressed, the factor of colour discrimination was often but subtly used, and the subject of economic and political independence became a constant theme in Chinese political writings.

Perhaps the most significant response to the new situation was the elaboration of a new theoretical framework which partially broke away from the original tenets of Marxism-Leninism.[84] Instead of reiterating the cosmic aspects of Marxist theory, of stressing the linkage between European working class struggles and national liberation movements, or of giving equal importance to all the conflictory situations that the Marxists perceived as being rampant in the world, the Chinese projected a zonal picture of the international system in 1963. While ritually enumerating all the "fundamental contradictions in the contemporary world,"[85] they arrived at the conclusion that the prime component of the contemporary proletarian world revolution[86] was the Third World, where the levels of exploitation and discontent had soared, and where the potential for revolutionary explosions had become tangible.

The Chinese apparently perceived the Third World as the area of greatest political and revolutionary opportunity in international politics. They viewed it as a world where old political orders and alliances were crumbling, where new friends could be won, and where new alliances could be forged. The Beijing government saw in the increasingly uncertain and volatile conditions of Asia, Africa, and Latin America its best diplomatic opportunity to influence the contemporary world scene and to use its limited resources towards the attainment of its foreign policy objectives.

But what precisely could China do to implement such a policy? How could she design her policies to reach these goals? And what type of operational diplomacy could she elaborate to advance her interests?

Like most revolutionary governments, China's behaviour in regard to the outside world was influenced by two objectives: as a nation conditioned by revolutionary ideas, the staging of revolutions in the Third World appeared to be a desirable objective; but, as a state among other states—with a long traumatic history of external domination—national independence and national security were important goals for which establishment of relations with other governments was necessary.

The operationalisation of a policy to move in the direction of these two goals (revolutionary and diplomatic) has often led Marxist-oriented governments into assuming contradictory positions. While one policy was designed to gain effective hold over revolutionary movements, the other was aimed at developing relations with newly independent governments—which often served to perpetuate them when the objective was to bring about their demise.

It can of course be argued that these contradictions really do not exist, that this is a figment of the imagination of those who tend to think in abstractions, and that notwithstanding the revolutionary orientations of a government, it will invariably opt for national interests in the event of a real conflict. While such reasoning may be valid in the long run, it does not appear to hold water for the day-to-day actions and initiatives, when revolutionary governments often find themselves hovering between revolutionary and classical diplomacies without noticing any apparent damage to either of the two objectives.

Third World Communism—Revolutionary Diplomacy

To reach out to the Third World Communist parties, the CCP initiated a major rhetorical campaign by elaborately explaining its new theoretical framework. At the same time, its escalatory polemical assaults directed at the Soviet Union contained considerable argumentation concerned with Soviet "revisionism" and the irrelevance of the Soviet revolutionary model to the developing countries.

Initially Communist parties did not really know how to respond to this new development. Their first reactions therefore were of considerable bemusement and ambivalence. The ideological defiance of the Soviet Union—hitherto revered as the great land of socialism—by another and equally prestigious Communist country generated uncertainty and demoralisation among Communists all over the world. That this was normal and even unavoidable would seem evident when one takes into account the fact that the monolithic character and the intellectual certitude that had so far characterised the international Communist movement had been a source of considerable psychological and intellectual security, giving the movement necessary strength and dimension.

This, however, did not last long; for soon after this initial period, Communist parties reacted to the new and difficult situation dichotomously. On the one hand, the parties generally began to manifest varying signs of a marked domestic orientation, of showing greater initiative in autonomously determining their own policies, and of responding more independently to their own national problems. On the other hand, the mounting and contending pressures from Moscow and Beijing to choose sides generally resulted in the development of competing groups in Third World countries and in the adoption of either a pro-Moscow or a pro-Beijing position on a wide array of international and ideological issues.

In Asia,[87] the Chinese position was generally favoured by a majority of parties, with the exception of South Asia (India, Pakistan, Nepal, Sri Lanka) where the Soviet line held sway although these countries were also by no means completely spared the problems of factionalism. In the first place, China's geographical and cultural proximity to other Asian countries permitted her to communicate effectively and convincingly with Asian Communists regarding the relevance of her revolutionary experience. Second, the experiment of modernisation carried out by the CCP was more appealing to its counterparts in Asia. And third, the Chinese, despite their enthnocentrism, were perhaps more skillful in the diplomatic handling of Asian Communists than were the Soviets, who, due to their long period of dominance, had become unconcerned about Asian sensitivities.

In Africa,[88] where Communism was much less firmly installed, the Soviet Union appeared to command the loyalty, if perhaps not always the sympathy, of most African groups professing a commitment to Marxism-Leninism. With the exception of small pro-Beijing groups in Mozambique, Angola, South Africa, Somalia, Sudan, a faction in Congo, and a handful of disaffected members of the *Parti Africain de l'indépendance* (Senegal) most of the parties had lined up behind the Soviet Union. Here the Chinese party was obviously at a disadvantage. The factors that had favoured China in Asia were missing in Africa. The differences between China and Africa were too great, cultural proximity did not exist, and the relevance of the Chinese model to Africa was doubtful. Moreover, the Soviet Union had a head start over the Chinese in the development of trade union activities, in the formation of Communist cells and cadres, and in the exercising of a marked influence over the African parties through the Communist parties of the colonial powers which had played a significant role in founding them during the colonial period.

In Latin America too, the Chinese impact was severely limited. The bulk of the Communist parties, having a long tradition of subordinating their interests to those of the Soviet Union,[89] generally sided with Moscow and stressed their firm opposition to ideas emanating from Beijing. The Sino-Soviet dispute, however, did create some rumblings of discontent within the Latin American Communist movement against Moscow, and even led to the emergence of pro-Beijing organisations in Brazil, Peru, Chili, Bolivia, and Paraguay, the principal function of which was to distribute Chinese political literature and to stress the relevance of the Chinese strategy to Latin America.[90] Their influence was limited, however. In fact, it has even been argued that the actual withdrawal of Maoist members from the Communist parties rendered the former weak and ineffective, with no great hope of their having any great impact.[91]

China's influence among the established Communist parties of the Third World countries was thus essentially limited. The bulk of them were much too dependent upon Moscow to adopt an independent line. Nonetheless, the Sino-Soviet dispute did have some impact on the Third World Communist parties, even on those which continued to maintain their pro-Soviet loyalties. Though most of them supported the Soviet line on external issues, their strategy and tactics insofar as internal issues were concerned had become more responsive to the internal situation and appeared to take less account of Soviet views than before. This autonomous posture in domestic matters should have been a source of potential strength, since one of the major elements that had hitherto obstructed the development of the Communist parties was precisely this image of dependence and subservience to Moscow; but this new potential was blocked by the development of hostile fragments within the Communist movements, thereby making them even more ineffective and more marginal than before in the political lives of their respective countries.

Third World States—Classical Diplomacy

Asia

The Chinese focus on the Third World was not only ideological, it was also diplomatic, the principal purpose of which was to reach out to the newly independent countries.

The three Asian Communist states—Outer Mongolia, North Korea, and North Vietnam—were naturally prime targets. Many of the initiatives taken were directed towards them, with the specific object of bringing them into the Chinese orbit. In the first place, China probably considered them easy to manipulate, in view of the fact that Communist parties were already at the helm of affairs and the similarities between their socio-economic conditions and those of China would make the Chinese model of development appear more relevant to them than Asian countries dominated by other socio-economic systems. Second, if China were to gain influence over

246

them—at least in the cases of North Korea and North Vietnam, situated as they were on the periphery of China—this would facilitate the task of effectively communicating with other countries of Asia. Third, it would help to swing the non-ruling Communist parties towards Beijing, as the Chinese, in this case, would be able to show to them that since the Soviet model was not acceptable to Asian Communists already in power, by the same token, it could hardly be relevant to the others in Asia.

The Soviet hold over Outer Mongolia was too tight to permit any disengagement. All the Chinese initiatives in 1960—and they were numerous [92]—did not succeed in breaking the firm hold established during years of Soviet domination.[93] Moreover, the Mongolians themselves, traditionally fearful of China, were uncertain of her ultimate intentions regarding the existence of their country as an independent state.

With North Korea, however, ties were forged. Agreement was reached on a wide spectrum of ideological and foreign policy issues. A long-term loan of 420 million roubles was given in October 1960 for the period 1961-64, and a Treaty of Friendship, Cooperation, and Mutual Assistance was concluded during the same year.[94]

Relations with North Vietnam were expanded. The first signs of some convergence became obvious with the speech given by Le Duan, Secretary General of the Lao Dong, the North Vietnamese Communist Party, on 14 March 1963. Many of the ideas proclaimed on this occasion were strikingly close to those of the Chinese,[95] and these were widely disseminated by the *People's Daily* and by Beijing's Foreign Languages Publishing House.

Neither of the two countries, however, were really pulled into the Chinese orbit. The Sino-Soviet dispute had made it possible for them to keep themselves out of the grasp of the two Communist giants and to develop wide leverage in their relations with both of them. But the nature of the response and the degree of leverage acquired by the two peripheral countries was different. Whereas Kim il-sung, the North Korean Premier, had changed his standpoint a number of times between 1960 and 1966, visibly swinging from a pro-Soviet position to a neutral one, and from a neutral to a pro-Chinese position, before moving on to an independent attitude,[96] North Vietnam displayed, during the same period, a remarkable degree of subtlety and a talent for using nuance in the Sino-Soviet dispute. While veering towards a position of greater manoeuvrability, she gave the impression of being pro-Chinese and pro-Soviet at the same time. If "modern revisionism" was publicly attacked to appease the Chinese, profound gratitude was simultaneously expressed to the Soviet Union for having consistently supported the Vietnamese cause.[97]

By far the most dramatic diplomatic offensive was directed towards the non-aligned countries. Their burgeoning role within the international system encouraged Beijing to initiate a series of bold steps to resolve some of the seemingly intractable issues that had hitherto damaged China's relations with most of them.

247

Burma was the first country to benefit from this new policy. The intractable border differences, which had cast a cloud over the relations between the two countries since 1958, were settled by Beijing's sudden decision to seek an agreement on the basis of the "fair and equitable" compromise proposals that the Burmese government had put forward in the summer of 1959. It is noteworthy that under the agreement concluded on 1 October 1960, the much-maligned McMahon Line, thereafter considered the "traditional customary line," was accepted with only minor alterations.[98]

In return for this major concession made by the Chinese, Burma signed a Treaty of Friendship and Mutual Non-Aggression, under which both the parties agreed "not to take part in any military alliance directed against the other contracting party."[99] Although the successful conclusion of the treaty was publicly hailed as a firm reiteration of the "Five Principles of Peaceful Coexistence," the Burmese leaders were less enthusiastic about it than their Chinese counterparts—for by signing such an accord, Rangoon had formally limited Burma's freedom of action in her own defense—a freedom of action which a small country normally is not prepared to renounce unless and until she is persuaded to do so by the political power and the military strength of a powerful neighbour.

With Nepal, the border differences that had partially ruffled relations between two countries and had generated a measure of apprehensive uncertainty in Nepalese politics were resolved in March 1960, when Prime Minister B.P. Koirala visited China. In the Chinese capital, after a formal welcome, a boundary agreement was concluded under which China made the major concession of agreeing that the five-hunderd-mile border separating the two countries "shall be scientifically delineated and formally demarcated through friendly consultations on the basis of existing traditional customary lines."[100] On the same occasion, a three-year economic agreement was also concluded, under which China agreed to give a "free grant" of $21 million to cover "equipment, machinery and materials, techniques and other commodities."[101] In stipulating the terms of this agreement under which Chinese technicians would work, Beijing avoided the conditions to which the Nepalese had hitherto objected in other aid programmes and thereby ostensibly demonstrated to the Nepalese that their objections had been justified. The travelling expenses and salaries of technicians were to be paid by China. The agreement also stipulated that the Chinese technicians in Nepal would receive living expenses sufficient for a standard of living equal to that of their Nepalese counterparts.[102]

In Indonesia, the Chinese government took prompt initiatives to settle the difficult problem of overseas Chinese residing there. With remarkable rapidity it arrived at an amicable arrangement for the implementation of the Dual Nationality Treaty concerned with overseas Chinese, and at the same time promptly acquiesced to draconian measures taken by the Indonesian government against Chinese residents.[103] A Treaty of Friendship was

248

also concluded (April 1961) under which both parties, reiterating their desire to establish friendly relations, agreed to respect each other's independence, sovereignty, and territorial integrity, and decided to "further" strengthen economic and commercial ties.[104]

With Kampuchea, the problem of overseas Chinese suspected of illegal activities allegedly inspired by Beijing was resolved. During his visit to Pnom Penh in May 1960, Zhou Enlai suddenly accepted their deportation to China[105] and publicly expressed his gratitude to the Kampuchean government for pursuing a friendly policy towards overseas Chinese. In his view, this could "serve as an example" to other Southeast Asian countries where similar problems existed.[106] At the same time, he supported Kampuchea's policy of "strict neutrality", stating that the disputed islands off the southern coast of Kampuchea belonged to the Royal Kingdom and not to South Vietnam, and made it clear that if Kampuchea were the subject of aggression "from whichever direction," China would stand by her side.[107] During Sihanouk's December 1960 visit to Beijing, he was given an elaborate welcome, and relations between China and Kampuchea reached a high point with the conclusion of a Treaty of Friendship and Mutual Non-Aggression.[108]

Towards India, too, important initiatives were taken in 1960 to seek a compromise on the question of disputed borders. After a series of incidents had increased tension between the two countries, Zhou Enlai proposed to Nehru that "the Prime Ministers of the two countries hold talks in the immediate future."[109] At the meeting, which was finally held in April 1960, Zhou proposed an interesting and perhaps not-too-unreasonable bargain in which India would drop her claim to Aksai Chin in the north west in exchange for formal Chinese recognition of the McMahon line in the north east.[110] Although it was not accepted by the Nehru government for a number of domestic reasons, the fact that such an offer was made was by itself an indication of China's desire to search for a compromise.

The Chinese attitude towards Laos also underwent a significant change. This became particularly evident after the *coup d'état* in August 1960, as a result of which a neutralist government was once again installed under the leadership of Souvanna Phouma. For Beijing—which had broken all ties with the preceding government—this was obviously a "new development"[111] which merited not only a close watch but a friendly response in order to keep the Laotian pendulum from once again swinging to the right. Therefore, when the new government announced its intention to forge ties with Beijing, the latter immediately announced that it was "ready to take corresponding measures to facilitate the realisation of this aim."[112] Diplomatic relations were therefore re-established and an element of warmth became increasingly discernible in the relations between the two countries.

The apparent interest in Asia was not limited to non-aligned countries. It was also directed towards some of the nations which had allowed their fates to hinge upon the West and which were, at the same time, prepared to maintain minimal relations with China.

With remarkable rapidity, attacks on Pakistan disappeared from the Chinese press. The U-2 incident was quickly passed over,[113] border differences were resolved, a trade agreement was concluded, and a general understanding was reached on diverse international issues. By 1963, according to some reports, even a military understanding had been reached under which China was expected to come to the aid of Pakistan in the event of any attack from India.[114]

With Tokyo, China moved away from its previous line of not seeking any economic relations as long as political relations were not normalised.[115] In a statement made on 27 August to the head of the China-Japan Trade Promotion Association, Zhou Enlai, while still insisting on establishing trade relations on a government level, held out some hope of resuming economic relations on a private level.[116]

Africa

The African continent also became an important target of revolutionary and diplomatic manoeuvres in the early 1960s. The process of de-colonization had become too widespread and the national liberation movements too accelerated to be ignored by China.[117]

In the Chinese perception of the 1960s, the centre of revolutionary activity had clearly shifted to Africa,[118] where diverse developments were "shaking the foundations of Western imperialism"[119] and where all the international contradictions had become increasingly obvious. The continent, declared a secret bulletin of the Chinese army:

> Is now both the centre of the anti-colonialist struggle and the centre for the East and the West to fight for the control of the intermediary zone, so that it has become the key point of world interest. The general situation is the forced withdrawal of old colonialism from Asia, or at least a large part of Asia and the changing of the last battlefield to Africa.[120]

Interestingly, Chinese interests were no longer cluttered by ideological considerations. Most of the principal writings were concerned neither with the roles of the Communist parties nor with making any searching analyses of class struggles. As late as July 1960, when Soviet analysts were busy stressing the unreliability of the African national bourgeoise and the need for independent working class action, the underlying issue for the Chinese was the armed national struggle, of which the bourgeoisie was considered an integral part. In fact, the developments in Africa were compared to the Boxer Rebellion, the Chinese Revolution of 1911, and the movement of May 1919.[121] As the political department of the Chinese army declared:

Africa at present is mostly occupied with fighting imperialism and colonialism. Its fight against feudalism is not so important, and, moreover, its role in the socialist revolution is in a dormant phase. The important part of its activities lies in its national revolution and in making the United Front spread everywhere in the continent.[122]

However, while stressing the national liberation aspects of revolutionary movements, they did not ignore the eventual possibility of socialist revolutions in Africa. As Marxists, the Chinese were convinced that in the long run the "embryo of national people's revolution in these countries will become a people's revolution, give rise to Marxists, form political parties of the proletariat, and go towards socialist revolution."[123] This, however, was only an eventual possibility with which China did not appear to be very concerned at the time. The principal focus was on nationalist revolutions. Therefore, all the rhetoric that was used by the Chinese leaders and by the Chinese press regarding the revolutionary potential of Africa was essentially limited to the African task of obtaining complete independence from outside control. For example, when Zhou Enlai openly declared, during his 1964 African trip, that the continent was "ripe for revolution,"[124] he was primarily thinking of complete African de-colonization, under which the influence of outside powers would be completely removed. But the Chinese revolutionary rhetoric often conjured up frightening visions of violent Communist upheavals among Africans and led to serious misunderstandings regarding Chinese intentions in Africa. Whereas, for most leaders of the continent, the commencement of de-colonization meant that Africa had or was in the process of having her revolution, for Chinese leaders it was only the beginning of the nationalist process, which would be really completed only when all Soviet and US influences were completely removed.

Based upon their own experience, the Chinese were first of all attracted by the armed struggles in Africa. In their view, this was the only effective way by which a clean break could be made with the past. The Algerian armed struggle naturally took pride of place in Chinese revolutionary thinking.[125] On numerous occasions, it was repeatedly stressed that the Algerian struggle had set a brilliant example for the liberation of the African people. Therefore, when the Algerian provisional government was established in the autumn of 1958, it was immediately recognised. Economic and military assistance was quickly sent to Algeria.[126] In fact, during visits to China of different delegations representing the provisional government,[127] detailed arrangements were believed to have been made for the financing of arms purchased in the Middle East and Eastern Europe, and for the training of selected Algerian officers in China.[128]

Support was also extended to the liberation struggle led by the *Union des Populations du Cameroun* (UPC). Here China was also in an advantageous position insofar as the UPC leaders, who had received Marxist training during their long association with the French *Confédération Générale des*

Travailleurs and the West African *Rassemblement Démocratique Africain* had turned to Beijing as a result of their disappointment with the moderate policy pursued by Moscow. The leader of the UPC, Dr. Felix Moumie, who had studied in the Soviet Union and Czechoslovakia, had switched his allegiance to Beijing once it became apparent that the Soviet Union was eager for him to seek power through elections.[129] In 1959 and 1960 he made two trips to Beijing and thereafter died mysteriously in Switzerland of "an overdose of rat poison administered by an unknown person."[130]

China's consistent partiality for violent revolutions in Africa was also discernible in other areas where, for various internal reasons, armed conflicts had broken out. In Zaire, where, in the aftermath of Lumumba's assassination, armed rebellions had erupted in many provinces, the Chinese did not hesitate to support them. The former Education Minister in Lumumba's cabinet, Pierre Mulélé, tried for example, to generate an armed revolt in Kwilu province after his return from Beijing.[131] The rebellion differed from anything previously seen in Africa. While Mulélé concentrated the leadership in the hands of the youth of Kwilu, he gave a social character to the movement by seeking the support of the peasants. Soon after, a much more widespread revolt was initiated by Lumumbist leaders like Gaston Soumialot and Christophe Gbenye, who operated from Burundi and Congo respectively. Both these wings of the Congolese rebellion received direct and open support from Chinese in terms of propaganda, financial aid, and arms.

In the Portuguese colonies of Angola, Mozambique and Guinea, liberation movements also received assistance from the Chinese. The Angola movement, led by Roberto Holden, radically shifted its orientation from a pro-American bias to a pro-Beijing stance. In December 1963, Holden met Chen Yi in Nairobi, and a few weeks later he declared that a radical change in the front's policy was imperative. He had abandoned hope of getting support from the "hypocritical" Western countries whom he accused of helping "our enemies". In contrast, the Communists had assured him that "we can have whatever we need in arms and money."[132] In the beginning of January 1964, Holden formally announced the Angolan government-in-exile's decision to accept assistance from the Chinese and from other Communist countries.[133]

The change of front in Angola was paralleled by a similar development in Mozambique. Before January 1964, Beijing supported the Mozambique National Democratic Union, a rival to the Liberation Front of Mozambique headed by Eduardo Mondlane. Until then, Mondlane had been regarded as pro-American and in some quarters as an American agent. In January 1964, he accepted an invitation to visit Beijing. On his return from the Chinese capital, he declared that he had been "very much impressed by the enthusiasm of the Chinese people towards the national liberation movement in Africa and their willingness to support the African peoples' struggle."[134] In February of the same year, the media organ of the Liberation Front condemned the United States and Great Britain for supporting Salazar's regime. There is little doubt that the correct explanation of why Mondlane and Holden turned to Beijing for support was that they had grown increasingly disillusioned with Washington, which was not prepared to annoy the Portuguese government because of the American military base in the Azores Islands. They were furthermore embarassed by the pro-Western label which had been given to them, and they realised the need to show better results if they were to survive as leaders.[135] In fact, as early as May 1963, Mondlane warned the US government that if it did not extend open support to the liberation movement, the Mozambique Liberation Front would have no choice but to turn to the Communist world.[136]

If the Beijing leaders gave support to national armed struggles in Africa, they did not ignore the importance of diplomatic initiatives on the continent. Many countries had already gained their political independence, and it was naturally considered important to develop close relations with them. Interestingly enough, Beijing, despite the projection of a revolutionary posture, was careful to cultivate state relations with all those who were willing to reciprocate. Close economic and political relations were, however, also established with those African states which, at least in the early 1960s, had developed an image of belonging to the radical spectrum of African politics with a strong bias against the West. The most important of these where Ghana, Guinea, Mali, UAR, Algeria, Burundi, Congo and Zanzibar. With all of these countries cultural agreements were signed and trade was developed, and economic assistance was made available to them. Towards all of them, the Chinese demonstrated considerable skill in the application of their essentially limited funds and technicians.

The Chinese thus were able to establish some influence in these countries. In Burundi, for example, they established an embassy quite disproportionate in size to what would be consistent with any normal interest in such a state.[137] An important commercial agreement was signed on 22 October 1964 between the two countries, as a result of which Chinese goods flooded the Burundi market.[138] The leading personalities of the country were constantly invited to the Chinese embassy, and, according to one report, money was lavishly distributed.[139] By far the most important Chinese activity was the important material support extended to refugees—the Watusi from Rwanda, who belonged to the same tribal group as that which resided in Burundi. Financial assistance, according to some reports, was given to them, and a training camp was established by the Chinese in Murore for 10,000 Watusi refugees.[140] The small state also became an important centre from which the Chinese kept contact with the rebels in Zaire.

In Congo the Chinese embassy also became a dominant force. Less than 18 months after the overthrow of President Youlou,[141] the government's party, The National Revolutionary Party, openly supported China's foreign policy and the principles of "scientific socialism". More than fifty officials of the Chinese embassy, most of whom were specialists in some technical field, were assigned to work closely with a specific ministry or organization ranging from those dealing with agriculture to children's groups.[142] The weekly, *Dipanda*, published by the governement, was actively advised by the *New China News Agency*. The radicals in the national revolutionary movement pushed aside the Catholic groups and formed Chinese-type labour and women's movements, making use of the paramilitary organization of young people called the "Jeunesse" to terrorize and sometimes eliminate their opponents.[143] Even in the economic sphere, China's role had become increasingly dominant. In 1964, Beijing gave a $20 million loan to set up small-scale industries and allocated a $5 million loan to help the regime balance its budget. Each of these ten-year loans was interest-free.[144]

In the Central African Republic, close relations were forged by opening a fabulous Chinese exhibition in Bangui,[145] by exchanging a number of educational and cultural delegations, and by establishing close contact with some of the leaders of the single political party, particularly its general secretary, Charles Ondoma.[146] It was even reported that Chinese experts were helping the Central African Republic leaders create a popular army, presumably to downgrade the influence and power of the existing army.[147]

Ties were also forged with the three radical states of black Africa, Ghana, Guinea, and Mali.[148] With Guinea, close relations were established in the aftermath of Guinean independence in October 1958. Ambassadors were exchanged, and high-level visits and cultural exchanges were arranged. In September of 1959, President Sekou Touré visited Beijing and signed a treaty of friendship, an agreement for cultural cooperation, an economic and technical cooperation agreement, and a trade agreement. The terms of economic assistance offered were extraordinarily generous, and the publicity with which the occasion was celebrated was most unusual in the cordiality of its tone.

With Mali, Beijing signed a trade and payments agreement, made a substantial interest-free loan, and established an embassy; and with Ghana, diplomatic relations were established as soon as she became a republic in July 1960. Nkrumah went on a state visit to Beijing, where he concluded a ten-year friendship treaty, received an interest-free loan of nearly $20 million, signed a trade and payments agreement and received other promises and assurances. That China was successful is evident from the numerous declarations made by the leaders of the three countries underlining the importance and the relevance of the Chinese model of nation-building and economic development.[149]

There were still other states of Africa with which China developed close ties. There was the island of Zanzibar, for instance, to which important military and technical assistance was given.[150] There was Somalia which had become heavily dependent on Beijing for military and economic assistance.[151] There were also the states of Tanzania and Zambia, which were increasingly turning to Beijing for support and assistance.[152]

China's policy in Africa was initially aimed at giving all political and economic struggles an anti-US orientation. The charge of neo-colonialism had been persistently directed at Washington. Beijing consistently attempted to persuade the Africans that their real enemy was not necessarily British, French, or Portuguese imperialism, but the United States, and that, in their fight for independence, they were "confronted with a new and fiercer enemy—US, imperialism,"[153] which was out to "enmesh the whole of Africa, particularly the newly independent African countries."[154] US friendship for Africa, Beijing continuously asserted, was a "knife hidden behind a smile", and it was further maintained that in fact the United States coveted the "rich mineral deposits and agricultural resources of Africa."[155] Even as late as 1965, when the Sino-Soviet dispute was escalating, the principal thrust of Chinese rhetoric in Africa was directed against the United States. When China was insisting on the postponement of the second Bandung conference to avoid a Soviet presence at the meeting, the Chinese underlined that the purpose of the conference was to "promote the struggle of the peoples of Asia and Africa against imperialism, colonialism, and neocolonialism headed by the United States."[156]

In 1966, however, the Soviet Union became a significant factor in China's African policy. With the aggravation of relations between the two countries, China's political and diplomatic activities were devoted to the task of curbing the Soviet influence on the continent. The one-front strategy directed against Washington was then transformed to a two-front strategy directed against the two superpowers. One wonders whether this new policy, though it remained apparent in Chinese rhetoric, had not operationally given way even before 1966 to a one-front strategy directly solely against the Soviet Union. From various Chinese actions, it would seem that this was the case.

From the Chinese point of view, this attitude did not seem unrealistic. Beijing viewed the conflict between the US and Africa as unavoidable, which would one day end in the decisive erosion of US influence on the continent. This process might need support, but history would inevitably perform this task. The case of the Soviet Union was, however, different: long before the Chinese Communists appeared on the international scene, the Soviet Union had successfully projected a revolutionary image. Obviously it was difficult to tarnish this image, and in the Chinese estimation, a greater effort and more subtle propaganda were required to attain this goal.

Latin America

Chinese sights also turned on Latin America in the early 1960s: the flow of propaganda material increased sharply, radio programmes were intensified, newspaper correspondents were despatched to the region, an office of *New China News Agency* was established in Havana with branch offices manned by non-Chinese personnel in Argentina, Brazil, Colombia, Equador, Peru, and Venezuela. A Chinese-Latin American Friendship Association was set up in Beijing in 1960 to promote Latin American travel to China.[157]

Initiatives were also taken to establish diplomatic relations. Newspaper correspondents were assigned the delicate task of initiating contacts with Latin American political figures who were suseptible to Chinese advances and who were powerful enough to influence decision-making processes in their countries.

Notwithstanding these efforts, no real breakthrough, however, was made in the hemisphere. With the exception of revolutionary Cuba, none of the countries manifested any major interest in establishing political ties with Beijing. Most of the governments were indeed too dependent on their powerful northern neighbour, and some of them, though eager to become disengaged from Washington, did not see any real political or economic advantage in taking the calculated risk of turning to Beijing. What protection and what assistance, they wondered, could China give to them in the event of US harrassment after they had developed relations with China? Hardly any. Obviously the risks were too great and advantages too few. The conservative character of many of the Latin American regimes also contributed to the absence of any major developments in diplomatic relations. The fear that a Chinese diplomatic presence might contribute to the expansion of left-wing movements understandably developed among these countries as well; and the Chinese pattern of making repeated revolutionary declarations and of warmly receiving Latin American revolutionary leaders only enhanced official Latin American apprehension regarding Beijing's intentions in the area.[158]

Unlike in Asia and Africa, therefore, China did not make any major diplomatic breakthrough in Latin America. Her relations were limited to Cuba, where Fidel Castro's victory in January 1959 sparked a prompt and enthusiastic response from the Communist world, including China.

Evidence that the Cuban Revolution was received with great panache can be found in the statements that appeared in the Chinese press. On 4 January 1959, the *People's Daily* spoke of the "national democratic movement of the Cuban people."[159] On 22 January, Peng Chen, member of the Political Bureau of the CCP, underlined "the common aspirations and interests" of the Chinese and Latin American peoples,[160] and on 25 January a resolution passed at a Beijing mass rally held up Castro's victory as "a great inspiration to the national revolutionary movements, not only in Latin America but also in Asia and Africa."[161]

The initial Cuban response to Chinese overtures, however, was prudent. Despite Che Guevara's June 1959 statement that Cubans had been influenced in their struggle against Batista by Mao's military strategy,[162] the new government did not make any effort to establish relations with

Beijing during the first year. Havana's attention in foreign affairs immediately after the Revolution was focussed either on the escalating tension
with the United States or on developing relations with the non-aligned
nations with which the Cuban leaders discerned a community of interest.[163]
Only when US-Cuban relations reached a point of no return by the spring
of 1960 and the Cuban leaders needed firmer protection than what was
offered by non-aligned countries, was a concerted attempt made to adopt a
socialist posture internally and to openly turn to the Socialist bloc countries
externally. Soviet and Chinese aid and friendship under the new circumstances was evidently viewed as vital.

It was thus in the summer of 1960 that ties began to develop between
Havana and Beijing. In July 1960, Odon Alvarez de la Campa, the Foreign
Affairs Secretary of the Cuban Labour Federation, travelled to China. At
the conclusion of his visit he signed a joint statement with Chinese trade
union leaders supporting the Beijing party line.[164] At about the same time,
the two countries signed a commercial agreement which the *People's Daily*
praised as an example of good relations between states "with different social
systems."[165]

During the ensuing months, the Cuban leaders continued to press for
Sino-Cuban amity, reaching a milestone on 2 September 1960 when Castro
expressed the Cuban National Assembly's "free and sovereign will to
establish relations with the People's Republic of China."[166]

The Chinese responded generously and promptly. Arriving in Beijing
after having returned empty-handed from Moscow, Che Guevara was
offered a generous trade agreement under which the Chinese agreed to
purchase one milion tons of Cuban sugar per annum and to give credit of
$ 60 million to Havana.[167] The loan was to be used to finance exports of
complete industrial plants to Cuba and "other technical aid to help to
develop its economy."[168]

In fact, so great was China's desire to maintain and to develop relations
with Cuba that, after an initial period of hesitation, she—though slowly—accepted Castro's proclamation that his revolution was socialist in
character. In October 1961, the Chinese leaders accepted the thesis that a
"thorough national and democratic revolution had been carried out" in
Cuba,[169] and that the Cubans was "dauntlessly and steadily carrying
forward their revolution along the path of socialist development chosen by
themselves."[170] In March 1962, the Chinese considered that Cuba had
"embarked on the road to socialism"[171] and in January 1963, the *People's
Daily* clearly expressed the view that the significance of the Cuban Revol-
tion lay in the fact that "after thoroughly completing the tasks of national
democratic revolution, it courageously led the Cuban people on the socialist
path and set up the first socialist country on the American continent."[172]

There were obviously a number of factors that contributed to the
improvement of Sino-Cuban relations. In the first place, the Chinese and

the Cubans shared many views regarding the nature of people's war. The Cuban organizational ability and revolutionary experience appeared to be more similar to that of the Chinese than that of the Russians. Both were firm partisans of the effectiveness of armed struggle: it was, in their view, the only viable road to power in a majority of countries in the Third World. Each had openly expressed its opposition to those forces in the international Communist movement who advocated a "peaceful path to power." The Castroites and Maoists furthermore agreed that revolutionaries everywhere must combine forces against the common enemy, US imperialism. They also concurred that the Third World was the arena for the most crucial struggle with the common enemy.

Second, there was a striking similarity in their perception of the international situation. Still fresh from their revolutionary experiences, the Cubans, like the Chinese, were firm partisans of a militant and aggressive policy, of promoting revolutions everywhere, and of believing that the main contradiction of the day was the conflict between the oppressed of the Third World and US imperialism. The Soviet performance during the missile crisis of October 1962 supported the growing conviction among Cuban and Chinese decision makers that Moscow was becoming as a much a "paper tiger" as the United States appeared to be at the Bay of Pigs.

If Castro was eager to cultivate relations with Beijing and was even prepared to a publicly support the Chinese argument that violent revolutions in a "majority of the Latin American countries" were necessary,[173] he was nonetheless unwilling and unable to put Cuba completely within the Chinese orbit. Unwilling because of his determination to safeguard Cuban independence from the two Communist giants; unable because of his increasing dependence on Russian political, economic, and military support, particularly after 1963. Evidently, the Soviet Union was in a position to give far greater and far more effective political and economic support than China. Furthermore, the increasing Soviet military strength put Russia in a far better position to offer a measure of military protection than China. Consider the missile crisis of 1962: notwithstanding the humiliating Soviet withdrawal of her missiles in the face of a decisive US ultimatum, it was nevertheless evident that Washington had to take into account the Soviet factor when formulating its Cuban policy.

Therefore, notwithstanding their firm and revolutionary contempt for all forms of revisionism, by 1963 the Cubans found themselves moving unavoidably in the direction of neutralism in the Sino-Soviet dispute, avoiding any fixed positions on many controversial issues, and making efforts to keep the two Communist giants happy. Undoubtedly this was a difficult task, but the Cuban leaders were successful during 1963 and most of 1964. Che Guevara summed up the Cuban position in August 1963:

> For us, the Sino-Soviet dispute is one of the saddest events. We do not participate in this dispute. We are trying to mediate. But as it [the dispute] is a fact, we inform our peoples about it and it is discussed by the party. Our party's attitude is not to

analyse who is in the right and who is not. We have our own position, and as they say in the American movies, any resemblance is purely coincidental.[174]

By 1964, China had been able to forge bilateral ties with Cuba and had been able to assist the Cubans in the maintenance of their neutrality in the Sino-Soviet dispute. On the face of it, this may not seem a significant development, but considering the absence of any relations before 1960 with a country such as Cuba—which was geographically distant and of which China neither had any historical experience nor any knowledge—the achievement may not seem that unimpressive.

Thus within a period of four years after the inauguration of a well-focussed Third World policy in 1960, China was able to establish wide-ranging ties with many countries of Asia, Africa, and Latin America. In many of these countries she was able to generate a wide interest in herself, an accomplishment no other Third World country had been able to achieve, and in most of them she had undoubtedly left a vital impact—no mean achievement for a nation which only two decades earlier had been struggling for her stability and survival.

SetBack: 1965-1969

But once again this did not last—for by the mid-1960s Beijing's relations with the Third World had considerably deteriorated, leaving the Middle Kingdom again in a state of isolation. Almost everywhere in Africa, Latin America, and Asia, strident voices were raised against China's policies, and almost everywhere in these regions, a general apprehension regarding Chinese domination became increasingly evident.

In Africa, the decline of Chinese influence was as striking as had been its meteoric rise in the early 1960s. One country after the other decried her policies and took appropriate measures to diminish her activities. The total number of African nations with which China maintained formal diplomatic ties fell from a high of eighteen in 1964-1965 to a low of thirteen in 1969.

The most advanced centre of Chinese activity, Burundi, expelled Chinese diplomats in January 1965 because of their alleged involvment in the assassination of Prime Minister Pierre Ngendamdumue.[175] They were also accused of having encouraged the Congolese rebellion from Burundi, of having supported Tutsi refugees from neighbouring Rwanda,[176] and of having established control over trade unions and youth organizations.[177] Although Beijing was finally absolved from any responsibility in the shooting of Ngendamdumue and was assured by the new Prime Minister of his intentions to re-establish formal relations as soon as the situation in the country "returned to normal," diplomatic relations were not restored.[178]

In West Africa, the governments of Niger, the Ivory Coast, and Upper Volta, supported by Madagascar, issued a formal declaration in which they severely condemned Chinese penetration in areas south of the Sahara and reprimanded some African states for having permitted subversive agents to organize training camps in their territories.[179] In Kenya, the National African Union, the only political party authorized to function, recommended in July 1965 breaking off diplomatic relations with China on the ground that her embassy in Nairobi had become a centre of subversive activities.[180] Though such intentions were not realized by the government, a number of Chinese nationals, including the Third Secretary of the embassy, were expelled in March 1966. The most serious setback to China, in Kenya, however, was the cancellation by the government of Zhou Enlai's visit to Nairobi in 1966, the dismissal from the government of pro-Chinese Vice President Oginga Odinga in April 1966, and the expulsion of the Chinese chargé d'affaires in June 1967.

In Cairo, a group of Egyptian dissidents who were known to have contacts with the Chinese embassy were arrested in 1965 on charges of attempting to overthrow Nasser and to establish a people's republic. The trial was held privately, and a NCNA correspondent and a Chinese military attaché were discreetly asked to leave as a result of their alleged participation in the conspiracy.[181]

Zambia and Tanzania, major recipients of Chinese economic and technical assistance to establish a 1,042-mile railway link between the two countries, became more guarded against any Chinese attempts to influence their policies. Kuanda of Zambia reacted sharply against Chinese attempts to disseminate Maoist propaganda in the country, particularly in the schools in November 1967, frequently criticized the wrangling between Moscow and Beijing, and opposed any attempts to draw African states into the whirlpool of Sino-Soviet quarrels. Nyerere of Tanzania, though having excellent relations with Beijing and receiving considerable Chinese aid, avoided becoming too closely associated with Chinese policies and made it clear that his country had no exclusive friendship with either the East or with the West and that Tanzania's friendship with China would never be a bar to the development of contacts with a wide range of other countries.[182]

Even in the small state of Congo where Chinese influence appeared to have become dominant, Beijing received a serious setback. The pro-Chinese Prime Minister Lissouba was replaced by Noumazaley, who, according to some reports represented the pro-Soviet tendency in his party,[183] and in January 1968, three pro-Chinese ministers were dismissed in a major government reshuffle. Six months later, Beijing's influence was further weakened when a military government took over and immediately disbanded the Chinese-trained militia and youth movement. Since then, the new government formed by Ngouabi has increasingly looked to the Soviet Union for guidance in shaping the party, the armed forces, and the judicial organs of the country.

Perhaps China's most serious rout on the continent of Africa was the military upheavals in West Africa. The *coup d'état* in Dahomay and in the

Central African Republic in 1966 culminated in these countries breaking off diplomatic relations with Beijing.[184] The revolt in Ghana in February 1966—which occurred while Nkrumah was travelling in China—led to the decline of Chinese influence in the country, including the expulsion of 200-250 Chinese technicians and the closing down of a substantial Chinese-led military camp for the training of saboteurs about 140 miles from Accra.[185] After nearly seven months of mutual protests and accusations, diplomatic relations were also suspended on 20 October. The Chinese characterised this action as "part and parcel of the present anti-China adverse current set in motion by imperialism and international reaction."[186]

In Mali, the new regime formed in November 1968 disbanded the Chinese-trained People's Militia and ejected Chinese technicians from the Chinese-built cigarette and match factories near Sobuta. It also placed the Chinese embassy in Bomako under surveillance for a short period.

In Latin America, too, China's stock declined. Cuba began to show unobstrusive signs of siding with Moscow in the Sino-Soviet dispute. By the end of 1965, Che Guevara, a critic of Soviet policies, had been eased out, and an agreement was reached between the Castroites and the Communists concerning the strategy to be followed in Latin America.[187] The Soviet news by that year began to receive a wide and favourable presentation in the Cuban press, and a number of declarations were made by Castro himself underlining the importance of Soviet assistance to Havana.[188] The most compelling evidence, however, of the Moscow-Havana rapprochement appeared in March 1965 when the Cuban Communist party despatched a delegation to the Soviet Union to attend the meeting of the Consultative Council of the Communist parties, notwithstanding the fact that Beijing had denounced it in strong terms. The joint communiqué issued at the end of the meeting condemned all factionalist activities, whatever their character and source, and accepted the Soviet proposal to convene an international conference.[189]

The Cuban *volte-face* can be attributed to a number of factors. In the first place, it was increasingly evident by the mid-1960s that Cuba had become heavily dependent on Moscow. In addition to military aid (which was free), Soviet economic aid mounted to about $ 300 million a year. All of Cuba's oil and wheat came from the Soviet Union, and all her tractors (some 40,000) were imported from the Soviet Union or her allies.[190] Furthermore, Moscow had re-equipped sugar mills, built electricity plants, hospitals, factories, irrigations plants and roads in Cuba. According to the US government, the Cuban capital debt to the Soviet Union had reached the high figure of $ 1.5 billion by 1969.[191] Second, the political and military protection offered by Moscow was equally considerable. Notwithstanding the setbacks encountered as a result of the missile crisis, the Cubans were well aware that the protection offered by the Soviet Union was decisive for their survival. Third, the Russians had shown that they were more prepared than the Chinese to put up with some Cuban autonomy on political issues—as long as the Cubans basically acknowledged Soviet leadership. Obviously, such an arrangement was more acceptable to independent Castroites than the increasing Chinese insistence on complete support, especially on international Communist issues.

The lines of communications between Havana and Beijing, on the other hand, were fast becoming tenuous. To the Chinese leaders, it had become abundantly clear by the mid-1960s that Castro was no longer neutral in the rapidly escalating Sino-Soviet dispute, and that he had decided to link Cuba's fate to that of the Soviet Union.

China's reaction to the new situation was true to the pattern she had established. While encouraging Albania to publicly—although indirectly—warn the Cubans against pursuing such a Soviet-oriented policy,[192] the Chinese initially manifested their disagreement by simply ignoring developments in Cuba. With a determination that is typical of mobilized regimes, Cuban news was blocked out of the Chinese press between January an May 1965.[193] Even when Havana openly blasted the United States for having bombarded North Vietnam and for having intervened in the Dominican Republic in 1965, the Chinese press completely ignored the Cuban reactions.[194] Cuban economic development, hitherto given pride of place in the Chinese press, was also virually ignored. Only one article appeared in the *People's Daily* on Cuban economy during the first six months of 1965.[195]

The difficulties between the two countries did not remain muted, however; with the further exacerbation of relations, the Chinese became sluggish in providing economic assistance, and at the same time, they intensified the distribution of their propaganda literature to the Cuban army officers through the embassy in Havana.[196] It was even alleged that the Chinese diplomats directly approached Cuban officers "to win them over, either for the purpose of proselytism or perhaps for the purpose of intelligence."[197]

The most serious sign of deterioration in Sino-Cuban relations, however, was Castro's dramatic disclosure at the Tricontinental Conference on 2 January 1966 that the Chinese were cutting their purchase of Cuban sugar by 200,000 tons and were planning to sell Cuba only 135,000 tons of China's much-needed rice, instead of 285,000 tons. On the same occasion, it was announced that, due to the US embargo, Cuba had no other source of procuring rice, so the rations in the country would have to be reduced by half.[198] A responsible official in China's Ministry of Foreign Trade denied that his government had ever agreed to supply Cuba with 250,000 tons of rice "on a long-term basis" and questioned Castro's motives for having made such an announcement on the eve of the Tricontinental Conference.[199] Castro responded angrily to the Chinese leaders, charging them with having engaged in economic brutality and with having displayed contempt for his country. In February, he declared:

262

It was no longer a matter of more or fewer tons of rice. . . though it affected that, too—but a matter of very much greater importance, fundamental to peoples, namely whether in the world of tomorrow, the powerful countries will be able to take on themselves the right to blackmail, exercise extortion against pressure, commit aggression against, and strangle smaller peoples; whether there will also prevail in the world of tomorrow which revolutionairies are struggling to establish, the worst methods of piracy, oppression, and filibustering that have been introduced into the world since the emergence of class society. . .[200]

At the Tricontinental Conference held in Havana in January 1966, the Sino-Cuban dispute reached its highest point; on this occasion, skillfully coordinated Soviet and Cuban manoeuvres isolated the Chinese and prevented them from making the conference a platform for their customary denunciations of revisionism.[201] For instance, when the Chinese delegate criticised the preliminary political report presented by Youssef el-Sebai, Secretary General of the Conference, as too weak-kneed, the head of the Cuban delegation replied, "We Cubans, who have been carrying on a struggle against the United States for seven years, do not need to receive an anti-imperialist lesson from anybody."[202]

In the aftermath of the Tricontinental Conference, the real Cuban determination to disengage from Beijing became increasingly evident. The main thrust of the new Cuban arguments was now focussed more on the political and ideological factors that separated Latin America from Beijing rather than on the factors that united them. One of the most striking examples of this new line was the encouragement given to Regis Debray in 1966 to write a book sharply distinguishing the Cuban from the Chinese model.[203] Although all potential or existing rivals in the revolutionary movements were attacked, principal criticism was directed against China, warnings were given against the dangers inherent in the blind emulation of "Asian models," and a concerted attempt was made to distinguish Latin American conditions from those of China. In fact, it was stated that many of the guerilla movements in the Western hemisphere had failed because they followed principles generally developed in Asia. Lenin's concept of the party as the vanguard of the proletariat and the leaders of the revolutionary struggle, argued Debray, was not relevant to Latin America,[204] and it was really not necessary, as the Chinese suggested, to wait until all conditions for a revolution existed since the "insurrectionary nucleas can create them."[205]

Thus, by 1965-66, the Chinese and the Cubans had drifted apart, and the nation that was hitherto considered a trail-blazer for other countries in Latin America was surrounded by total obscurity in the Chinese press. Other countries and other revolutionary processes became more important. The Dominican patriots, the student revolts in Brazil, Equador, Bolivia, the peasant seizure of lands, the steady development of Marxist-Leninist parties, and revolutionary organizations in many countries in the area were now deemed more worthy of note than developments in Cuba.[206]

It was, however, only during the height of the Cultural Revolution that

263

the Chinese press directly challenged some of the theoretical tenets advanced by Regis Debray. On 22 February 1968, Anna Louis Strong, an American Communist living for many years in China, presented a critique of Debray's book. In her *Letter from China,* she asserted that he had come forward to sell what he called revolution now that the people were preparing for people's war. She charged him with advocating that there was no need "to organize the masses, to build a party, to build an army, to study theory, to organize a broad united front, to make a base area or prepare for a protracted war—all that is needed is a few men with guns."[207] On 26 July, 1968, Beijing carried an article criticising Debray by name. The item in question was an extract from *l'Humanité Nouvelle,* the organ of pro-Beijing French Communist party. The objective of Debray's book, charged the article, was to attack Marxist-Leninism and Mao Zedong's thought and to deny the universal significance of Mao's theory.[208]

Thus by the late 1960s, Beijing had lost virtually all influence in Cuba. But this was much more than a simple diplomatic loss; the snapping of all ties with Havana had resulted in the closure of one of the most important channels for the establishment of relations with the rising Castroite movements in many countries of Latin America.

Even in Asia, where China had hitherto exercised great influence, her authority showed definite signs of declining. Outer Mongolia, which was playing Moscow against Beijing in 1959 to win greater leverage, was now settled firmly within the Soviet orbit. The Soviet Union had established missile bases to defend the vast Mongolian border, and had concluded a new treaty of mutual defense in 1966 under which the signatories agreed to take "all necessary steps," including military measures, in order to ensure the "security, independence, and territorial integrity of the two states."[209]

The North Korean warmth towards China all but evaporated, and staunch attacks on revisionism which used to characterize the North Korean press gave way to frequent warnings about the dangers of leftist opportunism, dogmatism, and sectarianism.[210] Breaking all ties with Moscow, even during the Sino-Korean honeymoon, was apparently too costly for North Korea. The slow-down of Soviet assistance seriously affected her ability to fulfill the annual quotas of her Seven-Year Plan,[211] and the complete cessation of Soviet military assistance forced the regime to concentrate on building up Korea's armament industry, thereby causing serious shortages of manpower and raw materials in other branches of industry. Furthermore, Korea's inordinate commitment to China had cost her a considerable number of options in foreign affairs. Such a situation might have been necessary during the earlier period, but in the mid-1960s, when the international situation had become less tense and when disengagement from the two super-power appeared to have become the objective of many small nations, Korean commitment to Beijing had indeed become a burden.

264

In North Vietnam, too, actions indicating disengagement from China became increasingly evident. The number of denunciations of "modern revisionism" in the press dropped in 1965 and almost completely disappeared a year later. An independant stance became more and more apparent on a number of issues. Relations with Moscow improved. This began with Kosygin's visit to Hanoi in February 1965. The occasion was used by the Russians to lure Hanoi away from Beijing by agreeing to give military assistance which "increased markedly with every month."[212] In 1965 there were other important visits in both directions. There was the visit of Le Duan and General Giap to Moscow in April 1965, during which the question of military assistance was discussed.[213] There was the visit of Le Thang Ngi, the Vietnamese Deputy Prime Minister, to Moscow in July 1965, during which military and economic agreements were concluded. And then there was the arrival of Shelepin in Hanoi, accompanied by General V. F. Tolubka, Commander of the Soviet strategic military force.

The North Vietnamese, Lao Dong party's relations with Moscow were also becoming closer, while those with the CCP were becoming increasingly distant. While the party attended the 23rd Congress of the CPSU in 1966, Beijing denounced it. While the Chinese boycotted the Czeckoslovakian, Mongolian, and other party congresses, Hanoi attended all of them. While the Chinese condemned the pro-Vietnamese appeal of the Karlovy Vary Conference of European Communists in April 1967 as a sham, North Vietnam welcomed it, and while the Chinese opposed all negotiations with the United States, North Vietnam agreed to open the peace talks with Washington and Saigon in Paris in 1968.

In non-Communist countries, Chinese authority also declined considerably. With Indonesia, relations cooled after the abortive *coup d'état* in September 1965, in which the pro-Beijing Communist party appeared to have been actively involved.[214] A groundswell of popular discontent against China surged up in the country, leading to the overthrow of Sukarno and the decimation of the Indonesian Communist party. Perhaps the most tragic consequences of the *coup* was the resurgence of a massive anti-Chinese campaign, including the massacre of thousands of Chinese in North Sumatra, the closing down of Chinese schools, the boycotting of Chinese shops, the suppression of Chinese organizations, and the execution of innumerable acts of vandalism. The diplomats of the two countries returned to their respective capitals.

With Burma, relations deteriorated seriously after the decision of the overseas Chinese to openly propagate the principles of the Cultural Revolution.[215] The Sino-Burmese agreement on economic and technical cooperation was abrogated on 6 October 1967 and all of the 412 Chinese experts working on different projects were returned to Beijing.

With Kampuchea, events took a turn for the worse when the Chinese technical experts in the country, carried away by the euphoria of the

Cultural Revolution, interfered in the internal affairs of the country.[216] Prince Norodom Sihanouk accused the Chinese in September 1967 of having worked to make young Kampucheans "docile instruments of subversion and Communist propaganda to convert the Kampuchean people to the Chinese Marxist faith."[217]

Nepal also began to show signs of disenchantment with Beijing in the aftermath of pro-Maoist propaganda disseminated by Chinese technicians.[218] Disregarding Nepalese warnings, the Chinese provoked an attack on their pavilion at a fair in Kathmundu. The ill-will generated by the incident contributed considerably in ruining the favourable image the Chinese had previously enjoyed in the country.

One might ask why these setbacks occurred. Why did this tension develop with some countries and why did China drift apart from the others? How is it that, notwithstanding the deployment of considerable effort, China was unable to maintain her influence of the early 1960s? Was it too much of a strain and too much of an effort for Chinese diplomacy to change from a continental-based strategy to a more global one? Was this isolation from the Third World an outer manifestation of all these burdensome strains and efforts?

First of all, the domestic turmoils connected with the Cultural Revolution occupied the attention of the Chinese leadership. Their involvement in this "closely locked contest for life or death"[219] was so great and so time-consuming that it diminished the level of China's activity in the Third World. Even the Chinese Ministry of Foreign Affairs, hitherto uninvolved in most domestic crises, became a victim of conflicting pressures during the Cultural Revolution. Foreign Minister Chen Yi personally came under heavy criticism from the Red Guards, and appeared to exercise, at least for some time, only a token control over his department.[220]

Second, the rapid deterioration of the internal situation could not fail to have a spillover effect on whatever was left of China's already reduced foreign policy activity. Following the intensification of intra-party conflict, practically all the foreign students—mainly from the Third World—studying in China were ordered to leave, almost all the key Chinese diplomatic personnel was recalled, and a number of foreign embassies were indiscriminately victimized. Other incidents included an attack on a Soviet ship in Dalian Harbour, the burning of the British legation and assaults on Indian diplomats. Moreover, incidents were also fomented by Chinese diplomats in foreign countries—indeed, during the twelve months prior to 1967, as many as 32 nations were involved in some type of crisis or incident concerned with Beijing.[221] But even more alarming for the developing world was the belligerent tone of many declarations emanating from Beijing. If Lin Biao was optimistically predicting the success of revolutionary upheavals—obviously based on the Chinese model—the communiqué of the 11th Plenary Session of the 8th Central Committee of the Communist Party was calling people to struggle against "imperialists" and "reactionaries".[222]

Third, the Sino-Soviet dispute made the task of Chinese diplomacy far more difficult than was the case before. China had to dissipate her limited strength to contain not only US influence but also that of the Soviet Union, whose image of progressiveness was still firmly established among the Third World countries. In fact, Chinese activities in her area seemed to suggest that she was more concerned with countering Soviet influence than that of the United States. The declarations made, the visits undertaken, and the front organizations created after 1965 were principally directed against the Soviet Union. Obviously this objective was by no means easy; the type of arguments needed to convince the Third World to contain Soviet influence were different and rather more difficult to formulate than those required to counter the United States. To suggest, as the Chinese did, that the Russians had restored capitalism, that they had become indifferent to national liberation movements, and that they were essentially motivated by "social imperialist" ideas in their foreign policy, was at variance with enduring perceptions of the Third World elitist groups regarding the Soviet system.

If the Soviet Union had become the principal target of Chinese polemical attacks, the United States was certainly not spared during the Cultural Revolution. The denunciations against Washington were still vitriolic and Chinese policy was still aimed at containing and contending American influence in many parts of the Third World. For any nation, the uphill and quixotic task of simultaneously trying to contain the two superpowers would have been difficult; for a deeply riven nation like China it was simply disastrous. Her exorbitant ambitions were at odds with her operational ability.

Fourth, in their determination to undermine Soviet influence, the Chinese leaders had forcibly introduced the Sino-Soviet dispute into all Third World organizations of which both were active members.[223] Such tactics invariably caused these conferences to degenerate into a Sino-Soviet wrangle, as a result of which discussions of the important problems for which the meetings were convened, were either postponed or side-tracked. All this was received with either great misgivings or considerable irritation by many countries of the Third World.[224] At the Afro-Asian Solidarity Conferene in Moshi in February 1963, ignoring all appeals from the Soviet delegation to avoid public debate on divisive issues, the Chinese carried on a ruthless "struggle" against the "white" Soviet delegation.[225] At the fourth meeting held in Algiers in March 1964, the same tactics were pursued, leading a member of the Kenyan delegation to complain:

> We are not Marxists-Leninists and most of us have never read a single line of *Das Kapital*. So what interest do you have in our participating in your doctrinal quarrels? When I am eating a sandwich, I have had enough of being accosted by someone who asks me what I think of the Soviet positions and, when I am drinking coffee, by someone who questions me about the Chinese arguments. I would like to be able to eat in peace.[226]

At the Tricontinental Conference held in Havana in January 1966, the Chinese attacks against the Soviet Union were coolly received by most of the delegations.[227] Again at the preparatory meeting of the Second Afro-Asian Conference in 1965, despite the general consensus to invite Moscow to participate in the conference, China refused to accept Soviet participation. In the end, however, the issue of inviting Russia was unceremoniously resolved by the military *coup d'état* that overthrew the Ben Bella government on 19 June, a few days before the conference was due to open.[228]

Fifth, in an age where the level of political influence is often linked with the quantity of economic assistance that is given by a nation, China faced the uphill task of having to compete with giants such as the United States and the Soviet Union. She evidently did not possess the economic power to give large-scale assistance or to develop important trade relations with the Third World countries. The Chinese slogan of "self-reliance", though appealing, was unpalatable to them in view of their rising economic needs, which, for the time being, could be met by the Soviet Union and—or the United States. Even militantly leftist governments realized the imperative need to develop or maintain ties with the developed world. Ghana, despite her allegiance to socialism under Nkrumah, sought foreign capital to accelerate economic development. Algeria, notwithstanding her close ties with Beijing, eagerly sought ties with Moscow and Paris. And Guinea, under Sekou Touré, in addition to her economic relations with socialist countries, felt the need to turn to Paris for the aid and trade which France had suddenly stopped in 1958.

Sixth, China in the 1960s was not a major power. She did not possess the necessary military power to make effective moves in areas which happened to be remotely situated. Africa and Latin America were the far-away areas. Even parts of Asia, though proximate, were nonetheless far enough away to make it possible for the Middle Kingdom to influence the behaviour of a target country. Any political or military support that she might decide to extend to her friends could not, therefore, have the same effectiveness as assistance emanating from the Soviet Union or the United States. It could only be marginal.

Finally, China's successive nuclear explosions had generated a feeling of bemusement among many of the Third World countries. While some of them expressed satisfaction and even pride at the remarkable fact that a developing nation had finally broken the nuclear monopoly of the West and the Soviet Union,[229] many expressed a feeling of uneasiness at this development, not because China had gone nuclear but because she continued, unlike other nuclear powers, to belittle the dangerous consequences of a nuclear holocaust.[230]

Thus by the late 1960s, China was left in a state of unparalled isolation. Her influence had indeed suffered considerable retrogession. Paradoxically, this state of affairs became evident just at the time when the Third World had begun to show signs of unity, mutual cooperation, and a common determination to obtain much-needed concessions from the developed countries—a process the Chinese had consistently recommended and from which they were excluded during the Cultural Revolution. Although this process of transnational cooperation and consultation among the developing nations was inaugurated at the Cairo Conference on Economic Development in 1962,[231] it took concrete shape at the different UNCTAD conferences held in Geneva (1964), New Delhi (1968), and Santiago de Chili (1972),[232] where widespread resentment was voiced against the unequal nature of economic relations between the developed and undeveloped countries, and a consensus had begun to emerge on a wide range of concrete demands to be presented to the Western world. Simultaneously, it had also become increasingly clear that the majority of the Third World countries, while receptive to the objective of introducing socio-economic structural changes into their societies, were not prepared to emulate the Chinese revolutionary model. Having long been influenced by winds of nationalism, they sought to formulate their own models of growth, which, though less well-conceptualised, were, at least in their eyes, more responsive to national needs and aspirations.

This total setback in and complete isolation from an area such as the Third World introduced a new element into the Chinese domestic debate during the tumultous years of the Cultural Revolution. Undoubtedly it gave an additional weapon to the moderates within the contending Chinese leadership to attack the hard-liners and in all probability it was this failure in international relations that finally resulted in a tilting of the balance in favour of the moderates and contributed to the inauguration of a new debate regarding China's role in the international system. As a result of this almost year-long process, the Chinese redesigned their perception of and adopted a new policy towards the Third World.

New perceptions and New Goals: 1970-1976

In the new Chinese perception,[233] the Third World was no longer considered a distant and distinct group of countries with which relations had to be developed but as an area of which China constituted an integral part. "Like the overwhelming majority of the Asian, African, and Latin American countries," declared Qiao Guanhua, head of the Chinese delegation to the 26th Session of the UN General Assembly on 15 November 1971, "China belongs to the Third World."[234] Mao Zedong personally declared on 22 June 1973 that "We all belong to the Third World and are developing countries,"[235] and two days later Zhou Enlai followed suit by repeating Mao's phrase.[236] Furthermore, within the wider framework of the international system which was now perceived by the Chinese as having become tripolar (divided into the First, Second, and Third Worlds) as a result of new alignments and realignments, the Third World was assigned an even more important position as representative of change than had been the case in the early 1960s. "The awakening and the growth of the Third World" was not only considered "a major event" in day-to-day contemporary international relations where its role was becoming "ever more significant",[237] but it was also viewed as the main motivating force "impelling forward the wheel of history."[238] It was in this part of the world, according to an often-used Chinese formula, that "countries want independance, nations want liberation and people want revolution."[239]

The Chinese operationalization of this new world-view was quite rapid. Soon after the domestic convulsions resulting from the excesses of the Cultural Revolution had been brought under control in 1969, Beijing returned to diplomatic and trading arenas with vigour, imagination and attention to the appropriate conventions. Ambassadors recalled during the Cultural Revolution were either re-assigned to old posts or despatched to new ones;[240] diplomatic relations were established with a number of additional Third World countries (see Table 6.1); trade resumed its upward growth pattern (see Table 6.2); economic and technical cooperation agreements were concluded with a number of countries; and the aid programme was given a boost by the Chinese commitment of $ 709 million in 1970—sum greater than that offered by the Soviet Union.[241]

New paradigms of China's foreign policy strategy also became visible. First, the confrontation on two fronts, hitherto still a dominant feature of Beijing's policy, was replaced by a focus on only one front—the Soviet Union. Admittedly, the formal Chinese rhetoric continued to employ the two-superpower formula, but by the early 1970s, Moscow had clearly become the main, target of Chinese operational diplomacy. Every major occasion was seized to assert that capitalism had been restored in the Soviet Union, that she had been transformed into "a social imperialist country" and that she had become even "more dangerous than the United States as a source of world war."[242]

Almost everywhere in the Third World, the lynchpin of Chinese strategy was thus to support all governments that had adopted a critical attitude towards the Soviet Union, irrespective of their socio-economic systems and irrespective of their socio-political orientations. The main enemy was the Soviet Union, and any contradictions or differences that China might face or which might develop with any other country were considered marginal.

The adoption of such a fixed anti-Soviet strategy led the Chinese to peculiar and apparently uncomfortable situations, such as supporting or normalising relations with Pinochet in Chile, the Shah in Iran, Marcos in the Philippines, Mobutu in Zaire, and Franco in Spain. It also led them to regard with approval the US military or political presence in the Third World, particularly in Asia and Africa. Rather than oppose the US, as they had done in the past, the Chinese considered her presence a necessary evil to be tolerated for the time being as a countervailing force against the Soviet Union.[243] In fact, they often found themselves in the unenviable position of

Table 6.1. *Establishment of Diplomatic Relations by China with Third World Countries in 1971-1972*

Equatorial Guinea	October 1970
Ethiopia	November 1970
Chile	December 1970
Nigeria	February 1971
Kuwait	March 1971
Cameroon	March 1971
Sierra Leone	July 1971
Iran	August 1971
Lebanon	November 1971
Peru	November 1971
Rwanda	November 1971
Cyprus	December 1971
Senegal	December 1971
Malta	January 1972
Mexico	February 1972
Argentina	February 1972
Mauritius	April 1972
Guyana	June 1972
Togo	September 1972
Maldives	October 1972
Chad	November 1972
Malgasy	November 1972
Jamaica	November 1972
Dahomay	December 1972

Table 6.2. *PRC trade with Third World Countries (U.S. $ millions)*

Total yearly turnover	
1971	945
1972	1,365
1973	2,076
1974	2,860
1975*	2,690

* Preliminary

Source: *Current Scene*, 12 (1974) and 9 (1975).

criticising Washington for not being sufficiently vigorous in its policies towards the Third World.

The second major component of Chinese diplomacy vis-à-vis the Third World was reflected in the encouragement China extended to the development of relations between the Third and Second Worlds. To the Chinese leadership this seemed to be not only possible as a result of the disappearance of colonialism, but was also viewed as a highly desirable goal in forestalling all Soviet attemps to exercise hegemonial control over small- or medium-sized powers. Since the 1960s, and particularly after the Cultural Revolution, China therefore ceaselessly supported the development of viable and meaningful relations between regional organizations belonging to the Second World and those created by the Third World countries.[244]

Third, the ideological component in Chinese diplomacy was considerably diluted and was largely replaced by policies designed with an eye to pragmatism and national interest. Most of the declarations, speeches, and theoretical writings were still full of ideological rhetoric, but almost the entire spectrum of China's operational diplomacy was emptied of its ideological content. The gap between theory and practice became wider. In view of this it is futile to argue endlessly about ultimate Chinese intentions, about the role of Marxism in Chinese diplomatic behaviour, and about the longterm perceptions that the Chinese may have of the world. What appears to be important to note is that the pattern of Chinese diplomacy had increasingly acquired the garb of conventionality, national interest, and pragmatism.

However, notwithstanding the considerable attention she has paid to the Third World, China has not been able to have a major impact on the area. In fact, it would seem as if this has declined. The globalisation of Chinese interests, China's manifestation of interest in the politics of modernisation, and her fluctuating domestic upheavals have introduced such unevenness into her foreign relations that it has become difficult to effectively play the role she has assigned to herself. Her active participation in the UN system, her continuous efforts to seek a countervailing power against the Soviet Union, and her attempts to react to all crises, compounded with the fact that her military and economic clout, though impressive, is still limited, does not permit her to exercise an effective role. China has, therefore, been unable to tilt any balances or manage any crises in the Third World, and she has often found herself in the peripheral position of issuing rhetorical statements without having any real capacity to influence the outcome of a crisis. In the Middle East conflicts, despite the support and assistance she extended to the Arab states and different Palestinian organizations, her point of view has hardly prevailed.[245] In most of the conflicts she was unable to have any major impact and in none of them was she able to establish a credible diplomatic position for herself from which she could influence the evolution of the conflict. Her material aid to the area was limited and her political presence almost nonexistent. Even in the case of the Palestinian guerilla movement, among which she enjoys some esteem, her actual influence is minimal. In fact, it considerably declined after the October 1973 war when the Soviet Union was not only able to demonstrate her credibility as an ally against Israel but also her strong support for the Palestinian cause. In the Bangladesh war of 1971, notwithstanding all the statements and all the military aid extended to Pakistan, China was either unable or unwilling to intervene to tilt the balance.[246] In Angola, despite her significant efforts to extend military aid, including training of militants of the National Front for the Liberation of Angola, she had to withdraw, abandoning all hopes of remedying the highly critical situation that her political friends were faced with in their conflict with the Popular Movement for the Liberation of Angola (which was supported by the Soviet Union).[247] In Dhofar, the Chinese supply of arms to the Peoples Front for the Liberation of the Occupied Arabian Gulf in 1969 did not have any material effect in tilting the balance. This policy was finally dropped in exchange for the establishment of diplomatic relations with the Shah's government in Iran, which was actively involved in suppressing the revolt. Even the crisis in neighbouring Vietnam, where China's role could have been decisive, Beijing decided to adopt a prudent attitude. Despite all the rhetorical support extended to the Vietnamese liberation movement, China avoided all confrontational situations. Mao Zedong personally made it clear that his country would not intervene in the conflict as long as the United States did not attack China.[248] This position was retained during the Cultural Revolution when China had neither the energy nor the resources available to alter it, and thereafter she cautiously groped towards establishing a closer relationship with Washington. In fact, from March 1972 until their decisive victory, the Vietminhs, having shifted from manpower-intensive tactics to the use of heavy weapons, relied almost completely on the most sophisticated SAM missiles to defend Hanoi and Haiphong, and employed the latest model Russian tanks and fuel to power the heavy equipment.[249]

China After Mao: 1976

The gap between Chinese rhetorical declarations and operational policies regarding the Third World became even wider after the death of Mao Zedong. Although developments in the Third World continued to receive pride of place in Chinese declarations and publications, internal and external imperatives accentuated the need for greater involvment in domestic issues on the one hand, and wide-ranging global problems on the other, thereby reducing the already limited resources available for any real concentration on the Third World.

This involvement was catalysed by the following developments: in the first place, the difficult problem of succession, including the arrest of the "gang of four" in October 1976 stimulated a process of monumental domestic convulsions, leaving the post-Maoist leadership only reduced possibilities for involving China to any significant degree in international affairs, least of all in the Third World, which, despite its ideological importance, —did not appear to be of major significance to Chinese interests at the time. This by no means is intended to imply that China's press coverage of foreign affairs had declined or that she had turned her back on the rapidly changing international situation; it only means that like most states facing major domestic difficulties and, at the same time, making the transition from a continental-based strategy to a global one, China faced a credibility problem in her actual capacity to influence or manage a crisis. China's intervention in Vietnam in February 1979 could be considered in this context. In many ways it was a failure. After a thirty-day massive military incursion into Vietnamese territory, she withdrew her troops without having seriously hurt the Hanoi regime or without having forced Vietnam to abandon Kampuchea (where she had toppled the pro-Beijing regime of Pol Pot in December 1977, subsequently becoming firmly installed there). Other major areas of conflict also reflect this reduced capability to take effective action. Whether in the horn of Africa, the liberation movements of Southern Africa, or the highly explosive developments in the Persian Gulf, China remains largely a spectator of events with very little real capacity for tilting the balance in favour of those political forces to which she gives rhetorical support.

Second, China's diplomacy continued to be principally focussed on the Odyssean and global task of undermining her principal opponent, the Soviet Union. The countervailing power of the weak and noncommittal Third World Countries in the power game could only be marginal. The importance of the United States and Europe, on the other hand, was evident—for in addition to their traditional and pronounced anti-Sovietism, they possessed the necassary clout to effectively challenge Moscow.

Third, having abandoned the autarchic policies of self-reliance, the post-Maoist leadership increasingly viewed the forging of economic and technological ties with the outside world as vital for the modernisation of China. A number of seminars and conferences were organized throughout China underlining the new leadership's awareness that the economic well-being of the nation hinged on more trade and on greater importation of science and technology. "There should be," declared Hua Guofeng "a big increase in foreign trade"[250] and the Minister of Trade Li Qiang went even further by declaring that "in the course of modernising China's agriculture, industry, national defence, and science and technology, we must learn from the advanced technology and experience of the West European countries in industrial and agricultural production."[251] Here again the importance of non-communist developed countries was evident, since they possessed what China needed for the attainment of her goal of modernisation.

The confluence of all these factors has thus further accentuated the marginality of the Third World in China's operational diplomacy. Her rapid ascension in global politics and her growing involvement in most international issues has certainly contributed to the projection of her image as a major power, but at the same time it has decreased her interest and, given her limited resources, reduced her capacity for influencing Third World politics.

Conclusions

The importance of the Third World has been consistently upgraded by the Chinese since the revolution: from its position low on the rungs of the international ladder in the early 1950s, it was ranked in the early 1960s with other important forces of the international system, and in the 1970s, was promoted to the multi-dimensional role of a preponderant force. But in operational terms, the Chinese interest in the Third World has not kept pace with this perception. In fact, it has diminished. By the early 1960s, the growing Chinese involvement in the international power game limited China's capacity to act in these areas. This widening gap between increasing interest and decreasing activity was principally due to the fact that China's real capacity was seriously strained.

The gap between formal explanations and the more tangible components of Chinese diplomatic behaviour has also widened. Although the formal reasons proffered to bring about an erosion of superpower influence in the Third World retained a high ideological content, the real determinants of China's policy were increasingly to be found in the domains of national interest.

The chasm also appears to have broadened regarding the levels of Chinese interest in different geographical areas. Although the Third World has been increasingly given pride of place in numerous Chinese declarations, and although it was viewed as the principal component of the international system, the imperatives of modernisation and national security have increasingly pushed China to focus her attention on the developed world.

Notes

1. Amaury de Riencourt, op cit., p. 111.
2. Ibid., p. 109.
3. Victor Purcell, *The Chinese in Southeast Asia* (London: Royal Institute of International Affairs, 1951), p. 200.
4. René Servoise, "Les relations entre la Chine et l'Afrique au XV siècle", *Revue Française d'études politiques Africaines,* 6 (1966).
5. K. M. Pannikar, *India and China* (Bombay: Asia Publishing House, 1957).
6. The 1927 Brussels Congress of Oppressed Nationalities and the regular meet-

ings of the Comintern gave the Chinese national and Communist leaders an opportunity to establish contact with their Asian counterparts.

7. C. Martin Wilbur, op cit.

8. Jawaharlal Nehru, *A Bunch of Old Letters* (Bombay: Asia Publishing House, 1958), p. 442.

9. Steven M. Goldstein, "The Chinese Revolution and the Colonial Areas: The View from Yenan, 1931-41", *The China Quarterly*, 75 (1978).

10. Harold Z. Schiffrin, *Sun Yat-sen and the Origins of the Chinese Revolution* (Berkeley: University of California Press, 1968).

11. Chiang Kai-shek, *China's Destiny* (New York: Roy Publishers, 1947).

12. See, *Selected Works of Mao*, op cit.; Robert Payne, *Mao Tse-tung* (New York: Pyramid Books, 1966); Stuart Schram, *Mao Tse-tung* (London: Penguin Books, 1966).

13. *Selected Works of Mao*, Vol. II, op cit.

14. Anna Louise Strong, "The Thought of Mao Tse-tung", *Amerasia*, 6 (1947), pp. 161-162.

15. *New China News Agency*, 23 November 1949.

16. *Le Monde*, 30 November 1949.

17. Full text in V. B. Karnik ed., *Indian Communist Party Documents 1930-1956* (Bombay: The Democratic Research Service, 1957), p. 48.

18. *People's China*, 10 October 1950.

19. Ibid., 16 January 1950.

20. For background information on Asian Communists, see A. Doak Barnett (ed.), *Communist Strategies in Asia: A Comparative Analysis of Governments and Parties* (London: Pall Mall Press, 1963).

21. Liu Shaoqi's speech at the World Federation of Trade Unions held in Peking in 1949; *New China News Agency*, 23 November 1949.

22. *Bolshevik*, 12 (1947).

23. For details on non-alignment, see K. P. Karunakaran (ed.), *Outside the Conflict: A Study of Non-Alignment and the Foreign Policies of Some Non-Aligned Nations* (New Delhi: People's Publishing House, 1963); J. W. Burton (ed.), *Non-Alignment* (London: Andre Deutsch, 1966); Leo Mates, *Non-Alignment, Theory and Current Policy* (Belgrade: The Institute of International Politics and Economics, 1972); Bahgat Korany, *Afro-Asian Non-Alignment in the Contemporary International System. A Pre-Theory* (Geneva: Institut Universitaire de Hautes Etudes Internationales, 1975).

24. K. M. Pannikar, *In Two Chinas. Memoirs of a Diplomat* (London: Allen and Unwin, 1955).

25. Ibid.

26. *People's China*, 16 September 1951, p. 39.

27. Ibid., 10 October 1951.

28. See Melvin Gurtov, *China and Southeast Asia—The Politics of Survival: A Study of Foreign Policy Interaction* (Baltimore: The John Hopkins University Press, 1975); also see William C. Johnstone, *Burma's Foreign Policy: A Study in Neutralism* (Cambridge, Mass: Harvard University Press, 1963).

29. *Le Monde*, 5-6 October 1952.

30. *Survey of China's Mainland Press*, 1000 (1952).

31. Ibid.

32. Jean Lacouture and Philippe Devilliers, *Indo-Chine 1954* (Paris: Le Seuil, 1960).

33. The Ministry of Foreign Affairs, *Afro-Asia Speaks from Bandung* (Djakarta: The Ministry of Foreign Affairs, 1955), p. 64.

34. Ibid.

35. Ibid.

36. G. V. Ambekar and V. D. Divekar (ed.), *Documents on China's Relations with South and Southeast Asia 1949-1962* (Bombay: Allied Publishers Private Ltd, 1964).

37. For details about overseas Chinese, see C. P. Fitzgerald, *The Third China* (University of British Columbia, 1965);Victor Purcell, op cit.

38. Herbert Passin, *China's Cultural Diplomacy* (London: The China Quarterly, 1962).

39. See Ministry of Information and Broadcasting, *Panchsheel* (New Delhi: Ministry of Information, 1957).

40. Cited by William C. Johnstone, op cit., p. 99.

41. Michael Leifer, *Cambodia, The Search for Security* (London: Pall Mall Press, 1967).

42. Fred Greene, *US Policy and Security of Asia* (New York: Mc Graw-Hill 1968).

43. Jawaharlal Nehru, *Speeches,* Vol. 3 (New Delhi: Government of India and Publications Division, 1958).

44. See David A. Wilson, "China, Thailand and the Spirit of Bandung", *The China Quarterly,* 30 and 31 (1967).

45. Latif Ahmed Sherwani, et al, *Foreign Policy of Pakistan: An Analysis* (Karachi: The Allied Book Corporation, 1964).

46. Fred Greene, op cit.

47. See supra.

48. Among those expelled included the Governor of Zhijiang Province, the Governor of Qinghai Province, the Deputy Governor of Anhui Province, and the Deputy Minister of Supervision.

49. *People's Daily,* 8 June 1957.

50. See Franz Schurmann, *Ideology and Organization in Communist China* (Berkeley: University of California Press, 1966).

51. Niu Chung-huang, *China Will Overtake Britain* (Peking: Foreign Languages Press, 1958).

52. *People's Communes in China* (Peking: Foreign Languages Press, 1958).

53. Yu Chao-li, "Chinese People's Great Victory in the Fight against Imperialism", *Peking Review,* 38 (1959).

54. Liu Shaoqi, *The Victory of Marxism-Leninism in China* (Peking: Foreign Languages Press, 1959).

55. *Dix glorieuses années* (Peking: Editions des langues étrangères, 1960), pp. 305-306.

56. For details on the Chinese attitude, see Omar Ali Amer, *China and the Afro-Asian Solidarity Organization 1958-1972* (Geneva: Institut Universitaire de Hautes Études Internationales, 1972).

57. Nehru was wary about the conference and is reported to have discouraged members of his party from participating in it; see *Est et Ouest,* 189 (1958).

58. Ibid.

59. *Afro-Asian People's Solidarity Conference* (Moscow: Foreign Publishing House, 1958); also see *Le Monde,* 27-28 December 1957 and 3 January 1958.

60. *Afro-Asian Solidarity Movement* (Cairo: Permanent Secretariat of the Afro-Asian People's Solidarity Organization, 1962).

61. "China, the Arab World and Africa. A Factual Survey 1959-1964", *The Mizan Newsletter,* 5 (1964).

62. *People's Daily,* 16 May 1958.

277

63. *Peking Review*, 33 (1959), p. 9.
64. Ibid., 30 (1959), p. 18.
65. Ibid.
66. *The China Quarterly*, 1 (1960); *New China News Agency*, 8 October 1959.
67. *Al Ahram*, 3 October 1959.
68. *Peking Review*, 50 (1959), p. 10.
69. *Documents on the Sino-Indian Boundary Question* (Peking: Foreign Languages Press, 1960).
70. Frank N. Trager, *Burma: From Kingdom to Republic* (London: Pall Mall Press, 1966).
71. Ibid.
72. Donald Zagoria, *Sino-Soviet Dispute 1956-1961* (New York: Atheneum, 1966).
73. Edgar Snow, *Red China Today. The Other Side of the River*, Revised and updated (New York: Random, 1970), p. 412.
74. See Roderick MacFarquhar (ed.), *The Hundred Flowers* (London: Stevens and Sons, 1960).
75. Li Fu Chun's address to a conference of cadres in Chungking, 16 May 1957; *New China News Agency*, 17 May 1957.
76. Liu Shaoqi, op. cit., p. 4.
77. On 26 August 1975 Tass announced that the Soviet Union had successfully tested "an intercontinental multi-stage ballistic rocket", and on 4 October of the same year, Moscow announced the launching of the first satellite.
78. Excerpts from Mao's 18 November 1957 speech in Moscow; for details see Mao Zedong, *Imperialism and All Reactionaires are Paper Tigers* (Peking: Foreign Languages Press, 1958), p. 28.
79. For details see Chapter 1.
80. *Selected Works of Mao*, Vol. IV, op. cit., p. 105.
81. Ibid., p. 104.
82. See Chapter 1.
83. For a Soviet view of new Chinese analysis, see B. Soborov, "Peking and the 'Third world': Mounting Contradictions", *Far Eastern Affairs*, 2 (1975); A. Kruchinin, "Third World in Peking's Foreign Policy Strategy", ibid., 3 (1976); B. Zanegin, *Nationalist Background of China's Foreign Policy* (Moscow: Novosti Press Agency Publishing House, n.d.).
84. For details, see Chapter 1.
85. *The Polemic on the General Line of the International Communist Movement*, op cit., p. 7.
86. Ibid.
87. For background information, see Robert A. Scalapino (ed.), *The Communist Revolutions in Asia: Tactics, Goals and Achievements* (Englewood Cliffs, New Jersey: Prentice Hall, 1969); Richard Lowenthal (ed.), *Issues in the Future of Asia: Communist and non-Communist Alternatives* (New York: Praeger, 1969); A. Doak Barnett, *Communist Strategies in Asia: A Comparative Analysis of Governments and Parties* (London: Pall Mall Press, 1964).
88. For background information, see Colin Legum, "Africa's Contending Revolutionaries", *Problems of Communism*, 2 (1972); Sven Hamrell and Carl Gosta Widsteand (ed.), *The Soviet Bloc, China and Africa* (Upsala: The Scandinavian Institute of African Studies, 1964).
89. For background information, see Robert J. Alexander, *Communism in Latin America* (New Brunswick, N. J.: Rutgers University Press, 1957).

90. See Ernest Halperin, "Peking and Latin American Communists", *The China Quarterly*, 29 (1967); Cecil Johnson, *Communist China and Latin America 1959-1967* (New York: Columbia University Press, 1970).

91. Ernest Halperin, loc cit.

92. Zhou Enlai visited Ulan Bator in May 1960 and signed a Treaty of Friendship and Mutual Assistance to "consult with each other on all important international questions of common interest." A loan of 200 million roubles was given to Mongolia on this occasion; for details, see *Peking Review*, 23 (1960).

93. For details, see Bagaryn Shirendyb (ed.), *History of the Mongolian People's Republic* (Cambridge, Mass: Harvard University Press, 1976).

94. *Peking Review*, 42 (1960).

95. *Vietnam News Agency*, 14 March 1963.

96. Ho-Min Yang, "North Korea between Moscow and Peking", *Conference Papers*, Vol. 2, Seventh International Conference on World Politics in the Netherlands in 1969, (unpublished); Joseph C. Kun, "North Korea: Between Moscow and Peking", *The China Quarterly*, 31 (1967).

97. Le Duan, *On Some Present International Problems* (Hanoi: Foreign Languages Publishing House, 1964), Second edition; also see P. J. Honey, *Communism in North Vietnam* (London: Ampersand, 1963).

98. For complete text, see G. V. Ambekar and V. D. Divekar, op cit.

99. For complete text, see *Victory for the Five Principles of Coexistence: Important Documents on the Settlement of the Sino-Burmese Boundary* (Peking: Foreign Languages Publishing House, 1960), p. 30.

100. For complete text, see Ambekar and Divekar, op cit.

101. Ibid.

102. Ibid.

103. For complete text of the treaty and subsequent declarations by both the sides, see ibid.

104. Ibid., p. 63.

105. See M. Smith, *Cambodia's Foreign Policy* (Ithaca: Cornell University Press, 1965).

106. *Peking Review*, 20 (1960), p. 33.

107. *Peking Review*, 19 (1960).

108. Ambekar and Divekar, op cit.

109. *Sino-Indian Boundary Question* (Peking: China Foreign Languages Press, 1962), p. 47.

110. See Naville Maxwell, *India's China War* (London: Jonathan Cape, 1970).

111. *People's Daily*, 19 August 1960.

112. *Peking Review*, 29 November 1960.

113. The U-2 spy plane downed by the Russian took off from Pakistani, territory.

114. K. Sarwar Hasan (ed.), *Documents on the Foreign Policy of Pakistan* (Karachi: Pakistan Institute of International Affairs, 1966).

115. See Chapter 4.

116. Ambekar and Divekar, op cit.

117. Between 1960 and 1965, no fewer than 29 colonies gained independence, with 16 of them emerging in 1960 alone; for details about China's policy in Africa, see Alan Hutchinson, *China's African Revolution* (London: Hutchinson, 1975); John K. Cooley, *East Wind over Africa: Red China's African Offensive* (New York: Walker and Company, 1965); Bruce Larkin, *China and Africa 1949-1970* (Berkeley: University of

California Press, 1971); Zbigniew Brezezinski, *Africa and the Communist World* (Stanford: Stanford University Press, 1959).

118.   Feng Chih-tan, "The Awakening of Africa", *Peking Review,* 27 (1960).

119.   J. Chester Cheng (ed.), *The Politics of the Chinese Red Army* (Stanford: Hoover Institution on War, Revolution and Peace, 1966).

120.   Ibid., p. 484.

121.   Ibid.

122.   Ibid.

123.   Ibid.

124.   *New China News Agency,* 3 February 1964.

125.   G. P. Despande, "China and the Liberation Wars: A Case Study of Algeria", *The Institute for Defense Studies and Analysis Journal,* 6 (1972).

126.   Ibid.

127.   For details regarding delegations to Beijing during the period, see "China, the Arab World and Africa, A Factual Survey 1959-1964", *The Mizan Newsletter,* 5 (1964).

128.   *Revue Militaire d'Information,* 4 (1960).

129.   Fritz Schatten, *Communism in Africa* (New York: Praeger, 1966).

130.   Robert Counts, "Chinese Footprints in Somalia", *The Reporter,* 2 February 1961, p. 32.

131.   *The African Mail,* 10 January 1964.

132.   *New York Times,* 4 and 7 January 1964.

133.   Ibid.

134.   Joseph Massinga, *Attempts towards Decolonization of Angola, Mozambique and Rhodesia* (Unpublished thesis submitted to the University of Geneva, 1973).

135.   Harry Heintzen, "Angola, Mozambique leaders turn to China", *New York Herald Tribune,* 8 January 1964.

136.   Mondlane addressed a memorandum to this effect to the US. Government in May 1963.

137.   *New York Times,* 5 February 1965.

138.   *Survey of China's Mainland Press,* 3326 (1964), p. 24.

139.   *La Tribune de Genève,* 29 June 1965.

140.   See John Cooley, op cit.

141.   See Fulbert Youlou, *J'accuse la Chine* (Paris: La Table Ronde, 1966).

142.   *New York Times,* 6-7 March 1965.

143.   Cooley, op cit.

144.   *New York Times,* 6-7 March 1965.

145.   *Le Monde,* 4 January 1966.

146.   Ibid.

147.   Ibid.

148.   Pierre Martens and Paul F. Smets, *L'Afrique de Péking* (Brussels: P. Martens and P. Smets, 1966).

149.   Ibid.

150.   Cooley, op cit.

151.   Alan Hutchinson, op cit.

152.   George T. Yu, *China and Tanzania: A Study in Cooperative Interaction* (Berkeley: University of California Centre for Chinese Studies, 1970).

153.   Cited by V. P. Dutt, *China's Foreign Policy 1958-1962* (New York: Asia Publishing House, 1964), p. 274.

154.   Statement by Mao Zedong on 28 November 1964; text in Daniel Lyons, S. J., and Stephen Pan, "The Road to Paris" *Voice of Peking* (New York: Twin Circle

Publishing Company, 1967), p. 178.

155. Cited by V. P. Dutt, op cit., p. 275.
156. *People's Daily,* 29 October 1965.
157. For background information, see Cecil Johnson, op cit.; Daniel Tretiak, "China and Latin America: An Ebbing Tide in Transpacific Maoism', *Current Scene,* 5 (1966); Cheng Ying-Hsiang, *Idylle Sino-Cubaine. Brouille Sino-Soviétique* (Paris: Armand Colin, 1973).
158. Cecil Johnson, op cit.
159. *Survey of China's Mainland Press* 1930 (1959), p. 26.
160. Ibid.
161. Ibid., 1942 (1959), p. 21.
162. Cecil Johnson, op cit.
163. For details, see Robert Scheer and Maurice Zetlen, *Cuba, An American Tragedy* (London: Penguin Books, 1964).
164. Full text in *Peking Review,* 29 (1960).
165. *Survey of China's Mainland Press,* 2308 (1960).
166. *Declaration of Havana* (Peking: Foreign Languages Publishing House, 1962).
167. *Peking Review,* 49 and 50 (1960).
168. Ibid., also see Che Guevara, *Le rôle de l'aide étrangère au développement de Cuba* (Havana: Editorial en Marcha, 1962).
169. *Survey of China's Mainland Press,* 2588 (1961), p. 33.
170. Ibid., 2594 (1961), p. 39.
171. Ibid., 2726 (1962), p. 29.
172. Ibid., 2892 (1962), p. 28.
173. Chang Ying-Hsiang, op cit.
174. *Revolucion,* 2 August 1963.
175. *New York Times,* 5 February 1965.
176. The Tutsi refugees had been the traditional feudal overlords of Rwanda and had been ejected by the Bahatu peasantry who formed 85 per cent of the country's population before independence in 1962.
177. Pierre Martens and Paul F. Smets, op cit.
178. Ibid.
179. E. Mendiaux, *L'Afrique sera chinoise* (Brussels: Sineco, 1965).
180. *Le Monde,* 30 July 1965.
181. Alan Hutchinson, op cit.
182. See George Yu, op cit.
183. *The Times,* 5 January 1966.
184. Pierre Martens and Paul F. Smets, op cit.
185. Ibid.
186. Partial text in *Peking Review,* 4 November 1966, p. 38.
187. An agreement had been reached at the Havana conference of Latin American Communist parties held in November-December 1964; see Bruce Jackson, *Castro, the Kremlin and Communism in Latin America* (Baltimore: The John Hopkins Press, 1969).
188. *Soviet News,* 22 May 1965 and 9 June 1965.
189. Ibid.
190. For details, see Hugh Thomas, *Cuba or the Pursuit of Freedom* (London: Eyre and Spottiswood, 1971).
191. Ibid.
192. Daniel Tretiak, loc cit.

193. Ibid.
194. Ibid.
195. Ibid.
196. See Castro's statement of 6 February, 1966; complete text in *Peking Review,* 9 (1966).
197. Ibid., p. 21.
198. "Fidel Castro on Trade between Cuba and China", *Prensa Latina,* as cited in the *Global Digest,* 4 (1966), pp. 92-98.
199. *Peking Review,* 3 (1966).
200. Ibid., 9 (1966), p. 22.
201. For details see, Albert Paul Lentin, *La Lutte Tricontinentale: impérialisme et la révolution après la conférence de Havane* (Paris: François Maspero, 1966); also see Council of the Organization of American States, *Report of the Special Committee to Study Resolution III and VIII of the Eighth Meeting of Consultation of Ministers of Foreign Affairs on the First Afro-Asian-Latin American Peoples Solidarity Conference* (Washington D.C.: Pan American Union, 1966).
202. Albert Paul Lentin, op cit., p. 49-51.
203. Régis Debray, *Révolution dans la Révolution: Lutte armée et lutte politique en Amérique Latine* (Paris: François Maspero, 1967).
204. Ibid.
205. Ibid., p. 39.
206. *New China News Agency,* 1967.
207. Anna Louise Strong, *Letter from China* (Peking: Foreign Languages Press, 28 February 1968), p. 4.
208. "Marxism-Leninism, Mao Tse-tung's Thought is Universal Thought". *Peking Review,* 30 (1968).
209. Full text in *Milestones of Soviet Foreign Policy* 1917-1967, op cit., p. 251.
210. See Joseph C. Kun, "North Korea between Moscow and Peking", *The China Quarterly,* 31 (1967).
211. In October 1966, the time limit for fulfilling the plan was extend by three years.
212. I. D. Ovsyany, et al, *A Study of Soviet Foreign Policy* (Moscow: Progress Publishers, 1975), p. 71.
213. Ibid.
214. Arnold C. Brackman, *The Communist Collapse in Indonesia* (New York: W. W. Norton, 1969).
215. Peter Boog, "The China-Burma Rift. An Analysis", *Current Scene,* 17 (1967).
216. Jan Taylor, *China and Southeast Asia: Peking's Relations with Revolutionary Movements* (New York: Praeger, 1974).
217. Cited in *Current Scene,* 20 (1967), p. 10.
218. *New China News Agency,* 8 July 1967.
219. Editorial in *People's Daily,* 5 June 1966.
220. Stephen Pan and Raymond J. de Jaegher, *Peking's Red Guards: The Great Proletarian Cultural Revolution* (New York: Twin Circle Publishing Company, 1968).
221. Robert A. Scalapino, "The Cultural Revolution and Chinese Foreign Policy", *Current Scene,* 13 (1968); also see François Joyaux, "Révolution Culturelle et Politique Extérieure Chinoise", *Politique Etrangère,* 1 (1968).
222. *The Decision of the Central Committee of the Chinese Communists Concerning the Great Proletarian Revolution* (Peking: Foreign Languages Press, 1966).
223. For details, see Omar Ali Amer, op cit.

224. Z. Brzezinski, *Africa and the Communist World,* op cit.
225. *Mizan Newsletter,* 5 (1964).
226. Quoted in *Le Monde,* 28 March 1964.
227. Albert Paul Lentin, op cit.
228. Algeria was strongly attacked for having convened the conference despite Chinese opposition, see *People's Daily,* 25 October 1965.
229. B. N. Chakrovarthy, "Political and Strategic Consequences of Chinese Nuclear Power", Background Paper No 1 for Seminar on Nuclear Weapons and Foreign Policy, in New Delhi in November 1966.
230. See the "detonation statement"; text in *Peking Review,* 42 (1964).
231. See *The Conference on the Problems of Economic Development* (Cairo: General Organization for Government Printing Press, 1962).
232. B. Gosovic, *UNCTAD: Conflict and Compromise* (Leiden: Sijthoff and Noord-hoff, 1972).
233. For details, see Chapter 1.
234. *Peking Review,* 47 (1971).
235. Ibid., 26 (1973), p. 3. He made this statement on the occasion of a meeting with Colonel Traore, the head of the Mali state.
236. Welcoming the head of Mali, Zhou Enlai said: "China and the African countries are all developing countries, and we all belong to the Third World"; ibid., p. 8.
237. Zhou Enlai, "Report to the Tenth National Congress", ibid., 35 and 36 (1973).
238. Cited in *Far Eastern Affairs,* 3 (1976), p. 83.
239. The Chinese representative's speech at the United Nations ECAFE session; *Peking Review;* 14 (1974), p. 22.
240. In 1970 ambassadors were sent to North Korea, Mali, Sudan, UAR, Sri Lanka, Somali, South Yemen, Cuba, and Iraq.
241. Altough there were subsequent cutbacks in new pledges, a foreign aid policy remained active, measured in terms of the number of nations drawing aid and the scope of Chinese medical, agricultural, and other missions abroad; for details, see John Franklin Copper, "China's Foreign Aid in 1976", *Current Scene,* 6-7 (1977).
242. *Peking Review,* 45 (1977).
243. The only exception was Taiwan.
244. For some details, see Chapter 2.
245. For some details, see Moshe Ma'oz, "Soviet and Chinese Relations with the Palestenian Guerilla Organizations" *Jerusalem Papers on Peace Problems,* No. 4 (Jerusalem: The Hebrew University of Jerusalem, 1974).
246. Mohammad Habib Sidky, "Chinese World Strategy and South Asia: The China Factor in Indo-Pakistan War", *Asian Survey,* 10 (1976).
247. David B. Ottoway, "China, Russia Vie in Sending Arms to Rival Angola Groups", *International Herald Tribune,* 24 June 1975.
248. Edgar Snow, "Interview with Mao", *New Republic,* 7 (1965).
249. Sheldon Simon, "Peking and Indo-China. The Perplexity of Victory", *Asian Survey,* 5 (1978).
250. Hua Guofeng's report on the work of the government delivered at the National People's Conference on 26 February 1978; see *Peking Review,* 10 (1978).
251. "Interview with Minister Li Chiang", *China's Foreign Trade,* 3 (1978).

Chapter 7

TOWARDS A GREAT POWER STATUS

Since the Revolution, China's role in world politics has grown continuously, so much so that within a span of thirty years she has come to be ranked among the major powers. The area of her interest and the field of her activity is no longer confined to her continent. They have become global, with manifestation of interests in developments everywhere and with active involvement in the central strategic balance of the international system.

It seems appropriate at this point to briefly explore whether this globalisation is commensurate with China's capacity to credibly play such a role. Does she possess the military, economic, and political power to effectively face the international situation? Can one argue that a country like China is attempting to achieve what is disproportionate to her real capability?

China is clearly a developing country. With a per capita income of not more than $152[1] she can hardly be compared to the two superpowers. Faced as she is with agonizing problems of modernisation, she is at the moment far from possessing levers of powers even remotely comparable to the United States and the Soviet Union.

Yet China has become a weighty factor internationally and has been recognised as such by those who dominate global politics. In fact, much of her diplomatic activity during these thirty years—even when she was at her weakest—revolved around the superpowers and was largely influenced by the actions and the reactions emanating from the central strategic balance. China has also successfully constituted herself into an important element in the diplomatic calculations and foreign policy objectives of the superpowers. In the first twenty years after the revolution, the United States has, for example, attempted to contain her. Since the Nixon presidency, the American administration has been seeking her out in order to establish viable counterbalances against Moscow. The Soviet Union, on the other hand, after a long period of friendship with China, is living in considerable fear of a Sino-American entente.

This unique and paradoxical phenomena is an indication that underdevelopment and an impactful foreign policy are not as mutually exclusive as they have been made out to be. For a nation as large, as populated, and as mobilised as China, it is possible to play a significant role in international politics despite a situation of underdevelopment. All attempts to rank China in terms of such indicators as per capita income, which is almost

1/15th that of Kuwait or literacy rates, which are equal to that of Burma or Lebanon, or productivity of population, which is probably no higher than that of Brazil or Nigeria are valid in terms of assessing China's level of modernisation but are misleading insofar as effectiveness in foreign affairs is concerned.

None of these handicaps and signs of underdevelopment kept China from stalemating the Americans during the Korean War in 1950, from tilting balances in favour of Ho Chi-Minh in 1950 as well, from defeating India in 1962, or from deterring the Russians from taking any major action in the Sino-Soviet border dispute in 1969. Furthermore, none of the agonizing problems of modernisation have stopped China from taking important initiatives in Africa, Latin America, and Europe. It could be argued that for a nation to play a major role in international affairs—as the preceding chapters have shown—a number of indicators closely linked with power are essential. In addition to size and population, with which China is more than well-equipped, a nation needs military strength, exploitable economic resources, and a stabilised domestic situation.

China's military strength is considerable. She has one of the largest armed forces in the world—even more than the United States and the Soviet Union combined. The bulk of this manpower is a ground force which is now the largest in the world, with 3,600,000 men as against 750,800 in the American army and 1,825,000 in the Soviet army.[2]

With her actual military strength, China is able to defend her frontiers and provide assistance to neighbouring and even distant countries. She can also infiltrate guerilla units into nations on her periphery and apply large-scale pressures to most of them. She can also apply large conventional military land forces to a Korean-type operation.

It has been argued that the Chinese army is badly equipped and that her weaponry is at least twenty years behind that used in most of the developed countries, and in the event of a conflict with an well-equipped adversary she would be seriously handicapped. But this backwardness is not inherent. It is linked to the choice made by the Maoist leadership to maintain a non-professional, people's army, since a high degree of political consciousness was viewed as more effective than a professional army concentrating on military theory, expertise, and sophisticated weapons.

However, now that China, in the post-Maoist phase, has moved away from this concept and appears to have clearly opted for modernisation, with the intention of professionalising the army and of producing and acquiring sophisticated weapons, there is no reason why China should not be able to remove this handicap. It should be one of the least difficult of objectives for a mobilised nation to achieve, since all that is needed is a decision and the determination to re-allocate the appropriate resources for this purpose. This apparently has been done.

International conjuncture is also favourable to China on this question. Recent Soviet expansionism has finally led the Western world to lift

286

restrictions on supplying China with appropriate and sophisticated technology. Though Moscow has been successful in making the European powers hesitate in disbursing sophisticated arms, it would seem that the international situation is not conducive to this kind of restraint. Even the United States, which had given the green light to her allies but was reluctant to embroil herself in arms assistance, has taken the first step—after the Afghan crisis—to provide China with military support equipment.

China is also in the process of becoming a nuclear power with a credible capability to play the atomic game with other nuclear powers. The considerable progress that she has already made in the field can be gauged from the fact that (a) she has already conducted twenty-five nuclear tests since 1964, not with plutonium, as had been expected, but with uranium-235, which implies the possession of a highly specialised technology; (b) a Chinese theatre nuclear force is already operational and is capable of reaching large parts of the Soviet Union and Asia; (c) she has stockpiled weapons, both fission and fusion-types, probably amounting to some two to three hundred; (d) medium-range ballistic missiles with a range from 600-700 miles and intermediate-range ballistic missiles with a range of 1500 to 1750 miles are already operational; (e) a multi-stage intercontinental ballistic missile (ICBM) with a range of 3000-3500 miles has been developed and an ICBM, believed to have a range of 8000 miles, has already been used (and tested) to launch a satellite.[3]

China's great progress in this field can be gauged from the facts that about two decades earlier the level of her nuclear technology was lower than that of India and her dependence on the Soviet Union was umbilical.

In the field of economic growth too, China appears to have made some visible strides in certain sectors. If one were to evaluate her overall economic development between 1952-1972 in terms of growth rate, her performance is not very impressive; for her gross national product, which was estimated to be $299 billion in 1975 has increased only by 3.5 per cent, her agricultural growth rate has not exceeded 1.9 per cent, and her industrial production has been in the vicinity of 8.5 per cent.

But this is not an adequate indicator to evaluate and assess real economic performance; a nation may have only a modest overall growth but considerable growth in certain strategic sectors which are viewed as vital for an effective foreign policy.

In a contemporary world, where the energy resources, and generative capacity of a nation is a key determinant of her economic and political strength, her military might and her populations' well-being, China has indeed made remarkable progress. The annual production of coal, for example, has increased from 32.4 million metric tons in 1949 to 605 million metric tons in 1978, making her probably second only to the Soviet Union in coal production. Her oil production has increased from 0.1 million metric tons in 1949 to 100 million metric tons in 1978. This remarkable development has made it possible for China to make the heady transition from oil importer to oil exporter, thereby marking a new chapter in China's hydrocarbon industry; and her annual production of electric power has shot up from 4.3 billion kilowatts in 1949 to 162 billion kilowatts.[4] China has thus become the fifth largest energy consumer in the world. Although she is behind the United States and the Soviet Union, she is almost at par with Japan and West Germany, and slightly ahead of Great Britain.

Similar trends are also discernible in some of the other important sectors of the Chinese economy. A number of metallurgical bases, for example, have been either further developed or created in different parts of China: in Anshan, in the city of Wuhan, in Baotou and in the province of Gansu. China's steel production has increased from 0.6 million tons in 1950 to 31.7 million metric tons in 1978. Her index of machinery output also presents an impressive picture. It has grown faster than industrial output as a whole, reflecting the insensitivity of this sector to even shifts of inter-sectorial emphasis, whether agriculture or industry.

But more important than her economic performance is her potential. The latest discoveries indicate that China possesses an abundance of natural resources in coal, iron, and oil, the three most important branches of the natural resources family. Her coal resources have been estimated at 11 trillion tons, an amount equal to one third of the known world reserves. In the field of oil resources, it is reported that she has about 10 billion tons[5] in reserve. It has been even suggested that China's offshore reserves might rival those of the Middle East—at 50 billion tons or more. Such an estimate, if correct, would make China first in a worldwide ranking of resources.[6]

But merely the possession of natural resources is not enough. It is important that they be accessible and that the country be capable of using them in a practical way. Here again China appears to be in a fortunate position. The abundant deposits of coal and iron resources are located in easily accessible areas in the central, northern and northeastern parts of the country. And the oil resources located in the distant northwestern regions have become accessible by the construction of the Lanchou-Xinjiang railroad extending China's highway network and by the building of pipelines from several oil fields to the oil refineries.

It is perhaps too early to pass any definite judgment concerning the practical utilisation of resources. But considering the fact that the political system of the country makes it possible to concentrate control of all resources in the hands of the controlling board of the state, one could perhaps venture to suggest that there too China should be successful. Admittedly many nations with similar socio-economic structures have "made mistakes, bungled assignments, and ruined the best of plans,"[7] but it should be noted, that they eventually attained their objectives on the economic front, even if it took them more effort than the competitive Western capitalist societies.

Her broad-based political system makes it possible for China to project herself effectively into the international system. It gives her the strength necessary to avoid any major digressions from her foreign policy goals. Admittedly it is no longer possible to sustain the belief that the Chinese regime was immune from internal crisis. The Cultural Revolution and the fate of many leaders, including the recent trial of the "Gang of Four", have shown that conflicts and crises are as much a part of Chinese politics as they are of other systems. But they are nonetheless not the great nullifiers of foreign policy goals to the same degree as they are in pluralistic societies. Moreover, crises in China are disparate and relatively infrequent, unlike in the Western societies where they are institutionalised, and unlike in the Third World countries where they are endemic.

The combination of all these factors, compounded with the important fact that China is led by a highly motivated leadership with clear-cut objectives regarding China's role in the world, has placed her in the ranks of the superpowers, though by no means at the same level.

For decades, the half-sleeping nation watched helplessly as the powers of the day seized her coastal areas, dominated her economy and belittled her ancient but mature civilization. Now that she has at last awakened, her role in the central strategic balance of the international system has become crucial.

Will she rise to still greater heights? Will she eventually acquire a status equal to that of the superpowers? Only time will tell. But considering the facts that China possesses all the important prerequisites for becoming great, and that since time immemorial the world has continuously witnessed the rise and fall of civilizations, such a possibility can hardly be excluded.

Notes

1. Ambassador Chen Chu gave this figure to the UN General Assembly's Fifth Committee; see *International Herald Tribune*, 28 September 1979. This was increased to $ 210 and then raised to $ 230, see Ibid., 22 December 1980.
2. The International Institute of Strategic Studies, *The Military Balance 1979-1980*. (1979).
3. Ibid.
4. See "The Trend and Pattern of Economic Growth" in Joyce K. Kallgren's (ed.), *The People's Republic of China After Thirty Years: An Overview* (Berkeley: University of California Press, 1979).
5. See, Victor P. Petrov, *China: Emerging World Power* (Princeton: D. van Nostrand Company 1967); also see Selig S. Harrison, *China, Oil and Asia; Conflict Ahead* (New York: Columbia University Press, 1977).
6. Ibid.
7. Victor P. Petrov, op.cit., p. 125.

SELECTED BIBLIOGRAPHY

1. Sources

Documents

Ambekar, G. V. and Divekar, V. D., *Documents on China's Relations with South and South-East Asia 1949-1962* (Bombay: Allied Publishers Private Ltd., 1964).

Department of State, *American Foreign Policy 1950-1955, 1956, 1957*, and subsequent annual volumes (Washington D.C.: US Government Printing Press, 1957).

United States Relations with China, with Special Reference to the Period 1944-1949 (Washington: US Government Printing Press, 1949).

Foreign Languages Press, *Important Documents Concerning the Question of Taiwan* (Peking: 1955).

In Refutation of Modern Revisionism (Peking: 1958).

Huit ans de lutte des volontaires du peuple chinois pour resister à l'agression et pour aider la Corée (Peking: 1958).

Oppose the Revival of Japanese Imperialism (Peking: 1960).

Long Live Leninism (Peking: 1960).

Chassons les impérialistes américains de l'Asie (Peking: 1960).

The Sino-Indian Boundary Question (Peking: 1962).

Prolétaires de tous les pays unissons-nous contre l'ennemi commun (Peking: 1963).

Peaceful Coexistence – two Diametrically Opposed views (Peking: 1963).

Oppose the US Occupation of Taiwan and the "Two Chinas" Plot (Peking: 1965).

The Polemic on the General Line of the International Communist Movement (Peking: 1965).

Important Documents Concerning the Question of Taiwan (Peking: 1965).

Confessions Concerning the Line of Soviet-US Collaboration Pursued by the New Leaders of the CPSU (Peking: 1966).

Struggle against Imperialism and Revisionism to the Very End: A Collection of Documents from the Visit to China of the Albanian Party and Government Delegation (Peking: 1966).

A New Page in the Annals of Sino-Japanese Relations (Peking: 1972).

The Tenth National Congress of the Communist Party of China (Peking: 1973).

Gittings, John., *Survey of the Sino-Soviet Dispute: A Commentary and Extracts from the Recent Polemics 1963-1967* (London: Oxford University Press, 1968).

Hasan, K. Sarwar, (ed.), *Documents on Foreign Relations of Pakistan: China, India, Pakistan* (Karachi: Pakistan Institute of International Affairs, 1966).

US Congress, House of Representatives Subcommittee on Asian and Pacific Affairs, *Hearings on United States-China Relations. A Strategy for the Future* (Washington D.C.: US Government Printing Press, 1970).

US Congress, Senate Committee on Foreign Relations. *Hearings on US Policy with Respect to Mainland China* (Washington D.C.: US Government Printing Press Office, 1966).

Ideological Writings

Lin Piao, *En avant sous le drapeau rouge de la ligne générale du parti et de la théorie de Mao Tse-Toung* (Peking: Foreign Languages Press, 1961).
Long Live the Victory of People's War (Peking: Foreign languages Press, 1965).
Liu Shaoqi, *How to be a Good Communist* (Peking: Foreign Languages Press, 1961).
— *The Victory of Marxism-Leninism in China* (Peking: Foreign Languages Press, 1959).
— *Collected Works of Liu Shaoqi (Liu Shao Chi)* (Hongkong: Union Research Institute, 1968-1969).
Lo Jui-Ching, *The People Defeated Japanese Fascism and They Can Certainly Defeat US. Imperialism* (Peking: Foreign Languages Press, 1965).
Mao Zedong *Selected Works of Mao Zedong* (Peking: Foreign Languages Press, 1965-1970), 5 Vols.
Peng Tchen, *Conference à l'Académie Indonésienne des Sciences Sociales Aliarcham* (Peking: Foreign Languages Press, 1965).

Memoirs

Acheson, Dean, *Present at the Creation* (New York: Norton, 1969).
Chiang Kai-Shek, *Soviet Russia in China: A Summing-up at Seventy*, Revised, abridged Edition (New York: Farvar, Straus and Giroux, 1915).
Kissinger, Henry, *White House Years* (Boston: Little Brown and Company, 1979).
Kruschev, N. S. *Kruschev Remembers*, (London: Penguin, 1977).
Micunovic, Veljko, *Journées de Moscou 1956-1958: Un Embassadeur de Tito au Kremlin* (Paris: Robert Lafont, 1979).
Nixon, Richard, *The Memoirs of Richard Nixon* (London: Arrow, 1978).
Pannikar, K. M. *In Two Chinas: Memoirs of a Diplomat* (London: Allen and Unwin, 1955).
Yoshida, Shigeru, *The Yoshida Memoirs: The Story of Japan in Crisis* (Westfort, Conn. Green Wood Press, 1963).

2. Studies

China's Perception of the World

Bloodworth, Dennis, *Chinese Looking Glass* (London: Penguin Books, 1967).
Etiemble, *Connaissons-nous la Chine?* (Paris: Gallimard, 1964).
Fairbank, John King, (ed.), *The Chinese World Order: Traditional China's Foreign Relations* (Cambridge: Harvard University Press, 1968).
Fitzgerald, C. P., *The Chinese View of their Place in the World* (London: Oxford University Press, 1969).
Granet, Marcel, *La Pensée chinoise* (Paris: Albin Michel, 1968).
Hou, Wai-Lu, *A Short History of Chinese Philosophy* (Peking: Foreign Languages Press, 1959).
Lin, Yutang, *The Wisdom of China*, Edited and annotated (Bombay: Jaico Books, 1955).
Marx, Karl and Engels, F., *On Colonialism* (Moscow: Foreign Languages Press, n.d.).
Ness, Peter Van, *Revolution and Chinese Foreign Policy: Peking's Support for Wars of National Liberation* (Berkeley: University of California Press, 1971).

Northop, F. S. C., *The Meeting of the East and the West* (New York: Macmillan, 1946).

Ojha, I. C., *Chinese Foreign Policy in an Age of Transition: The Diplomacy of Cultural Despair* (Boston: Beacon Press, 1969).

Riencourt, Amaury, de, *The Soul of China,* Revised edition (New York: Harper and Row 1965).

Schram, Stuart, Mao Tse-Tung (London: Penguin, 1966).

Scwartz, B., *Chinese Communism and the Rise of Mao* (Harvard: Harvard University Press, 1951).

Snow, Edgar, *Red Star over China* (New York: Grove Press, 1961).

Teng, Ssu-yü and Fairbank, John K., *China's Response to the West: A Documentary Survey 1839-1923* (Cambridge: Harvard University Press, 1954).

Vissiere, Isabelle and Jean-Louis, *Lettres édifiantes et curieuses de Chine par des missionaires jésuites 1702-1776,* Chronologie, introduction, notices et notes (Paris: Garnier-Flammarion, 1976).

Wilson, Dick, (ed.), *Mao Tse-Tung in the Scales of History* (Cambridge: Cambridge University Press, 1977).

China and the Soviet Union

Baby, Jean, *La grande controverse Sino-Soviétique 1956-1966* (Paris: Grasset, 1966).

Beloff, Max, *Soviet Policy in the Far East 1944-1951* (Oxford: Oxford University Press, 1953).

Bettati, Mario, *Le conflit Sino-Soviétique,* 2 vols., (Paris: Armand Collin, 1971).

Borisov, O. B. and Koloskov, B. T., *Sino-Soviet Relations 1945-1973: A Brief History* (Moscow: Progress Publishers, 1975).

Brzezinski, Z., *The Soviet Bloc, Unity and Conflict* (New York: Praeger, 1961).

Carrere d'Encausse, H. and Schram, S. R., *L'URSS et la Chine devant les révolutions dans les sociétés pré-industrielles* (Paris: Armand Collin, 1970).

Clemens, Jr., Walter E., *The Arms Race and Sino-Soviet Relations* (Stanford: Hoover Institution Publication, 1968).

Clubb, Edmund O., *China and Russia: The Great Game* (Columbia University Press, 1971).

Crankshaw, Edward, *The New Cold War: Moscow v. Peking* (London: Penguin, 1963).

Doolin, Dennis J., *Territorial Claims in the Sino-Soviet Conflict. Documents and Analysis* (Stanford: Hoover Institution Studies, 1965).

Fetto, François, *Chine-URSS,* 2 vols., (Paris: Plon, 1964 and 1966).

Ginsburg, G. and Pinkele, C., *The Sino-Soviet Territorial Dispute 1949-1964* (New York: Praeger, 1978).

Griffith, W. E., *The Sino-Soviet Rift,* Analysed and documented (London: Allen and Unwin, 1964).

Hamrell, Sven and Widstrand, Carl Gosta, (eds.), *The Soviet Bloc, China and Africa* (Uppsala: The Scandinavian Institute of African Studies, 1964).

Hudson, G. F., Lowenthal, Richard and MacFarquhar, Roderick, *The Sino-Soviet Dispute* Documented and analysed (New York: Praeger, 1961).

Klein, Sidney, *Economic Aspects of the Sino-Soviet Dispute* (Hongkong: International Studies Group, 1966).

Leong, Sow-Theng, *Sino-Soviet Diplomatic Relations 1917-1926* (Canberra: Australian National University Press, 1976).

Louis, Victor, *The Coming Decline of the Chinese Empire* (New York: Times Books, 1979).

293

McLane, Charles, B., *Soviet Policy and the Chinese Communists 1931-1946* (New York: Columbia University Press, 1958).

Mehnert, Klaus, *Peking and Moscow* (New York: Mentor, 1964).

Meray, Tibor, *La rupture Moscou-Pékin* (Paris: Robert Laffont, 1966).

Middleton, Drew, *The Duel of the Giants: China and Russia in Asia* (New York: Scribner's New York, 1978).

Oksenberg, Michel and Oxnam, R. B., (eds.), *Dragon and Eagle. United States-China Relations: Past and Future* (New York: Basic Books, 1978).

Rubinstein, Alvinz, (ed.), *Soviet and Chinese Influence in the Third World* (New York: Praeger, 1975).

Salisbury, Harrison E., *The Coming War between Russia and China* (London: Pan, 1969).

Saran, Vimla, *Sino-Soviet Schism. A Bibliography 1956-1964* (New Delhi: Asia Publishing House, 1971).

Sergeyeva, E. A.,*Vneshnaya Politika i Vneshnepoliticheskaya Propaganda Rookovodstva* (Moscow: Nauka Publishers, 1978).

Sladkovski, M., et al., *Léninisme et la Chine moderne* (Moscow: Les Editions du Progrès, 1974).

Thornton, Richard C., *The Comintern and the Chinese Communists 1928-1931* (Seattle: University of Washington Press, 1969).

Yakovlev, A., *World Socialist System and National Liberation Movement* (Moscow: Novosti Press Agency Publishing House, n.d.).

Yurkov, S. G., *Peking Novya Politika* (Moscow: Politizdat, 1972).

Zagoria, Donald S., *The Sino-Soviet Conflict 1956-1961* (New York: Atheneum, 1966).

Zanegin, B., *Nationalist Background of China's Foreign Policy* (Moscow: Novosti Press Agency, n.d.).

China and the United States

Ballantine, Joseph W., *Formosa: A Problem for United States Policy* (Washington DC: Brookings Institution, 1952).

Barnds, William J., *China and America: The Search for a New Relationship* (New York: New York University Press, 1977).

Barnett, A. Doak, *A New U.S. Policy Toward China* (Washington DC: Brookings Institution, 1971).

Blum, Robert (Edited by A. Doak Barnett), *The United States and China in World Affairs* (New York: McGraw-Hill, 1966).

Borg, Dorothy, *American Policy and the Chinese Revolution* (Princeton: Princeton University Press, 1950).

Cohen, Warren I., *American Response to China: An Interpretative History of Sino-American Relations* (New York: John Wiley and Sons, 1971).

Dennett, Tyler, *Americans in Eastern Asia: A Critical Study of the Policy of the United States with Reference to China, Japan and Korea in the 19th Century* (New York: Macmillan, 1922).

Dulles, F. R., *American Policy Toward Communist China 1949-1969* (New York: Thomas Y. Cromwell, 1972).

— *China and America: The Story of their Relations since 1784* (Princeton: Princeton University Press, 1946).

Esherick, John S., (ed.), *Lost Chance in China: The World War II Despatches of John S. Service* (New York: Randon House, 1974).

Fairbank, John King, *China Perceived: Images and Policies in Chinese-American Relations* (New York: Alfred A. Knopf, 1974).

— *The United States and China,* New edition completely revised and enlarged (New York: Viking Press, 1966).

Griswold, A. Whitney, *The Far Eastern Policy of the United States* (New York: Harcourt, Brace and Company, 1938).

Hsiao, Gene J., (ed.), *Sino-American Détente and Its Policy Implications* (New York: Praeger, 1975).

Jo, Yung-hwan, (ed.), *Taiwan's Future* (Hongkong: Union Research Institute for Arizona State University, 1974).

Kalichi, Jan, *The Pattern of the Sino-American Crisis* (New York: Cambridge University Press, 1975).

Kintner, William R. and Copper John F., *A Matter of Two Chinas: The China-Taiwan Issue in US Foreign Policy* (Philadelphia: Foreign Policy Research Institute, 1979).

Kuzmin, V.V., *Kitaii v strateghii amerikanckovo imperializma* (Moscow: International Relations, 1978).

MacFarquhar, Roderick, *Sino-American Relations 1949-1971* (London: David and Charles Ltd. for the Royal Institute of International Affairs, 1972).

Service, John S., *The Amerasia Papers: Some Problems in the History of US-China Relations,* Research monograph (Berkeley: Center for Chinese Studies, University of California Press, 1971).

Shewmaker, Kenneth E., *Americans and Chinese Communists 1972-1945: A Persuading Encounter* (Itacha: Cornell University Press, 1971).

Sullivan, William A., (ed.), *Doing Business with China: American Trade Opportunities in the 1970s* (New York: Praeger, 1974).

Terrill, Ross, (ed.), *China and Ourselves: Explorations and Revisions by a New Generation* (Boston: Beacon, 1969).

Tong, Te-Kong, *United States Diplomacy in China 1844-1860* (Seattle: University of Washington Press, 1964).

Topping, Seymour, *Journey Between Two Worlds* (New York: Harper and Row, 1972).

Tsou, Tang, *American's Failure in China 1941-1950* (Chicago: University of Chicago Press, 1953).

Tuchman, Barbara W., *Stilwell and the American Experience in China 1911-1945* (New York: Macmillan, 1971).

— *Notes From China* (New York; Collier, 1972).

Whiting, Allen S., *China Crosses the Yalu River: The Decision to Enter the Korean War* (New York: Macmillan, 1960).

Young, Kenneth T., *Negotiating with the Chinese Communists: The United States Experience, 1953-1967* (New York: MacGraw-Hill, 1968).

China and Japan

Bamba, Nobuya, *Japanese Diplomacy in a Dilemma. New Light on Japan's China Policy 1924-1929* (Vancouver: University of British Columbia Press, 1972).

Beasley, W. G., *The Modern History of Japan* (London: Weidenfeld and Nicholson, 1963).

Beckmann, George, *Modernization of China and Japan* (New York: Harper and Row, 1962).

Boyle, John H., *China and Japan at War 1937—1945: The Politics of Collaboration* (Stanford: Stanford University Press, 1972).

Duus, Peter, *The Rise of Modern Japan* (Boston: Houghton Mifflin, 1978).

Guillain, R., *Japon, troisième Grand* (Paris: Editions du Seuil, 1969).

Halpern, Abraham M., *Peking and the Problem of Japan 1968-1972*, Professional paper no. 99, (Arlington, Virginia: July 1972).

Hellman, Donald C., *Japan and East Asia: The New International Order* (London: Pall Mall Press, 1972).

Hsiao, Gene T., (ed.), *Nonrecognition and Trade: A Case Study of the Fourth Sino-Japanese Trade Agreement*, Asian Studies Occasional paper, Series no. 1 (Edwardsville: Southern Illinois University Press, 1973).

Jain, L. K., *China and Japan 1949-1976* (New Delhi: Radiant Publishers, 1977).

Jansen, Marius B., *The Japanese and Sun Yat-sen* (Cambridge, Mass.: Harvard University Press, 1954).

— *Japan and China: From War to Peace 1894-1972* (Chicago: McNally College Publishing Company, 1978).

Kato, S., *The Japan-China Phenomenon: Conflict or Compatibility* (London: Paul Norbury, 1974).

Langer, Paul F., *Communism in Japan: A Case of Political Naturalisation* (Stanford: Hoover Institution Press, 1972).

Lee, Chae-Jin, *Japan Faces China: Political and Economic Relations in the Postwar Era* (Baltimore: John Hopkins University Press, 1976).

Livingston, Jon, et al, (eds.), *Postwar Japan: 1945 to the Present* (New York: Pantheon Books, 1973).

Mendl, Wolf, *Issues in Japan's China Policy* (London: Macmillan, for the Royal Institute of International Affairs, 1978).

Morley, James W., *Soviet and Chinese Communist Policies towards Japan* (New York: Institute of Pacific Relations, 1958).

Reischauer, E. O., *Japan Past and Present* (New York: Knopf, 1953).

Sansom, G. B., *The Western World and Japan* (New York; Alfred A. Knopf, 1950).

Scalapino, Robert A., *The Japanese Communist Movement 1920-1966* (Berkeley and Los Angeles: University of California Press, 1967).

Shao, Chuan Leng, *Japan and Communist China* (Kyoto: Doshisha University Press, 1967).

China and Europe

Actafev, G. B., et al. (eds.), *Kitaii i kapitalisticheskie strani europi* (Moscow: Isdatelctvo Nauka, 1976).

Dallin, Alexander (ed.), *Diversity in International Communism* (New York: Columbia University Press 1963).

Deutscher, Isaac, *Russia, China and West 1953-1966* (London: Penguin, 1970).

Godson, Roy and Haseler, Stephen, *"Eurocommunism": Implications for East and West* (London: Macmillan, 1978).

Griffith, William E., *Communism in Europe. Continuity, Change and the Sino-Soviet Dispute* (Cambridge. Mass.: M.I.T., 1966), 2 vols.

Lévesque, Jacques, *Le conflit sino-soviétique et l'Europe de l'Est* (Montreal: Les Presses de l'Université de Montreal, 1970).

Lewis, Flora, *A Case History of Hope: A Story of Poland's Peaceful Revolutions* (New York: Doubleday, 1958).

Majonica, Ernest, *Bonn-Peking. Die Beziehungen des Bundersrepublik Deutschland sur Volksrepublik China* (Stuttgart: W. Kohlhammer, 1971).

Mehnert, Klaus, *Peking and the New Left. At Home and Abroad* (California, Berkeley: University of California 1969).

296

Padovani, Marcelle, *La Longue Marche: le P.C. italien* (Paris: Calmann-Levy, 1976).
Stahnle, Arthur A., (ed.), *China's Trade with the West. Political and Economic Analysis* (New York: Praeger, 1972).
Stephenov, A. I., *F.R.G. i kitaii* (Moscow: Mezdhunarodnie Otnoshenia, 1974).
Zogladin, V., *Europe and Communists* (Moscow: Progress Publishers, 1977).

China and the Third World

Amer, Omer, *Communist China and the Afro-Asian People's Solidarity Organisation 1958-1967* (Geneva: Graduate Institute of International Studies, 1971).
Barnett, A. Doak, *Communist China and Asia: Challenge to American Policy* (New York: Vintage, 1960).
Brezezinski, Z., (ed.), *Africa and the Communist World* (Stanford: Stanford University Press, 1964).
Buchan, Alastair, (ed.), *China and the Peace of Asia* (London: Chatto and Windus, 1965).
Chao, Howard H. S., *Histoire sans fin* (Hong Kong: Phoenix Press, 1966).
Cooley, John K., *East Wind over Africa: Red China's African Offensive* (New York: Walker and Company, 1965).
Debray, Régis, *Essais sur l'Amérique Latine* (Paris: François Maspéro, 1967).
— *Revolution in the Revolution? Armed Struggle and Political Struggle in Latin America* (New York: Grove Press, 1967).
Despande, G. P., *Chinese Foreign Policy in Africa 1949-1964* (New Delhi: Jawaharlal Nehru University, 1970).
Garaudy, Roger, *Le problème chinois* (Paris: Éditions Seghers, 1967).
Guevara, Che, *Guerilla Warfare* (New York: Monthly Review Press, 1961).
Hevi, John Emmanuel, *An African Student in China* (London: Pall Mall Press, 1963).
— *The Dragon's Embrace: Communist China in Africa* (London: Pall Mall Press, 1967).
Johnson, Cecil, *Communist China and Latin America 1959-1967* (New York and London: Columbia University Press, 1970).
Labin, Suzanne, *Menaces chinoises sur l'Asie* (Paris: La Table Ronde, 1966).
Larkin, Bruce D., *China and Africa 1949-1970: The Foreign Policy of the People's Republic of China* (Berkeley: University of California Press, 1971).
Lentin, Albert-Paul, *La lutte tricontinentale: impérialisme et révolution après la conférence de la Havane* (Paris: François Maspéro, 1966).
Lessing, Pieter, *Africa's Red Harvest* (New York: John Day, 1968).
Mertens, Pierre and Smets, Paul F., *L'Afrique de Pékin* (Bruxelles: P. Mertens and P. Smets, 1966).
Neuhauser, Charles, *Third World Politics: China and the Afro-Asian People's Solidarity Organization* (Cambridge, Mass.: Harvard University Press, 1968).
Nielsen, Waldemor A., *The Great Powers in Africa* (New York: Praeger, for the Council on Foreign Relations, 1969).
Richer, Philippe, *La Chine et le Tiers Monde* (Paris: Payot, 1971).
Simon, Sheldon W., *The Broken Triangle: Peking, Djakarta and the PKI* (Baltimore: John Hopkins Press, 1969).
Schatten, Fritz, *Communism in Africa* (London: Allen and Unwin, 1966).
Youlou, F, *J'accuse la Chine* (Paris: La Table Ronde, 1966).

Harrison, Selig, S., *China Oil and Asia; Conflict Ahead* (New York: Columbia, University Press, 1977)

Kallgren, Joyce K. (ed.), *The People's Republic of China after Thirty Years: An Overview* (Berkeley, California: Institute of East Asian Studies University of California, 1979)

Leo, Yueh-Yun Liu, *China as a Nuclear Power in World Politics* (London: Macmillan 1972)

Petrov, Victor P., *China: Emerging World Power* (Princeton: D. Van Nostrand Company Inc., 1967)

Vaclar Smil., *China's Energy Achievements, Problems, Prospects* (New York: Praeger 1976)

The Military Balance 1980-1981 (London: The International Institute for Strategic Studies 1980)

3. Articles

China's Perception of the World

Bedeski, R. E., "The Evolution of the Modern State in China: Nationalist and Communist Continuities", *World Politics*, 27 (1975).

Deleyne, J., "Ideologie et développement en Chine populaire", *Tiers Monde*, 15 (1974).

Hervouet, G., "Perceptions occidentales de la Chine contemporaine: l'analyse de la politique étrangère chinoise dans la littérature spécialisée", *Etudes Internationales*, 5 (1974).

Hook, B., "Historical Perspectives on China's New Diplomacy", *Asian Affairs*, 61 (1974).

Koloskov, B., "Foreign Policy Concepts of Maoism", *International Affairs*, 2 (1976).

Leng, S. C., "China and the International System", *World Affairs*, 138 (1976).

Myasnikov, V., "Ideological Bankruptcy of Peking's Falsifiers", *Far Eastern Affairs*, 1 (1979).

Tang, P. S. H., "Mao Tse-tung Thought Since the Cultural Revolution", *Studies in Soviet Thought*, 13 (1973).

Yahuda, Michael B., "Chinese Conception of Their Role in the World", *Political Quarterly*, I (1974).

— "The Chinese View of a New World Order", *Millennium*, I (1978).

China and the Soviet Union

Alexeyev, I. and Apalin, G., "A Soviet Assessment of China", *Coexistence*, 15 (1978).

Azar, Edward E., "The USSR, China and the Middle East", *Problems of Communism*, 3 (1979).

Badour, W., "La Chine et l'URSS—Liens entre politique interne et politique externe", *Etudes Internationales*, 3 (1972).

Beskrovny, L., Tikhvinsky, S. and Khrostov, V., "On the History of the Formation of the Russo-Chinese Border", *International Affairs*, 7 (1972).

Fitzgerald, C. P., "The Dispute between China and the Soviet Union", *Australian Quarterly*, December (1963).

Grigoryeva, E. and Kostikov, E., "Maoist Speculations on the 'Unequal Treaty' Conception", *Far Eastern Affairs,* 3 (1975).

Horn, R. C. "China and Russia in 1977: Maoism without Mao", *Asian Survey,* 17 (1977).

Hudson, G. F., "Moscow and Beijing: Seeds of Conflict", *Problems of Communism,* 5 (6) (1956).

Iurkov, S. G., "50 let sovetsko-kitaiskikh otnoshnenii", *Problemy Dol'nego Vostoka,* 2 (1974).

Katona, P., "Sino-Soviet Relations", *Yearbook of World Affairs,* 26 (1972).

Koloskov, B., "Foreign Policy Concepts of Maoism", *International Affairs,* 2 (1976).

Lowenthal, Richard, "Diplomacy and Revolution: The Dialectics of a Dispute", *China Quarterly,* 5 (1961).

Lukacs, George, "Reflections on the Sino-Soviet Dispute", *Studies on the Left,* 4 (1) (1964).

Mosely, Philip E., "The Chinese-Soviet Rift: Origins of Portents", *Foreign Affairs,* 42 (1) (1963).

Schleisinger, Rudolf, "Observations on the Sino-Soviet Dispute", *Science and Society,* 27 (3) (1963).

Sen, Mohit, "Great Divide in Communist Ideology", *India Quarterly,* 20 (4) (1964).

Shirayev, Y. and Yakovlev, A., " The Socialist Community and Its Peking Ill-wishers", *Far Eastern Affairs,* 4 (1977).

Tang, Peter S. H., "Moscow and Peking: The Question of War and Peace", *Orbis,* 5 (1) (1961).

Thornton, Thomas P., "Peking, Moscow and Under-developed Areas", *World Politics,* 13 (4) (1961).

Ukraintsev, M., "Maoist Ideology and Peking's Foreign Policy", *International Affairs,* 5 (1975).

Waller, D. J. and Donaldson, R. H., "A Comparison of the Current Chinese and Soviet Central Committees", *Studies in Comparative Communism,* 6 (1973).

Whiting, Allen S., " 'Contradictions' in the Moscow-Peking Axis", *Journal of Politics,* 20 (1) (1958)

China and the United States

Ali, M., "The New American Attitude towards China", *Pakistan Horizon,* 24 (1971).

Barnet, A. Doak, "Military-Security Relations between China and the United States", *Foreign Affairs,* 3 (1977).

Billa, Krupadanam J. B., "The 'Nixon Shock' and its Consequences: Sino-American Reconciliation", *China Report,* 5 (1979).

Brown, R. G., "Chinese Politics and American Policy: a New Look at the Triangle", *Foreign Policy,* Summer (1976).

Clubb, Edmund O., "Sino-American Relations and the Future of Formosa", *Political Science Quarterly,* March (1965).

Cohen, Warren I, "The Development of Chinese Communist Policy towards the United States 1922-1933", *Orbis,* 1 (1967).

— "The Development of Chinese Communist Policy towards the United States 1934-1945", *Orbis,* 2 (1967).

Devane, Richard T., "The United States and China: Claims and Assets", *Asian Survey,* 12 (1978).

Eckstein, Alexander, "China's Trade and Sino-American Relations", *Foreign Affairs*, 1 (1975).

Emmerson, J. K., "American and Chinese Rediscover Each Other", *Pacific Community*, 2 (1971).

Engelborghs-Bertels, M., "Le communiqué de Shanghai et la politique extérieure de la Chine", *Revue des pays de l'Est*, 2 (1972).

Fairbank, John K., "American China Policy" to 1898: A Misconception", *Pacific Historical Review*, 4 (1970).

— "East Asia: Our One-China Problem", *The Atlantic Monthly*, 9 (1976).

— "The New China and the American Connection", *Foreign Affairs*, 51 (1972).

Gelber, H. D., "The United States and China", *International Affairs*, 46 (1970).

Guhin, Michael A., "The United States and the Chinese People's Republic: A Non-Recognition Policy Reviewed", *International Affairs*, January (1969).

Hsiung, James C., "US Relations with China in the post-Kissingerian Era: A Sensible Policy for the 1980s, *Asian Survey*, 8 (1977).

Jo, Yung-Hwan, "China and America", *China Report*, 1 (1979).

Joyaux, F., "Chine-Etats-Unis: Dix ans de détente", *Mondes Asiatiques*, 16 (1978-1979).

Lampton, D. M., "The US image of Peking in Three International Crisis", *The Western Political Quarterly*, 26 (1973).

Ledovsky, A., "The Fiasco of US Plans of Intervention in China and Alienation of Manchuria", *Far Eastern Affairs*, 1 (1979).

Levine, Steven I., "China Policy during Carter's One Year", *Asian Survey*, 5 (1978).

Morgenthau, H. J., "The United States and China", *International Studies*, 10 (1968).

Nixon, Richard M., "Asia After Vietnam", *Foreign Affairs*, 1 (1967).

Pillsbury, Michael, "US-China Military Ties", *Foreign Policy*, 20 (1975).

Pye, Lucien, "Bringing Our China Policy Down to Earth", *Foreign Policy*, 18 (1975).

Solomon, R. H., "Thinking Through the (US)-China Problem", *Foreign Affairs*, 56 (1978).

Thompson, Jr., James, C., "On the Making of US-China Policy 1961-69: A Study of Bureaucratic Politics", *China Quarterly*, 50 (1972).

Titov, A., "Peking and its American Lobby", *Far Eastern Affairs*, 4 (1978).

Tuchman, Barbara, "If Mao had come to Washington: An Essay in Alternatives", *Foreign Affairs*, 1 (1972).

Worden, Robert L., "A Perspective on US-China Relations since the Shanghai Communiqué", *Asian Profile*, 1 (1979).

Young, Kenneth T., "American Dealings with Peking", *Foreign Affairs*, October (1966).

Zanegin, B., "Sino-US Rapprochement: What It Is and Why", *Far Eastern Affairs*, 1 (1975).

China and Japan

Baerweld, H. H., "Aspects of Sino-Japanese Normalisation", *Pacific Community*, 4 (1973).

Bandura, Y., "The Sino-Japanese Alliance Runs Counter to Peace Interests", *International Affairs*, 8 (1979).

Cheng, T., "The Sino-Japanese Dispute over the Tiao-yu-tai (Senkaka) Islands and the Law of Territorial Acquisition", *Virginia Journal of International Law*, 14 (1974).

Current Scene, "A Japanese View of China", Current Scene, 1 May (1964).

Davies, D., "Will Japan's Accomodation with China work?"
Pacific Community, 4 (1973).

Dennis, T. Yasutomo, "Sato's China Policy, 1964-1966", Asian Survey, 6 (1977).

Eto, Shinkichi, "Japan and China—A New Stage", Problems of Communism, 6 (1972).

Holdsworth, R. "Japanese Peace Treaty Negotiations with the Soviet Union and China", Millenium, 5 (1976).

Hong K. Kim, "Sino-Japanese Relations Since the Rapprochement", Asian Survey, 7 (1975).

— " 'Anti-Hegemonism' and the Politics of the Sino-Japanese Treaty. A Study in the Meki Government's China Policy", Korea and World Affairs, 4 (1977).

— "The Tanaka Government and the Politics of the Sino-Japanese Civil Aviation Pact", World Affairs, 137 (1975).

Hsiao, G. T., "The Sino-Japanese Rapprochement—A Relationship of Ambivalence", China Quarterly, 57 (1974).

Hudson, G., "Japanese Attitudes of Policies towards China in 1973", China Quarterly, 56 (1973).

Jan, G. P., "The Japanese People and Japan's Policy towards Communist China", Western Political Quarterly, 22 (1969).

Kaushik, B. M., "Japan-China Peace Pact: Problems and Prospects", China Report, 11 (1975).

Lee, Chae-Jin, "The Japan Socialist Party and China, 1975-1977", Asian Survey, 3 (1978).

Mendel, D. H., "Japanese Public Views on Taiwan's Future", Asian Survey, 3 (1975).

Michimasa, Irie, "Communist China's Nuclear Power and the Security of Japan", Journal of Social and Political Ideas in Japan, 2 (1965), selected articles 1964.

Oguro, Kazuo, "How the 'Incrutables' Negotiate with the 'Inscrutables': Chinese Negotiating Tactics vis-à-vis the Japanese", China Quarterly, 79 (1979).

Shinchiro, Shiranishi, "A New Era Comes to Japan-China Relations: The Potential for Economic Cooperation", Japan Quarterly, 1 (1979).

Simon, Sheldon, "Maoism and Inter-party Relations: Peking's Alienation of the Japan Communist Party", China Quarterly, 35 (1968).

Sinha, Mira, "The Sino-Japanese Peace Treaty: Moscow Loses Round One to Peking", China Report, 4 (1978).

Seiichi, Tagawa, "A New Era Comes to Japan-China Relations: Don't Forget the Well-Diggers", Japan Quarterly, 1 (1979).

Takeuchi, Yoshimi, "A Return to Sino-Japanese Problem", Journal of Social and Political Ideas in Japan, 2 (1965), selected articles 1964.

Trivière, L., "Quand le Japon renoue avec la Chine", Études December 1972.

Uchida, K., "A Brief History of Post-war Japan-China Relations", The Developing Economics, 9 (1971).

Vishwanathan, S., "The Japan-China-URSS Triangle: A view from Tokyo", India Quarterly, 31 (1975).

China and Europe

Aczel, Tamas, "Hungary: Glad Tidings from Nanking", China Quarterly, 3 (1960).

Adie, W. A. C., "Chinese Relations with Eastern and Western Europe", Wilton Park Journal, 6 (1970).

301

Alexeyev, I., "Peking's European Policy", *International Affairs*, 1 (1976).

Avesenev, Y., Karshinov, V. and Potymkina, E., "China's Foreign Trade", *Far Eastern Affairs*, 4 (1975).

Biegel, Alfred, "The Sino-West European Connection", *Military Review*, 1 (1976).

Bouc, Alain, "Peking Now Wants a United Europe", *The Atlantic Community Quarterly*, 2 (1972).

Braine, Bernard, "China and the European Community", *China Now*, 76 (1978).

Bressi, Giovanni, "China's Foreign Policy: Western Europe", *European Review*, Spring (1973).

— "China and Western Europe", *Asian Survey*, 10 (1978).

Broadbent, K. P., "China and the EEC: The Politics of a New Trade Relationship", *The World Today*, 5 (1976).

Caldwell, Malcolm, "China View on the Common Market", *China Now*, 32 (1972).

Chung, Ho, "De Gaulle's New Challenge", *Peking Review*, 13 (1966).

Dreyer, Peter, "The China Trade: Will EEC Agreement Mean Increased Business?", *European Community*, 1 (1978).

Dumesnil, Claude, "Les relations entre la Chine et les pays de l'Est", *Revue du Marché Commun*, 2 (1975).

Dziewanowski, K., "Communist China and Eastern Europe", *Survey*, 77 (1970).

Esslin, M. J. "East-Germany: Peking-Pankow Axis", *The China Quarterly*, 3 (1960).

Findorff, W. B., "China and the European Community", *Aussenpolitik*, 2 (1973).

Gorce, Paul-Marie de la, "Les relations entre la Chine et l'Europe occidentale", *Études Internationales*, 1 (1970).

Henning, Vent Hans Myran, "The Bonn-Peking Connection Overview of the Trade and Treaty Relations", *Issues and Studies*, 12 (1975).

Henri, E., "German Revanchists and Peking. Essays and Reminiscences", *Far Eastern Affairs*, 2 (1975).

Hsia, Cung-Mao, "Maoist-oriented Communist Parties and Their Splinter Organizations. An Instrument of Revolution", *Issues and Studies*, 4 (1977).

Hubert, Agnès, "Le sens du rapprochement CEE-Chine: Pragmatisme Commercial et Alliance Stratégique", *Revue du Marché Commun*, 211 (1977).

Jen, Ju-Ping, "Sovereignty and Independence of Balkan Countries Brook No Encroachment", *Peking Review*, 43 (1974).

Kun, Joseph C., "Peking's View of Western Europe", *Radio Free Europe Research*, 5 April (1972).

Kux, Ernest, "China and Europe", *Current Scene*, 5 (1973).

Labedz, Leopold, "Poland: The Small Leap Sideways", *China Quarterly*, 3 (1960).

Larin, A., "Britain in China's Foreign Policy", *Far Eastern Affairs*, 3 (1979).

Lin, Kuo-Shuan, "Maoist Communist and the EEC", *Asian Outlook*, 15 July (1973).

Liu, William H., "Britain's China Policy", *China Report*, 5 and 6 (1978).

Löwenthal, Richard, "Der Einfluz Chinas auf die Entwikklung des Ouest-West Konfliktes in Europe", *Europa-Archiv*, 10 (1967).

Milligan, Stephen, "EEC - China Trade Pact", *European Community*, 6 (1978).

Notes et Études Documentaires, "Les relations Franco-chinoises 1945-1973", *Notes et Études Documentaires*, 4014-4015 (1973).

Ojha Ishwer, C., "A Comparison of China's Policies towards Western and Eastern Europe Covering the Period after the Czechoslovakian Invasion", *Asia Quarterly*, 2 (1975).

Reisky de Dubnic, Vladimir, "Germany and China: The Intermediate Zone Theory and the Moscow Treaty", *Asian Quaterly*, 4 (1971).

Rybakov, V., "Behind the Scenes of Peking's Peace Strategy", *International Affairs*, 11 (1972).

Stankovic, Slobodan, "Croatia's Economic Relations with China, *Radio Free Europe Research*, 1466 (1972).

Tretiak, David and Gabor, Teliki, "The Uneasy Alliance: The Sino-Yugoslav Rapprochement and Its Implications for Sino-Albanian Relations", *Current Scene*, 15.10 (1977).

Tung, Fan-Hsiang, "Britain's Shaky Labour Government", *Peking Review*, 6 (1966).

Yao, Hien-Keng, "British Strategy East of Suez", *Peking Review*, 9 (1966).

Younger, Kenneth, "The Western Attitude to China", *The China Quarterly*, 10 (1962).

China and the Third World

Adie, W. A. C., "China and the Developing Countries", *Yearbook of World Affairs* (1966).

— "Chou En-lai on Safari", *China Quarterly*, 18 (1964).

Alba, Victor, "The Chinese in Latin America", *China Quarterly*, 5 (1961).

Apalin, G., "Peking and the 'Third World' ", *International Affairs*, 12 (1972).

— "Peking and the 'Third World' ", *International Affairs*, 3 (1976).

Belyaev, I., "Peking's African Policy", *Far Eastern Affairs*, 3 (1975).

Borisov, V., "Beijing's Expansionist Plans in South East Asia", *International Affairs*, 6 (1979).

David, D., "La République de Chine et les 'cinq centres'", *Annuaire du tiers monde*, (1974-1975).

Despande, G. P., "China and the Liberation Wars: A Case Study of Algeria", *The Institute for Defense Studies and Analyses Journal*, 1 (1972).

Halperin, Ernst, "Peking and the Latin American Communists", *China Quarterly*, 29 (1967).

Halpern, A. M., "The Chinese Communist Line on Neutralism", *China Quarterly*, 5 (1961).

Joyaux, F., "La politique chinoise en Amérique latine", *Projet*, December (1969).

Kapasov, M., "Peking Seeks Hegemony in Southeast Asia", *Far Eastern Affairs*, 4 (1978).

Kapur, Harish, "China and the Third World", *Mizan*, 11, 6 (1969).

Khachaturov, K., "Maoism in Latin America", *International Affairs*, 3 (1979).

Klein, Donald W., "Peking's Diplomats in Africa", *Current Scene*, 36 (1964).

Kruchinin, A., " 'Third World' in Peking's Foreign Policy Strategy", *Far Eastern Affairs*, 3 (1976).

Lee, Joseph J., "Communist China's Latin American Policy", *Survey*, November (1964).

Leifer, M., "China and Southeast Asia", *Pacific Community*, 1 (1977).

Marchand, Jean, "La République Populaire de Chine et l'Afrique Noire", *Revue de Défense Nationale*, 20 (1964).

Mikhailova, M., "The Bandung Principles and China's Great-Power Course in the 'Third World' ", *Far Eastern Affairs*, 3 (1975).

Näth, Marie-Louise, "PRC policies towards South and Southeast Asia", *Current Scene*, 18, 7-8 (1975).

Prybyla, Jan S., "Communist China's Economic Relations with Africa", *Asian Survey*, 4 (1964).

Ratliff, William E., "Chinese Communist Cultural Diplomacy towards Latin America 1949-1960", *The Hispanic American Historical Review*, February (1969).

Schneyder, Philippe, "Péking à l'assaut du tiers monde", *Revue Militaire d'Information*, April (1960).

Soborov, B. "Peking and the 'Third World': Mounting Contradictions", *Far Eastern Affairs*, 2 (1975).

Sofinsky, V. and Khazanov, A., "PRC Policy in Tropical Africa (1960-1970)", *Far Eastern Affairs*, 3 (1978).

Suarez, Andrés, "Castro between Moscow and Peking", *Problems of Communism* September-October (1963).

Tretiak, Daniel, "China and Latin America. An Ebbing Tide in Trans-Pacific Maoism", *Current Scene*, 5 (1966).

Yi, Li-Yu, "People's China Relations with Asian and African Countries", *International Affairs*, March 1959.

Yu, George T., "Sino-African Relations: A Survey", *Asian Survey*, 7 (1965).

— "China and the Third World", *Asian Survey*, 11 (1977).

Wang, Yu San, "People's Republic of China in Latin America", *Asian Profile*, 6, 4 (1978).

Weis, Ude, "China Trade and Aid with the Developing Countries of the Third World", *Asia Quarterly*, 3 - 4 (1974).

Towards Great Power Status

Macioti, Manfredo, "The P.R. China: A Technological Power in the Making", *Asia Quarterly*, 4 (1979)

— "Developments in Mainland China 1949-1968", *American Association of Petroleum Geologists Bulletin*, 8 (1970)

Meyerhoff, A. A., "China's Petroleum Potential", *World Petroleum Report* 1975.

Needham, J., "Science Rebom in China", *Nature*, 31 August 1978.

Woodord, Kim, "People's China and the World Energy Crisis", *Stanford Journal of International Studies* (Spring 1975)

INDEX

Lenin, V. I., 21, 28
Levchenko, S., 143
Liang Qichao, 5, 105, 159
Libya, 88
Liebknecht, Karl, 20
Li Xiannian, 87
Lin Biao, 11, 139, 266
Liu Quang, 274
Liu Shaoqi, 77, 276
Lodge, Henry Cabot, 64
Lomé convention, 200
Lukman, 29
Lumumba, P, 252
Luxembourg, 193
Luxembourg, Rosa, 20

Macao, 163
Mac Arthur (General), 229
Madagascar, 259
Madiun revolt, 230
Mahan, Alfred Mayer, 64
Malaysia, 227
Malaya, 230, 233
Mali, 253, 254, 261
Manchuria, 18, 19, 27, 65, 68, 104, 107, 161
Manchu dynasty, 2, 18, 105, 160
Maoist groups, 177
Mao Zedong, 7-9, 23-25, 28, 29, 35, 37, 49, 57, 69, 73, 76, 77, 79, 85, 87, 117, 121, 128, 129, 177, 189, 194, 198, 201, 209, 210, 226, 227, 232, 238, 264, 269, 273
  on contradictions, 7-8
  on developmental models, 8
  on revolutions in colonies and semi-colonies, 8-9
  on Soviet Union, 8
  and second United Front Strategy, 23-24
  and Sino-Soviet dispute, 42
Marshall, George, 69, 70
Marx, K., 35
Marxism, 24, 160, 162
Marxism-Leninism, 5-7, 10, 13, 25, 29, 124, 168, 169, 176, 177, 189
Matsumura, Kenzo, 118, 120
MBFR, 184
McCarthysism, 73
McMahon Line, 248
Mecca, 239

Meiji period, 105, 106
Middle East, 92, 234, 238, 251, 272, 288
  -crisis in (1958) 38
Middle Kingdom, 3, 101, 103, 157, 229, 259, 268
Mif, Pavel, 24
Miki government, 141
Mikoyan, Anastas, 130
Mintoff, Dom, 194
Miyamoto, Kenji, 124
Modernisation
  Chinese, 160, 206
  Japanese, 104
Mondale, Walter, 93
Mondlane, Eduardo, 252, 253
Mongolia, 2, 18
  Inner, 107, 229
  Outer, 26, 246, 247, 264
Moscow Consultative Conference, 174
Most-favoured-nation-clause, 203
Moumie, Dr. Felix, 252
Mozambique, 245, 252
Mulélé, Pierre, 252
Muraviev, Nicholas, 17
Mutual Security Treaty (Japan, USA), 111
Mutual Security Treaty (1954) (US-Taiwan), 87, 89

Nagy, Imre, 166
Nakasone, Yasuhira,
Nanjing, 66
Narita Tomoni, 129
Nasser, G, 239, 260
Nationalism, 21, 160, 161, 162
National Liberation Movements, 10, 11, 243, 250, 251
National People's Congress (April 1959), 40
National Revolution Movements, 254
NATO, (North Atlantic Treaty Organization) 183, 192, 198
Natsir, Mohammed, 231
Nehru, J, 232, 235, 249
Nepal, 245, 248, 266
Netherlands, 231
New Delhi, 239
New England merchants, 63
New Fourth Army, 24
New Fourth Army Incident, 24

309

311

West Berlin, 207, 209
Washington Conference for the limitations of armaments, 66, 107
Western Europe, 121, 147, 164, 176, 177, 178, 181, 183, 185, 191 ff
Western industrial powers, 3
West Germany, 288 (see also Federal Republic of Germany)
West Wind, 241
Woodcock, Leonard, 88
World Federation of Trade Unions, 42, 171
World Peace Council, 171
World War II, 226, 230, 231
World War III, 234
Wuhan, 118, 288

Xinjiang, 48, 49, 229

Yalta, 26, 69
Yalu River, 229
Yamagata, Aritono, 104
Yano, 141

Yen, W.W., 26
Yenan, 24, 68, 225
Yong-lu, 158
Yoshida government, 110-114, 130
Yoshiro, Inayama, 134
Youlou, 253
Young, Kenneth Th. 75
Yuan, Shikai, 107
Yugoslavia, 28, 164, 165, 169, 170, 172, 175, 186, 188 ff

Zaïre, 252, 253
    Mobutu in, 270
Zambia, 254, 260
Zanzibar, 253, 254
Zhang, Zhidong, 159
Zhou Enlai, 40, 42, 49, 70, 72-74, 80, 82, 85, 87, 112-114, 118, 120, 134, 135, 168, 199, 200, 209, 228, 232, 233, 239, 249, 250
    African trip, 251, 260, 269
'Zhou, Hongqing, 122
Zumwalt, Elmo, 87

313

ABOUT THE AUTHOR

Harish Kapur is Professor of International Relations at the Graduate Institute of International Studies, in Geneva, Switzerland, He is also Director of the Asian Centre of the Graduate Institute. Before joining the Graduate Institute, he spent a year (1961-1962) at the Harvard Russian Research Centre as a Research Associate and worked as Assistant legal Advisor for four years (1957-1961) at the office of the United Nations High Commissioner for Refugees.

Publications are:

Soviet Russia and Asia 1917-1927: A Case Study of Soviet Policy Towards Turkey, Iran and Afghanistan.
The Soviet Union and the Emerging Nations: A Case Study of Soviet Policy Towards India.
The Embattled Triangle: Moscow-Peking-New Delhi.
China in World Politics.

COLOPHON

letter: baskerville 3.75/4.00 mm; 3. 25/3.50 mm
setter and printer: Samsom Sijthoff Grafische Bedrijven
binder: Callenbach
cover-design: Jan Jonkers

314